ATLANTIC DOUBLE-CROSS

ROBERT WEISBUCH

ATLANTIC DOUBLE-CROSS

American Literature
AND
British Influence
IN THE
Age of Emerson

The University of Chicago Press · Chicago and London

ROBERT WEISBUCH is professor of English at the University of Michigan in Ann Arbor and the author of *Emily Dickinson's Poetry,* also published by the University of Chicago Press.

The University of Chicago Press, Chicago 60637
The University of Chicago Press, Ltd., London
© 1986 by The University of Chicago
All rights reserved. Published 1986
Printed in The United States of America

95 94 93 92 91 90 89 88 87 86   5 4 3 2 1

LIBRARY OF CONGRESS CATALOGING-IN-PUBLICATION DATA

Weisbuch, Robert, 1946–
Atlantic double-cross.

   Includes bibliographies and index.
   1. American literature—English influences.
2. American literature—19th century—History and
criticism.   3. English literature—19th century—
History and criticism.   4. Literature, Comparative—
American and English.   5. Literature, Comparative—
English and American.   I. Title.
PS159.E5W4   1986   810'.9'003   86-6922
ISBN 0-226-89149-6

For Louise

CONTENTS

CONTENTS

PREFACE: THE AMERICAN'S SECRET

In his book on Hawthorne, Henry James lists with grisly insistence "the absent things in American life." Such listings of American cultural lacks had been a commonplace for fifty years on both sides of the Atlantic. For Americans they served as an excuse. For Englishmen, they constituted an indictment. For James, as our first Euro-American, they were excuse and accusation at once and they were something more: an American boast. After his most ambitious enumeration of absences, James expresses shock at his compilation. "An English or French imagination" would find "appalling" some such list; it seems an "indictment . . . shedding an almost lurid light." The Old World writer would believe that "if these things are left out everything is left out." But, quicksilver, James undercuts his sense to add, "The American knows that a good deal remains; what it is that remains—that is his secret, his joke, as one may say."[1]

In beginning my attempt to describe this saving secret, this cosmic joke by which American writers could laugh off the burden of Britain, I need to emphasize that Hawthorne's contemporaries did not possess the confidence evinced by James in hindsight. They worried that there might be no secret at all and that the joke might be on them. They engaged in a simplistic debate over the secret's hiding place; and yet the final result of this debate, despite the naïveté of its warring attitudes and the impossible clumsiness of its terms, was to create an American secret which in truth was not a priori existent anywhere.

The disputants of this dialogue may be termed the party of mimesis and the party of consciousness, and the two most imaginative women of Hawthorne's time may be made to represent each party in a diametrical disagreement. Commenting on the impediments to a national literature, Margaret Fuller remarks with devastating simplicity, "We cannot have expression till there is something to be expressed."[2] But Emily Dickinson, while creating a poetry unprecedented in its refusal of "somethings," of external, situational particulars, writes with equally bold simplicity, "Subjects hinder talk" (L, 397).

The party of mimesis, when it was not counting the missing aspects of American life, was ever nominating somethings to fill imagined absences: the Hudson for the Thames, the Catskills for Mount Olympus, colonial battles for epic wars, the Indians for gothic Italian villains. The party of consciousness met all such nominations with scorn. John Knapp demurred from the materialistic recipe for a national literature by stating, "It boots nothing what things have happened, if men have no delight in thinking of them."[3] The objection was not so much that Niagara Falls was insufficiently grand or even inadequately storied or that Indian history was not available as indigenous to an American culture under development by European offspring. Rather, the party of consciousness found impossible the notion that merely new materials lead automatically to a new literature. It would be more to the point to describe the Lake District of Wordsworth and Coleridge from a distinctly American vantage than to exclaim over Niagara by the inherited conventions of European literature. Walt Whitman approvingly quotes a *London Times* editorial occasioned by Bryant's death to this effect: American writers "may talk of the primeval forest, but it would generally be very hard from internal evidence to detect that they were writing on the banks of the Hudson rather than on those of the Thames."[4]

The disagreement finally had to do with the grounds for literary creation. Edward Everett proclaims the Transcendentalist counter-recipe for a national literature in defining the source of poetic power: "It comes from within. It springs from beneath the wand of their genius [the genius of finite spirits imaging the Great All-powerful Intelligence]. No matter how cold, and barren, and desolate the scene;— they fill it with life and motion; with interest and passion. They strike the desert rock and it flows with the full tide of fancy." Or, as Thoreau more economically says, "The theme is nothing, the life is everything."[5]

Living in a postromantic world that tends to afford imagination priority over nature and living more immediately in a post-Structuralist world that has emptied the signifieds, we enroll in the party of consciousness without hesitation. We probably would do so wherever and whenever we lived, for the program of the American party of mimesis is patently nonsensical in the assumption that objects and events produce literature. Its apparent ignorance of the transformations demanded of consciousness would embarrass the most reality-minded of the great theorists of mimesis.

Had its sophistication been greater, however, the party of mimesis still would have been defeated by the mere era in which the debate took place, for it occurred at a time when, in Europe, imitative theories of art had been overthrown decisively by expressive theories. The new dictum, as M. H. Abrams documents it in *The Mirror and the Lamp,* holds that "A work of art is essentially the internal made external. . . . the primary source and subject matter of a poem, therefore, are the attributes and actions of the poet's own mind; or, if aspects of the external world, then these only as they are converted from fact to poetry by the feelings and operations of the poet's mind."[6]

Not a heyday for positivists, then. But if the party of mimesis was defeated, defeat meant a subordination of the American objective, not a banishment. The great connoisseur of consciousness himself appears literal-minded in his famous list:

> No state, in the European sense of the word, and indeed barely a specific national name. No sovereign, no court, no personal loyalty, no aristocracy, no church, no army, no diplomatic service, no country gentlemen, no palaces, no castles, nor manors, nor old country houses, nor parsonages, nor thatched cottages, nor ivied ruins; no cathedrals, nor abbeys, nor little Norman churches; no great universities nor public schools—no Oxford, nor Eton, nor Harrow; no literature, no novels, no museums, no pictures, no political society, no sporting class—no Epsom nor Ascot![7]

James can join the party of mimesis to the party of consciousness. The skillful sweep of his itemization—from formal institutions through social classes to signs of age in the landscape—makes clear that he is not mourning the absence of particular items but of the historical sense and social sensibility these items might go to create: not so much materials for the imagination to work upon as aspects of the imagination itself.

James's merging illustrates the true alternative to the impossible choice-makings posed by the party of mimesis and the party of consciousness. (Once we acknowledge our own pro-consciousness biases, statements such as Everett's that attempt to establish creativity as independent of any social nexus are fully as naïve as any of the statements of crazed verisimilitude on the part of mimesis-spokesmen.) Both parties spring into existence from a common fear, which James terms cultural thinness; both parties assume that this thinness, this lack of a shared history, will block literary production unless it can be gotten around; and the extremity of claims made for outer and inner resources measures the degree of this shared anxiety. Possible solutions to this problem would be solutions indeed. That is, a radically new, distinctly American literature would depend on neither the mere recording of American externals nor on a doing-away with all externality in the name of pure consciousness; it would depend instead on the drawing of new relations between matter and mind, fact and vision.

In chronicling this achievement from the viewpoint of Anglo-American literary relations, this study confronts three dangers at least. Perhaps the most dissatisfying aspect of theories of American literature consists in the claiming as uniquely American certain themes and strategies that are universal even as stated or common to many literatures if generalized a bit. My very topic should aid against such false or fuzzy claims of uniqueness by requiring close comparisons. And it should help me to avoid a connected danger, the enumeration of American literary characteristics without any explanation for their existence. This lack of explanation allows for operatic melodrama and cheap mystification, as if a New World Spirit, rising from the Mississippi or descending from Ktaadn, were performing strange doings on the human psyche. Again, my topic wards against this danger by encouraging considerations of literary and social history.

But the necessary attempt to say how a literary quality came to be courts a third danger, which I see as absolutely unavoidable: the drawing of a causal sequence rife with reduction. Willy-nilly, the construction of an argument, in its linear progression, becomes a claim for the process of creation. I would ask my reader to free himself sufficiently from this progress so as not to imagine that every American writer in the nineteenth century experienced first this and then that in the temporal manner by which one idea in my argument leads to another.

At the same time, my argumentative strategy is a choice based on biases, and I am aware of some of them. I believe that the American writer begins from a defensive position and that the achievements of British literature and British national life are the chief intimidations against which he, as American representative, defends himself. Further, while I would not and cannot legislate mystery out of creation, I believe that the Anglo-American struggle proves shapings of an American literature to be more consciously deliberated than they are usually considered. And finally, I believe that the American writer achieves whatever literary independence he can by realizing the benefits of a correlative law between social and literary forms, a law that Raymond Williams succinctly states:

> Most stable forms, of the kind properly recognizable as collective, belong to social systems which can also be characterized as relatively collective and stable. Most mobile, innovative, and experimental forms belong to social systems in which these new characteristics are evident or even dominant. Periods of major transition between social systems are

commonly marked by the emergence of radically new forms . . . it is common to find, as in the case of genres, apparent continuations or even conscious revivals of older forms, which yet, when they are really looked at, can be seen to be new.[8]

Generalized, my view of Anglo-American literary relations concerns the joys and sorrows of both British cultural stability and American instability. The British nineteenth century hardly would appear to Englishmen a proof of national stability. But the worries occasioned by social upheaval would goad the British into pressing more insistently their advantage, however relative, of cultural continuity.

Here, telescoped, is the explanatory sequence that derives from these assumptions. American writers required of themselves literary qualities that would set their works apart from European and particularly from English literary models. The British told them over and again that they would fail in this endeavor because America lacked a sufficiently full history. The consequences of such an absence, they argued, were many and disastrous: little to commemorate and an insufficient passage of time to allow for the mythic enlargements of fact on which much epic and romance depend; no national identity and thus none of those national manners (what Lionel Trilling in our century would define as a culture's barely discernible, but indispensible "hum and buzz of implication")[9] that imbue life and literature with myriad associations; and no social classes (both because of the democratic ethic and the lack of a common national identity from which differences are developed) with the attendant possibilities of representative characterization.

American writers, in their propensity to turn to England as the nearest, most relevant comparative model, would find themselves in reluctant agreement. They would become aware of absences not only external in America but within, in the environment of their imaginations. They could neither pretend to a history that had not occurred nor alter at will the resultant flimsiness of a social-associational fabric. They had no choice, then, but to redefine the very meanings of history and society and to reconsider the relation of either to the creation of literature.

In the course of these rethinkings, there evolved new models of history and the subordination of history to other constructs of centrality or authority. These rethinkings would be enabled by or accompanied by or result in distinctive, seemingly new patterns of thought. (Here in particular I would avoid cause-and-effect language.) The introspective, self-conscious bent of whatever Puritan-derived heritage the American had in him and the awareness that he was setting out to solve a problem were added to the writer's usual interest in his mental strategies to make him especially conscious of his method. Indeed, in its search for external national matter, the searching intellect could become part (often a majority part) of that matter.

An impressive variety of alternative histories and alternatives to history evolved, but all of them were informed by two attitudes, both of them social and literary at once. The first I will call actualism. By it, absences become virtues. To the extent that American history was brief and the American present consequently undefined, possibility could flourish. For the first time in a long time, literary vision could be socially implemented. If, as the American writer had discovered, history could be created by thought, so too thought could create a living history. History could be imagined as a creative invention and then implemented. Actualism, then, meant reverse verisimilitude, life modelled on the mind's design. And from within the actualist attitude, British writers—even and especially the high romantics, with their "perhaps," "but," and "in a sense" habits and their turn inward after the disappointments of the revolution in France—would seem hypocritical, tame, and cowardly. For by the standards of an actualist attitude, the British did not mean what they said.

American actualism is confident, assertive, and programmatic; but a different, sometimes contradictory attitude develops alongside it, one that is nervous, exploratory, and fragmented. It is an ontological insecurity that, when capitalized upon, becomes an epistemological daring. It too is the product of a short history and an underdefined cultural present that deny to members of the national community the assumptions about themselves, their cultural environment, and, by extension, the universe that European cultures provided their generations. Alternately, one could say that the American was freed from the perceptual narrowing created by these inherited assumptions. But ontological insecurity equally develops from a rebellion by wayward thought against the driving dogmatics of actualism; and, as the real nation more and more disappoints, a searching skepticism becomes something of a solace to the disappointed devotee of actualist hope. Yet the epistemological worry, like the utopian assurance, can be shaped to criticize a British moderation. The motto of ontological insecurity is Emerson's "Man Thinking"; from its vantage, English literature may be characterized scornfully as "Man Having Thought" or "Man Letting the Past Think for Him." British assurance can seem stupid and secretly frightened, its wisdom a low common sense guarding against mysteries better admitted and puzzled over.[10]

In this sequence of American responses, the British serve first as threatening catalysts and last as targets of the attitudes catalyzed to answer their threats. The strong British sense of history humiliates the American writer into developing his own, or an answering substitute for one, which is capable of making British attitudes seem small and British texts circumscribed and incomplete. Of course, contemporary criticism eschews such pejoration to achieve a serene neutrality. But, as Harold Bloom has insisted, latecomers cannot afford the luxury of neutrality: the muse, if she is to arrive for them at all, arrives embattled. This is particularly so for the American writers of the nineteenth century in their relation to English literature. As Edward Tyrell Channing remarked by analogy, "The Romans worshipped Greece after they had conquered her,"[11] and the American ascension was far too doubtful to allow for the worship of Britannia.

My purpose is not to endorse pejoration but to define differences, in part by examining the need for pejoration. The American writer derogates his British contemporary or near-contemporary because he needs to do that. He could allude to Chaucer or to Spenser or to Milton in a friendly, even worshipful spirit because he could consider the centuries of British literature before the establishment of America as a common inheritance. Indeed, as this notion is a half-truth, he could employ early British literature in the service of his own meanings without the fearfully competitive spirit by which, say, a Blake or a Wordsworth incorporates and challenges Milton. It is with the more recent British writers that the American has his quarrel, with those Englishmen who are crowding his books off the stalls in New York, and, more crucially, who are crowding his own potential idea out of his dominated brain. With the English romantics, the American undertakes a complex, subtle argument similar in its revisionary rites to the argument those very English romantics take up in relation to Milton. It is only with his absolute contemporaries, the Victorians, that the temperature of the debate reaches to a fever for the American. And then, the American engages in savagings of a brutality that we usually associate with the ultimately flippant and historically unimportant feuds of theorists of the theatre. But these contests, crude as they may seem in relation to the usual influence-battlings, partake of their deep seriousness, for the American is compelled by a conviction of a British yoke so enslaving upon his thought that his art will be doomed to humiliated imitation if he does not violently throw off that yoke.

But in saying this we must be mindful of our own preconceptions. We live at a moment in critical history that belatedly has adopted the demonic worldview of much of our century's literature. We are given to credit compulsion and hatred and to discount freedom and gratitude. By the 1970s, for instance, T. S. Eliot's image of the literary tradition as an agent of strenuous nurturing had been challenged and successfully overthrown by an idea of literary tradition as burdensome, preventive, anxiety-arousing.[12] When individuals as utterly different as Walter Jackson Bate and Harold Bloom write major books within a few years of each other[13] to promulgate this (to us) more real-seeming notion of the literary past, we must acknowledge that we are in the grips of a muscled zeitgeist. We no longer image the new writer seeing further by virtue of his elevation upon the shoulders of the giants of the past. Instead, we see him as trampled under the feet of those giants or as creating a Perseus-shield to battle the giants by viewing and striking at their distorted reflections. Eliot's chemical analogy of the tradition as a table of elements all-restructured by each new work's addition seems suddenly bloodless and even, in its cold way, sentimental. Something had happened to us.

What happened was the partial overthrow of the important belief that literature offers an alternative to the values of official society, replete with an elevated and bloodless history. Earlier, literary creations had been assumed to illustrate or reflect beliefs. With romanticism, these creations became a belief: the individual work as the sign of consciousness uncloaked, as mind and life purified and perfect; all works, the tradition, as a kind of race-consciousness poised against governments and machines. In short, we believed in the romantic idea of culture against society. Now, increasingly, we do not believe in the separated elevation of literature, much less in its effective opposition. We speak of literary production and assert the power of history and the unconscious on a newly resultant, powerless or struggling literature.

We must not give way to all of this utterly. How inviting it would be to view Anglo-American literary relations from 1830 to 1860 as a family drama in the quasi-Freudian manner that has become (literally) second nature to us. How inviting and how bigoted! I mostly have eschewed that analogy (not entirely; it is contributory as one trope among a multitude that Americans and Englishmen would employ) because it reduces complications to a puerile paradigm. It, like equally inviting Marxist formulae, would make compulsion everything, when the American's secret is not alone a survival-strategy. The compulsive need to overcome British literary influence for reasons of pride or even for reasons of sufficient personal and national selfhood is real and strong; but it is absolutely accompanied by an American idea that, beyond all the circumstances created by a social nexus, there is a permanent life, a being-in-the-world that is mysterious and fructifying.

That is part of what James means by the American's secret. The struggle against a British cultural hegemony makes the secret explicit, known to its beholders. The British provide the goad for the Americans to find it out. But it was there, James and I think, in some nascent form all along. And by its very nature, sponsoring a kind of negative capability to counterbalance the egotistical sublimes of self and nation, the secret adds an element of play to the savagery characterizing the American debunking of imported British wisdoms.

We are put in the presence of a contradiction. British insults encouraged anew the Puritan-derived idea of each individual as a microcosm of America and of America as the completion in secular reality of God's design for humanity. This is nationalism made larger and more personal than a European ever would experience it. And yet the American's secret, his recognition that what we call reality is exactly and only that, a named thing, thought's marshalling choice of a set of possibilities amidst unthought others, makes him too self-aware of his own tropes to accept the nationalist feud all-solemnly.

Both ways the contradiction invites us to qualify the sense of relations among authors as an embattled world of its own. The American merging of individual and nation prevents us from accepting Harold Bloom's cheerful setting aside, in some ways like Eliot's own, of social considerations to focus on "the writer in a writer." We cannot separate out what these writers will not. And the "yes, but" toleration in American writers of all models keeps us from fixing upon competition as the only truth of our tale.

Indeed, there is a huge, rough agreement between American and British writers in the nineteenth century. Each nation, with Britain chronologically and influentially in the lead, produces a literature intolerant of the habitual understandings of its culture's daily social life. The Americans adopt an awareness, generally European but (to the Americans, for whom Europe often reduces to England despite all Germanic influences) specifically British, of the loss of a theological compact that had informed and bounded individual consciousness and action. Both British and American writers would glory in the freedom won by this theological decline and would be frightened by the emptiness it created. Writers of both nations would be worried in particular by a loss of security and power occasioned by this decline of a shared ethic; and they would experience the loss as writers by contrast to their visionary predecessors who could operate within, or at least in meaningful relation to, the cultural-theological field of opinion. Yet the writers of each culture also would argue for an enlargement of the purpose of secular writing and would attempt an educative literature to supply what religion had lost. One could go on extensively to list further every major tenet of romantic thought as imported from Britain to America.

But such a large agreement itself impels the American to look for major national differences within its area or to challenge its boundaries. On one side of the agreement, the American challenge would be to extend the visions of the English romantics to everyday historical living with an unprecedented literalness. On another side, the American would challenge British hopes for human and national redemption—the sense of a decisive human Fall being shared—by exposing to a withering skepticism the common understandings that British hope sometimes accepted uncritically, for instance the existence of the individual ego or selfhood. Thus, roughly, Emerson, Thoreau, and Whitman on the first side and Poe, Hawthorne, and Melville on the second.

After citing my misgivings then, after acknowledging the many instances of Anglo-American friendships and the reality of global or at least Western movements of thought that are transnational, after confessing our new prejudice of viewing influence in terms of contest, and after insisting that meaningful difference must arise out of a primary unity, still I find enmity the keynote of Anglo-American literary relations in the mid-nineteenth century. There was a war, after all; indeed there were two for the generations of Americans directly preceding Emerson's. There was a quarrel of nation and colony, and another of nation and nation. It is too innocent to equate political and literary histories; but it is more innocent still to discount any effect of the political upon the literary. Besides, the literary facts, as I see them, prove the preponderance of enmity. Of course, there are agreements: meaningful difference depends on initial likeness. But enmity is the keynote because American writers chose to dramatize difference and to devalue Anglo-Saxon agreement. The recent characterization of influence as anxiety was Emerson's as well; and it is no accident that Bate and Bloom are, in Emerson's high sense, American scholars.

My procedure throughout is to pair a general discussion with a particular case-study. Each case-study is meant to be an illustration in depth of the major features I have argued for in the foregoing chapter. This does not quite work. Each case-study exceeds its bounds and illustrates much from elsewhere in the study as well. But the assigning is not arbitrary any more than it is perfect.

Once we begin to consider specific cases, a fourth difficulty must be added to the three earlier noted. The scholar of influence may bind himself to what is provable by textual allusion or historical document. Such literalism kids itself, however, in that one easily can imagine the most profound influence as bearing not a single specific textual echo.[14] And the tendency in such studies is to provide a mountain of facts that, like any mountain, has nowhere to go. Literalists tend to cower before implication. The opposing extreme eschews all data for opinion. This is a lesser fault, and no fault at all if a sensitive intelligence informs the opinion. An opinion, as Harold Bloom has shown us on hundreds of occasions, may be right.

But I will try to differentiate among kinds of influence and to make the scope of my claims obvious. Nowhere am I bringing together texts that merely happen to illuminate each other by juxtaposition. That can be a useful exercise, but it has no place in the present study. In each case, I am making a claim for authorial awareness, for purpose. Within that understanding, though, we need to pay attention to differences of scope and intent to judge what matters. A single, isolated allusion is less consequential than an organized series of allusions; and inspiration, which may or may not evidence itself at all by allusion but which informs the total being of a work, is more consequential still. Or again: an allusion may be friendly, with the intent of clarifying or broadening something in the present text by invoking an earlier text, with no effect of derogating that source; or an allusion may be competitive and parodic, employing the words of an earlier text to challenge them by a ridiculing alteration or by the changed context of the surroundings in the new text. My business here is not to provide a classificatory system for judging influence but only to make some sample distinctions. These imply that there is no escape from critical subjectivity possible unless at the utter loss of critical power; but they also imply that the critic, by contemplating the extensive range of one text's references to another text and by determining the friendly or challenging intensity of those references, can prevent the connection-seeking intellect from committing utter cheats upon itself.

I have tried to be honest and capacious. That I have failed to be comprehensive will be obvious at every moment. In particular, it will be noted that I am employing the adjective "American" as if there is at present no furious debate over the relation of that adjective to women and minority writers. The Americans I here discuss are members in good standing of what is being termed (crazily, given its recent and still-shaky academic approval) the traditional canon. I have rounded up the usual suspects because these are the writers who most engage me and those who, I believe, will continue to engage intelligent readers whatever new figures join their company. Nonetheless, I hope my work will be suggestive for others who are better educated to consider as such the writings in the nineteenth century of women, native Americans, Afro-Americans, and other minorities. I would hypothesize that, to the extent such writers identified themselves as members of an oppressed group, they encountered a double bind. They would see themselves oppressed by the oppressed so to say; they would join in the American attempt to defend New World possibilities against British taunts but they would also need to define those New World possibilities away from any homogenizing American ideal that would not recognize their particular social identity.

Here, as in many other regards, this study has been written in the full confidence that I do not know enough. There is too much to do and too little has been done in the area of Anglo-American comparative study. We have thousands of articles on specific pairs of writers. We have studies of the travel books written by English and American author-voyagers. We have biographical investigations of transatlantic meetings. We have accounts of the rise of American literary nationalism. We have in abundance theoretical considerations of Anglo-American difference. But we do not have any book that investigates texts intensively to get at a characterization of Anglo-American influence. We will need many more books after this one to get to a satisfying assurance of major understanding. I am aware always here of neglected and important instances—a full book could be written on Trollope and the Americans, for example—and I am aware more sadly of absent powers of synthesis.

Nonetheless, I will boast that this study represents something new. It means to inaugurate a new field, or subfield, of literary study. The conventional habits by which departments of English and comparative literature organize themselves have made for a vacancy where a rigorous study of Anglo-American literary relations should have been occurring. Without a fabricated humility, then, I beg for the correcting and completion of this study by others.

What follows is simply a beginning attempt to account for the shocks I experienced when I first recognized that English and American books of the nineteenth century were so like and unlike as to force me to enlarge what I hitherto meant by the term literature.

Abbreviations

Dickinson's poems are reprinted in accordance with Thomas H. Johnson's choice of variants in his one-volume edition, *The Poems of Emily Dickinson*. Boston: Little, Brown, 1960. References to this edition in the text are followed by the number of the cited poem.

Quotations from Dickinson's letters are taken from *The Letters of Emily Dickinson*, ed. Thomas H. Johnson and Theodora Ward. 3 vols. Cambridge: Harvard University Press, 1965. References to this edition appear in the text in parentheses with the abbreviation *L* followed by the number of the cited letter.

Quotations from Emerson's published works up through *Essays: Second Series* are taken from *The Collected Works of Ralph Waldo Emerson*, ed. Alfred R. Ferguson. Vol. I, *Nature, Addresses, and Lectures*, ed. Robert F. Spiller and Ferguson. Cambridge: Harvard University Press, 1971. Vol. II, *Essays: First Series*, ed. Joseph Slater, Ferguson, and Jean Ferguson Carr. Cambridge: Harvard University Press, 1979. Vol. III, *Essays: Second Series*, ed. Slater, Ferguson and Carr. Cambridge: Harvard University Press, 1983. References to this edition appear in the text with the abbreviation *CW* followed by volume and page number in parentheses.

Quotations from Emerson's published works after *Essays: Second Series* are taken from *The Complete Works of Ralph Waldo Emerson*, Centenary Edition, ed. Edward Waldo Emerson. 12 vols. Boston and New York: Houghton, Mifflin, 1903–4. References to this edition appear in the text with the abbreviation *W* followed by volume and page numbers in parentheses.

Quotations from Emerson's journal and notebook entries are taken from *The Journals and Miscellaneous Notebooks of Ralph Waldo Emerson*, ed. William H. Gilman, Alfred R. Ferguson, George P. Clark, Merrell R. Davis, Merton M. Sealts, Harrison Hayford, Ralph H. Orth, J. E. Parsons, A. W. Plumstead, Linda Allardt, and Susan Sutton Smith. 14 vols. Cambridge: Harvard University Press, 1960–. References to this edition appear in the text with the abbreviation *JMN* followed by volume and page numbers in parentheses. Where necessary, I have quoted from the earlier edition of the *Journals*, ed. Edward

Waldo Emerson and Waldo Emerson Forbes. 10 vols. Boston and New York: Houghton Mifflin, 1909–14. References to this edition appear in the text with the abbreviation *J* followed by volume and page numbers in parentheses.

Quotations from Hawthorne's works are taken from *The Centenary Edition of the Works of Nathanial Hawthorne,* ed. William Charvat et al. 12 vols. to date. Columbus: Ohio State University Press, 1962–. References to this edition appear in the text with the abbreviation *CE* followed by volume and page numbers in parentheses.

Quotations from Thoreau's journal are taken from *The Journal of Henry David Thoreau,* ed. Bradford Torrey and Francis H. Allen. Vols. VII–XX of *The Writings of Henry David Thoreau,* Walden edition. Boston: Houghton, Mifflin, 1906. The volumes of the Journal are also numbered I–XIV, and this numbering is employed in the text. References to this edition appear with the abbreviation *J* followed by volume and page numbers in parentheses.

Elsewhere in the text, popular editions are cited for the reader's ease. These editions are noted individually.

Acknowledgments

The two books mentioned in the preface, Bate's *The Burden of the Past and the English Poet* and Bloom's *The Anxiety of Influence,* have been basic to my understanding of this subject. The title of the first chapter is intended to acknowledge my debt to Bate's work; and Bloom's passionate commitments to poetry and to his own sense-makings emboldened me to take on a large task.

This book was initiated during a year when I was supported by a generous fellowship from The American Council of Learned Societies, and a Rackham Summer Research Fellowship from The University of Michigan aided its completion. But its origin goes back further, and more personally, to my graduate years at Yale University, where I studied British and American Literature of the nineteenth century with A. N. Kaul. There, too, I studied American Romanticism with James McIntosh, who remains my great mentor now that, by the luckiest of circumstances, we are colleagues at The University of Michigan. A four-year continuing conversation from that time with my then-schoolmate Richard Brodhead also informs these pages, and this book extends back over a distance of fifteen years in friendship to him.

In the intervening time, this project has benefited decisively from conversations with John Elder of Middlebury College, Kerry Charles Larson of The University of Michigan, Robert Parker of The University of Illinois, Patricia Sharpe of Simon's Rock School, James Wheatley of Trinity College, and Bryan Wolf of Yale University. Michael Davitt Bell of Williams College and Eric J. Sundquist of The University of California, Berkeley, served as wonderfully sympathetic and acute readers. John Knott, chairman of English at The University of Michigan, has supported the project in every way imaginable. And my colleagues George Bornstein, Russell Fraser, James Gindin, and Ira Konigsberg have badgered and encouraged me as only dear friends can.

Louise Wicks Freymann, my wife, persuaded me to simplify the syntax of hundreds of sentences. Readers should join me in gratitude to her, for what follows was all the more twisty in its original form. In the simple language of strong love, I dedicate this book to her.

R. W.

One

THE DIMENSIONS OF INFLUENCE

I

THE BURDEN OF BRITAIN
AND THE AMERICAN WRITER

Had Emerson expected gods in trousers? At thirty, unaccomplished, unemployed, and incompletely focused, he visited the greatly accomplished English writers—Landor, Coleridge, Carlyle, Wordsworth—and tenderly cherished his disappointment.

> Many things I owe to the sight of these men. I shall judge more justly, less timidly, of wise men forevermore. To be sure not one of these is a mind of the very first class, but what the intercourse with each of these suggests is true of intercourse with better men, that they never *fill the ear*—fill the mind—no, it is an *idealized* portrait which always we draw of them. Upon an intelligent man, wholly a stranger to their names, they would make in conversation no deep impression—none of a world-filling fame—they would be remembered as sensible, well-read, earnest men, not more. Especially are they all deficient, all these four,—in different degrees but all deficient,—in insight into religious truth. They have no idea of that species of moral truth which I call the first philosophy. (*JMN*,IV, 78–79)

Emerson goes on to confess that Carlyle *had* dazzled him, but not so blindingly as to have prevented the American from finding his necessary attitude. Here and henceforward, Emerson celebrates a disillusion with the great as a first motion toward self-trust and self-realization. On the boat carrying him home to America, looking west with his back to England, Emerson thought upon his first book. He would title it *Nature,* as if no one ever had written before him.

From this private note, too, Emerson would derive a chief attitude of his influence-refusing essays, "The American Scholar," "The Divinity School Address," "Self-Reliance," "History," and "The Poet." The accomplishments of the past are not prohibitive in their grandeur; they are minute in comparison to the unaccomplished possible. "The books which once we valued more than the apple of the eye, we have exhausted," Emerson will write in "The American Scholar." "What is that but saying that we have come up with the point of view which the universal mind took through the eyes of one scribe: we have been that man, and have passed on" (*CW*, I, 66). The great men of the past, none of them, can equal the glory of Central Man, whose wholeness within each self reveals every historical hero to have been only a brilliant splinter. The great men are instructive most in having forsworn instruction themselves. Everything is left to be done.

Nothing remains to be done; or, if something does remain, it cannot be achieved in barren, culturally new America. To these twin fears, Emerson's journal entry speaks. Personal realization and public accomplishment, the burden of history and the potential for the *now* to become itself are Emerson's huge concerns; but British literary influence is the linchpin. Ten observations on Emerson's brief entry can characterize the negotiations between American and British writers in the nineteenth century.

1. Most largely, Emerson assumes a British domination of American letters that stifles native thought. That assumption prevailed by an easy margin over the sanguine attitude of those American loyalists who saw British literature as a model. But even their minority view served to publicize the nationalist ideal by arguing against it. In all, British literary imperialism is the chief issue in American critical thought through the Civil War.

In a verse written in 1788, Philip Freneau demands,

> Can we never be thought to have learning or grace
> Unless it be brought from that damnable place
> Where tyranny reigns with her impudent face? . . .

There is a moral urgency here in the castigation of British influence. There is bombast too—that is typical of the nationalist rhetoric—but, clearly, British domination is not merely an aesthetic issue. Likewise, in Charles Brockden Brown's novel, *Clara Howard*, the young Philip Stanley, because he reads British books, comes to scorn himself as "American peasantry," for "our notions are more the offspring of the books we read than of external circumstances." Twenty years later, Bryant complains "With respect to the prevailing style of poetry at the present day in our country, we apprehend that it will be found, in too many instances, tinged with a sickly and affected imitation of the peculiar manner of some of the late popular poets of England." In 1832, Longfellow berates American writers: "instead of coming forward as bold, original thinkers, they have imbibed the degenerate spirit of modern English poetry." In 1838, Orestes Brownson cries, "We write as Englishmen, not as Americans. We are afraid to think our own thoughts, to speak our own words, or to give utterance to the rich and gushing sentiments of our own hearts. And so it must be so long as we rely on England's literature as exclusively as we have hitherto done." After another quarter of a century, Brownson will discover drearily that he can repeat himself: our literature "lacks spontaneity, is imitative, and, for the most part, imitative of the English." And of a minor novel he says, "none but an American could have written it; for none but an American could have shown us the same evident effort to write like an Englishman. . . ." Meanwhile, during the forties, Nathaniel Willis and George P. Morris write hopefully, "What more natural than that we should tire of having our thinking done for us in London, our imaginations fed only with food that is Londonish. . . . The country is tired of being *be-Britished*." Most American books, Margaret Fuller says simple, "were English books," and Emerson in "Culture" speaks of "this tape-worm of Europe" (*W*, XI, 535). All is hopeless, Walt Whitman editorializes in 1847 in the Brooklyn Eagle, "as long as we copy with a servile imitation, the very cast-off literary fashions of London . . ." And in 1869, Lowell laid down the same law: "We are worth nothing except so far as we have disinfected ouselves of Anglicism."[1]

Such expressions should be seen less as statements of absolute fact than as conveyors of a conjecture that took on the assurance of myth: despite the real claims of Brown or Irving or Cooper, we have no distinctly American literature; and that is because we have been swamped by the British. The near-dismissal of American authors by the most fervent nationalists may appear contradictory, but it only italicizes the degree of American difference they required.

There was no colonial American literature in the view of the nineteenth century. We do not believe that now. We study Winthrop, the Puritan divines, Edwards, and Franklin as literary writers. But that is because we have reasserted a larger definition of literature than the previous century would allow. Through the Renaissance, Raymond Williams tells us, "literature" had meant "reading ability and reading experience." But the term shrunk through the eighteenth century to denote only "creative" or "imaginative" works free of direct claims upon facticity.[2] Benjamin T. Spencer's research on pleas for a national literature locates just such a shift in America between the 1780s, when literature still referred to any intellectual publication, and the age of Emerson, by which time literature meant exclusively belles lettres.[3] Since belles lettres in the American eighteenth century consisted in grotesque imitations of Augustan couplets by dull gentlemen, the century past appears a failure so complete as to afford no hope at all.

Charles Brockden Brown seems to us now a powerful exception at the turn of the century, and the claims we make for him as the inventor of American romance were put forward first during the Emerson era. But in the present context, it matters more that Brown himself stopped writing fiction after six productive years and issued this familiar complaint: "Our books are almost wholly the productions of Europe and the prejudices which infect us are derived wholly from this source."[4] Likewise the case of Washington Irving in the next generation. Whatever Irving's real achievement, the question he encouraged did not concern his indigenous originality but the British source of his inspiration: was it Dean Swift, Addison and Steele, Sterne, or Scott?[5]

This is not to say that excessive imitation on the part of American writers was merely a paranoid fear. Irving *did* imitate British models (and, we now realize, German ones as well and more closely). But this also is not to say that a self-conscious nationalism comes into being only with Emerson, for Irving fictionalizes the shock of revolutionary change even while he pleads for an American transformation of European models rather than an absolute break. Irving characterizes a prerevolutionary Rip Van Winkle as something of a would-be European man of leisure who lacks appropriate funds and lives on the wrong continent. He hunts, fishes, and frequents a Scriblerus-like club "which held its sessions on a bench before a small inn, designated by a rubicund portrait of His majesty George the Third." As punishment more for his un-American sloth than for sloth in general, this figure of cultural nostalgia is placed into a trance by bowlers—a game associated more with England than Holland—who yet "reminded Rip of the figures in an old Flemish painting. . . ." And his postrevolutionary waking occasions a series of culture shocks that are temporarily quieted when Rip spots the familiar portrait of King George at the inn: "but even this was singularly metamorphosed" into the figure of General Washington.[6] This metamorphosis is part of Irving's complex commentary: it is not simply a new portrait after all, and it displays continuity as much as it does revolution, the continuity at least of a need for heroes that withstands all democratic leavenings. But shock is the story's point; and Rip is, however imperfectly, remade a free citizen. Nonetheless, he is so remade, and Irving's rational commentary occurs, via an imitation of a German legendary tale that Irving acknowledges as his source at story's end.

This is crucial, for while we can cite particularly American qualities in his writing and can consider his intriguing double-mindedness concerning Anglo-American questions, we cannot find in Irving an American literary form, a uniquely shaped national imagination. That is what Emerson and his contemporaries cannot locate in Irving or anywhere. The prologue to Royall Tyler's successful 1787 comedy, *The Contrast*, represents the problem with a perfect unconsciousness.

> Exult each patriot heart!—this night is shewn
> A piece, which we may fairly call our own;
> Where the proud titles of "My Lord! Your Grace!"
> To humble Mr and plain Sir give place.[7]

But those English neoclassical couplets do not give place, and they ruin Tyler's overt claim. Likewise, Tyler's subplot hero bristles when his British counterpart calls him a servant. He refuses the status and provides a stirring lecture on freedom and upward mobility. But he *is* a servant, or something servantlike; more importantly, he is relegated to the subplot, while the man he will not call master parades solely in the main plot, and he himself is characterized as a bumpkin. Huck Finn is still a century from being.

Much stronger writers than Tyler suffered confusions. For instance, it is a startling fact that James Fenimore Cooper, before he became considered the American Scott, attempted to become the American Jane Austen. Cooper began his career by responding to Austen's *Persuasion* with the remark, "I could write a better book myself." This better book, as unfortunate as its imitative title, was *Precaution,* an irritatingly awkward treatment of English country life. By the next year, Cooper had adopted Scott. The American despised this comparison and often wrote harshly of Scott; but then he should not have chosen, in *The Spy,* to have dramatized a historically important conflict (the revolution) between opposing components of a single race as mirrored in a family conflict. In the same year he wrote *The Pilot* as, in his words, "a sort of provocation to dispute the seamanship of 'The Pirate,'" a work by Scott.[8] As for the Leatherstocking novels, Scott himself, in his introduction to *Rob Roy,* had compared the conflict between Augustan England and wild Scotland to the American conflict between whites and Indians. As the Leatherstocking series progressed over twenty years, Cooper increasingly and importantly replaced Scott's social context with the image of an individual man's self-discovery in the wilderness, a substitution drawing on Puritan captivity narratives and other frontier materials; he more greatly emphasized Indian mythology and more finely described a distinctly American landscape.[9] It is a literary progress that seems to enact in anticipation the Turner thesis. But it is not enough.

Cooper's ultimately high achievement could not make a sufficient American mark, perhaps because he never utilized influence with transformative control. In one of his last tales, "The Crater," he set out to escape Scott by rewriting Defoe's *Crusoe*. But each time that he draws on Defoe, he forgets his own narrative: his hero, in listing the advantages and disadvantages of his situation, so repeats Crusoe's list that he appears to forget he is accompanied by a friend; later, taken ill, the hero, like Crusoe, drinks himself into a stupor and awakes determined to think more of religion in the future—but Cooper's hero, unlike Crusoe, has been deeply, loquaciously Christian throughout the narrative.[10]

2. Cooper's worst imitations would seem to enact what Emerson's entry implies, the potential scattering of a native imagination by British influence. In such an atmosphere, the issue of influence would be as theoretical as a hammerblow. Emerson's easy dismissal of these great men is attractively audacious, but it is attended by a certain bravado. Thus our second law: frank acknowledgments of indebtedness became emotionally fraught and nigh impossible. And thin excuses for American failure abounded.

It is in Poe, in the aspect of Poe's career so troubled and low that it makes all the more impressive his great writings elsewhere, that we discover the ultimate confusion created by the burden of Britain. Poe's outright plagiarisms and close paraphrases of British periodicals in his reviews and aesthetic writings signify a terrible sense of inferiority. It was in relation to Charles Dickens, however, that Poe became most embattled.

He began by charging Dickens with having plagiarized from Joseph Neal's *Charcoal Sketches* (Dickens, conclusively, never read Neal); to play fair, he accused Marryat, again not just wrongly but with a malicious naïveté, of plagiarizing Dickens's *Oliver Twist;* he himself took a warm personal note from Dickens, in which Dickens told him how Godwin had written a story backwards, beginning with a desired concluding effect, and claimed the information about Godwin as his own. In "The Philosophy of Composition" Poe would obliterate Godwin as well, to claim backward composition as his own invention. The next year, in false amends, he quoted Dickens's letter directly, but misquoted it badly to support his own view of ratiocination. In another article, Poe claimed to have predicted in an earlier review the entire plot of *Barnaby Rudge* from a reading of the first installment. "The man must be a devil," Poe claimed Dickens wrote of him to the review's publisher. No, not a devil, just a liar: Dickens wrote no such note: Poe made five predictions on *Rudge,* four of which were entirely incorrect; and at the time of the review, he had seen a good deal more of *Rudge* than he later claimed. And finally, Poe was convinced that Dickens had written an anonymous review in which he charged that Poe's poems plagiarized from Tennyson's. Dickens did not write the review; and the review did not accuse Poe of plagiarism. (In his unnecessary defense, Poe noted rightly that his volume had preceded Tennyson's, but went on to charge that countless American poets had plagiarized indeed from Tennyson.)[11]

By treating Poe's plagiarisms as a witty hoax or an unethical procedure, we obscure the important issue which is this study's topic. Seen in the total context of the Anglo-American struggle, Poe's entire obsession with plagiarism, because of which he was publicly accusatory of other writers when he wasn't himself thieving, results from wild yet culturally explainable misunderstandings of influence and originality; and those misunderstandings in turn image the brightest, most fiery hell threatening the American writer confronted with the British achievement.

The fear that misshapes Poe and, to a lesser extent, the entire period is simple and brutal. It is that America, to judge by its literature, does not significantly exist. Against that fear, the nationalists would wedge a particularly whiny version of the idea of British domination, the theory of a colonialist hangover: "the mother country exerts an almost absolute spiritual dominion over the colonies, which may be continued long after events shall have severed the political ties which bind them together," Brownson writes,[12] and this gives all responsibility for the perceived literary dearth to "that damnable place."

More often a separate excuse was conjoined with the idea of a continuing and cringing colonial loyalty: Americans have been too busy forming a nation and conquering a continent to write literature. When Charles Brockden Brown writes, "A people must secure a provision of absolute necessities before they think of conveniences; and must enjoy conveniences before they can indulge in the agreeable arts of life," one might overlook the fragile assumptions. When Bryant repeats this idea several years later—"our citizens are just beginning to find leisure to attend to intellectual refinement, to indulge in intellectual luxury"—one may remain hopeful. But one must be allowed a grin when Brownson, after another twenty years, reiterates, "We have had a savage world to subdue, primitive forests to clear away, material interests to provide for. . . . There is a literature in the American soul, waiting for a favorable moment to burst forth." The alibi soured. When Longfellow repeated it, he removed its solace by worrying that the noted exigencies had created in the national character "an aversion to everything that is not practical, operative, and thorough-going," a criticism that Dickens would repeat and that Hawthorne would make the basis for "The Artist of the Beautiful." Lowell is frankly dismissive: "However else our literature may avoid the payment of its liabilities, it can surely never be by a plea of infancy."[13]

Even the amount of writing about the lack of writing became an embarrassment. Theodore Parker finds "a great deal of criticism upon very little poetry"; Emerson and Fuller, in initiating *The Dial,* commend a new national literary spirit but confess, "this influence appears not yet in new books so much as in the higher tone of criticism."[14]

The comic aspects of this angst should not detract from the serious worry at heart. Mircea Eliade recounts the cosmogonic myth of an Australian tribe in which two brothers, who are the tribe's mythological heroes, emerge from the earth, see animals and plants, and name them. "That is to say, from that moment, because they had names, the animals and plants began to *really* exist."[15] Bryant proclaims of the New World:

> These are the gardens of the Desert, these
> The unshorn fields, boundless and beautiful,
> For which the speech of England has no name—[16]

But neither yet has the speech of America a fitting name for New World vistas. The inappropriate, transported speech of England must be accused as the enemy preventing an American lexicon. Otherwise, the nation was simply unpoetical, the country no culture but an opportunistic enterprise, an economic arrangement. The excuse of British literary hegemony often stood between American intellectuals and, in one important sense, nonexistence.

3. The fear of Old World influence is at heart then the fear of Britain specifically. When we return to Emerson's journal entry, we note that he ostensibly is attacking any humbling glorification of "wise men"; but the wise men are, and do not merely happen to be, English poets and essayists. Three years before his journey, Emerson had written more generally that every man must "fully trust his own share of God's goodness," in which case "Let him scorn to imitate any being, let him scorn to be a secondary man, . . ." (*JMN,* III, 199). But the 1834 journal entry is Emerson's first major mention of particular men; and their identities teach us to translate fears of "the Old World," "Europe," and even "the past" into "England." Thus the minor poet, Eaglesfield Smith, writing soon after 1800, makes the characteristic switch: "The same sun which shines on the Old World illumines the New. . . . The Ameri-

cans eat, drink, walk, sleep, study, and think, in the same manner as English man."[17] Eighty years later, when Henry James lists all that America lacked and Europe possessed in Hawthorne's time— "no Eton College, no Oxford"—the translation holds.

More rangingly, in American admonitions against imitating the thoughts of any other man, that other man is eventually and inevitably defined as an Englishman. After a general plea, by the early middle of "The American Scholar," Emerson is inveighing against the imitators of Shakespeare, Chaucer, Marvell, and Dryden. Explicitly, he is not worrying about Homer or Rabelais, Boccaccio or Goethe.

What of other national literatures, of Germany in particular? Surely Goethe matters for Emerson and for Thoreau and Melville as well, and all of German idealistic philosophy matters for all of the American romantics. But the literatures and ideas of other nations are consequential most often at second hand, as imported into the English language by such Englishmen as Coleridge and Carlyle. History, language, and education argue that American responses to England must be more fraught than to other lands, and of an entirely different cast. This is true to such an extent that references to non-British Europe could be seen as an escape. That is Longfellow's hope, as expressed by an approved character in *Kavanagh:* "We shall draw from the Germans, tenderness; from the Spaniards, passion; from the French, vivacity,—to mingle more and more with our English solid sense. And this will give us universality, so much to be desired." (Notice Longfellow's phrase "*our* Englsh solid sense." Only the English influence is involuntary, automatic, inherited.) Brownson says, more plainly, "We must bring in France and Germany to combat or neutralize England, so that our national spirit may gain the freedom to manifest itself."[18]

History, language, education—each of these links to England is ambivalent. Americans hungry for a heritage could adopt prerevolutionary British history as their own to whatever extent was comfortable. But postcolonial American history would find the contemporary mother country suffocating and possessive. Of the three American wars before 1898, the two that were not internal had England as the enemy; and English sympathy for the South in the Civil War (in literary examples, Carlyle's forthright support of slavery, Dickens's editorship of a journal solidly pro-Southern, and Arnold's waffling) did nothing to ameliorate the conviction that Great Britain was the great problem in foreign relations for the United States. As for the shared language, it served as a continuous reminder of consanguinity; but the progressively widening gaps in usage, the constant barrage of British ridicule toward American English, and the American notion that the New World needed new words to bespeak it, all led to Oscar Wilde's famous comment on "the barrier of a common language." The educational inheritance as well, with its practical dependence on British masterpieces and textbooks, would lead more to resentment than gratitude.

4. This leads to another observation so obvious that it might be overlooked. Emerson's entry encourages an antagonistic model of Anglo-American literary relations. Something better than blockage and subterfuge might be brought forth by an acceptance of enmity. Insult could catalyze the imagination.

Robert E. Spiller argues rightly that the American romantics, lacking a potent native version of the neoclassicism that served the English romantics so well as an enemy, found their required opposition in the British literary hegemony.[19] It certainly enables Emerson in this entry, once he discovers an attitude toward it. That attitude is dramatized in the first quoted sentence—"Many things I owe to the sight of these men"—where Emerson's verb "owe" sets up expectations of an avowal of indebtedness that are rudely undercut. He owes his inspiration not to the visionary sight of these men but to his own sighting of their visionary inadequacies. We have seen that refusals to imitate and acknowledge the British are not always under such rhetorical control as Emerson wields, nor can such a short, straight line between rebellion and success usually be drawn. But both the continuing richness of English literature and the plentiful taunts of British periodicals went to encourage a creative anger in America that in turn helped to create the very native literature whose absence was its own starting-point.

English periodicals were helpfully savage. Relentlessly, the English reviews made sure that Americans would be aware of their national failure. Sydney Smith's famous 1820 query, "In the four quarters of the globe, who reads an American book?" is only one example of a tradition of blunt insult stretching before and after. *The Quarterly,* probably Southey, 1809: "No work of distinguished merit in any branch has yet been produced among them; . . ." *The British Critic,* 1818: "The Americans have no national literature, and no learned men." *Colburn's New Monthly Magazine,* 1827: "To talk of the literature of America is to talk of that which has no existence." *The Athenaeum,* 1831: "this want of originality in American literature is, we think, likely long to continue. . . ." *The Westminster Review,* 1860: "For almost every work of note which has been produced there, the mother nation can show a better counterpart." As for crediting the British domination of

American thought as a discouragement to a New World literature, the British agreed, but gave the domination a special, threatening twist: reviewing Irving's *Sketch Book*, the *Literary Gazette* remarks with sympathetic condescension, "The charges of borrowing from English literature are allowed, but with as little blame. From what other source can any American borrow? He has no native literature. He has even no material for the foundation of a native literature."[20] And the English knife cuts more deeply because the hand holding it is prodigious. In a five-year period around 1850, English literature could boast of *The Prelude, In Memoriam, Wuthering Heights, Dombey and Son, Bleak House,* and *Vanity Fair.*

Yet during roughly that same five years and shortly after, *Walden,* the first edition of *Leaves of Grass, The Scarlet Letter, The House of the Seven Gables,* and *Moby-Dick* managed to be written. Americans learned that the efficacious response to British taunts consisted not in a war of words in periodicals but in embedding counterthrusts within literary works of sufficient ambition to refute the British insults by their total being. Then, the greater the immediate British achievements, the greater might be the American return.

To illustrate with a most modest example, Poe, as we have seen, would appear silly in seeking an association with Dickens. But once he moves Dickens into his own vision and criticizes him thereby, he is at least lively. One of Poe's erroneous predictions concerning *Barnaby Rudge* he sought to right, or write: Dickens's raven never did become the symbol of infernal despair Poe expected, and thus Poe's "Raven." Dickens's "The Clock Case: A Confession Found in a Prison in the Time of Charles the Second" is bettered by "The Black Cat." "The System of Dr. Tarr and Professor Fether" replied sardonically to Dickens's praise of a progressive Boston mental hospital and his disgust with the Blackwell Island asylum in *American Notes.* Poe takes a furthest step in the history of influence here; Dickens is made the main character, duped by inmates who have taken over the hospital's administration.[21]

Herman Melville's career provides a more impressive exemplum of national revenge as an imaginative good. Alone among the American romantics, he is essentially antagonistic toward the English romantic poets. His early "Fragments from a Writing Desk" are full of a general Byronism; but by the time he writes *Pierre*, Byron is limned as a frightening figure of a demonic, incestuous urge. The Melville of *Pierre* is mostly out for Wordsworth, however. In a cascade of allusions, Pierre's maddeningly naïve sentimentality is linked to Wordsworth's landscapes; meanwhile, Wordsworth's relation to his sister, like Byron's to his, has an allusive role in Pierre's quasi-incestuous romance; and the then-circulating rumors concerning Wordworth's desertion of his French mistress and their child are cruelly incorporated into the "secret portrait" of Pierre's publicly upright father. Next, Melville attacks what seems to him the facile transcendence of "Resolution and Independence." In the tale "Cock-A-Doodle-Doo," a rooster replaces the leech-gatherer as the emboldening daemon of a despairing narrator who hilariously misquotes Wordsworth:

> Of fine mornings
> We fine lusty cocks begin our crows in gladness;
> But when eve does come we don't crow quite so much
> For then cometh despondency and madness.[22]

The members of the indigent family that owns the cock die one after the other, die happily to the cock's crowing, but die—the cock seems finally not to embolden but to suck their life-spirit; and the narrator, equally obsessed, lets his worldly affairs slide into ruin, becoming indigent himself. A damnable impracticality is one of Melville's charges against Wordsworth; a callous disregard of real suffering based on social—thus human and remediable—injustice is another. Melville finds Wordsworth's figure of the leech-gatherer (wrongly—we are considering here a blatant case of deliberate misreading) a cowardly use of symbolism as an escape from a real questioning of social ills. Melville did not stop here with Wordsworth in his lifelong attempt to exorcise himself of the optimisms that he found magnetic and disastrously betraying: in *The Confidence Man*, Wordsworth is one of the bromide-peddlars—the tenth chapter is entitled "Ode on the Imitations of Distrust in Man"—and in *Clarel*, the character Derwent, named after the river of Wordsworth's youth, is a shallow affirmer.

But Melville would mock equally a too easy despair. In "The Aeolian Harp," he adopts Coleridge's title to describe a still-floating wrecked ship that is "Saturate, but never sinking,/ Fatal only to the *other!*"[23] In many of Coleridge's poems, a joyless speaker blesses the Other by pronouncing visionary hopes no longer available to himself. Melville mockingly reverses and reduces the Coleridgean attitude into a self-pitying despair drowning others in its discouraging malaise.

Melville had his peaceful interludes in which allusions do not criticize the source but illuminate the Melvillian character attached to the allusion. Coleridge's "Mariner" is employed variously in *Moby-Dick*, most strikingly to dramatize Ahab's failure to bless nature in "The Symphony." Shelley's Prometheus is yet another visionary hero set off against Ahab, to Ahab's and not Shelley's detriment. But *Moby Dick* is not everywhere peaceable. "The Cassock" ridicules Carlyle's hope of updating religion in the "Church Clothier" chapter of *Sartor Resartus;* and the entire work serves as a critique of Carlyle's overorganized rhetoric of yea and nay.

In each of the sections that follow, I will incorporate a particular case-study, and in every one of these examples an American writer follows Melville's basic pattern of aggressive, parodic response. Melville himself, watching Dickens apparently steal from Hawthorne's romances and from one of his own, attempts to devastate *Bleak House* in the brief space of "Bartleby the Scrivener." Whitman savages the culture-ideal of Matthew Arnold in "Democratic Vistas." Thoreau sets himself in explicit opposition to Coleridge while implicitly contesting Wordsworth in *Walden*. Emerson stands Carlyle on his head in refusing the idea of history as providing emboldening models as he answers *On Heroes, Hero-Worship, and the Heroic in History* with *Representative Men*. Whitman's 1855 "Song of Myself" completes and rudely corrects the 1850 *Prelude*. This emphasis on repudiation does not mean that I endorse that view which sees influence invariably as a matter of primal hordes or poets as patricidal (or, in our case, fratricidal) cannibals. Influence is not everywhere contentious and deadly; but it is predominantly so in the particular circumstances we are considering. The clever title of Stephen Spender's book, *Love-Hate Relations,*[24] best characterizes the entire Anglo-American drama; but in the mid-nineteenth century, the edge must be given to hate.

Melville is exemplary as well in the trickiness of his attributions. Perhaps all writers, in their desire to be original more than revisionary, mask sources; but the American writer is especially circumspect, to the point that Melville must make a joke of this secrecy in himself. In *Moby-Dick*, Ishmael describes an albatross and appends a self-defeating note declaring that he had not then read Coleridge's "Wild Rhyme." By his agreement with Coleridge concerning the bird's spectral spirituality, "I do but burnish a little brighter the noble merit of the poem and the poet." Yet the text is less laudatory. It reads "Not Coleridge first threw that spell; but God's great unflattering laureate, Nature"; and in his note Melville goes on to attribute the bird's supernatural aspect solely to its whiteness, an aspect that Coleridge does not emphasize.[25] In attributing his inspiration to Nature rather than to Coleridge and then in kidding himself for so doing, Melville implies the corollary to the proposition that insult catalyzes the imagination: the imagination, even in its like, insulting reply, tends to disguise its inspiring target or to name it only subtly.

We might expect the American writer to obscure an influence, but why would he leave implicit a challenge? In small part because the demands for an utterly new literature in the New World are so extreme as to render even argument against the British a slur upon absolute authorial individualism: such arguments are reactive in a world that wishes not to be re-anything. But nothing can advertise itself as innovative without positing a notion of the conventional against which it asserts itself. Some of these battles are hidden, then, at once to disguise contention and, more, to emphasize it. That is, the contest with the British writer is left implicit for the same reason that a trope does not explain itself in a paraphrase—because it is finally more present and precise when left imaged.

5. Contemporaries matter most. This is still another facet of Emerson's journal entry that needs emphasis precisely because it is explicit. The writers against whom Emerson inveighs are living writers. Granted one wouldn't expect him to party with the dead. But he might have written some thoughts upon visiting Westminster Abbey or have commented on Shakespeare or Milton. We tend to think of the problems of influence as hauntings by the living dead. Cultural lateness and repetition syndromes beset the new writer as he cowers in the face of a mighty past. This is not so in the Anglo-American argument. Shakespeare and Milton belong to a heritage that could be considered, however giddily, common because it was essentially pre-colonial. It is the contemporary or near-contemporary British writer who threatens his American counterpart: he who monopolizes the attention of the American reading public and proves in his every success the attraction of the British way. The more contemporary, the more threatening is the English writer. Emerson is elsewhere instructive in this: he becomes suddenly more admiring toward Wordsworth when he can think of him in the past tense, as the great poet of a previous generation, rather than as a living personality.

To put the tenet another way, the further past, the more sanguinary the influence. Thus far I have mentioned no examples of medieval or Renaissance British literature as influences upon the American writer, and that is because the early periods were not influential in threatening ways. Emerson quotes Milton occasionally; Hawthorne often provides psychologized versions of Spenserian romance (and he did name his daughter Una), and Milton's Eden is often played upon in Hawthorne's works; Melville's employment of Shakespeare and, more generally, Elizabethan dramatic form in *Moby-Dick* is well known, Spenser runs importantly through "The Encantadas," Milton is sometimes paraphrased when Melville wishes to invoke the Christian myth or challenge its values,[26] and *Clarel* is a modern version of Chaucer's pilgrimage.

But I exclude earlier English literature from the Anglo-American struggle on the grounds that it neither provoked a struggle nor provided a primary shaping force for American writers. This may seem a dubious contention given Melville's assertion that "we want no American Miltons" or Emerson's complaint that "Milton is too literary" (*CW*, III, 22) to qualify as the ideal poet. Thoreau, charging that English literature "breathes no quite fresh and, in this sense, wild strain," pointedly adds, "Chaucer and Spenser and Milton, and even Shakespeare, included. . . ." And Whitman worries that Shakespeare's plays would hold back the progress of a democratic consciousness because he "belongs essentially to the buried past" and his works "belong in America just about as much as the persons and institutes they depict."[27]

But as Benjamin Spencer avers, Whitman's was a minority opinion. More representative was Cooper's attitude: "The authors, previously to the revolution, are common property, and it is quite idle to say that the American has not just as good a right to claim Milton, and Shakespeare, and all the old masters of the language, for his countrymen, as an Englishman." Lowell says, more aggressively, "we should be strongly inclined to question any exclusive claim to Shakespeare on the part of our respected relative, John Bull" (who, Lowell adds, called Shakespeare bizarre in his lifetime and thereafter bowdlerized his plays). Shakespeare "sprung from the race and the class which colonized New England" and the American democracy realized the dreams of "the puritan and republican Milton, . . ."[28]

Uncharacteristically, many Englishmen agreed with this claim. When a proposal to erect a monument to Shakespeare at Stratford-upon-Avon was refused because Washington Irving was a member of the proposing committee, the English were as vociferous as some Americans in protesting that decision. And when the American literary anthologist Rufus Griswold termed Milton "the most American" of all writers, the *Westminster Review* seconded the claim: "are not his immortal books on State and Church politics the very fixed and undecaying expression of the American ideas on these subjects?"[29]

These opposing views of earlier English writers may seem a typical difference of opinion between strong and ambivalent literary nationalists; and the British, in granting Shakespeare and Milton to Americans, generally did so in the condescending context of comforting Americans who surely had no native writers of worth. But when we turn to literature proper, the controversy ends: apart from Twain's

Connecticut Yankee, I find very few instances of an American writer alluding to Chaucer, Spenser, Shakespeare, or Milton in such a way as to challenge that writer's vision.

Medieval and renaissance English poets more often enter American literature with honor, to provide helpful contexts for understanding. Many of the details of Milton's Eden are alluded to in "Rappaccini's Daughter," not to criticize the poet but Rappaccini, a scientist whose hybrid creations are attempts to supplant God's nature with his own. Just so, Hawthorne, in that story with an Italian setting, alludes to Dante: Rappaccini's daugher is named Beatrice, and the young Giovanni views her first with the same voyeuristic lust that accompanies Dante's first view of his Beatrice. Unlike Dante, however, Giovanni remains incapable of transforming that lust into an idea of Beatrice as an exemplar of God's beauty of creation. My point here is that Hawthorne employs Milton and Dante identically, to reflect on his characters rather than to quarrel with their ideas. The Englishness of the one doesn't matter. Similarly, in *Benito Cereno,* Melville plays upon *Othello* by making the gullible man of action a white American and the viciously cunning deceiver, "subtle Babo," a black man. This reverses and attacks racial stereotypes and perhaps even what Melville considers Shakespeare's uncritical application of them; but, as the story itself concerns the endless inversions of victim and victimizer throughout history, Melville's reversal of Shakespeare's characters serves more as an extension of the tale's pattern of inversions than as an influence-freeing swipe. Again, in *Moby-Dick,* conventions of Elizabethan tragedy simply provide an appropriate form for the Ahab portion of Melville's tale.

One can see such allusions as distinguished most by their ease and friendliness. Spencer notes that Renaissance literature would seem to many American literary nationalists "akin to the temper of young America."[30] Further, such allusions defended against British charges of American provincialism. In fact, just as Walter Jackson Bate has remarked that Scottish writers of the eighteenth century could look back to Renaissance English literature with less anxiety than the English, "less crushed than the English themselves by the weight of the great English past, but still in love with its tradition and eager to share in the mystery of its fertility,"[31] so too could nineteenth-century American writers—though with one or two qualifications carried over from the ill will of the contemporary situation. Despite these qualifications, it is possible to see the American employment of early English literature just as Bate sees the English Augustan employment of classical models, as an escape from a nearer and thus more threatening period of influence: for the Augustans the Renaissance, for the Americans British romantic and Victorian literature. No less an American literary nationalist than Evert Duyckinck avers of England, "Our past is hers, and let no man under-value the sacred influence of Ancient Times, when rivalries are forgotten, jealousies have disappeared. . . ."[32] Duyckinck's rivalries and jealousies refer to the relation of English and American literature in and of his time; his "Ancient Times" include all of English literature to 1776.

Or perhaps not quite to then, for we must deal with the case of the missing British century in American romanticism. Notice that when Cooper claims an American share in all of British literature before the American revolution, he specifies Shakespeare and Milton; other commentators, as we have seen, add a mention of Chaucer and Spenser. Where is Pope? Where, in fact, is English neoclassicism? It is buried in the American eighteenth century. Then, Pope had numerous American imitators; Freneau called him, incongruously, "heav'nly Pope." But, as we have said, the imitations were poor. To the nineteenth-century American, they were embarrassingly poor. The nearly unanimous, painful verdict of these later Americans that America had produced no great literature was a total, if tacit, denunciation of American neoclassicism. More, an Augustan consciousness could do nothing with raw America. As Spencer comments, "in the shadow of the neoclassical ideal America became a dull land whose inelegance rendered it unfit to inspire or receive literary treatment"; reciprocally, the British world treated by Dryden, Swift, and Pope was more foreign to nineteenth-century America than Chaucer's or Milton's England. There were a few exceptions. We will note Hawthorne's employment of neoclassical prose style, though the employment is deliberately misleading; American schoolboys studied Addison assiduously—and then perhaps never again; Noah Webster termed neoclassicism the "most splendid era of English literature"[33] in his old age, but Webster's dictionaries democratically substituted common and changing usage for Dr. Johnson's fixed meanings.

Neoclassicism could not serve even as a whipping boy. There was a spate of attacks on it following the War of 1812, led by Edward Channing, the Harvard professor of rhetoric who would instruct Thoreau. But the English romantics had performed the neoclassical exorcism and, after a time, American writers would simply dismiss neoclassicism mildly and in passing. In contrast with a romantic tradition that he traces from Goldsmith through Goethe to Carlyle (and, implicitly, himself), Emerson in "The American Scholar" finds "the style of Pope, of Johnson, of Gibbon . . . cold and pedantic." The newer tradition, in contrast, "is blood-warm. Man is surprised to find that things near are not less beautiful and wondrous than things remote. The near explains the far" (*CW*, I, 68). Having thus so inadequately summarized Coleridge's critique of neoclassicism, Emerson quickly passes on. In so doing, he indicates the basic American romantic response to Augustan England: you bother me only a little, but do go away.

In contrast, the English romantic poets and Victorian poets, novelists, and essayists are omnipresent in nineteenth-century America, will not go away without a fearful fight, and will return immediately after every dismissal. Careful definitions and extended commentaries on particular works can wait, but a further distinction must be made here. The American response to English romanticism is exactly what we have been taught by Walter Jackson Bate and Harold Bloom to expect when we go looking for profound influence: a complex of acceptance, extension, and completion, subtle misreading, cunning transformation, troubled refusal. The American response to the English Victorians, on the other hand, neither Bloom nor Bate nor anyone else could prepare us for. It is virulent. It consists in angry refutation, destructive undoing by parody, deliberately wild misreading, and outright competition. Melville alone seems to treat the romantics as his compatriots would treat only the Victorians; Poe is more typical in this. We noted Poe's deep difficulties with Dickens and with the aesthetic ideas of the early Victorian periodicals, where he seems able only to copy or to vociferate. A suddenly more mature Poe—indeed the great Poe—emerges in dialogue with the romantics. Drawn, most reasonably, to Coleridge and Shelley, the two most self-divided of the English romantics, the two like himself most worried by incongruities of perspective, he adopts and emends Coleridge's philosophical ideas in his critical writings, employs "Kubla Khan," "The Eolian Harp," and "The Ancient Mariner" in many of his poems and in *Pym*, bases "Eleonora" on the imagery of "Adonais," and gives "Alastor" a happy ending in "The Domain of Arnheim." His arguments with Wordsworth's great Ode and its pre-existential myth in his "Stanzas" and throughout *Eureka* are equally intricate.

Poe and other American romantics became far more aggressive toward the Victorians, first, because it was the Victorians who were monopolizing the attention of American readers. Thus American writers became something of a guerrilla band hacking away at a usurping force. Second, America had a thin past and Americans a thin historical consciousness: the New World was a Now World, and the Victorians were present tense. Third, Victorian writers made their social, political, and theological ideas more immediately apparent than did their romantic predecessors: they were more available to argument and, further, the very openness of their views made Americans suspicious that Victorian thinkers were missing a metaphysics, a quid pro quo the romantics could not be suspected of neglecting. Finally—and later we will consider this issue in its deserved richness—the ideas, attitudes, and expressive forms created by the English romantics coincided remarkably if roughly with the ideas, attitudes, and forms of an American democratic ideal rooted in a similar Protestantism; many of these were the very elements the Victorians attacked in their English predecessors and themselves overturned. Indeed, many Victorians described the romantics and the Americans in near-identical images, as dreamy children. The Victorian response to romanticism served to make the Americans more conscious of a partial kinship with the romantics while it also made them more aware of their differences with the Victorians. At times it is not difficult to imagine that the English romantics are afforded a postmortem opportunity to reply to Victorian pejorations against them through the voices of the Americans.

6. We return to Emerson's entry to complicate the foregoing predictors of literary violence. Anglo-American influence is always more than personal and individual. A British writer will be engaged and attacked to the extent that he is seen as nationally representative. Obviously, the four writers mentioned by Emerson are taken more as a composite type than as individuals. They are a type of the idealized wise man but we have seen that they also are a type of the English writer. In turn, when Emerson begins *English Traits* by recounting in detail his visits to these men, the English writer becomes a metonym for England. Emerson's Coleridge is "A short, thick old man" who dirties his cravat and suit by taking snuff. He busies his conversation with furious comments on narrow, sectarian controversies. His discourse "was often like so many printed paragraphs in his book—perhaps, the same,—so readily did he fall into certain commonplaces." Emerson describes the visit finally as "rather a spectacle than a conversation" and Coleridge seems less transcendental than subhuman. Wordsworth is far more pleasant, easy in conversation and gentle in manner. But "To judge from a single conversation, he made the impression of a narrow and very English mind; of one who paid for his rare elevation by general tameness and conformity" (*W*, V, 10,14,24). Emerson has more good to say of these poets and of England than these summaries suggest, but the faults of Coleridge and Wordsworth—a bigoted narrowness, cranky old age, an overwilling accommodation to the most ordinary, trivial reality—are the limitations

Emerson finds in every aspect of English life. For reasons we will explore, American writers tend to fix on one or another Englishman as The English Spokesman—Wordsworth first, then Carlyle, Dickens, Arnold, and Tennyson; and they tend to fuse the qualities of a literary work with an idea of the national character.

Anglo-American influence is not only extrapersonal but sometimes counterpersonal. Emerson greatly admired Carlyle as a thinker and loved him as a man. Yet Emerson saw him—had to see him, as an American viewing an English writer—in terms of "the magnificence of his genuis and the poverty of his aims" (*JMN*, X, 553). Whitman had reason to love Tennyson, who was unfailingly kind and generous to him, and yet Whitman would see him as the poet of feudalism and the aristocracy, just as England to him was the nation of the past and of unjust privilege. Typically, then, the American depersonalizes the Englishman, focusing upon what Harold Bloom calls "the writer in a writer," and then personifies those literary tendencies into a national caricature. Ordinary friendship and enmity have nothing to do with this process, and that is why the biographical studies of Anglo-American literary relations ultimately count for little.

Nor is genuine achievement a guarantee that a British writer will figure in American responses once those responses are literary. Byron and his works were famous and infamous in America; American travellers who met Byron sent back excited reports. Yet, aside from some casual citations of Byronism as proof of English decadence, Byron is not wrestled with. And that is because the expatriate renegade seemed too cosmopolitan and countercultural to be made nationally representative. Thoreau wrote in a college essay, "twelve lines . . . of his poetry contain more true religion than was ever possessed by any or all of his calumniators"[34] and asks in a journal entry the next year, "What was it to Lord Byron whether England owned or disowned him, whether he smelled sour and was skunk-cabbage to the English nostril or violet-like . . . ?" (*J*, VII, 62). But Thoreau's attitude suggests that Byron is a violet to him in part *because* his countrymen deem him skunk-cabbage.

In all, then, American writers took the native, Puritan-derived habit of seeing the special man as a microcosm of his culture and transported this cultural synecdoche to England. En route, of course, the microcosm's portent was reversed, from an exemplum of the Puritan ideal to an admonition against adopting one or another Englishman who was England for America.

7. English literature constitutes a failure of nerve. It too-readily accommodates itself to a fallen world. This is the particular shaping of

the English representative evidenced in Emerson's journal entry and at large. Emerson's complaint that the men he met lacked "moral truth" has a deceptively conservative sound. But at this moment in his life, having retired from his Unitarian pulpit, Emerson is busy enlarging his idea of morality to make it mean the realization of Spirit potential within each being. The idealism of his Englishmen is insufficiently capacious; and, such as their ideals are, these men who "make in conversation no deep impression" fail to realize their ideals in their daily lives. Emerson may not have expected gods in trousers, but this is what he demanded: if not the writer as God, then the writer as visible saint. He will not abide the compartmentalization of life; no more than Milton will he praise a fugitive and cloistered virtue. He will demand in addition that authorial virtue stretch beyond the bindings of books. Emerson's own eventual choice of vocation as secular preacher and Thoreau's Walden experiment are only the most obvious examples of an emergent American demand for a literal, first-person enactment of literary vision.

Making it new will mean making it real; and the real will be defined more in opposition than in fidelity to the status quo of everyday existence. This latter the British romantics will be charged with accommodating, the Victorians with absolutely battening on. When Americans go on the attack, they charge invariably against an English literature that in every pejorative sense is too narrowly literary and commonplace (delusively real) at once.

This condemnation of British insincerity gives some force to such an odd bagatelle as Hawthorne's "P's Correspondence." In this apparently slight story, a mad letter-writer describes living British writers as if they were dead: "I had expectations from a young man—one Dickens. . . ; but the poor fellow died shortly after commencing an odd series of sketches, entitled, I think, the Pickwick Papers"; and more cruelly, the actually aged Wordsworth is reported to have "died only a week or two ago." But the dead Romantics are rendered alive and all-too-well, having disowned any heterodoxy to arrive at the famous British accommodation. Byron, reconciled with his wife, is expurgating *Don Juan* to make "a moralized version," and he "now combines the rigid tenets of Methodism with the ultra doctrines of the Puseyites." Shelley is engaged in a "vindication of the Christian faith" with special emphasis on the greatness of the Church of England—now a minister, he views his earlier poetry as the lowest steps of a staircase that are equally "essential to the support of the whole as the highest and final one resting upon the thresholds of the heavens" (CE, X, 369–70,374,366,364,362). Even the characteristic downward direction of Shelley's visionary imagery has been reversed in his accommodation.

Hawthorne's tale may be a slight joke, but it is also a subtle one based on an instinct of much of what we have sketched in the British-American literary quarrel. The living Victorians belong so fully to the deadening party of the past that they are made dead and past; the American writer speaks of his British contemporaries as if they belong to a prior age because the social system to which, despite their criticisms of it, they contribute is outmoded and because their socially conditioned attitudes prevent a different future. The English romantics are made by Hawthorne to linger on, but this constitutes no approval as their earlier, less apparent tendencies to compromise their values are made notorious. In all, we begin to collect a constellation of images: British writer-Britain-outmoded past-deadening present-unfounded repute-conventional living-blinkered literature.

The organization of my topic—in its claim that American writers of this period not only had to confront the single situation of British literary dominance but that they often shared formulae for confronting it—depends upon usefully relating the tragedy-minded American romantics who work principally in fiction to the church-without-walls visionary celebrants who write poems and essays. The sharing of attitudes that we have seen between Emerson and Hawthorne is a beginning. So too is Melville's characterization of the British as unthinking hedonists, who even in their hedonism settle for too little. The elderly London bachelors in "The Paradise of Bachelors" inhabit the place where the heroic Knights-Templar once sat and unconsciously chronicle a terrible decline as they gorge themselves upon gross heaps of food in a pathetic sublimation of libido and a selfish cancelling of heroism. Similarly, the English Captain Boomer, having lost an arm to Moby Dick, refuses to join with Ahab in his fiery quest, finds the whale's malice mere awkwardness, considers Ahab crazy, and heads home to tea and crumpets—a discounting, unthinking accommodation that for once makes Ahab's mania appear preferable to a slavish common sense.

Yet it would be foolish to deny differences. Hawthorne and Melville insist, of course, on the despair-provoking abyss between the philosophic and moral ideals of thought and the bewildering negations of psychological and circumstantial necessity in the world of action. The tragic is defined for them by an acknowledging of the unfordable gaps between what Melville's Plinlimmon in *Pierre* terms the horological and the chronometrical, and an equal recognition of the human need, always frustrated, to conquer the contradictions. The difference is de-

cisive, for in Hawthorne and Melville the Emersonian ideal of living
out one's vision can be made to seem, as in Ahab, a calamitous solip-
sism. But this difference in Hawthorne and Melville does not lead to a
favoring of English moderation. It leads instead to a view of English
thought as bromidic and superficial.

Emerson himself examples this alternate attack against the un-
philosophical English complacence, just as Hawthorne and Melville
are capable of adopting the Emersonian demand of visionary literalism
in the all's-fair aggression against Britain. Emerson was not so engaged
by Dickens' generation of English novelists to enter into fictional debate, much less like Poe to make Dickens a duped character. Nonetheless, his passage on Dickens in *English Traits* perfectly summarizes the
critique of Dickens which Poe, Hawthorne, and Melville would dramatize. "Dickens, with preternatural apprehension of the language of
manners and the varieties of street life, with pathos and laughter, with
patriotic and still enlarging generosity, writes London tracts. He is a
painter of English details, like Hogarth; local and temporary in his
tints and style, and local in his aims." His limitation is repeated in
Thackeray, who perversely teaches us that "we must renounce ideals,
and accept London." For Emerson, exactly as for Poe, Hawthorne, and
Melville, the Victorian novelist is the very type of the "good Englishman" who "shuts himself out of three-fourths of his mind, and
confines himself to one-fourth" (*W*, V, 246,247). "There is cramp limitation in their habit of thought, sleepy routine," Emerson writes of
Englishmen, and of English writers most. They are guilty of "the suppression of imagination" and operate always "in the absence of the
highest aims" to become finally "incapable of an inutility" (*W*, V,
305,255,251). Accommodating, then, can apply both to short-cir-
cuited thought and to an acceptance of a conformist experience. To
attack the Victorians in their place of greatest pride—earnestness—is
sufficient inducement to make merge the two American parties.

Emerson provides half of a final, clinching comparison as he
moves to figures who concern his enterprise far more than Dickens or
Thackeray. When Emerson demands, as he does repeatedly in his great
early essays, that we subdue learning and look directly to nature for
inspiration, he himself is looking instead to the English romantics who
had first and recently put forward this same advice, Wordsworth and
Coleridge. Wordsworth's genius is "the exceptional fact of the period. . . . He had no master but nature and solitude"; Coleridge "wrote
and spoke the only high criticism in his time." But the latter praising is
qualified in terms we might predict: Coleridge "fell into *accommoda-
tions;* and . . . narrowed his mind in the attempt to reconcile the gothic

rule and dogma of the Anglican church with eternal ideas." The praise itself (this is from *English Traits* again) seems affordable: Wordsworth "has written longer than he was inspired"; Coleridge failed to achieve a single masterpiece and this "seems to mark the closing of an era" while the national refusal of interest in his philosophical writings "is the surest sign of national decay, when the Bramins can no longer read or understand the Braminical philosophy" (*W*, V, 257,248,257,249).

Thus, to the extent that England has failed its best representatives or, alternately, to the extent that Wordsworth and Coleridge represent a ruined past, Emerson acknowledges, applies, extends them; to the extent that they remain inhibiting he repudiates them.

Emerson is serving here as half of what I hope is a surprising comparison, for his mate from a generation beyond is Henry James, that man most unlikely to be grouped with him. Yet James's critique of Browning is of a kind with Emerson's jibes against the British writers who concerned him. James came to know Browning and both admired and wondered at him. In a letter he wrote of Browning, "The poet and the 'member of society' were, in a word, dissociated in him as they can rarely elsewhere have been. . . ." James turned this observation into a story, "The Private Life," and Browning is the likable chief character of it. That Browning's dissociation of sensibility can be tolerated, even admired, suggests James's distance from the earlier demands of American romantics for making the visionary actual; but his view of Browning's split self as being strange-unto-unaccountable takes us back to Emerson's meetings with Coleridge and Wordsworth.[35] An Englishman, we must remember, might find the totalization of art on the surface of one's life equally unaccountable.

8. Beyond the specifics of Emerson's journal entry lies the fact that he wrote it at all. The Englishmen he visited wrote nothing so charged upon their visitor; Carlyle aside, they wrote nothing at all about Emerson. This too is representative, for my book's title, in its nonvernacular meaning, is itself a cheat, a double-cross. The Americans matter far less to their British contemporaries than the British do to the Americans. While I am confessing, let me admit that another purpose of the present chapter has been, by a plethora of examples, to establish the extraordinary frequency of American attempts, in works of literature proper, to refuse and refute English models. When we reverse our procedure to look for American influences in British texts, we are not devoid of examples; but this is not a matter of numbers, for the examples one and all lack the refusing force to which we have become accustomed on the other side of the Atlantic.

At first glance, we might mistake the situation for an apparent equality. Clarence Gohdes reports that "from 1840, and perhaps earlier, on to the end of the century the English people read more books by American authors than by all the writers of the European continent combined." Between 1856 and 1875, 7.5 percent of the new books offered for sale in England were of American origin; in the period 1881–1889, the figure rose to nearly 9 percent.[36] During the nineteenth century, Englishmen wrote travel books on America as often as Americans returned the dubious favor (dubious because the travel books themselves were grudging appreciations at best and perpetuated a war of charges, responses, and countercharges that seemed less and less to depend upon firsthand, open-minded observation). For every journalled journey to England by an Emerson and a Hawthorne, there is a journalled journey to America by a Dickens and a Trollope. Further, while Melville sends a Redburn and several unnamed narrators of his tales to England, and Hawthorne attempts a British romance, Dickens sends Martin Chuzzlewit to America and Thackeray writes *The Virginians*. Even the predominantly negative reception accorded the major American writers by British reviews might bode well for an argument claiming a British unease in accepting American influences.

But this is illusion. When we reverse our procedure to look for American influences upon British writers, we find no repetition of the threatened, feisty American response to British literature.

Here is what we have. Despite the rage of American journalists toward Matthew Arnold when he lectured on Emerson during his 1883–84 tour of America and said "We have not in Emerson a great poet, a great writer, a great philosopher-maker," Arnold held Emerson in high repute. In that same lecture he would praise Emerson in the well-remembered phrase, "He is the friend and aider of those who would live in the spirit." "I always found him of more use than Carlyle," Arnold wrote late in his life to his sister. Elsewhere, he described Emerson's essays as "the most important work done in prose in the nineteenth century," but this praise occurs long after Emerson had ceased to be an active influence.[37] R. H. Super, the current editor of Arnold's work, has supported by specific and telling example the earlier contention of Tinker and Lowry that "the mood and ideas of Arnold's early poetry often reflect his reading of Emerson."[38] But in this there was more of the ephebe learning his craft than of the anxious, influence-freeing struggle we might expect from a rationalist encountering a transcendentalist; and in his mature work Arnold simply forgot about Emerson. Earlier, even Carlyle had not been compelled into making literary his differences with Emerson.

Hawthorne is the one American romantic who may have given as much as he got in terms of influence. He contributes to Dickens's *Bleak House* in significant ways, which we will detail in the subsequent chapter. Further, George Eliot called Hawthorne "a great favourite of mine." She and Lewes had reread *The Scarlet Letter* together seven months before she began *Adam Bede,* and the influences are several. In this work—never before, never again—she restricted the action of each chapter to a single scene, Hawthorne's procedure in his tale of Hester. Eliot's Hetty Sorrell (full name Hester), like Hawthorne's heroine, bears an illegitimate child and maintains a tortured silence at her trial. More generally, like Hawthorne's Hester, Hetty possesses a "rich, voluptuous, oriental" nature. Indeed, an anonymous writer compared the two writers (though not as specifically as we have done) in the *North British Review,* in an article entitled "Imaginative Literature: The Author of Adam Bede and Nathaniel Hawthorne." We know that Eliot read this article, but it did not deter her. In *Silas Marner,* Silas, like Hester, is the victim of a grim theology and has removed himself (though more fully than Hester) from the community to live in a simple cottage by the woods. We also find that in *Silas Marner,* as nowhere else in Eliot, important events in a character's past remain obscure until near the novel's end, a technique of meaningful suspense that she may have adopted from *The Scarlet Letter* or, more probably, *The Blithedale Romance,* which she also had read. Later, in *Middlemarch,* Dorothea, like Hester, marries a much older, unattractive, and vengeful scholar: Casaubon is partly modelled upon Chillingworth. But in *Middlemarch* there is no broader structural influence from Hawthorne.[39]

Hawthorne's influence continues unto Hardy's *Tess,* in which critics have found allusions to Hester and Dimmesdale in Tess and Angel Clare.[40] But Hawthorne jumped via Browning from novelistic to poetic influence. Hawthorne had adapted Browning's poem "Porphyria's Lover" in his legend of Alice Pynchon and Matthew Maule in *The House of the Seven Gables.* Browning clearly returned the favor in his poem "Mesmerism" by borrowing several elements invented by Hawthorne for that legend, independent of the earlier Browning poem. Years later, when Browning created his only American speaker of a dramatic monologue, such was the force of the Hawthorne-American-mesmerism association that his speaker is "Mr. Sludge, the Medium," and in his monologue, along with his other literary errors, Sludge mentions "Hawthorne, the poet."[41] Again, this is a nice tidbit, made more pleasant by the knowledge that Hawthorne and Browning became personal friends and that Browning provided some editorial aid to Hawthorne's daughter when Una sought to publish Hawthorne's unfinished romance *Septimus Fulton* after her father's death; but as a tidbit, it provides nothing of influence-struggle.

The case of Whitman and the British does, though not much: certainly not when Hardy quotes from "Crossing Brooklyn Ferry" at the beginning of that section of *Tess* in which the Hawthorne allusions occur, or even when Angel Clare mentions Whitman by name and takes on a Whitman-influenced democratic ethic. With Swinburne we come closer to a case of influence truly influential. He was perhaps Whitman's first sympathetic British reader, taking issue with the harsh English reviews of Whitman's first (1855) edition of *Leaves of Grass* by asserting that "there are jolly good things in it." He disliked the "bluster" of the 1860 poems but greatly loved the poem later retitled "Out of the Cradle Endlessly Rocking." In his study, *William Blake,* he carefully (and very aptly) compared the two poets in terms of their hatred of tyranny, their confidence in the emergence of a universal democracy, and their emphases on intertwined political and sexual freedoms. He found Blake more profound, Whitman to emit a "sweeter air." Swinburne later underlined reservations he always had held concerning Whitman ("the prophet in him too frequently subsides into the lecturer") when he imagined a "Whitmania" abroad in England. But Swinburne's volume "Songs Before Sunrise" incorporated Whitman more fully than any other British writer incorporated any other American. He had spoken some years earlier of attempting "a book of political or national poems as complete and coherent in its ways as . . . Drum Taps . . . "; later, he worried momentarily that the title of his volume might be too close to Whitman's "Songs at Parting"; and, in his description of the volume, "an appeal from the suffering European democracy to the triumphant American," we have one of very few British examples of a writer connecting an American literary influence to the national American character, as the Americans relentlessly did with the British—this despite the fact that the Americans would present themselves as national representatives while the British would not.[42]

But even in Swinburne's relation to Whitman, there is more unclouded influence than there is anxiety. In Gerard Manley Hopkins's relation to Whitman, on the other hand, anxiety was so great that it cancelled influence. Hopkins admitted to a surface similarity in the two poets' long poetic lines and irregular rhythms. Indeed, in 1882, Hopkins called Whitman's mind more like his own than that of any other living man's. But he despised the similarity, for he thought Whitman "a very great scoundrel" and his similarity to Whitman only proof of something frighteningly unregenerate in himself. In language that bespeaks severe libidinal repression, Hopkins "desired" to read Whitman but, as a good Victorian, "determined not to." How he then gained his knowledge of Whitman we must wonder at. Instead of reading Whitman, Hopkins wrote of him. In the sonnet, "Andromeda," he speaks of the Church as threatened by "A wilder beast from West than all were, more/Rife in her wrongs, more lawless, and more lewd." We cannot know if Hopkins knew that the poet to whom he was referring would take the terms of such an insult as high compliment. Nor, though this beast of the west may be both Whitman and an America he represents, can we definitely count this another case of a poet-nation conjunction, for Hopkins's reaction to Whitman is so personal, extreme, and split that it seems less literary than morally self-involved. In any case, Hopkins was honest in asserting that Whitman's verse did not influence the form of his own; and if the thought of Whitman is repressed in all but this sonnet, it is so repressed as to be simply absent from the rest of Hopkins' poetic endeavor.[43]

I have not spent even these relatively few pages to make the case that the American influence on English literature of the nineteenth century was meaningless. This second survey holds meaning in two ways. First, we can see from it that an American influence began only in the fifties and that it increased in power and in the unease that it caused (however low at its greatest height) as the century progressed. Of course, it may be argued that most of the American writers with whom I am dealing did not write their major works until the forties and fifties. But Brown, Irving, Cooper, and Poe left not a trace on English literature per se, though they were noticed by British periodicals; and this absence is not caused by their lesser power as writers than the Americans who followed them so much as by the British dismissal of all American writing during their time. This dismissal was withdrawn gradually. Gohdes notes that the British periodicals slowly became more welcoming toward new American writers; more importantly he notes that during the last two decades of the century, British publishers "brought out at least thirty-five editions or issues of one or more volumes by Poe, twenty by Whitman, nine by Melville, twenty by Thoreau, fifty by Lowell, sixty by Irving, fifty by Cooper, seventy by Holmes, ninety by Hawthorne" (predictably leading the pack) and, among similar examples, "sixty by Mark Twain." Poe had a belated influence, by their own accounts inspiring Rossetti to "The Blessed Damozel," Stevenson to *Treasure Island,* and Conan Doyle to his detective fiction.[44] Whitman in his lifetime became a cult-hero of the young aesthetes; and in Birmingham in the nineties, a new religious

sect, the Labour Church, viewed Whitman as a messiah, and congrega-
tions read his poems in unison as part of its service.[45] Over the same
decades in America, there was progressively more American literature
of value, and more Americans were reading the literature of their countrymen. By the end of the century, the Anglo-American literary relation
had become more equal and (probably as a consequence) more friendly. American writers of the 1920s also would have intense dealings
with the British, but by then the issues and their cultural backdrop
would be almost entirely different.

But save the more or less happy endings for late in the century. The
other meaning carried by our second survey, when compared to the
first, only points up how fraught the Anglo-American relation was for
Americans by showing how mild it was for the British. Even when an
American influence was profound or anxious, for British writers American influence was exactly what British influence was not for Americans: in Gatsby's phrase, just personal. Indeed, one-on-one cases, even
with the American penchant for seeing each treated Englishman as
representative of English culture, do not provide a complete picture of
Anglo-American influence battles on the American side, as I have argued; but significantly, one-on-one cases, generally gracious incorpo-
rations which are never seriously microsocial, are all that we find on
the English shore.

9. The literary battle against Britain is persistent and its indirect
effects are far-flung. As I just indicated, we have here a tale of the
nineteenth century, only that but all of that; and this angst toward the
British persists long after the amazing American creativity of the two
decades before the Civil War. Emerson's journal entry is representative
again. Preceding the passage I have quoted, at the beginning of his
entry, Emerson thanks God for having "comforted and confirmed me
in my convictions." And we know from his earlier entries that Emerson
was prepared to devalue the great. But however prepared Emerson
claims to have been for the shortcomings of the writers he was about to
visit, a certain shock runs through his rhetoric: "I shall judge more
justly, less timidly . . . forevermore." Emerson is learning what he already knew; he would be compelled to learn it many times again. The
British influence and the American unease toward it would demand a
ritual repetition of debunking, on Emerson's part and on the part of
others, before and long after this one entry. Like death in Donne's holy
sonnet, the British domination is rhetorically defeated in thought only
to rise up, be defeated anew, and rise up again.

We can dramatize this persistence by skipping ahead thirty-five years from the time of Emerson's voyage to England to a moment when Samuel Clemens views Charles Dickens at a public reading and makes strikingly like witness:

> This was Dickens—Dickens. There was no question about that, and yet it was not right easy to realize it. Somehow this puissant God seemed to be only a man, after all. How the great do tumble from their high pedestals when we see them in common flesh, and know that they eat pork and cabbage and act like other men. . . . I was a good deal disappointed in Mr. Dickens' readings. I will go farther and say, a great deal disappointed.[46]

Twain's emphatic, "go farther" repetition bespeaks the same delight Emerson experienced in his debunking, the same relief too, and the same necessity.

In *The Quest for Nationality*, Benjamin Spencer omits any extended consideration of Twain along with Emily Dickinson "simply because they left scant record of their participation in the quest for nationality. . . ."[47] To the contrary, Twain seems almost anachronistic in his struggle with the British. His attacks upon Scott in *Huckleberry Finn* and elsewhere broaden into an Emersonian worry with an America that refuses its fresh self for Old World pretensions. His less recognized relation to Dickens is more full by far: the newspaper sketch "Mark Twain Overpowered" burlesques Little Nell's characterization; Tom's calf-romance with Becky Thatcher in *Tom Sawyer* parodies David Copperfield's courtship of Dora; *Life on the Mississippi* responds to Dickens's *American Notes;* Twain's Huck often parallels and sometimes parodies Dickens's Pip. At times, Twain is happy with Dickens: he often mentions the Circumlocution Office of *Little Dorrit* in his satires, and the characterization of Colonel Sellers in *The Gilded Age* is based on Micawber. But these mixed attitudes and this degree of involvement with Dickens suggests a persistence more than a cessation of the Anglo-American hostility. The characteristic forms of the hostility continue as well: *A Connecticut Yankee* limns contemporary England by moving aspects of it to a feudal past.[48]

Spencer is more completely right concerning Dickinson's lack of participation in any deliberate creation of an American literature. But that makes her works a perfect example for our second kind of claim for the extensive range of the shaping power of the Anglo-American battle, as we find important traces of it even in the poet who truly is unconcerned with it.

As a local instance, here is the second stanza of a Dickinson poem which mourns the tendency of the Godlike self to refuse its potential:

> The Heroism we recite
> Would be a normal thing
> Did not ourselves the Cubits warp
> For fear to be a King—(1176)

Nothing in the poem relates directly to a self-injurious American humility in the face of the British tradition. True, "Cubits" is a more familiar term in England, where it began its career by passing into Old English from Latin; "King" is a British-European reference; "recited heroism" is seen in the poem's context as an unfortunately bookish, exclusionary limit—we could, if we would, make ourselves heroes of life while now we only read of heroes in literature and consider them extraordinary because illogically we fear the greatness within all of us. These are gestures—especially the last, as it takes up the American demand to live out vision, which we noted earlier—that tempt us to relate the stanze to our topic. That temptation should be resisted, however, as the poem is applicable to any number of situations; "ourselves" is too universal here to be read as "Americans," much less "American writers." Dickinson's poems rid the referential. Further, the term "Cubits" occurs most importantly in the Biblical warning, "Man cannot by taking thought add a cubit to his stature"; and it is primarily against such Christian humility that Dickinson protests. Nonetheless, the stanza's highly probable source is Emerson's comment: "As long as our people quote English standards, they dwarf their own proportions. . . . . . As long as our people quote English standards, they will miss the sovereignty of power" (*W*, VI, 62–63). Emerson's "dwarf" becomes Dickinson's "warp," "sovereignty of power" becomes "King," "English standards" perhaps becomes an English standard of measurement, "Cubits." More significantly, the poem's basic idea, that we refuse our potential, constitutes both the charge against British literary thought and the feared American result should Americans humbly allow British dominion to continue. Dickinson's poem is not about such issues; but they are informing, present everywhere in the vista of a poet who proclaims "I see—New Englandly—" (285).

This example is merely a suggestion of the more important ways in which the Anglo-American quarrel leaves its traces upon Dickinson. (It would have done so even if Dickinson's brother Austin had not delivered an Amherst College commencement oration entitled "The Elements of our National Literature.") We will employ Dickinson's poems frequently as test cases to sound the far reverberations of the Anglo-American quarrel. For were we considering the quarrel merely as a clash that involved a few important writers for some of their hours and then ended, we would be "warping the cubits" of its import; my claim is rather that this clash led American writers to shape their works in particular ways that continued to influence American literature even when the tension with English models was not immediate.

10. We return, at last, to Emerson's journal entry to acknowledge that it is, literally at least, the result of a journey, and that it germinates, years later, in a travel book. We need to note the genre of travel books as an important aspect of the Anglo-American battle, even while I choose not to treat them in any detail in this study. Peter Conrad's *Imagining America* is the best of several recent works on the subject;[49] but I am excluding full consideration of these books because my chief concern here is to take the quarrel's measure in the great literary works of the period. None of the travel books is quite sufficiently great, though *English Traits* comes close. I long to be convinced otherwise.

The travel books tend toward the petty and nasty in the quarrel. The great literature is less nasty only because its ideas are more profound. The question of nastiness must occur when one confronts a literary situation lined up like a killing war. Are insecurity and aggression the bases of our subject? No more wholly than love and peace, for one can say that American writers strike out against England because England is Emerson's "best of actual nations" (*W*, V, 299) and the American writer is catalyzed by a sense of how decisively failed our world is and has been. The gap between the potential best and the realized best, not a low competitive lust, makes the American write against the Englishman. Well, no: low competition is there as well. There are perfect fits in our issue, places where high- and low-mindedness deliciously merge. We need not bring the sceptical realism of the Derrideans to our task nor need we adopt the flower-ethic to which contemporary humanisms often reduce. Just so, Freudian paradigms are greatly tempting but finally worth resisting, for this is a quarrel rich enough to speak in every tone, by any number of tropes.

Is the goal superiority or equality, dominion or fair play? That is a question you refrain from asking of a dominated nation, out of tact and because there is no answer. The more idealistic choices fail to figure the anger of the dominated: the negatives of hatred fail equally to acknowledge the mind's freedoms and the heart's affections. The alternatives are contradictory and inextricable. And so we conclude, as we began, with Emerson. Here he acknowledges a transatlantic fight but has it issue from a guarantee of equality that is its goal as well: "Courage consists in the conviction that they with whom you contend are no more than you. If we believed in the existence of strict *individuals,* natures, that is, not radically identical but unknown, unmeasurable, we should never dare to fight" (*J,* IV, 257). Englishmen, Americans, we are all souls radically like in spirit. Thus luckily we can to war.

2

Melville's "Bartleby" and the Dead Letter of Charles Dickens

I

Beyond a list of laws and a survey of examples, Anglo-American literary relations can be comprehended by a full consideration of a single case. I am going to engage here in the critical counterpart of what the anthropologist Clifford Geertz calls "thick description." This tale of three authors, by its very twistings, is the unavoidable initiation into the jungle of American influence-fighting.

One subscriber to *Harper's* would have taken a particular interest in that magazine's serial publication of Charles Dickens's *Bleak House*. Herman Melville, more than other readers, would have kenned the many effects of Hawthorne's first two book-length romances upon Dickens's novel. Dickens's very title might not have been sufficient to alert him to this influence. But Hawthorne's announced moral in *The House of the Seven Gables*—"the truth, namely, that the wrong-doing of one generation lives into the successive ones" (*CE*, II, 2)—was being repeated in Dickens's Chancery suit of Jarndyce and Jarndyce; so too Dickens's Chancery was illustrating anew Holgrave's complaint, that "a Dead Man, if he happens to have made a will, disposes of wealth no longer his own" and thus "A dead man sits on all our judgement seats" (183). Likewise, that "impalpable claim" of the Pynchon family to a vast Western territory that "resulted in nothing more solid than to cherish, from generation to generation, an absurd delusion of family importance" (19) would have its match in the Chancery suit's undermining of the moral sense and emotional sanity of Richard Carstone and many other *Bleak House* characters. Still, likeness is not influence. Only when Melville read the early installment in which the servant Mrs. Rouncewell rehearses to her grandson Watt the curse of the seventeenth-century radical Lady Dedlock upon the Dedlock progeny—"I will walk here, until the pride of this house is humbled. And when calamity, or when disgrace is coming to it, let the Dedlocks listen for my tap!"[1]—would the case be made. Dickens's language echoes too nearly the curse of the seventeenth-century Matthew Maule for Melville to have ignored the link: "old Matthew Maule, it is to be feared, trode downward from his own age to a far later one, planting a heavy footstep, all the way, on the conscience of a Pynchon" (20).

From that point, Dickens's heroine, Esther, would seem more and more a redaction of Hawthorne's Phoebe, both of them young women of radiating innocence in need of a deepening trial to become fully humanized. Indeed, the complaints of modern critics (and it is easy to imagine Melville sharing these complaints) are alike toward each. Phoebe, that "nice little housewife" by Hepzibah's praise, is "more like a ray of sunshine than like a person" and "quite unbelievable," says Hyatt Waggoner; Esther is "almost cloyingly unselfish, noble, and devoted, and rather tiresome in her domestic efficiency," says Edgar Johnson.[2] Their suitors, Holgrave and Woodcourt, make important appearances with climactic corpses, Judge Pynchon and Lady Dedlock, which bring near to consummation their loves; and the reformed reformer Holgrave ends where Woodcourt begins and remains, as, in Jarndyce's description of Woodcourt, "a man whose hopes and aims may sometimes lie above the ordinary level, but to whom the ordinary level will be high enough, after all, if it should prove to be a way of usefulness and good service leading to no other" (618). And both couples finally depart to rural new homes, pastoral Edens. "They transfigure the earth, and make it Eden again," Hawthorne writes of his couple (307); and the second Bleak House is replete with "the shadows of the apple-trees . . . sporting on the grass . . ." (648). In this scene, Dickens's Ada imagines her infant growing up to think of his father as "ruined by a fatal inheritance, and restored through me" (624). Jarndyce earlier tells Esther, "we can't get out of the suit on any terms for we are made parties to it, and *must be* parties to it, whether we like it or not" (73): and in both works a simulacrum of original sin, engendered by bad human choices but coming to look like a deterministic, imposed Fate, is ameliorated by these second Edens.

Melville, engrossed as he was by Hawthorne, would have seen these and other aspects of *Bleak House* as adapted from *The House of the Seven Gables*. Of course these are partial resemblances and there is much, a great deal more, in Dickens's novel that bears no relation to Hawthorne's romance. There is in *Bleak House* as there is not in *The House of the Seven Gables* an illegitimate child born of a passionate romance to a woman who suffers the guilty keeping of a secret concerning the child's paternity. In *Bleak House* and not in *The House of the Seven Gables* there is an elderly man, "black" in appearance, dimeyed but acutely perceptive, cold, formal, and inscrutable in demeanor, who combines the roles of pertinacious investigator of secret guilt and self-ordained agent of retribution. You have guessed my trick, for I have been paraphrasing an article by E. Stokes on the relation of *The Scarlet Letter* and *Bleak House*. Lady Dedlock combines the roles of Hester and Dimmesdale; Tulkinghorn, even in the chief images which reveal his nastiness, is modelled upon Chillingsworth.[3] This too Melville would have noticed far before any of us source-hunting scholars.

But I imagine also that Melville did not overrate the profundity of this case of influence. Melville would have been surprised and delighted to find Dickens, the writer who monopolized contemporary fictional taste more in America than he did in Britain, imitating to some degree the writer Melville had nominated three years earlier as the American Shakespeare. And at moments Melville could sound the raucous note of literary nationalism, as he did in his famous article on Hawthorne: "no American writer should write like an Englishman or a Frenchman; let him write like a man, for then he will write like an American. Let us away with this leaven of literary flunkeyism toward England. If either must play the flunkey in this thing, let England do it, not us." But Melville signs the article "a Virginian Spending July in Vermont," thus betraying, as he always does when he takes the guise of a Virginian, a sense that he is speaking with a naïf's blinded enthusiasm. And in the midst of such enthusiasm, Melville exaggerates his tone to a point where it satirizes, though never wholly undercuts, itself: "I was much pleased with a hot-headed North Carolina cousin of mine, who once said, 'If there were no other American to stand by, in literature, why then I would stand by Pop Eamons and his *Fredoniad,* and til a better epic came along, swear it was not very far behind the *Iliad.*' Take away the words, and in spirit he was sound."[4]

Melville, then, would not be so patriotically deluded as to see Dickens becoming Hawthorne's and America's literary flunkey. For there is much in *Bleak House* that truly does not have anything to do with any of Hawthorne's works; the whole of it is far more profoundly related to Dickens's own earlier writing and at every moment the book is, even stridently, Dickensian. Dickens had incorporated Hawthorne so that Hawthorne's quavering sense of far and metaphysical significance could be grounded in a social nexus. This transportation was especially effortless in regard to *The House of the Seven Gables,* for that, as many readers have noticed, is Hawthorne's most English-seeming, even Dickensian work. We see the Dickens stamp locally in sentimental or humorous minor characters like Uncle Venner and Ned. We hear the Dickens tone throughout in the chatty, satirically wise, rhetorically playful and grandiloquent narrative voice. Hawthorne never writes like this elsewhere: "Rise up, Judge Pynchon! The morning sunshine glimmers through the foliage, and, beautiful and holy as it is, shuns not to kindle up your face. Rise up, thou subtile, worldly, selfish, iron-hearted hypocrite, and make thy choice, whether still to be subtile, worldly, selfish, iron-hearted, and hypocritical, or to tear these sins out of thy nature, though they bring the life-blood with them" (283). Such a passage resembles less anything in Hawthorne than any number of passages in Dickens like this one from *Bleak House:* "Call the death by any name Your Highness will, attribute it to whom you will, or say it might have been prevented how you will, it is the same death eternally—inborn, inbred, engendered in the corrupted humours of the vicious body itself, and that only—Spontaneous Combustion, and none other of all the deaths that can be died" (346). With its neighborhood gossip, its abundance (which Henry James emphasized) of minute and often not-symbolic details, its greater emphasis on social and political history and its lesser one on psychology, this is Hawthorne's least American work. At times, in relation to *Bleak House,* Hawthorne's *House* seems afflicted by the fate that Harold Bloom categorizes as the rare case in which a subsequent text so subsumes its influential predecessor that the latter text comes to appear the source of the former.[5]

Still, Melville, reading *Bleak House,* would not have found Hawthorne topped, though he might have imagined something of a competition. He would have seen delightedly that, if Hawthorne's influence upon Dickens was shallow, it was present and wide. He would not yet have read the "Author's Preface" that Dickens added in August 1853 to the book publication of *Bleak House.* It ends with the single-sentence paragraph "In *Bleak House,* I have purposely upon the romantic side of familiar things" (xxxii) and thus echoes Hawthorne's prefatory definitions of the romance genre. Nonetheless, Melville would have seen enough to comprehend that Hawthorne had been noticed by Dickens. The winds of influence, momentarily and faintly perhaps but for a first important time, had shifted.

2

I am attempting, speculatively of course, to construe Melville's motive for the all-out attack on *Bleak House* that is "Bartleby the Scrivener." For that, I need to remain one moment longer with Hawthorne. For Hawthorne's most important influence upon Dickens may be negative, as providing Dickens with a model of what he did not wish to imitate.

One often-cited problem with *Bleak House* concerns the Lawyer Tulkinghorn's nearly motiveless desire to cause Lady Dedlock ill. The narrator does, in a brief passage, nominate envy as a possibility; and perhaps Dickens merely hopes to create an Iago-like absence of motive. But Tulkinghorn is so present and central—both to the novel's action and to its social criticism—that he seems oddly mindless even as the creation of a writer not primarily psychological in his orientation. More importantly, there is the problem with Esther, who to many readers still seems an unfortunate examplar. Too often still she appears to readers as the businesswoman of altruism, always cashing in. I say "still" because other interpreters have proven that Dickens provides Esther with a troubled psyche and that he locates much of her altruism in her troubles.[6] Esther is the child of the wrathful Calvinism her godmother enforced. She is taught that her instincts are sinful, more so than other people's, because of her tainted birth. She tells Jarndyce that one of her earliest remembrances has to do with her godmother declaring, "Your mother, Esther, is your disgrace as you were hers" (180) and that she dreams frequently of her blighted childhood. She speaks of "a terror of myself" (389) when she learns of her mother's identity; and she wishes, momentarily, to die. But this terror predates the disclosure of her identity and even the infliction of smallpox, which seems the visible manifestation of sin. It is what makes Esther dutiful unto agreeing to a marriage proposal, at once asexual and incestuous, from John Jarndyce. Esther refuses her sexuality so as not to perpetuate her mother's and her own sin. Her generosity, in part, is an attempt to undo or refute or outrace her guilt. Otherwise-intelligent readers fail to notice all this, however, and that is because the implied author seems so obviously to approve Esther at every moment. Dickens adopts a narrative stance at odds with the attempt to emphasize Esther's psychological reality: for instance, via the wholehearted praise of the usually skeptical Detective Bucket, "You're a pattern, you know, that's what you are—" (606).

The source for this ambivalence—at least one immediate source— is easy to locate. It concerns Hawthorne, and it is evidenced in a letter from Dickens to John Forster written in 1851: "I finished *The Scarlet Letter* yesterday. It falls off sadly after that first opening scene. The psychological part of the story is very much overdone, and not truly done I think."[7]

In short, his low (and wrong) opinion of Hawthorne's psychologizing scares off Dickens from attempting blatantly psychological fiction at the same time that it may encourage him to try his own hand at it. And both impulses coexist because Dickens is writing an adaptation of the basic personal situation of *The Scarlet Letter*.

In "Bartleby," as we will see, Melville implicitly yet fiercely attacks a kind of cowardly refusal on Dickens's part to dig for disturbing, obscure truth. Hawthorne's positive influence on Dickens affords Melville the sense that influence is at play and that he might join in. Hawthorne's negative influence on Dickens, the admonition against the psychological which he stirred in Dickens, furthers Melville's sense of what Dickens misses in experience and thus, however indirectly, provides him arms for an attack.

An attack it is, and here we need to distinguish clearly between two kinds of influence at least: Dickens's incorporation of Hawthornian elements, which is friendly, not profound, uncompetitive, more than a footnote to literary history but a great deal less than a major event; and Melville's parodic, competitive return upon Dickens, which *is* a major event, an attempt by one of the great American writers to propose an American difference, an American literary advantage.

But novelists are not all-intellect, much less all nationalist-intellect, and a more personal ire probably contributed to Melville's motive. In *Redburn* (1849), Melville had dramatized a drunken sailor's death by spontaneous combustion. We do not know with certainty that Dickens read Melville's *bildungsroman*. We do know, from Elizabeth Wiley's research, that Dickens may have found the idea of spontaneous combustion in an article on the phenomenon in an 1828 issue of the *Literary Gazette;* less likely in Charles Brockden Brown's *Wieland;* or, more probably, in Frederick Marryat's *Jacob Faithful.* Melville probably knew both of the latter himself, as Marryat's case also occurs aboard a ship;[8] and Dickens, in his Author's Preface, cites thirty cases on record, beginning in 1731. But in *Bleak House,* as only in the case of spontaneous combustion in *Redburn,* narrative suspense is initiated by notice of a mysterious, noxious odor. In *Bleak House,* the odor is first detected by Mr. Swills, "a comic vocalist, professional engaged by Mr. J. G. Bogsby," who immediately mentions the odor to one Miss M. Melvilleson, "a lady of some pretentions to musical ability, likewise engaged by Mr. J. G. Bogsby to sing at a series of concerts called Harmonic Assemblies or Meetings . . ." (347). Miss M. Melvilleson in an earlier passage had been described by a local gossip as "married a year and a half, though announced as Miss M. Melvilleson the noted syren"; and we are informed that her "baby is clandestinely conveyed to the Sol's Arms every night to receive its natural nourishment during the entertainments" (337).

Melville could hardly not have reacted to Krook's death by spontaneous combustion and to these passages concerning a namesake as a steal and a slap. Perhaps Dickens meant nothing but an inside joke acknowledging indebtedness—though it seems hardly a friendly joke or a frank acknowledgment.

The two passages abound with potential incitements, some of them unintended by Dickens. He indeed appears to have read Melville but it is unlikely that he would have known the first name of the mother of a relatively obscure young American romancer. Nonetheless, Miss M. Melvilleson seems to implicate Maria Melville. The hint of an illegitimate or covert child, perhaps intended by Dickens simply to imply that Lady Dedlock's predicament links her to a wide range of folk far outside of her aristocratic circle, could have rubbed irritatingly against Melville's sense of near-orphaning. This is speculative and relatively unimportant in comparison to the allusion's main thrust, which is to characterize Melville as a mediocre barroom warbler, an entertainer, a vulgarian. It would not be impossible for Melville to counterattack by viewing Dickens in those terms.

And Melville did give notice to these specific passages in "Bartleby." Bartleby's very name is a variation on Bogsby, the leader of the harmonic group in which Miss M. Melvilleson is employed. Dickens' misnamed tavern, Sol's Arms, may contribute to Melville's emphasis on the sunless, sky-occluded blockage of nature by the walls of Wall Street. Certainly the small, punning joke of Mr. Swills, that the noxious fumes emanating from Krook's room make him feel "like a post office, for he hadn't a single note in him" (347), is made weighty as the concluding rumor concerning Bartleby in Melville's story: that Bartleby had been "a subordinate clerk in the Dead Letter Office in Washington, . . ."[9] And the gruesome occasion of Krook's death for Swills' quip is hinted at by Melville's Lawyer's exclamation, "Dead letters! does it not sound like dead men?" (54).

To delay like a Chancery Lawyer no longer, here is the larger case in the suit of Melville and Dickens: Melville, motivated by Dickens's borrowing from Hawthorne and by the insufficiencies of Dickens's worldview in comparison to Hawthorne's, motivated too by Dickens's insulting reference to himself, contrives to delve deeper into life's sorrows within the space of a short story than Dickens can manage over hundreds of pages in an extremely long novel. Further, if one source of sorrow in Melville's story is seen as an ontological given, another resides with human choice: it results from the epistemological cowardice of shallow men at work in a shallow system dependent upon unquestioning, unthinking obedience. And Charles Dickens, who in *Bleak House* attacks a system's heartless failure to resolve questions, will be seen as representative of English realism's heartless failure to open questions. Melville's Lawyer, that "eminently *safe* man" (16), is Charles Dickens, an eminently safe writer who never delves beneath the social construct to question the abyss of existence.

3

But this is only the Lawyer's ultimate identification, and in the course of Melville's story he bears two other identities as well. In an important sense, he begins as Melville perusing Dickens, for "Bartleby the Scrivener: A Story of Wall Street" begins with implications of influence. The Lawyer announces as a general topic of interest law-copyists; and the drudge-work of mindless copying, given the context we are considering, gestures toward the chief anxiety of influence—that there is nothing but copying left for the self to write, nothing left for the self to be a self about. As a corollary to this anxiety of influence, the lawyer, en route to naming his topic, puts forth a claim of literary originality: "The nature of my avocations, for the last thirty years, has brought me an interesting and somewhat singular set of men, of whom, as yet, nothing, that I know of, has ever been written—I mean, the law-copyists, or scriveners" (16). Both the claim of originality and the partial, legal-minded disclaimer ("that I know of") are strangely irrelevant to the matter at hand unless we see the Lawyer here as representing Melville. This is an act of sweet revenge: if Dickens will not acknowledge Melville in copying Melville's idea of self-combustion, Melville's Lawyer will not have read Dickens. It is an especially smart jibe in that the first installment of "Bartleby" was published in *Putnam's Monthly Magazine* one month after *Harper's* had concluded the serialization of *Bleak House*. But the disclaimer is also a subtle announcement that a contest of influence is at play. When Melville's Lawyer mentions that, at the time of the story, he had been named Master in Chancery in the State of New York, not only is the most overt link to *Bleak House* forged but the issue of influence is further emphasized: Chancery is, in New York or London, the court that judges inheritence, and literary influence is a kind of inheriting.[10]

By this same reference to Chancery, the Lawyer sheds his identity with Melville to become a compendium of Dickens's mean-spirited legal figures in *Bleak House*. His very lack of a personal name suggests the degree to which his selfhood has been usurped by his occupation. The view from his Wall Street office, which he confesses to be "deficient in what landscape painters call 'life'" (17), defines his own severe limitations of view. In this unnatural, anti-natural bias he resembles the vampire-lawyer Mr. Vholes, about whom "there was nothing so remarkable . . . as his lifeless manner" (404). And in his refusal to take risks professionally, Melville's Lawyer becomes the counterpart to Tulkinghorn. He claims to "do a snug business among rich men's bonds, and mortgages, and title-deeds" (16) just as Tulkinghorn is "reputed to have made good thrift out of aristocratic marriage settlements and aristocratic wills" (8). Further, Melville's Lawyer boasts, "The late Jacob Astor, a personage little given to poetic enthusiasm, had no hesitation in pronouncing my first grand point to be prudence; my next method" (16–17). In this too he is like the patiently methodical Tulkinghorn, that "Mausoleum" (8) of secrets who is "always the same speechless repository of noble confidences" (126). No wonder that, to one of the employees of Melville's Lawyer, Ginger-Nut, "the whole noble science of the law was contained in a nut-shell" just as Dickens's Tulkinghorn rents rooms in a mansion "where lawyers lie like maggots in nuts" (99). When Bartleby's unblinking, unresponsive presence disturbs the Lawyer, his solution is to build yet another wall, a partition within the office. Like Tulkinghorn, "watchful behind a blind" (287), the Lawyer investigates Bartleby but refuses authentic emotional commitment in so doing. Finally, then, in his concern that the system go forward unruffled and in his simultaneous refusal to question the value and humanity of that system, Melville's Lawyer is not just Tulkinghorn or Vholes but Dickens's entire Chancery. The Lawyer is a mechanism within a mechanism to the extent that Bartleby's repetitive "I would prefer not to" (despite its subjunctive "would" which suggests his knowledge that his preference may not be respected) constitutes a major rebellion, for preference and the individuality it implies are outlawed by Wall Street.

In all of this, Melville is seconding Dickens in a critique of an absurdly abstracted system that not only ignores but attempts to replace an organic society. This is Melville seeing America as Dickens sees England, the only difference being Melville's insistence on the barrenness of American pragmatism as opposed to Dickens's insistence on British clutter unto chaos. Again, when Melville chronicles the Lawyer's attempts to salvage Bartleby, attempts that risk his "eminently *safe*" status not at all and mean to domesticate Bartleby into his unthinking world, he echoes Dickens' criticism of such self-serving charities as Snagsby's half crowns or Mrs. Jellyby's "telescopic philanthropy."

At his worst moments of epistemological and sympathetic refusal, the Lawyer is a Dickensian villain. By this, Melville both acknowledges his agreement with aspects of Dickens's social critique and asserts his own capacity to write in such a manner. But as an ostensible author, the Lawyer is identified with Dickens. As early as 1856 one reviewer, in the Boston *Daily Herald Traveller,* noted that "for originality of invention and grotesqueness of humor, Melville's 'Bartleby' is equal to anything from the pen of Dickens, whose writing it closely resembles, both as to the character of the sketch and the pecularity of the style."[11] And in our time, several critics have noticed the likeness, especially in terms of characterization. The characters in "Bartleby" are "all minor triumphs of solid Dickensian portraiture," Edward Rosenberg comments.[12] Turkey, Nippers, and Ginger-Nut—and even Bartleby—are named in Dickensian fashion. Each is characterized in Dickensian fashion by one or a few quirks.

Beyond the Dickensian characterizations, the Lawyer's self-satisfied tone imitates Esther at her least forgivable. But the narrative voice of Dickens himself is also adopted by Melville's Lawyer, in whom it becomes pompous and rationalizing. The story's action ends inside a Dickensian prison, while its rhetoric ends with a Dickensian exclamation: "Ah, Bartleby! Ah, humanity!"

This is a someways hollow and unfeeling exclamation on the Lawyer's part. Kingsley Widmer characterizes the Lawyer's successive attempts to deal with Bartleby as "common sense, authority, rationality, theology, prudence, pity, charity, resignation, flight, morality and even, at the end, reverence." The key term is "flight," for these approaches are all avoidances; the final exclamation, however much it displays an increase of compassion in the Lawyer, finally fixes Bartleby as, in Widmer's phrase, "an image of self-pity in a social tract." Widmer sees this as "the last moralizing and rationalizing gesture of a representative American,"[13] but it is equally an attempt to substitute the effulgent moralizing of Dickens for a more challenging view, one for instance that would not relegate Bartleby's ills to the woes of universal humanity without acknowledging the Lawyer's role in furthering those ills. Instead, the Lawyer seems to have fulfilled his opening boast, that he "could relate divers histories" of copyists "at which good-natured gentlemen might smile, and sentimental souls might weep" (16)—a Dickensian effect indeed. In all, if the Lawyer is both Dickens and Dickens's typical villain, then Dickens's solutions are being made part of the problem.

When the Lawyer becomes emotionally honest, he simultaneously ceases to write like Dickens. As the word "prefer" creeps into his vocabulary, the Lawyer is shown to contain a latent Bartleby within himself. And as Bartleby comes to be seen as the Lawyer's potential *doppelganger*, Dickensian prose is momentarily discarded:

> Again I sat ruminating what I should do. Mortified as I was by his behavior, and resolved as I had been to dismiss him when I entered my office, nevertheless I strangely felt something superstitious knocking at my heart, and forbidding me to carry out my purpose, and denouncing me for a villain if I dared to breathe one bitter word against this forlornest of mankind. (36)

These are the cadences, this the lexicon of Edgar Allan Poe. And Poe's tone is appropriate to the Lawyer at this moment. In one of his aspects, Bartleby represents the irrational will, however knowledgeable it is of its pending defeat; as the Lawyer for a moment generously acknowledges the irrational Bartleby, he simultaneously experiences the irrational within himself. Here, most temporarily, the unconscious is not trivialized in Dickensian fashion into a surface eccentricity but granted decisive power. And at that same moment—and only for that moment—the Lawyer abides by Melville's injunction to "write like a man, for then he will write like an American."[14]

To review: when the Lawyer ostensibly proclaims his literary originality, he covertly acknowledges Melville's debt to Dickens in a way that sets up a contest between the two writers. When the lawyer serves as a compendium of Dickensian villains, Melville seems to be flattering and following Dickens. But when the Lawyer simultaneously is seen to write like Dickens, Melville sours the flattery. And the Lawyer's actions in reference to Dickensian models follow the same pattern of allusion with a damning difference. For instance, Bartleby's "I would prefer not to" derives not only from Jo in *Bleak House* with his "I don't know nothink" but also and more from a character in Dickens's *Pickwick*. As J. Don Vann notes,[15] when Sam Weller has himself imprisoned for failing to pay a debt so that he can join his unjustly imprisoned master, Pickwick asks his servant to sit and receives the reply, "I'd rayther not now, sir." Later, Sam replies "Wery much obliged to you sir, but I'd rayther not," when Pickwick asks Sam to whom he owes his freedom so that he can pay off the loan. Vann considers Melville's allusion to Dickens another compliment to the British writer. God save us all from such compliments! Pickwick and Sam unite in criticizing the system that is victimizing them; Bartleby is victimized by a system of which the Lawyer is a proud integral. Sam consigns himself to prison because he is committed to Pickwick; the Lawyer merely visits his imprisoned servant, and Bartleby rightly refuses to credit the Lawyer's false commitment. These are merely differences. But Sam's self-sacrifice sentimentally praises class deference, or at least a loyalty transcending class. Melville's Bartleby politely refuses deference to the Lawyer throughout, and the lawyer, denying his responsibility, contrives to punish Bartleby via the authorities. By such allusions-with-a-difference, the Lawyer's toadyism is attributed to Dickens as well; Dickens's reformist anger is made to appear trivial while he unconsciously abets the class assumptions of the system he means to oppose.

Dickens's apparent liberal generosity is, then, finally a miserly, dismissive refusal to confront either the bases of social injustice or the full force of the unreason. Remaining on the plane of social morality, Dickens cannot resolve evil; his novel is ultimately ignorant of and irrelevant to life's deepest questions. Dickens is too easy; Melville implicitly says to him, as Ahab to Starbuck, "thou requirest the little lower layer."

4

Bartleby is that lower layer. Like Dickens's Nemo, he is a scrivener whose background is obscure, whose identity has been significantly nullified, and who embodies a terminal despair. He is present yet absent through Melville's story, as Captain Hawdon is absent, already dead, yet present as the center of mystery in Dickens's novel. Bartleby appears to be asleep but is discovered to be dead upon the Lawyer's final visit to him in the Tombs, just as Nemo appears asleep but is discovered to be dead upon Tulkinghorn's only visit to his room above Krook's rag-and-bottle shop. Even the lodgings of the two characters carry forth Melville's revisioning of Dickens. The New York City prison, whose light-obscuring walls Melville emphasizes, are merely the extension of the Lawyer's office on Wall Street with its walls that obscure comprehension and frustrate communication and sympathy. Bartleby lodges with the Lawyer, a symbol of the system, as Nemo does with Krook, the little Lord Chancellor whose evil disarray and selfish unconcern serves as an emblem for Chancery. And, as Charlotte Walker Mendez points out, both Bartleby and Nemo are victims who are simultaneously granted great spiritual power. Snagsby's wife misnames Nemo as Nimrod, the Bible's "mighty hunter before the Lord." Of him, Milton comments in Book XII of *Paradise Lost*, "he from rebellion shall derive his name." So too, Mendez argues, Bartleby is a rebel and mighty hunter.[16]

But Mendez incorrectly assumes that Melville grants Bartleby no real biographical history because he began to write his tale before that installment of *Bleak House* had been published in which is disclosed Nemo's identity as Lady Dedlock's youthful lover and Esther's father. In all probability, that installment had appeared as Melville began to write his tale; and surely Melville would have foreseen some such disclosure, as Nemo's identity is obviously a mystery to be solved. Melville's Lawyer, in his guise as a Dickensian writer who would explain all by the ordinary circumstances of social life, mourns that he cannot account for Bartleby in this manner: "I believe that no materials exist for a full and satisfactory biography of this man. It is an irreparable loss to literature" (16). Perhaps not. Because Bartleby's melancholy cannot be socially explained—even the Dead-Letter-Office explanation is a rumor and, if true, indicates a despair that is Kafkaesque, more ontological than social—we are made to pass through (not to ignore or discount but neither to stop at) Melville's social critique of a hardened America to pose ultimate questions about the trans-social failures of existence to provide a home for human beings.

Bartleby is suggestive and unsolvable: by this, Melville reopens the questions of existence that Dickens prematurely closes. As Melville writes in one of those chapters of *The Confidence Man* that imitate an eighteenth-century defense of novelistic technique, the "great masters" of fiction seem to present inconsistent characters only to resolve such inconsistencies with a facile neatness. "They challenge astonishment at the tangled web of some character, and then raise admiration still greater at their satisfactory unravelling of it: in this way throwing open, sometimes to the understanding even of school misses, the last complications of that spirit which is affirmed by its creator to be fearfully and wonderfully made."[17] Bartleby is ultimately inexplicable because reality, traced to its origins, is so. The so-called realist Dickens, by untangling webs and explaining Nemo, falsifies the man and the mystery of despair.

But the characterization of Bartleby also serves Melville's purpose of compacting, for the brevity of the story is a related aspect of Melville's critique of Dickens. Not only does Melville get at the "little lower layer," which Dickens cannot, but he can delve it deeply in a fraction of the length of *Bleak House*. The story can do so much in so few words because Bartleby is a multigeneric character. Often in Melville's works, a figure of common sense is assaulted by a phantom who carries with him obscure but essential truths contradictory to and far beyond the conventions of common sense. Both Queequeg and Moby Dick haunt Ishmael as Isabel haunts Pierre, as Babo and Benito Cereno haunt Amasa Delano, as Bartleby haunts the Lawyer. He haunts him doubly. Bartleby's assertion of the irrational will expresses the freedom of life that the Lawyer's world of walls refuses and combats. Yet the very assertion is couched in a negative statement; and Bartleby's pallid composure, his lack of physical movement, and above all his silences also image death as a consequence of the rejection of communication, empathy, questioning. As an angel of life, Bartleby offers the Lawyer an alternative; as an angel of death, Bartleby states an accusation and an admonition. But Bartleby is not only a symbol; he is also a fellow found of a Sunday morning in shirt-sleeves.

Dickens attempts to write an epic, traditionally defined as the story of all things, by exhaustively portraying society top-to-bottom. Melville tries for an encyclopedic fiction that can startle by its compactness. The range of Bartleby's characterization, from downtrodden person to transcendent principle; the range of the Lawyer's speculations upon him, from commonsense to supernaturalism; and the constant merging of the everyday and the metaphysically emblematic: together these create not the story of all things but all ways of thinking a story together, the typical form of American epic once such content-bound endeavors as Barlow's *Colombiad* are eschewed. Epic becomes epistemological, on which grounds "Bartleby" is more exhaustive, larger, than *Bleak House.*

In any attempt at the encyclopedic in Western writing, biblical myth is prerequisite; and the employment of biblical myth as a general context for understanding provides Melville a final, ultimate grounds for his critique of Dickens. In *Bleak House,* Chancery, and everything linked to it by selfishness, constitute Hell on earth. Boythorne overtly makes the comparison and George Rouncewell innocently comments upon the heat of the fire in the Smallweed parlor. But evil on itself back recoils, as spontaneous combustion, "inborn, inbred, engendered in the corrupted humours of the vicious body itself," metes out justice (346). And if that should not be enough, political apocalypse is threatened. Future Jos who are treated like dogs "will lose even their bark—but not their bite" (116); and the murder of Tulkinghorn by the French Mademoiselle Hortense suggests the possibility of an English counterpart to a French revolution. That is a grisly threat more than a wish, but it does put forth the assurance that evil will not maintain itself.

Esther's narrative provides a more gentle, gradual, happy alternative. There, Eden is lost, then recovered, in a myth of eternal return. Esther buries her doll in a garden but finds happiness at a school called Greenleaf; and her departure from the school for the slimy, unnatural world of London and Chancery is yet another expulsion from the garden. Esther's laborious "duty" is an analogue to the labor Adam and

Eve and all their children must undertake to achieve, at time's end, a better paradise. Such a paradise is realized in the second Bleak House upon which I commented earlier. Jarndyce's godlike presentation of the place to Esther and the Christlike surgeon Woodcourt makes the allusion plain: "My dearest, Allan Woodcourt stood beside your father when he lay dead—stood beside your mother. This is Bleak House. This day I give this house its little mistress; and before God, it is the brightest day in my life" (650). Having passed through the dark night of experiential initiation that climaxes with the viewing of her dead mother, Esther can attain a matured innocence. As she largely recovers from the smallpox inflicted upon her not so much by contact with Jo as with the constituted England, notions (including her self-hating own) of original sin get powerfully refuted.

Not so in Melville. Spiritually starved, Bartleby lies starved to death on "a soft imprisoned turf" enclosed by the walls of the Tombs, a turf that at once grounds a sense of Bartleby's incorruptible innocence (the Lawyer considers the grass a miracle tantamount to grass seed dropped by birds in a cleft of the eternal pyramids) and serves as a grotesque parody of pastoral recovery.

Melville's only allusion to scripture is likewise more skeptical. At one point in the narrative, the Lawyer is tempted to murder Bartleby. This temptation calls to his mind the case of "poor Colt," a Cain-figure given the name of the American weapons company, who slew his employee Adams (Adam and Adam's Abel at once) in a business office. The Lawyer resists the temptation "by recalling the divine injunction: 'A new commandment give I unto you, that ye love one another.' Yes, it was that which saved me" (43). The Lawyer does not love another, nor his whole self, and he saves no one. *Bleak House,* with Nemo's law-copying initiating one plot and the deadly hand of written wills of inheritance another, threatens and then dispels a final evil that arises from a crisis of failed communication. In "Bartleby" the threat is consummated.

This final difference delineated by Melville is not merely a matter of optimism and pessimism. It is part and parcel of Melville's general complaint against Dickens that he is in many ways too easy, a cheater upon the examination of despair. At best, Dickens simply dispenses bromides that are irrelevant and anachronistic. The Lawyer, modulating his fury in the prudent delay of a dash, early declares "that I consider the abrogation of the office of Master of Chancery, by the new Constitution, as a—premature act" (17). In consideration of the story's general view of American society, this sentence seems less an implicit boast of American superiority than a sly indicator that Dickens's concerns are being superseded. *Bleak House* is another dead letter.

It is not, of course. Melville's reading of Dickens's masterpiece discounts too much. Dickens's image of fog is tantamount to Melville's walls; Dickens's understanding of perceptual issues is greater than Melville will allow. His employment of a narrative alternation between the impersonal, satiric voice and Esther provides complementary insights—we need both criticism and faith—and complementary blindnessess: to the satiric voice, Lady Dedlock "has no children" (7) and is simply a freezing, pompous lady; and Esther is, like Jarndyce, ever disappointed in her idealistic view of people. So too, Dickens's affirmations are more nervously qualified, more tentative than Melville acknowledges. Even Esther ends, and ends the novel, on a note of unfortunate coyness that expresses an imperfectly repressed vanity. Told by her husband that she has more than recovered her beauty, she replies that she has some doubt of this, that Jarndyce and her husband and her children truly are beautiful, "and that they can do very well without much beauty in me—even supposing—" (665). The final long dash suggests that a completely happy ending is for the to-be-continued future, as Esther is never fully freed from her unhappy upbringing. Indeed, in *Bleak House* Dickens provides a catalogue of the failures of liberal humanism and the partial quality of its successes. He challenges himself and his deepest social faith by insisting upon the limitations and misunderstandings of his very best characters. *Bleak House* in itself, as many readers have emphasized, is Dickens' own harsh critique upon his previous novels. And Melville ignores just this self-doubting aspect of Dickens's work because it would bring Dickens closer to his own skepticism.

But the question that matters in any looming of an anxiety of influence, as Harold Bloom repeatedly argues, is not whether the present writer has read his precedessor fairly and well but whether his misreading is creative. I have tried to show that it is so for Melville in his reduction of Dickens. I would stress more that his is not a merely individual action. By a Puritan inheritance touched upon in chapter one and soon to be detailed, an American writer is almost always *the* American writer, a microcosm of his ideal culture. British writers do not consider themselves in this way so readily, but it is natural for Americans to see them so. It is not only that Dickens is America's favorite writer in Melville's time but that Dickens is *the* English novelist. Thus, it is not merely Poe and Hawthorne whom Melville is defending, though their indirect presences in "Bartleby" go to suggest a class action. Melville against Dickens is, for Melville, a representative case—the New World against Britannia.

But this occasions a last question. How can Melville commit an act of literary patriotism at the same time that he is negating by his social critique any number of American Adamic myths? In the relation of "Bartleby" to *Bleak House,* as in many of the *Piazza Tales* within themselves, America is viewed as merely the last outpost of a decaying Western civilization, a new start at a very old and very vicious game. America continues British corruption. It matters more that the English institution of Chancery is imitated in New York than that it is eventually abrogated. Similarly, while Turkey, "a dependent Englishman," is paired with the American Nippers, and while it is Nippers who prospers and Turkey who degenerates after the sun reaches its meridian, that is only to suggest where the action is moving, not that the action has improved. The Puritan errand into the wilderness surely had as its goal no nation of Nippers.

One might resolve the paradox simply by remarking on Melville's typical double-mindedness. Or, with just a bit more difficulty, one might propose with Sacvan Bercovitch that, from the late seventeenth century on, Americans in their Jeremiah-like way have emphasized the gap between the American ideal and its sunken social reality. The writer is intrinsically countercultural by that, upholding the ideal America against the American consensus.[18] Thus Melville could be pro- and anti-American at once, depending upon what we mean by American: upholding a literature of unsettling discontent against the assurances of both Dickens and Wall Street.

The allusion to dead letters examples this protesting patriotism. We noted earlier that the dead letters imply an America disastrously hypocritical in its pieties, for letters make up words and words letters by one pun, while by another the word is The Word. As I noted, the scriptural cry of Jesus, "A new commandment give I unto you, that ye love one another" is cited by, of all people, the Lawyer to explain why he did not murder Bartleby. But the Lawyer indirectly murders Bartleby and the Bartley principle of rebellion within himself. Melville condemns an America represented by the Lawyer as dead to the Word.

Yet in the lawyer's recourse to Dickensian sentimentality as a response to a heartless world, the British representative writer is savaged as well. In fact, if we question where the very image of dead letters originates, we can round upon the entire argument. The image comes from Charles Dickens, indeed from three sources in Dickens. One we have mentioned: the singer Bogsby's joke that the fumes from Nemo's death left him "like a post office, for he hadn't a single note in him."

Earlier, in *Pickwick,* Dickens had made another joke, when a bagman tells his landlord of an uncle's dream wherein the uncle entered a yard full of worn-out mail coaches. The landlord questions "what those ghosts of mail-coaches carry in their bags" and the bagman, himself a pun, punningly replies "The dead letters, of course."[19] By transforming these jokes to mean tragically, Melville is impatiently telling Dickens to get serious. In the third source, however, Dickens *is* serious: the dead letter that ultimately dooms Lady Dedlock. Yet even here Melville's borrowing is critical, for, as in the case of Nemo and Bartleby, Melville makes a temporal, temporary mystery into an ultimate and permanent one concerning being in the world.

But there is still another source for the dead letter in Melville's mind, and it allows us to round upon ourselves. Another dead letter is grasped by a man who, like Bartleby, works in an office of killingly dull routine. From this governmental post, he too, like Bartleby in Melville's words, "had been suddenly removed by a change in the administration" (54). The man, of course, is Hawthorne. His customhouse contains elements of both the dead-letter office and the Lawyer's office. And if he does not die as Bartleby does upon expulsion from that second office, he at least sees his jobless self in an extended metaphor as "the decapitated surveyor" (*CE,* I, 43). His dead letter is both Surveyor Pue's dry account of the tribulation of Hester Prynne and the "A." But Hester's "A," which Hawthorne recovers literally and then literarily, is alive. If the Lawyer is someways Dickens at his worst, Bartleby is a failed Hawthorne. Dickens deadens true inquiry, and Bartleby is deadened by a lawyer who imitates Dickens' apparent goodwill and his covert refusals to see. Only Hawthorne, and now perhaps Melville, can make the letter live, however burningly, in passionate accusation.

To this I would add a final complication. Melville's generation hears again and again the British taunt that, without a history, without both the social differentiations and the social cohesion and national identity provided by history, no literature is possible. For the British viewing America, as later for Gertrude Stein commenting on an unevocative town, "There is no there there." We can see now the little lower layer for the part of "Bartleby" that seems to coincide with the social critique of *Bleak House.* It is to affirm that America now has its sufficiency of classes and systems as much as England, and that we know this chiefly by the evil they create. Class and system prove an American presence; they provide the Dickensian Lawyer with all his literary material and Melville with some. But Melville knows that such presence is an emptiness and that the British taunts are invalid because literature depends not upon history but upon thought. Thank you

then, England and Mr. Dickens. To our despair, your dead letters finally have arrived. The letter of social conventions penned by British history is read and slavishly acted upon by the Lawyer and the American
mass—it is by that sense that Bartleby is made exactly what the lawyer
calls him, "A bit of wreck in the mid Atlantic" (39), a victim of Old
World corruptions all too successfully en route to America. But the
letter of literary manners written by Charles Dickens is read, reviled,
wrecked, and written against by an American author so that he can
write at all.

Two

WRITER, NATION, CULTURE

3

A LITANY OF CAUSES

I

What in the name of universal truth has a poet, Heidegger's "shepherd of Being," to do with such trivial facts as nationality? Why can't a poet consider himself simply and grandly a poet, not the American poet? There comes a moment—there come many—when the writer of a study on the American attempt to wrestle with British influence must rebel against the issue he is treating, must wonder whether the issue signifies. Don't serious writers, especially those of visionary intent, play at such a quarrel with their left hands while keeping their good rights free to grasp at the cosmos?

Not in America. Here, several forces combined to make an issue so apparently banal and tangential as literary nationalism absolutely central to what Harold Bloom calls "the *writer* in a writer." I will isolate these factors—the rise of nationalism, the separation-anxieties of political independence, the controversy concerning democracy, the many myths of the west, and the puritan-derived idea of the self as national microcosm—to investigate each; but in lived experience, they combined willy-nilly into an irresistible compound.

To initiate that investigation, it is well nonetheless to admit misgivings concerning nationalism in literature. In doing so, we will find our investigation already well under way; for a great many literary Americans of the period shared these misgivings, and the eventual failure of the anti-nationalists tells us something.

Humanity versus nation, abstract conceptions versus local integrities, art itself versus particular allegiances: "There are always, it seems," Geoffrey Hartman writes, "two genii fighting for the soul of the artist: two stars, or visions of destiny, or Genius and the genius loci."[1] We have heard from the second genius. Melville summarizes his message: "let America first praise mediocrity even, in her children, before she praises (for everywhere merit demands acknowledgement from everyone) the best excellence in the children of any other land."[2] But we have seen how quickly the genius loci can seem a genius more loco than loci, as Melville, with his usual double mindedness, turns satirically upon his own real nationalism by advertising Pop Emmons.

Now hear the genius of universality, if for the moment you will accept Benjamin Franklin as a rather portly spirit. His Poor Richard addresses the issue by analogy: " 'Tis methinks a poor Excuse for the bad Entertainment of Guests, that the Food we set before them, tho' coarse and ordinary, is *of one's own Raising, off one's own Plantation,* &c. when there is Plenty of what is ten times better, to be had in the Market."[3]

That is, national-minded writers like Melville and Emerson would disown the most simple- and literal-minded versions of their views, and meanwhile large numbers of anglophiles, Hamiltonians, and cosmopolites attacked all formulae for a distinct literature. Everyone, Franklin included, wanted literature to be written in America, but not everyone wanted an American literature. For every Young America club (that group led by the bizarre Cornelius Mathews, but founded by the New York Duyckinck brothers, Melville's publishers and the editors of the finest anthology of American literature in the fifties), there would be a periodical like *The Knickerbocker* that ridiculed nationalism in the name of "the poetry of the heart and the affections." A reviewer in the more moderate, Boston-based *North American Review* spoke for many in complaining that "an intense national self-consciousness, though the shallow may name it patriotism, is the worst foe to true and generous unfolding of national genius."[4] Lowell, as we have seen, wanted a literature free of foreign influence, but he was not passionate for an official American literature, as it too would enforce preconception. Let us expend our energies on creating a just commonwealth, he writes; "We can, in the meantime, borrow a great poet when we want one, unless the pleasure and profit which we derive from the works of a great master, depend upon the proprietary right in him secured to us by compatriotism." Longfellow, like Lowell truly interested in encouraging American writers but skeptical toward making a project of it, provides the fullest argument as he takes the character of a Mr. Churchill confronting a literary patriot:

> Mere nationality is often ridiculous. Every one smiles when he hears the Icelandic proverb, "Iceland is the best land the sun shines upon." Let us be natural, and we shall be national enough. Besides, our literature can be strictly national only so far as our character and modes of thought differ from those of other nations. Now, as we are very like the English, —are, in fact, English under a different sky, —I do not see how our literature can be very different from theirs.[5]

Unaware, Longfellow's elisions show us exactly what is impure in this anti-national universalism. What we call universal or natural is often no more than what is traditional or habitual—for the American writer, English literature. As Benjamin Spencer writes, "To accept English literature as the perfected organ of universal taste was also, even for many a literary nationalist, to accept the corollary of a universal English style, whose values and harmonies and usages had been fixed by the Augustans in permanent standards of elegance and correctness."[6] Whether universalism referred to reason, rules, taste, as it did in the Enlightenment, or to a spontaneous seeing of nature whole, as it did in the Romantic period, England seemed to center the universe.

We have here two related reasons for the failure of the universalist argument. It failed in the sense that the major writers who emerged in nineteenth-century America refused it. Emerson and Whitman, Melville and Hawthorne would acknowledge far more generously than would the programmatic nationalists their ties to England; but they also would work more assiduously at cutting those ties that bind and at asserting new-world differences that matter. What might be perceived immediately as the universal heart would turn out, on scrutiny, to beat British. And to accept as inevitable British-filtered universals was tantamount to defining the American writer as a latecomer. For a latecomer, the universe is never unmediated; he never sees with his own eyes.

This is precisely the dread at the center of all influence-anxiety, national and otherwise: not that the present writer will be unequal to his ancestors or that each past master has filled a possibility and thus removed it—these are real but secondary fears; it is the threat to originary selfhood that is their center and self. We know that the world seeming to begin with our birth has preceded us; and, to feel alive, we battle against that knowledge. We do so because of what Kenneth Burke calls "familial definition," the logic—neither true nor false but persistent—by which we equate essence with origin.[7] To discover the ultimate of a thing (say, a neurosis), we look for its beginning (perhaps a traumatic childhood experience). The further we exist from the origin, source, beginning, the less we exist essentially at all.

That is why every culture creates its own myth of creation and its own rites for re-enacting this creation, to battle late-middleness; and this local myth makes universal claims. The universal must be locally centered; to borrow a universal is an anomaly. Let Longfellow sneer at the saying, "Iceland is the best land the sun shines upon"; it is the expression of a law. "Any local goddess," Eliade writes, "tends to become *the* Great Goddess; any village anywhere *is* the 'Center of the World,' and any wizard whatever pretends, at the height of his ritual, to be the Universal Sovereign."[8] To get at the universal, America had to become centered in regard to it; to refuse that centering by considering Boston a suburb of London was an untenable alternative. Thus an argument that began by ignoring or defending the British influence ended by repudiating it: "Instead of studying Man," Brownson writes, "we have studied English liteature; . . ."[9]

There is one other, much simpler reason for the failure of a British-tinged universalism. It didn't work. It had been tried already, in the American neoclassicism of the eighteenth century, and found wanting. Universalism would persist but it would be transformed to accommodate nationalism by the union of Genius and genius loci.

If we define the term broadly, nationalism, as Eliade's observation makes clear, has existed from the beginnings of socialized time. It is more an inevitable of the imagination than a fact in political history. Perhaps that is why the rise of nationalism, like the rise of the English middle class, is variously ascribed to eight or ten different centuries. Nonetheless, it is fair to mark an increased emphasis on literary nationalism beginning with the Renaissance validation of modern Europe and peaking in the late eighteenth and early nineteenth centuries. This emphasis provided a particularly strong base for the tribal centralism that Eliade discerns in all times and places.

This narrower, literary nationalism, which Hartman cogently defines as "Art seeking Pop—art seeking its father figure in folk culture,"[10] was itself a chiefly German import of the 1810s. In 1813, the *Analectic* excerpted portions of Madame De Staél's *Influence of Literature Upon Society* in which she argued that the literature of any nation reflected its social, political, and religious character and modified that character in turn. Two years later, A. W. Schlegel's similar ideas appeared in *Port Folio;* von Humboldt, Herder, and Friedrich Schlegel, with his view of literature as a symbol-system conveying national character, gained belated currency with their versions of this concept. It is difficult now, when further history has associated nationalism with bigotry, militarism, and mindless patriotism, to see how this concept would seem sunny and freeing to the American romantics. But it helpfully devalued the old universalism—in Spencer's words, the new nationalism considered "the attempt to erect the 'rules' of any literary epoch into universals" as "a despotism of taste"; it encouraged a new universality based on the idea that "the beautiful and grand can be comprehended only through the external and modifying particulars necessary to their existence."[11] Unlike its subsequent vulgarization, it provided a relativist appreciation of different cultures, and a beleaguered and belittled American culture would accept happily such an offer of egalitarian appreciation.

American writers swallowed literary nationalism whole. By 1825, Bryant gave universality—"The passions and affections, virtue and vice, are of no country"—a nationalist corollary: the native writer "must show how the infinite diversities of human character are yet further varied, by causes that exist in our own country, exhibit our peculiar modes of thinking and action, and mark the effect of these upon individual fortunes and happiness." Longfellow paraphrased Frederick Schlegel enthusiastically through the thirties; and E. T. Channing set for a Harvard student the problem, "How Genius may be fully manifested in a . . . Literary Work, upon a Foreign or Ancient Subject, —and yet full justice done to the subject." The student was Thoreau, and he replied that while an author should see his subject, universal man, with a naked eye, "he must look through a national glass."[12]

That is the public record on literary nationalism, and it seems sanguine enough. I would suggest that it was as much a torture as an encouragement. In Europe, Raymond Williams notes, "national literature" deepened history into a tradition;[13] and, coinciding with the stricter sense of what constituted a literary work, this created disputes about who and what should be included. But Americans might envy such disputes as the embarrassment of riches. Instead, they were asked to celebrate a *Volksgeist* which had not yet developed, and they were asked to formulate a literary tradition from works not yet written.

The very valuation of original genius was a recent development, dating in England from Young and Johnson. Only then, William Wimsatt tells us, did literary worth come to mean "to be in on the threshold of literary history, to get there first, even if with the least."[14] Now, quickly, originality was coupled with nationalism to beget an extraordinary extrapersonal pressure. The search for a folk culture could lead Cooper to the frontier and, ambivalently, to American Indian mythology; it would inspire Emerson and Hawthorne to their revaluations of the Puritan theocracy. In that sense, the nationalist idea was a benign muse. In encouraging the writer to identify with his country, nationalism was neither benign nor malignant but simply part of our story. But in emphasizing nationality as a suprapolitical union and in assuming that all nationalities had a rich past, it made the British literary hegemony and the nonappearance of an American literature intolerable. Nationalism also supported without comfort the linking of those two facts.

2

Nationalist literary theory gained special piquancy in America because its importation followed so rapidly upon political independence. One might have expected the nation's brief federal existence to serve as persuasive justification for an absence of literary and folk traditions; instead, independence served to further shame. The phrase "American literature" became popular in the eighties and the first two national literary anthologies were published in the nineties; but the gap between political independence and success and literary dependence and failure was the main rhetorical idea to arise from the revolution. "America must be as independent in *literature* as she is in *politics*," Noah Webster wrote in the 1780s; nearly half a century later, the *New American Review* editorialized, "We have indeed shaken off her [England's] civil yoke, but we hug yet closer and closer the chains of intellectual bondage"; still, in 1845, Poe was crying "In letters as in government we require a Declaration of Independence," indeed "a Declaration of War," a "nationality that will throw off this [British] yoke." Bryant had found in the revolution the manifestation of a new spirit: "the general amibition to distinguish ourselves as a nation was not without its effect on our literature." Yes it was, Cooper sadly disagreed two decades later: "I know very well it is said, that the war of 1812 liberated the American mind from its ancient thralldom, and for a time it did; so did the war of revolution; but no sooner did things, in both instances, revert back to their ancient channels, than the habits of thought appear to have kept them company." Despite Freneau's totally sensible insistence that "political and literary independence" are "two very different things . . . the first was accomplished in about seven years, the latter will not be completely effected, perhaps, in as many centuries," the analogy and the literary failure to fulfill it held true for most. And like the myth of preventive British domination in which it was incorporated, the failed analogy became more threatening as the years piled up. Such Englishmen as Robert Southey jumped on the trope: "See what it is," he wrote to Landor, "to have a nation to take its place among civilized states before it has either gentlemen or scholars."[15]

But Southey's is a half-truth. If Americans could have dated their beginning surely at 1776 or 1783 or 1812, the embarrassment over the lack of a literature would have been less keen. Cotton Mather was speaking of "our little New-English nation" as early as 1702; and colonial scholars as different as Sacvan Bercovitch and Richard Slotkin have insisted on the degree to which pre-federal America had seen its destiny as distinct from Britain's and had begun to build prodigious myth-making structures as soon as colonization occurred. Yet much later, Orestes Brownson blamed the British hegemony on a colonial complex—"Colonists almost invariably regard the mother country as their moral and intellectual superior"—which had persisted long after independence as "a habit of looking to England for direction in nearly all cases which we have not yet wholly surmounted."[16] Daniel Boorstin argues persuasively that the nation did not experience itself as such even during the war of independence—in Virginia, it was "the Tobacco War"—or completely as such long after the war. Henry Steele Commager makes the distinction that "in the Old World the nation came before the state" while "in America the state came before the nation." He continues, "In the Old World nations grew out of well-prepared soil, built upon a foundation of history and traditions; in America the foundations were still to be laid, the seeds still to be planted, the traditions still to be formed." Robert Spiller says simply, "Political independence from England established the need rather than the actuality of cultural unity. And even in political terms, as George B. Forgie demonstrates, "throughout the early part of the nineteenth century it was a common observation that the Union was evanescent."[17]

Both views—that an American culture originates long before 1776 or that it fails to occur long after 1776—are supportable, depending upon one's definition of culture. Mather's phrase "New England nation" is itself ambivalent. In all, there was just enough of a culture dating from the seventeenth century to make worrisome the absence of more of one.

Independence brought with it another, nearly opposite fear. An American colonist could, if he wished, see himself as a part or extension of European culture. Now, by a willful act of rebellion, that prerogative seemed lost. Thence derives both Hugh Henry Brackenridge's purpose for his *United States Magazine,* to prove that America was "able to cultivate the belles lettres, even disconnected with Britain" and, conversely, such insistences as the historian Motley's that "Politically, we shall soon become a distinct nation—socially and morally we shall continue to be Europeans."[18]

This latter sentiment, as we have seen, did not carry, and nothing could disguise a certain guilt occasioned by what Brackenridge euphemistically called "disconnection." Englishmen and Americans alike spoke in metaphors that established a family drama. The historian Gerald Critolf paraphrases one version of that drama: "The colonies were John Bull's children. He had been indulgent and protective when they were growing and in danger. However, with the danger removed after 1763, he asked them to pay a share of the family bills. They claimed the right to help to determine the size of the payments, but father said, 'No,' and the children cut the family ties." And justly so, for the familial metaphor employed by Americans depends, as Jay Fliegelman argues, on an eighteenth-century transformation of the idea of family. Both Locke and the Scottish commonsense philosophers "insisted on a noncoercive rather than authoritarian model of the family" with a call for "filial autonomy" and an emphasis on the parental responsibility "to encourage that transition from adolescence to adulthood."[19] Something of this notion of justified rebellion against the father goes into Hawthorne's "My Kinsman, Major Molineux," though there the repudiated father figure is an uncle, not an Englishman but a colonial in the service of England who sleeps with a prostitute as an emblem of his national disloyalty.

The British figured these familial images differently, by the older authoritarian model. The usually pro-American *Monthly Review* scorned Jefferson's *Notes on Virginia* with the comment, "these *children of yesterday*, with the usual presumption of youth, affect to consider themselves as the most enlightened race existing. . . ." Many years later, on the eve of the Civil War, Matthew Arnold would write of Americans as children in need of "a moral lesson." Ruskin, as late as 1874, invoked the father-educator, wayward child analogy without any restraint at all:

> England taught the Americans all they have of speech hitherto. What thoughts they have not learned from England are foolish thoughts; what words they have not learned from England, unseemly words; the vile among them not being able even to be humorous parrots, but only obscene mocking-birds.

During the same period, in his conciliatory note to *North America*, Trollope, knowing exactly what he was about, would address Americans as "friends" whom "I call my cousins and love as brothers." Trollope need not have known W. E. Channing's angry reply to Heraud's insistence that Emerson was a disciple of Carlyle—"Emerson is a brother, not a son"—to know that he way paying Americans a high compliment by changing the metaphor.[20]

"Mother country" was the other epithet for Britain, but it made little difference. Brownson saw it as symbolizing the American attitude to Britain as "the superior and ruling nation" even after the revolution. "We wished for her approbation; we sought her sanction for what we had done and were doing; and were anxious that she should own that we had not been naughty children in running away from our mother and setting up for ourselves." It is the *father*-son relation that remains functional here except for the invocation of mercy. "We do not blame thee, elder World, nor really separate ourselves from thee," Whitman writes in "Song of the Exposition"; and he adds parenthetically, "Would the son separate himself from the father?"[21]

Whitman's rhetorical question may be a real one. And Brownson, even satiricially, makes a key point about the American anxiety over "running away" and a resultant search for self-justification. In fact, the revolution was only the latest example of a pattern going back to the Puritan emigration from England and reasserting itself whenever British rule was challenged.

Richard Slotkin describes this pattern most fully in *Regeneration Through Violence*. In regard to the homeland they had deserted the Puritan emigrants were placed in a position that finds a recent analogue in the position of American draft-resisters who chose to emigrate to Canada during the Vietnam War. The American Puritans had opted out of an accelerating crisis. They had left voluntarily, despite exhortations to remain. To create their City on the Hill, a secular representation of the City of God, "they had been compelled to breach and violate the ties of blood, custom, and affection that bound them to England." The continuing criticism directed at them by the English Puritans and royal magistrates further irritated their anxiety over this break. "To the Puritans who remained in England, they were men fleeing from the task of rebuilding the church in England. To the crown they were, potentially at least, political separatists seeking to escape from the requirement of civil law and duty."[22]

The Americans thus experienced a psychological necessity to practice remembered English ways, oppose Indian culture, and in all ways disprove the charge that they had deserted European civilization for American savagery. But they felt compelled as well to justify their project in itself as unique and uniquely ordained. This led in turn to a repudiation of England. The American Puritan, Sacvan Bercovitch writes, "had to prove the Old World a *second* Babylon; otherwise, his readers might consider it (along with America) to be part of the universal spiritual Babylon."[23] Thus at one moment the Puritan would affirm his Englishness by opposition to the Indian; at the next, he would link the Englishman to the Indian and place himself in lonely opposition to both.[24]

The ambivalences of the American partly explain the alternations in Puritan typological figures: between America as a desert place of trial in a drama of temporary exile from the failed promised land of England, a drama akin to the Babylonian captivity, and America as itself the promised land, the potential place of scriptural fulfillment.

These ambivalences also resulted in a colonial rhetoric Slotkin characterizes by "a tendency toward polemic and apology, in which the colonist simultaneously argued the firmness and stability of his European character and (paradoxically) the superiority of his new American land and mode of life to all things European."[25] This pattern of guilt-informed justification easily outlasted the Puritan heyday. The Declaration of Independence is informed by remembered rhetoric: "a decent respect to the opinions of mankind requires that they [the revolutionaries] should declare the causes which impel them to the separation." One should remember that, only twelve years prior to 1776, Americans had concluded a war in which they fought for several years side by side with the British, and successfully. While the French and Indian War had shown Americans how different they had become from the Englishmen with whom they shared ancestry, it also had raised their pride of membership in the British Empire. Simultaneously, the religious fervor of the Great Awakening recalled the original motives for emigration from Britain two centuries earlier. The postrevolutionary ambivalences toward British literary domination noted earlier in such writers as Irving and Lowell has much to do with these renewals of the initial separation anxiety.

So too, and more importantly, do the more anti-British attitudes. Political revolution had weakened the necessity for justification that depended on Americans proving themselves still essentially English. Simultaneously, it had strengthened that contrary claim for justification based on American uniqueness and superiority. Again, America superiority in the nineteenth century would mean primarily superiority to England. The British literary domination thus not only seemed to contradict independence; it positively frustrated and made ridiculous any claims for cultural superiority, forcing such claims embarrassedly into the future tense.

3

I have noted before this that the Anglo-American literary struggle was onesided in two related ways, both of them sad for the Americans: in the extreme British advantage and in the much greater and more emotional American involvement. In only one area was the British involvement nearly equal—where the argument became more explicitly political and social. The issue concerned the daring extensions of representative government and egalitarian social forms in the United States; in a word, democracy, a term once as controversial as it now is blandly honorific. That "once" is surprisingly recent. In 1874, a writer for the *Dublin Review* remarked: "We are apt to look on Yankees in the mass as vulgar, sectarian, swaggering, democratic, money worshipping folk. . . ."[26] Of course, American democratic idealism had not waited upon independence; but the revolution and subsequent documents of confederation, however much affected by prerevolutionary developments, yet gave a new, official reality to the ideals.

Here especially, one properly may question the literary centrality of such a clearly extraliterary concern. But facts quiet skepticism. Nearly every formula for an American literature included the challenge of translating democracy into literary modes. Melville, in defining the American writer as "a man who is bound to carry republican progressiveness into Literature as well as into Life," exemplifies this sentiment. Democratic demands are implied too in Emerson's well-known plaint, "We have listened too long to the courtly muses of Europe" (*CW*, I, 69). Brownson is characteristically specific, contentious, and extreme: English literature is excellent, but "it is not exactly the literature for young republicans"; just as "England is the most artistocratic country in the world," so "its literature is, with some noble exceptions, artistocratic"; it "overflows with servility to the great, and with contempt, or what is worse, condescension for the little." But Whitman takes Brownson further: Scott is "the noblest, healthiest, cheeriest romancer that ever lived," but he "and Tennyson, like Shakespeare, exhale that principle of caste which we Americans have come on earth to destroy."[27]

The British had a ready reply to this, and it was as far as possible from engaging them in a competition over which nation was more democratic: the American nation was ever so much more democratic, and that was precisely why the Americans were incapable of literature. From *The Athenaeum,* 1829: "We do not believe that America has a literature; we do not see that it has the germs of one; we do not believe that it can have one till its institutions are fundamentally changed." Such a conclusion was as telling as it was typical. The neutral De Tocqueville would second it: "The principle of equality not only diverts men from the description of ideal beauty—it also diminishes the number of objects to be described." And the Americans themselves were partly convinced. Cooper noted that democracy, contrary to expectations, had not encouraged "novelty and variety" but a certain sameness. He finds this sameness admirable, for Americans "are not only like each other, but they are remarkably like that which common sense tells them they ought to resemble." Nonetheless, "However useful and respectable all this may be in actual life, it indicates but one direction to the man of genius." Whitman worries likewise: "That primal and interior something in man, in his soul's abysms, coloring all, and, by exceptional fruitions, giving the last majesty of his . . . modern science and democracy appear to be endangering, perhaps eliminating." He goes on to see that this is mere appearance, that eventually democracy will provide even "greater individualities."[28] But when the poet who sees the ideal in the real and present is forced into the future tense, one can be sure that a wound has been endured.

More generally, the leading proof of democratic efficacy, a spectacular degree of national prosperity, caused more concern than pride when the issue was democracy's effect on culture. In *Unquiet Eagle: Memory and Desire in the Idea of American Freedom, 1815–1860,* Fred Somkin quotes John Adams's aphorism, "Human Nature, in no form of it, ever could bear Prosperity," and goes on to describe the internal debate over what he calls "Prosperity the Riddle." He shows that for every American who insisted that economic prosperity was the base and the predictor of cultural wealth, there was another who found prosperity a disastrous mischanneling of ambition away from the imaginative arts.[29]

One element of the British attack—the notion that only an aristocratic leisure class could produce literature or serve as interesting characters in it—was as weak as the American excuse that no literature had been created because the people were too busy conquering a continent. Bryant, for instance, could ridicule the argued necessity of aristocratic fictional characters by saying that a depiction of that class "whose only employment is to glitter at places of public resort, to follow a perpetual round of amusements, and to form plans to outshine, thwart, and vex each other" would confine the writer "to a narrow and most barren circle" and require of him "an undue proportion of heartlessness, selfishness, and vice in his pictures of society."[30] Here, as elsewhere in the Anglo-American relation, literary and social issues become indistinguishable; while Bryant defends the potential of a democratic American literature, he simultaneously attacks the reality of a class-oriented British society.

But the more general charge of democratic levelling was less easily parried. This charge is dramatized and specified in scores of Victorian novels. A recommended character in Mrs. Catherine Gore's *Peers and Parvenus* expresses the exemplary critique: to him, Americans "wish not only to bring every one to one common plan, but they desire even more—they wish to run their general rolling stone over all mental distinctions, and vulgarize their highest and best nature, by insisting on one common standard of familiar manners."[31] Eventually, American writers would find ways to capitalize on such a critique by boldly accepting it but changing its tone—as in Whitman's persona, self-described as "one of the roughs, a kosmos"; and they would be compelled to invent a literature less dependent on social class and circumstance and a literary model less dependent on mimetic assumptions. But my point here is simply this: the democracy debate, and especially the American sense of vulnerability in it, encouraged writers to identify not only with a mythy folk-culture but with contemporary, factual practices and institutions of government. In this, the American version of literary nationalism extended beyond the European renderings.

Throughout this section, I may seem to be hymning Yankee ingenuity, the ability of American writers and critics to turn problems into possibilities. That is indeed the cheerful portion of my meaning. But one might as easily see in this process a compelled, reactive defensiveness that would confine or delimit the possibilities of literary forms in America and occasionally misshape them by encouraging self-caricature.

I mention this now because, in the democracy debate alone, this negative effect was visited upon British literature. One would expect the most radical elements of British society to have cheered on American literary prospects as proof of democratic efficacy. That did occur to some extent, but weakly. Whig periodicals were ungenerous. Extreme liberals, who saw some of their programs realized in American, native Scotsmen, who empathized with the Americans out of their own historical suffering of British contempt, and journalists writing for the middle class, who imagined a sharing of aspirations between Americans and that class, were the most dependable enthusiasts—and they were entirely undependable. Clarence Gohdes, who has written the major study of nineteenth-century British reactions to American literature, generalizes: "always, whether radicals, Scotchmen, or panderers to Demos, there was a tendency on the part of a writer, once established, to assume the long-nosed attitude toward all things America."[32] Literary nationalism had its British effect; American rebellion and success hurt a national ego in which radicals, too, shared.

American democracy threatened England. The English reacted by defending the aristocracy and class distinctions in general far more confidently and aggressively than they would apart from the American issue. Apart from it, we know, Victorian English intellectuals were divided among themselves and yet unanimously concerned with adapting English traditions to accommodate contemporary aspirations. The

British came across to Americans as more unitary, hardhearted, and unregenerately reactionary and feudal than they were. This was particularly true in literature, which England's own democracy-anxiety infected. Apart from the notorious cases of Dickens and Arnold, there developed a continuing equation in Victorian fiction whereby Americans were identified, usually implicitly, with the rebellious British working class. Even when empathy was intended, impossible and ugly condescension toward both the British poor and the American average was the effect. In all, the British chose a literary stance toward democratic America that gave support and encouragement to the American equation of contemporary England with the past in the most negative senses: as anachronistic, outmoded, oppressively dead-in-life.

4

The myth of the west contributed to this trope in more subtle ways. The hoary idea that religion and culture progressed westward through history, like the sun, could be employed to suggest that the existence of America put England in the shade; England was finished, over. But the west myth is a complex one, and its literary application could threaten American writers as much as it emboldened them.

The Christian basis for the myth has an impressive source. As Edwin Fussell writes, "Christ Himself (according to St. Matthew) predicted that the Son of Man would spring from the East and flash across to the West."[33] The persistence of the myth's sacred aspect and another source of the myth are expressed in Christopher Columbus's interpretation of his discovery of America: "God made me the messenger of the new heaven and the new earth of which He spoke in the Apocalypse by Saint John, after having spoken of it by the mouth of Isaiah; and He showed me the spot where to find it." Local habitations always had been attached to the westward movement, but only with America was the fulfillment of that westward course localized. The American Puritans seized upon this notion as the very basis for their America; but one did not have to be an official Puritan for the idea to possess a powerful force. To Harriet Beecher Stowe, Cotton Mather's *Magnalia*, which she had read in her youth, validly set forth "the glorious future of the United States of America . . . commissioned to bear the light of liberty and religion through all the earth and to bring in the great millennial day, when wars should cease and the whole world, released from the thralldom of evil, should rejoice in the light of the Lord."[34]

Stowe's mention of "the light of liberty" importantly spreads the myth beyond the strictly sacred. But this is no innovation. The myth has its origin not in Christianity but in the solar symbolism of Egypt; and the revival of this symbology in Ficino and the Italian humanists insured the myth's extra-religious meanings. In fact, the nature of Christianity in itself encourages secular, historical applications of the myth. Christianity's chief innovation in relation to all previous religious life, Mircea Eliade contends, consists in "its valorization of Time—in the final reckoning, its *redemption* of Time and of History." The rites of earlier religions consisted in a "leap backward" by which time and history were abolished; Christianity renounces "the reversability of cyclic Time, it posits a time that is irreversible" and thus "strives to *save* history."[35]

Eliade himself does not mention Christian typology, most simply stated as the idea that all historical events are shadows of Christ's career on earth and that Christ's career itself is an anticipation of the Apocalypse; he rather emphasizes the Christian faith in history as a revelation. But typology, with its looking-forward, particularly lends subordinate secular meanings to the myth of the west. From there, a small but decisive move can render the secular meanings independent, as in the opening of *Sir Gawain* where the reign of King Arthur is seen to derive from a westward movement that begins with the founding, by Aeneus and his descendents, of a series of western kingdoms; or in Bishop Berkeley's "Westward the course of Empire takes it way . . . ."; or in the German idealist myth of an imminent third age that will renew and complete History.[36] Alternately, as with the American Puritans, the secular an divine promises of the west may become indistinguishable.

Thus, just as a Jonathan Edwards could follow Columbus and the Puritan divines in emphasizing the religious significance of the myth to America—"AMERICA is that Part of the World which is pointed out in the *Revelation* of GOD for . . . this glorious scene" of "the *millennium* state"—so a John Adams could emphasize secular progress: "There is nothing more ancient in my memory than the observation that arts, sciences, and empire have travelled westward; and in conversation it was always added since I was a child, that their next leap would be over the Atlantic into America."[37]

The poetic version of the myth, which centered on the figure of the muses and thus combined secular and religious emphases, was inherited by American writers from a British literary tradition that the America version of the myth would serve to devalue. Geoffrey Hartman documents the invocation of the west myth through three centuries of British literature: "From Milton through Thomson, Gray, Collins, and the Romantics, the idea of a Progress of Poetry from

Greece or the Holy Land to Britain is essential." But for the British, especially after the Enlightenment, the wild aspirations suggested by "Muse" and "West" had to be tempered and demystified by British mildness and rationality. "The poem becomes, in a sense, a seduction of the poetical genius by the genius loci: the latter invites—subtly compels—the former to live within via media charms."[38]

The Americans took several attitudes toward this British version of the myth. They could simply ally themselves with its mildness, as in the eighteenth-century poem inviting the Muses, whom a "Western course has pleas'd . . . all along," to "soft retreats" in a mild American landscape.[39] The anglophiles would go further, by citing the western myth as proof that America, as merely the latest extension of a process in which England is the immediate predecessor, should take over English literary habits. Crèvecoeur, in his famous passage, represents a middle, somewhat self-contradictory position adopted by many native Americans: "What then is the American, this new man? . . . *He* is an American, who leaving behind him all his ancient prejudices and manners, receives new ones from the new mode of life he has embraced, the new government he obeys, and the new rank he holds . . . Americans are the Western pilgrims, who are carrying along with them that great mass of arts, sciences, vigour, and industry which began long since in the east; they will finish the great cycle."[40] Crèvecoeur wavers between seeing the American as "leaving behind him" or "carrying along" the European past and its achievements.

More often, however, American literary nationalists would invoke the myth to argue that Britain had been superseded. Thoreau goes farthest in this: in "Walking" he equates the West with the Wild and argues that England never played its role in the westward movement precisely because its literature sought to make the muse mild: "English literature, from the days of the minstrels to the Lake Poets—Chaucer and Spenser and Milton, and even Shakespeare, included—breathes no quite fresh and, in this sense, wild strain . . . Her wilderness is a greenwood, her wild man a Robin Hood."[41] Thoreau here plays havoc with the British fear, emphasized in Hartman's account, that English poets had lost connections to the poetic source, that the westward movement had broken down.

No other American went so far as to argue that the sun of inspiration had hopped over the British Isles on its westward course. But in the contest of interpretations—has the British torch been passed on to America or has the American torch quenched the British—the more aggressive, anti-English attitude held sway. In America, the myth's apocalyptic connotations overwhelmed its implications of gradual progress, for the sun sets and history completes and transcends itself here. "Heaven or Europe," went the Puritan saying. If renewal and renovation were the keynotes, England was part of the Old World in need of renewal and renovation. John Adams thus quotes the lines seen by a friend who imagined them drilled on a rock by the first emigrants: "The Eastern nations sink, their glory ends/And empire rises where the sun descends." And an eighteenth-century poet anticipates Adams (or follows the imagined Puritan) in shouting that long after Britain should be laid in its grave, the arts would be perfected in "th'utmost Bourne/Of California."[42]

But, like the claims of separation and superiority to which it is related, this American-aggressive version of the myth falls prey to anxiety. It places a special pressure on the development of an American literature: in its apocalyptic expression, the myth demands a specially distinctive literature, one which would not so much follow from the literature of the past as it would break with that past to create a literary future that Old World literature would follow. This reversal, whereby American writers would influence others rather than be subject to influence themselves, is implied in Thoreau's national boast that also expresses an attendant anxiety: If America is not "the Great Western pioneer whom the nations follow. . . . . . to what end does the world go on, and why was America discovered?" Similarly, Thoreau will proclaim, "The Atlantic is a Lethean stream, in our passage over which we have had an opportunity to forget the Old world and its institutions." But he then adds, with some fear, "If we do not succeed this time, there is perhaps one more chance for the race before it arrives on the banks of the Styx; and that is the Lethe of the Pacific, which is three times as wide. . . ."[43]

Anxiety increases in proportion to the American claim: the failure of an American literature and culture will be disastrous not only to America but to the entire world, whose destiny is now America's. Given this extraordinary pressure, Emerson himself would retreat to Crèvecoeur's ambivalences in a manner especially reminiscent of the Puritan emigrants in their separation-anxiety. On his second trip to England, Emerson reports himself as telling Carlyle that "England, an old and exhausted island, must one day be contented, like other parents, to be strong only in her children." But in this same book, *English Traits*, he employs the myth of the west in its alternate (sequential rather than competitive) aspect, saying that the "American is only the continuation of the English genius into new conditions" (*W*, V, 277–78,36). Whitman, too, retreated to a moderate position. "Years ago I thought Americans ought to strike out separate, and have expressions

of their own in highest literature." He still believes this in 1881 but
with a qualification: "I see that this world of the West, as part of all,
fuses inseparably with the East" and thus, echoing but also reversing
Thoreau, "If we are not to hospitably receive and complete the inaugurations of the old civilizations, and change their small scale to the
largest, broadest scale, what on earth are we for?"[44]

Not for an absolute newness, apparently; Whitman retains to
some extent the idea of America as the western fulfillment, but fulfillment here is stated in the less threatening image of a magnification of
earlier cultures. When rhetoricians of the joyous extreme begin to
moderate their views, this mildness testifies to the myth's nerve-
wracking demands.

To comprehend this pressure fully, we must recall the demonic,
inverted version of the west myth. Richard Slotkin notes that this version alternated or even combined in Europe with the hopeful vision of
blessed Western isles. In it, the unsettled west represents a horrifying
regression into primitive savagery and a chaos both external and psychological. The west is the land of "the sunset, death, darkness, passion, and dreams"; it is "the world below consciousness."[45] It is this
frightening version of the myth against which the Puritan emigrants
had to defend their enterprise, this version that George Herbert employs to qualify his generous handing over of religion. In "The Church
Militant," he begins, "Religion Stands on Tiptoe in our Land,/Ready
to pass to the American Strand," but immediately adds:

> Yet as the Church shall thither westward file,
> So Sinne shall trace and dog her instantly:
> . . . .
> Thus also Sinne and Darkness follow still.
> The Church and Sunne with all their power and skill.

Keats invokes the negative myth with none of Herbert's balance when
he mourns the American habitation of his brother and sister-in-law in
his "Second Ode to Fanny Browne." He can wish only

> To banish thoughts of that most hateful land,
> Dungeoner of my friends, that wicked strand
> Where they were wreck'd and live a wrecked life;
> That monstrous region, whose dull rivers pour,
> Even from their sordid urns unto the shore,
> Unown'd of any weedy-haired gods;

Whose winds, all zephyrless, hold scourging rods,
Iced in the great lakes to afflict mankind: . . .

And so on, to the conclusion that, in America, "great unerring Nature
once seems wrong." That is, the negative west myth is sufficiently
strong to overcome the typical, Rousseau-derived romantic faith in un-
civilized nature. And Keats guarantees our awareness that he is refusing the more hopeful version of the myth by beginning the next section
of the poem with "O, for some sunny spell/To dissipate the shadows of
this hell!"[46] Alternately, in *Martin Chuzzlewit,* Dickens invokes the
negative myth to equate America not with Hell but Chaos. The pointedly named town of New Eden to which his hero journeys is a swampy
wilderness of disorder, disease, and all-too-civilized swindle. Thoreau's
equations of the west with the wild and the wild with "a spirit of
enterprise and adventure" that constitutes "the preservation of the
World"[47] is a canny defense because it takes up the elements of the
demonic myth but transforms them by lauding the wild.

Replies were possible, then; but the negative west myth, known by
Americans and constantly reiterated for them by any number of un-
friendly British travel books, specified in melodramatic detail the consequences of cultural failure. The west myth compels the individual
American writer's identification with the national destiny, but under a
threatening sign: for the west myth raises the bet on the success or
failure of American literature to an all-or-nothing, heaven-or-hell
proposition.

5

I admire Edwin Fussell's enthusiasm when he ascribes nothing less than
the production of American civilization to the "interpenetration of the
Western myth with the actual events comprising the expansion of the
United States";[48] every writer should feel strongly his topic. But I cannot agree with his claim. I do not see the myth of the west as prior to or
underlying the more nearly political causes for the American anxiety
toward British literary domination and for the tendency of writers in
America to see themselves as American writers. I am aware that myths
form an alternative history which usually counts more with the poetic
imagination than that public history formed by governments and their
actions. But these spheres of spiritual and legal history blend in America. They are merged by a Puritan-derived idea of America and of the
ideal American individual as a microcosmic carrier or representative of

divine perfection; and this cause of national identification, if any, *does* underlie or contain the others.

This American idea has been illuminated by Sacvan Bercovitch in a series of articles and books. He defines the American difference as a merging, unprecedented in its absoluteness, of national and spiritual aspirations. This union "yokes together the internal and external Kingdom of God by asserting the simultaneity of a geographic locale, America, and a mode of vision." Thus, for Urian Oakes, the president of Harvard, in his 1673 Election-Day address, "if we . . . lay all things together, this our Commonwealth seems to exhibit to us a *specimen,* or a *little model* of the *Kingdom of Christ upon Earth,* . . . wherein it is generally acknowledged and accepted."[49]

The Puritan synthesis depended on a new extension of Christian typology and a new insistence upon it. A first extension had occurred long before the Puritans with the birth of hermeneutics: by it, the Church fathers expanded the initial typological strategy, which interpreted the Old Testament as a foreshadowing of the New, into history after Christ, "casting His shadow forward to the end of time as well as backward across the Old Testament." For the Puritan, New England events were types of actions that had occurred already, in scripture; but they also came to be seen as fulfillments of scriptural promises which would lead in turn to the ultimate fulfillment of Apocalypse. And typology was extended to include not only major historical crises: the Puritan must "ratify his every experience, all his thoughts and feelings, by the infallible standard of holy scripture."[50]

This was not an intellectually abstruse system to the Puritan; it came to be his way of seeing, his attitude, often automatic rather than a planned strategy, just as Freudian psychoanalytic theory has become for us (with the attendant dangers of vulgarization in both cases). Bercovitch never fully explains why this "interaction between the literal event, spiritual parallel, and Christic referent" became so extensive and intensive in New England, but the reason is plain. Mircea Eliade generalizes on the utility of all myth in a manner immediately applicable to expatriate Englishmen, city dwellers used to a settled, highly civilized existence now facing a wild: "Myth assures man that what he is about to do *has already been done,* in other words, it helps him to overcome doubts as to the result of his undertaking. . . . One has merely to repeat the cosmogonic ritual, whereupon the unknown territory (= 'Chaos') is transformed into 'Cosmos,' becomes an *imago mundi* and hence a ritually legitimized 'habitation.' "[51]

We need only add to this Bercovitch's constant emphasis, that in America alone the personal life and the corporate ideal are made to merge. And the representative self who would carry out this enterprise could become manifest in confession as well as in confidence. In his reading of Puritan captivity narratives, which are full of doubts largely absent from the materials to which Bercovitch attends, Richard Slotkin reaches the like conclusion: "The sufferer represents the whole, chastened body of Puritan society." Even in the throes of separation-anxiety, the self remains representative, for the captive sees his bondage as a paradigm "of the self-exile of English Israel from England." Slotkin also helps us to credit Bercovitch's basic idea without accepting completely the centrality Bercovitch assumes for the writing of the Puritan divines. Frontier conditions could be seen to encourage collective narratives as much as could a typological mindset: "Usually the experience of initation is portrayed as an individual accomplishment, an experience of life which each man must come to in his turn. In America, however, the experience of initiation into a new life was shared by all members of colonial society simultaneously during a certain, relatively brief period of time." And this, too, would give rise to "a view of the individual experience as community experience in microcosm."[52]

These linkings of the spiritual to the national and the self to both were never forged fully in England. A sixteenth-century English Puritan like Foxe would gesture in that direction; but the fact of the Anglican Church would make him qualify his identifications of "sainthood with British citizenship" and reassert "the eternal conflict between the world and the kingdom." It was precisely a perception of that gap which led to Cromwell's rebellion; and yet even during the years of Puritan rule, the role of English nationality was limited. As Bercovitch paraphrases the English Puritan position, "The spiritual Israel *would* inherit the kingdom [of God]; the English Israel *could* clear away obstacles to Christ's return." Foxe's image of "the perishable ship of England" is countered by the American Puritan view of New England as "the world-redeeming ark of Christ," which might be buffeted but was guaranteed against shipwreck.[53]

Indeed, Bercovitch argues that the American Puritan decline did not result in any weakening of the self-nation-God triad. Instead, a certain osmosis occurred, as the Puritan rhetoric was adapted to secular considerations, which redoubled its influence as the American idea. Bercovitch sees it travelling through Edwards in a direct line to the American romantics; it is what makes American romanticism American. "Intermediary between the Puritan and God was the created Word of scripture. Intermediary between the Romantic and God was the creating imagination. Intermediary between the Transcendentalist and the Oversoul was the text of America. . . ."[54] So too, differences in

English and American romanticism can be seen as a seventeenth-century inheritance. While Blake would envision "Jerusalem in England's green and pleasant land," this political millennialism retreated quickly into what Meyer Abrams has termed "the apocalypse of imagination." With the failure of the French Revolution, mass action was renounced for a revolution of consciousness.[55] Again, we should not take that historical event as simply causal, for it could have been interpreted differently; a British habit of mind was ready to disconnect self and soul from nation.

The American romantics remained representative selves. Thoreau sees his brief westward hike as representative of the national migration westward and that migration as the fulfillment of the myth of the west. The autobiographical subject of Wordworth's great epic is the private mind while Emerson's mind *is* "The American Scholar," transpersonal. The American romantic persona, like its Puritan model, was based on the idea that "the country was not *like* its exemplary consciousness; it was that consciousness, . . ."[56]

Bercovitch's writings contribute greatly to our understanding of the phenomenon whereby the writer in a writer also meant the America in a writer to the New World imagination. They suggest another reason for the American equation of contemporary England with "the past": the failure of Cromwell's Protectorate and the British reaction to that failure closed the apocalyptic future to England, finished it as a regenerative nation—which, to the most secular-minded American, was what a living nation had to be. Bercovitch's writings also provide a historical basis for the American characterization of the British as limited, too commonsensical, and dead to ultimates in their refusal to consider England an elect nation: just so, in the American linking of self, nation, and God we find the root for the English perception that Americans are braggarts who rationalize a low materialism by imbuing it with high ideals. And, even if the Englishman refused to see himself or his heroes as representative, as microcosms of a national destiny, the American habit of doing so explains why American writers seized on single British figures as representative of British culture (to criticize writer and culture, since neither was redemptive-minded).

Given these helps, I must risk ingratitude by refusing one element of Bercovitch's argument. Jonathan Edwards is a thin thread by which to connect the American Puritans and romantics; and the appropriation of deep rhetorial tropes for self-serving political purposes in the eighteenth century is a typical tactic of propaganda that argues against, not for, the *living* continuation of an idea's original meaning and force. Bercovitch quotes Emerson's excited acknowledgments of the Puritans as proof of continuation: they formed "a bridge to us between the . . . Hebrew epoch, and our own," they insure "the greatness of the New World"; and, supposedly most telling, "What is this abolition and non-resistance . . . but a continuation of Puritanism. . . ?"[57] To me, Emerson's assertions imply not an unbroken line but a *re*-discovery. As Emerson's bridge between Israel and 1840, the Puritans are centered halfway between, at a greater-than-factual temporal distance from the present even while their influence is affirmed. Emerson's very ascription of Puritan origins to modern social causes seems more an attempt to make those causes rooted and respectable than a calm tracing. Why would the Puritan origins have to be advertised if they had not been, to some measure, interrupted or obscured?

I would propose instead that the Puritan idea of America became residual during the eighteenth century. It did not remain dominant, though Bercovitch is right to claim that it did not disappear or become archaic. Raymond Williams makes the distinctions we need:

> I would call the "archaic" that which is wholly recognized as an element of the past, to be observed, to be examined, or even on occasion to be consciously "revived," in a deliberately specializing way. What I mean by the "residual" is very different. The residual, by definition, has been effectively true in the past, but it is still active in the cultural process, not only and often not at all as an element of the past, but as an effective element of the present.

Williams then splits "the residual" in half: one aspect of residual value is largely incorporated into the dominant culture, and in this incorporation often suffers dilution or reinterpretation because the now dominant structures differ greatly from those which existed when the residual value was itself dominant; but a second aspect of residual value more closely retaining its original shape may have "an alternative or even appositional relation to the dominant culture, . . ."[58] Clearly, the Puritan ideas of the elect nation and the representative self split into these two aspects; and in their literary manifestation in the nineteenth century, it is the second aspect—with the original shape of the ideas modified by romanticism but largely unchanged—which showed itself.

I am suggesting, then, that these ideas were retrieved by the literary nationalists, or perhaps repurified. The ideas were not nostalgically "revived" because they remained, vulgarized, in the dominant culture and, in their more pristine form, retained a weak presence; but neither did they, in their original form and power, travel a direct route to Emerson and his contemporaries as Bercovitch implies. That is why I am reluctant to see the ideas of the elect nation and the representative self as the cause of all other causes in fomenting literary nationalism and in identifying the individual writer with the nation. Certainly they were causal; as the most completely native born, at once the most mythy and yet immediately applicable of the causes we have named, they may have played the leading role. But their retrieval occurred at a particular time: Spencer notes that only after 1789 did subtitles like "An American Ballad" or "An American Tale" proliferate, and fuller statements of American identity and destiny began to accumulate in the 1820s; only upon nationhood was the notion of the individual American who is simultaneously all of us and our collective historical-spiritual mission revived, in the many biographies of Washington; and this was the period that experienced the rise of literary nationalism, the democracy debate, the renewal of separation-anxiety. Thus the full-fledged reemergence of the attitudes of the elect nation and the representative self was caused by these other factors—themselves partly shaped and catalyzed by the residue of their earlier, Puritan formulations. Such turns and twists should warn us against the attractive alternative of assigning a single, most basic cause to the Anglo-American struggle. But we are not left with a disorganized, compromising eclecticism; rather, at every point we find the various motives for an American attempt to combat British literary influence overlapping with, blending into, reinforcing each other.

A final question remains to be raised concerning the identification of individual writers with America, the same question we raised concerning Melville alone in the previous chapter. How could this phenomenon coexist in the era that witnesses a remarkable surge of national distrust and in the same writers who most profoundly challenged the nation's dominant institutions and aspirations? Emerson often speaks against the American grain, Thoreau almost always. "Since Jefferson's time the forces of industrialism have been the chief threat to the bucolic image of America," Leo Marx writes, and those forces began to dominate "just at the time our first significant literary generation was coming to maturity."[59] How could writers identify so completely with an America which they simultaneously were growing to hate?

Because there were two Americas. Stephen Spender introduces an important distinction between *patria,* or the ideally true nation, and the actual nation.[60] Whitman, whose "Song of Myself" had claimed for America an unprecedented merge of *patria* and nation, was forced

finally to Spender's distinction. In a note to "Poetry To-Day—
Shakspere—The Future" (1881), he posits "two sets of wills to nations
and persons," one that "works from explainable motives—from teaching, intelligence, judgment, circumstance, caprice, emulation, greed"
and another, "perhaps deep, hidden, unsuspected, yet often more potent than the first . . . resistlessly urging on speakers, doers, commu-
nities, unwitting to themselves—the poet to his fiercest words—the
race to pursue its loftiest ideals." These wills interact, "producing
strangest results."[61] For Whitman, the perception of a fissure between
patria and nation provokes a retreat, though one in which *patria*, now
associated with something akin to both the soul and the unconscious,
predominates. More often, however, as the perceived gap between patria and nation increases, so too does the writer's identification with
the *patria*. This is especially the case in America, where the nation's
demand upon itself to manifest the *patria* in every moment and aspect
of the actual nation makes especially intolerable any gap: "We must
realize our rhetoric and our rituals," Emerson says in "The Fortune of
the Republic" (*W*, XI, 530), with words which might have been spoken
by Mather. Indeed, father and his contemporaries provided the richest
conceptions of the elect nation and the representative self in response
to the shared perception that their generation had witnessed a terrible
decline of Puritan faith.

Recall Williams's dictum: the residual, retrieved in its original,
consequential form, may have "an alternative or even oppositional relation to the dominant culture." Thus the American writer could locate
himself as America (in the sense of *patria*) and view the actual nation
as at a distressing distance from that center that he and the true America occupied; but all of the denigrations of the actual nation could not
budge him and his America from the center.

But I do not wish to gainsay the tensions experienced between
patria and nation by any of the American romantics. To the contrary,
these tensions were exploitable and American writers exploited
them—not only because these tensions produced anxieties but also
because an involvement with them afforded an escape from that literary anxiety we have been discussing. Everything we have considered
heretofore supports Leslie Fiedler's contention that, while Europeans
can see their world as given, "we Americans are plagued by the need to
invent a mythological version of Europe first, something against which
we can then define ourselves" and thus to "see ourselves not directly
but reflexively" as "the other's other."[62] Here finally was a crisis with
which the British had nothing to do, not directly; a wide-ranging prob-

lem that might be all-American. And so, while a deeply, wildly comic utopian vision had encouraged literary nationalism, only a sensed possibility of dystopic tragedy could complete its realization.

In all, how miserable to be a writer in nineteenth-century America: plagued by doubts as to the existence, much less the self-sufficiency, of a culture he could call his own; told over and again that his world afforded nothing for the imagination to begin upon; aware of his entrapment by models largely inappropriate to his existence, aware too that no past American could provide him a key for escape; at the same time, laboring under the millennial burden of creating a literature not merely new, but more new than any new literature had been, different by an apocalypse from what had been done, demand and incapacity reaching the pitch of scream together.

And yet how lucky, what a boon to be a writer at such a time in a land that was and was not yet America: gifted by English insults that would encourage replies, by pointed challenges that would suggest what he needed to find, in himself and his nation, to form a reply; assured by the myth of the representative self that his reply could bespeak the continent, that inhaling American air he might exhale an American culture; freed by a relatively empty literary past to believe that he could discover spaciously, every man his own Columbus; and emboldened by the millennial myth to imagine for this discovery a universal consequence of redemption that would suffuse lived experience with literary vision, every man, as Emerson prophesied, his own Christ. Oh then! could he achieve this, he might find himself out from under the burden of Britain, at the beginning with the Word; might say, as Whitman did,

> I conn'd old times
>
> I sat studying at the feet of the great masters
>
> Now if eligible O that the great masters
>   might return and study me.[63]

4

WHITMAN'S PERSONALISM, ARNOLD'S CULTURE

I

Matthew Arnold, remarked Walt Whitman, is "one of the dudes of literature";[1] and it is Matthew Arnold, not the always credited Thomas Carlyle, who is the rejected muse of Whitman's finest prose essay, *Democratic Vistas.* These two writers occupy extremes that their national fellows will qualify. But at this still early stage, it is well to write largely: and if Whitman and Arnold are more nationally hyperbolic than simply typical, they afford us a stressed if stretched difference. We have considered the social origins of the American need to define its literature away from British models. Through Whitman and Arnold we can consider the social differences which an American literature proposed and the English model of an ideal society which it refused. Indeed, these two writers are so variously representative that this chapter may serve as our center, exemplifying what we have said and anticipating what more we will need to say.

Whitman defines the chief problem of the New World as the attempt "to vitalize man's free play of special Personalism."[2] In saying this, he is himself playing upon and denigrating the phrase Arnold had made notorious in the five years prior to the writing of *Democratic Vistas,* a phrase that he was continuing to employ in ever varied contexts, "the free play of the mind upon all subjects." When in the same sentence Whitman terms this active mode Personalism, by which he means the deep self's unique yet universal identity, "the best that belongs to us," he plays upon another of Arnold's catch phrases, "the best that is known and thought in the world."[3]

Against Arnold's ideal of a self that rises above the freaks of individuality to absorb all ideas and sift for the best of them, Whitman proposes "the Me in the center," in whose midst "creeds, conventions, fall away and become of no account . . ." (394). To the author of "The Function of Criticism at the Present Time," Whitman replies, "The quality of BEING, in the object's self, according to its own central idea and purpose, and of growing therefrom and thereto—not criticism by other standards and adjustments thereto—is the lesson of nature"

(394). What Arnold desires, an intellectual impersonality, is too much with us already: "True, the full man gathers, culls, absorbs; but if, engaged disproportionately in that, he slights or overlays the precious idiocrasy and special nativity and intention that he is, the man's self, the main thing, is a failure, however wide his general cultivation" (394). "The whole scope of the essay," Arnold writes in his "Preface" to *Culture and Anarchy*, "is to recommend culture as the great help out of our present difficulties; culture being a pursuit of our total perfection by means of getting to know, on all the matters which most concern us, the best which has been thought and said in the world; . . ."[4] "The writers of a time hint the mottoes of its gods. The word of the modern, say these voices, is the word Culture" (395), Whitman notes in *Democratic Vistas*, perfectly aware that "these voices" must be identified with Arnold.

In *Matthew Arnold and American Culture*, John Henry Raleigh demonstrates that "Even as early as 1867, before the publication of *Culture and Anarchy*, Arnold was generally known as the apostle of culture and the condemner of the Philistine."[5] Whitman immediately opposes this word: "We find ourselves abruptly in close quarters with the enemy. This word Culture, or what it has come to represent, involves, by contrast, our whole theme, and has been, indeed, the spur, urging us to engagement" (395). This is as close as one could come to identifying Arnold as the inspiriting enemy without directly naming him. Further, all that Whitman writes is couched in the complaint that America "seems singularly unaware that the models of persons, books, manners, etc., appropriate for former conditions and for European lands, are but exiles and exotics here" (395); and much later in his life, in 1889, reacting to Arnold's comment that Lincoln lacked distinction, Whitman remarked, "Matthew Arnold was not in the abstract sense a damned fool, but with respect to the modern—to America—he was the damndest of damned fools—a total ignoramus—knew nothing at all. I know Arnold was not alone in this ignorance—. . ."[6]

Arnold becomes The European or The Englishman and the disastrously inappropriate nature of his leading idea becomes the proof of an American, democratic difference. In *Culture and Anarchy*, Arnold calls America "that chosen home of newspapers and politics" (*P*, 242), quotes approvingly E. Renan's criticism of Americans for "*their intellectual mediocrity, their vulgarity of manners, their superficial spirit, their lack of general intelligence*" (*P*, 241) and concludes, with some generosity, "America has up to the present time been hardly more than a province of England, and even now would not herself claim to be more than abreast of England, . . ." (149). Whitman's response is to accept and further the familiar criticism of a colonialist hangover—"Never, in the Old World, was thoroughly upholster'd exterior appearance and show, mental and other, built entirely on the idea of caste, and on the sufficiency of mere verbal acquisition—never were glibness, verbal intellect more the test, the emulation—more loftily elevated as head and sample—than they are on the surface of our republican States these days" (395)—and then to turn tables by making the American interest in Arnold his prime example of a national treachery.

Whitman had indeed begun *Democratic Vistas* with Carlyle and his noxious essay "Shooting Niagara: and After?" in mind. There Carlyle puts forth his ideal of a renewed heroic aristocracy in opposition to a "swarmery" of democratizing trends exemplified by America. The essay is full of his infamous racism:

> Essentially the Nigger Question was one of the smallest; and in itself did not much concern mankind in the present time of struggles and hurries. One always rather likes the Nigger; evidently a poor blockhead with good dispositions, with affections, attachments—with a turn for Nigger melodies, and the like—. . . The Almighty Maker has appointed him to be a Servant.

Or again:

> half a million . . . of excellent White Men, full of gifts and faculty, have torn and slashed one another into horrid death, in a temporary humour, which will leave centuries of remembrance fierce enough; and three million absurd Blacks, men and brothers (of a sort) are completely "emancipated": launched into the career of improvement—likely to be "improved off the face of the earth" in a generation or two![7]

No wonder that Whitman would be engaged by the age's single nastiest statement of Old World caste, even if Whitman was not always the militant abolitionist of "Song of Myself." (Indeed, in *Democratic Vistas* he appears to substitute a lengthy discussion of women's elevation for any mention of racial equality, as if to let the war's wounds heal.) In a footnote he remarks, "I was at first roused to much anger and abuse by this essay from Mr. Carlyle, so insulting to the theory of America," but goes on to admit that he "had more than once been in the like mood . . . and seen persons and things in the same light" (375n). Carlyle's essay improves upon reflection, "expressing as it does certain judgments from the highest feudal point of view" of "an earnest soul." Not gold, the essay is "good, hard, honest iron" (375–6n).

The footnote is disingenuous. Even if Carlyle's essay, itself as much a harsh critique of his nation's present situation as *Democratic Vistas* is of America, suggested to Whitman the stance of a Jeremiah, we can affirm with confidence that Whitman never for a moment had been "in the same mood" as Carlyle demonstrates in his essay's worst, most ignorant moments. Whitman is being polite toward Emerson's English hero: in the guise of making friends with the essay, he is dismissing it from more particular debate.[8]

Arnold replaced Carlyle as the enemy, once Whitman found himself drawn to his subject. In September, 1867, he had written to the editors of the *Galaxy*, "I have, in composition, an article (prose) of some length—the subject opportune—I shall probably name it *Democracy*. It is partly provoked by, & in some respects a rejoinder to, Carlyle's *Shooting Niagara*." Following its publication—and during a period when Whitman was sharply conscious of his rocketing reputation in England—he met with the magazine editors and then wrote to them in February, 1868 proposing an essay that "takes up the subject of *Democracy* where the article by that name in the *Galaxy* of December left it." Entitled *Personalism*, it will, Whitman writes, consider individuality, the ideal "American of the future," and the American woman. But he gives most space to its other aim: the essay "overhauls the Cultural theory, shows its deficiencies, tested by any grand, practical Democratic test—argues that the main thing wanted for the literary, esthetic, and moral areas of the United States is to institute what must result in copious supplies, among the masses of healthy, acute, handsome Individualities," the opposing principle of Personalism. A third section of the essay was already in mind, but Whitman did not publish "Orbic Literature" in the *Galaxy*. It appeared when he revised and combined the three articles as *Democratic Vistas*, published in 1871 as a book.[9]

Whitman could not have been privy to Arnold's completed *Culture and Anarchy* when he responded to Arnold most directly in "Personalism." But Arnold's "Introduction" and "Sweetness and Light" had been published in the *Cornhill* in July, 1867, and the succeeding five chapters in January, February, June, July, and September of 1868. In other words, Whitman may have read some of *Culture and Anarchy* before it was revised and published in book form in January, 1869. Certainly the earlier *Essays in Criticism* (1865) was available to him. In all, the major ideas and manner of Arnold's thought in *Culture and*

Anarchy were sufficiently familiar to Whitman and his readers that we can consider that work as tantamount to Whitman's goad.

2

Whitman switched his focus from Carlyle to Arnold, I believe, as Arnold, in this instance at least, was the worthier, more strenuous opponent. Because Whitman shared many of Arnold's views, his rejection of others would be more charged. There is, beyond ideas, a sharing of genre. Both works, like Carlyle's "Niagara," are Jeremiads. That is, both castigate the present situation of their respective nations in light of a disregarded ideal, with the hope that the ideal is not so lost as to be incapable of recalling the people to perfection. "We have founded for us the most positive of lands. The founders have pass'd to other spheres—but what are these terrible duties they have left us?" (410). Whitman is thus following in the Puritan tradition that Sacvan Bercovitch traces in *The American Jeremiad,* although the typical Puritan stress upon the biography of an exemplary forebear is replaced in Whitman's forward-looking "ideal American of the future," a substitution appropriate to a culturally early attitude that considers democracy "to be at present in its embryo condition" so that "the only large and satisfactory justification of it resides in the future, . . ." (392). Arnold, without such a native tradition to play upon, nonetheless complains that "I have been taken to task by the *Daily Telegraph,* coupled, by a strange perversity of fate, with just that very one of the Hebrew prophets whose style I admire the least, and called 'an elegant Jeremiah' " (88). Whitman inveighs against an America that has adopted every European corruption, though at heart it is the adoption that enrages him more than the corruption: "At present these States, in their theology and social standards (of greater importance than their political institutions) are entirely held possession of by foreign lands" (411). Arnold denigrates an England which vaunts freedom above value and which is intent upon acting without thinking sufficiently to determine in what right acting would consist—in all, a provincial England. Arnold's England is for him all too like the popular conception of America, as America for Whitman is all too like England. But they are themselves alike in their general argumentative stance, a similarity Whitman emphasizes by employing the famous Arnoldian rhetorical insistence "I say" followed by a repeated phrase throughout "Democratic Vistas" as he does nowhere else in his prose.[10]

But what Whitman and Arnold share most importantly has to do with the historical moment. Both view the middle to late nineteenth century as the moment at which the feudal is giving way to the modern. Arnold calls the present an "epoch of expansion," particularly open to new ideas as opposed to a "clinging to the established fact" (124). He is not entirely sanguine concerning "an epoch of dissolution and transformation"[11] for "as feudalism, which with its ideas and habits of subordination was for many centuries silently behind the British constitution, dies out, and we are left with nothing but our system of checks, and our notion of its being the great right and happiness of an Englishman to do as far as possible what he likes, we are in danger of drifting toward anarchy" (117). But ultimately he welcomes this "sense,—vague and obscure as yet,—of weariness with the old organizations," a sense that "works and grows" (228). Whitman does not worry the effects of the transformation but the lingering resistance to it—"feudalism, caste, the ecclesiastical traditions, though palpably retreating from political institutions, still hold essentially, by their spirit, even in this country, entire possession of the more important fields, indeed the very subsoil, of education, and of social standards and literature" (364–5). But he agrees with Arnold as to the terms of the transformation: "The United States are destined either to surmount the gorgeous history of feudalism or else prove the most tremendous failure of time" (363).

There are important differences here, to which we will return: Arnold is speaking of the next twenty years while Whitman wraps up all of the past in the term "feudal" and grandly enlarges America's import by positing it as the unbounded future; Arnold speaks of the transformation as a national one, but Whitman alone sees this same transformation as the reason for being of the nation; and Arnold tends to see the dissolution of feudalism as something to which we must react, whereas Whitman, despite his notation of a prevailing "atmosphere," sees the transformation as something we must achieve.

But the agreement—and here, I think, we best may speak not of influence but of agreement, as of views independently developed—extends to the consequences of feudalism's demise. Generally, these consequences consist in the individual's assumption of areas of thought and action previously determined by institutions. This leads, for Arnold, either to culture, defined not as social machinery but as an "inward operation" (P, 234) larger and more free than any institution, or to anarchy, "doing as one likes" (115,119). For Whitman, more wholly positive, the end of feudalism makes for "the simple idea that the last, best dependence is to be upon humanity itself, and its own inherent, normal, full-grown qualities without any superstitious support whatever" (374).

Again we note a difference that is more than an accident of phrasing: Arnold speaks of an activity, thinking, purified of the individual who performs it, while Whitman constantly images a bodily person as his ideal. Yet in Whitman's phrase "superstitious support" we note a further likeness. For Arnold, the creative-critical mind replaces religion by subsuming it. He notes the English tendency "to Hebraise, as we call it; that is, to sacrifice all other sides of our being to the religious self" (P, 238). He does not wish to disestablish national churches, for they quiet "private forms for expressing the inexpressible" and allow the individual by a tacit agreement to attend to the neglected "other sides of his nature" (P, 239).

Culture itself best surounds and subdues religion: "the worth of what a man thinks about God and the objects of religion depends on what the man *is*" and that in turn "depends upon his having more or less reached the measure of a perfect and total man" (P, 252). Arnold insists upon "the idea of perfection at all points," a goal that can be achieved not by dogma and priests but by culture (which is meta-theological as it is meta-everything) and a phalanx of those who realize their best selves, rise above the bigotries of class, and "make their distinguishing characteristic not their Barbarianism or their Philistinism, but their *humanity*" (146).

Whitman calls for a classless class, "of native authors, literatuses" (365): "The priest departs, the divine literatus comes" (365). For Whitman it is no matter of moderating the spiritual so that it does not reduce a multidimensional self but of realizing the spirit at all, "the identified soul, which can really confront Religion when it extricates itself entirely from churches and not before." There is a clear opposition here, for Arnold sees the Church as quieting spiritual egoism while Whitman argues that "only in the perfect uncontamination and solitariness of individuality may the spirituality of religion positively come forth at all" (398). But this opposition exists within a larger agreement, the need for an ethos strong but undogmatic, linked to the freedom and dynamism of consciousness. Thereby Whitman joins Arnold in a distrust of mere political progress: he issues an alarm "against the prevailing delusion that the establishment of free political institutions . . . do, of themselves, determine and yield to our experiment of democracy the fruitage of success" (369). Like Arnold's culture, Whitman's democracy is a prevailing spirit, an "inward operation" in Arnold's phrase, not a social engineering.

And despite his praise of the individually eccentric under the banner of personalism, so much at odds with Arnold's distrust of any one person's mutations of belief, Whitman with Arnold emphasizes the need for moral strength in his new scene of freedom. When he speaks of "a strong mastership of the general inferior self by the superior self," a self that recognizes "fairness, manliness, decorum" and is achieved by "regulation, control, and oversight" (421), Whitman most echoes Arnold and his notion of a best self. This *is* a moment of Arnoldian influence, beyond independent agreement. It is not in its conservatism representative of the whole of Whitman's essay and it is quickly relegated to the status of a "contingency"; nonetheless, Whitman replicates Arnold's worry of anarchism and provides by like internal means against it. "Morality," Arnold writes plainly, "is indispensible" (102), as he admits that some men of culture have failed in this. "The climax of this loftiest range of civilization," writes Whitman of literature, ". . . is to be its development, from the eternal bases, and the fit expression, of absolute Conscience, moral soundness, Justice" (415).

On the basic issue of the historical character of the age, then—as a time of transition from the feudal to the modern that opens up possibilities by courting new ideas; as a time that relies on the individual to replace religious dogma and hereditary custom with free thought and thereby enforces upon that individual new demands for ethical behavior—Arnold and Whitman agree. But we have seen already and will see far more that these agreements are partial. In our latest example, to cite another divergence following upon agreement, morality to Arnold appears to mean on one hand a guard against traditional kinds of licentious behavior and on another a rising above the bigotries of class. To Whitman, morality is only at times Arnoldian "regulation" while elsewhere it coincides with social, egalitarian justice.

Such partial agreements lead directly to difference and then to disgust. On the occasion of Arnold's visit to America, Whitman, writing in 1883, classed him with those who "do good—the deepest, widest, most needed good—though certainly not in the ways attempted—which have, at times, something irresistably comic."[12] Explicitly Whitman is referring to the ignorance of such visitors as Arnold toward an America they see only in a series of unrepresentative drawing rooms, but the notion that Arnold performs powerful good by engendering a ridiculing response returns us to *Democratic Vistas*. John Henry Raleigh summarizes Whitman's continuing attitude toward Arnold well: "Arnold, with his 'civilized' manner, seemed somehow effably effete to Whitman; and at the root of the poet's distaste there was undoubtedly a profound revulsion from the so-called 'genteel' tradition, . . ."[13] Thus Whitman would tell Horace Traubel that Arnold's poetry was "wonderful fine" porcelain or that "I can easily see how a

91

WHITMAN'S PERSONALISM, ARNOLD'S CULTURE

stylist like Arnold should find Emerson below the mark . . . But there's a higher thing than the pure stylist can ever know." His friend John Burroughs spoke so warmly of Arnold that Whitman was made to remark, "we must be in no haste to dismiss Arnold"; and Whitman said of an interview with the avowed Arnoldian Mrs. Florence Coates, "Mrs. Coates gave me the other side of him—the social side. the personal side, the intellectual side—the side of deportment, behavior— the side of which I ought perhaps most to hear about and did willingly and gladly hear of from her." But these are concessions to an enemy and have nothing to do with the Arnold present in *Democratic Vistas*. Of that Arnold, Whitman said when he died that he would not be missed; that was the Arnold, he said, who ever would be considered "one of the dudes of literature."[14]

The most obvious sources of Whitman's animus are also the least interesting and profound, for instance Arnold's alleged elitism: he is, to Whitman, foremost among that "damned set of roosters" who think "the dirt is so dirty"; "But everything comes out of the dirt—everything; everything comes out of the people, the everyday people, the people as you find them and leave them: not university people, not F.F.V. people: people, people, just people."[15] Included here is a jibe against that anti-democratic feeling that leads Arnold to speak of "American vulgarity, moral, intellectual, and social" or to equate, sneeringly, "the democracy" (108,109) with the working class (which is, of course, by making the classless ideal the property of a class, a serious sneer) or to trivialize civil liberties into an anarchic "doing as one likes," or, less consciously, to cling to class notions even as he renames the classes and seeks for a classless class of "*aliens,* if we may so call them—persons who are mainly led, not by their class spirit, but by a general *humane* spirit, by the love of human perfection" (146). The very name of aliens suggests how little Arnold can imagine a democratized England much as he claims to fear it or even, in some exalted sense, wish it—all equal as equally dispassionate intellectuals, a nation of Matt Arnolds. Such an Arnold must arouse the fury of a Whitman who "shall use the words America and democracy as convertible terms" and seek in them a global salvation (363).

Whitman and Arnold are sundered deep under all likeness in their assumptions of differing, even opposing national histories. However much a Jeremiah Arnold at times becomes, there is an underlying confidence throughout his prose of a world that has survived for a good long time and that will continue on forever. We have had our Hellenic ages and our Hebraic ages, our ages of free critical play and of moral action; now it is time to right the balance by Hellenizing, while some-

day we may need to Hebraize again. Cyclical, possibly spinning toward a perfect harmony and balance, Arnold's world is in no real
danger of dissolution despite his cry against anarchy. One hears in
Arnold the rich tone of an England that has done much and survived
all, the appreciation for the roll upon roll of history. The present moment is indeed dark and confused but, as in the final section of George
Eliot's *Middlemarch* entitled "Sunset and Sunrise," it is dark only because a new era is dawning: "a more free play of consciousness, an
increased desire for sweetness and light, and all the bent which we call
Hellenizing, is the master-impulse now of the life of our nation and of
humanity,—somewhat obscurely perhaps for this actual moment, but
decisively and certainly for the immediate future; and those who work
for this are the sovereign educators" (229). Hellenism gave way to
Hebraism, and in the Renaissance, Hellenism asserted itself once more
only to be too much subsumed by a still pervading Hebraism. But the
world survives periods of change and is refreshed by them.

Arnold's temporal sense tends toward the local rather than the
grand because of this confidence in the ongoing. To Hellenism belongs
no more than "the immediate future" (229), not a future conceived like
Whitman's as a from-now-on-unto-the-forever, a future that will bring
down the curtain upon the historical drama as it has played until now.
Arnold believes in time and the times; we must only obey the times
and, with a hardy pragmatism, be ready to reverse ourselves when time
again changes. "Now, and for us, it is a time to Hellenise, and to praise
knowing; for we have Hebraised too much, and have overvalued
doing" (*P*, 255). But the habits of Hebraism "remain for our race an
eternal possession" and we "must never assign to them the second
rank to-day, without being prepared to restore to them the first rank
to-morrow" (*P*, 255). Indeed, this temporal relativity, this refusal to
argue for any permanent values aside from wholeness, proves the supple, open nature of culture and defines it as dynamic consciousness
tuned to a dynamic world.

Arnold is not always so completely sanguine. He can imagine a
demonic alternative to a peaceful change. Instead of a new dawn of
sweetness and light, in "The Function of Criticism" he can consider his
own play of thought that of an alien: "My vivacity is but the last spar-
kle of flame before we are all in the dark, the last glimpse of colour
before we all go into drab,—the drab of the earnest, prosaic, practical,
austerely literal future. Yes, the world will soon be the Phillistines."[16]
Especially when he is confronted by the materialist boasts of a self-
congratulatory liberal optimism, Arnold can view the march of civilization ironically, as a return to primitive chaos. Thus the renaming of

the aristocracy as barbarians. But this is not so much a deep fear as a satirical whip. And Arnold proposes a different kind of temporal return to combat darkness, "a clue to some sound order and authority" which "we can only get by going back upon the actual instincts and forces which rule our lives," the high instincts of Hellenism (175). The mind for Arnold is what the domestic hearth is for such social novelists as Dickens, a great enclave against corruption that someday may spread itself to eradicate that corruption.

But Arnold is so comfortable within his English historical assurance that England's salvation rests only in catching up with the rest of Europe: "For more than two hundred years, the main stream of man's advance has moved toward . . . spontaneity of consciousness" while England, contretemps, has moved even further into "strictness of conscience" (175). For Arnold, time is a race toward perfection in which England need only stay abreast; but, as we will see, being with the time and not against it is a major Arnoldian principle.

Whitman, of course, sees England and Europe as the lingering corpse of feudalism. The dead cannot catch up to anything alive; and any American desire to catch up to Britain is a death wish. America must decide to die, as it appears to be doing by adopting British standards, or to choose for life by choosing for its democratic self. "To prune, gather, trim, conform, and ever cram and stuff, and be genteel and proper is the essence of our days" (394) and Whitman would have us live against the times as much as Arnold would have us live with them. Indeed, Whitman's most meaningful attack upon Arnold argues that he and his culture make this disastrously overcivilized lateness later: "My own criticism of Arnold—the worst I could say of him— the severest . . . would be, that Arnold brings coals to Newcastle— that he brings to the world what the world already has a surfeit of: is rich, hefted, lousy, reeking, with delicacy, refinement, elegance, prettiness, propriety, criticism, analysis: all of them things which threaten to overwhelm us."[17]

This is an "us" whom Whitman would define away from intellect, for to him Arnold's wholeness is ridiculously partial, bodiless and devoid of belief. "As now taught, accepted and carried out, are not the processes of culture rapidly creating a class of supercillious infidels, who believe nothing? Shall a man lose himself in countless masses of adjustments, and be so shaped with reference to this, that, and the other, that the simply good and healthy and brave parts of him are reduced and clipp'd away, like the bordering of box in a garden?" (395). Arnold pictures himself as a heroically embattled minority of one; Whitman sees Arnold as the latest victor in a procession of dudes whose ethic of fussy thought has triumphantly impoverished life. Arnold's careful and brilliant dialectics, his fence against both anarchy and the mechanical, become to Whitman "masses of adjustments." And Arnold's canny emphasis upon a contemplative method as prior to and larger than objects of belief becomes an "infidel" skepticism.

Whitman knows his Arnold. Much of Arnold's writing during this period defends his idea of culture against the charge of self-luxuriating quietism: "But what if rough and coarse action, ill-calculated action, action with insufficient light, is, and has for a long time been, our bane? What if our urgent want now is, not to act at any price, but rather to lay in a stock of light for our difficulties?" (116). Nonetheless, Arnold writes, the final aim of culture is "to *prevail*"; and Whitman, knowing him to hate him, asks in response, "Lastly—is the readily given reply that culture only seeks to help, systematize, and put in attitude, the elements of fertility and power, a conclusive reply?" (396). It is not, he implies, for Arnold's notion of the practical is not the really "practical life, the west, the workingmen, the facts of farms and jack-planes and engineers, and of the broad range of the women also of the middle and working strata, . . ." (396). For whom is this culture meant besides the privileged? It must be for all—"drawn out, not for a single class alone"—and its aim must be "to form, over this continent, an idiocrasy of universalism" (396).

"I do not so much object to the name, or word" of culture, Whitman writes, but by the time he is done with it, culture means in ways diametrically opposed to Arnold's usage. The culture of Arnold, which Whitman sums as "enlargement of intellect," is already "so overweening" that it needs no further promulgation but "a phrase of warning and restraint" (397). Just so, Whitman turns the tables to place a restraint upon the very ethic of restraint, which has become overzealous in its war against zeal. Whitman's *culture,* his "idiocrasy," is what Arnold calls "the bathos" (147), that acting upon subjective belief that is the worst result of "doing as one likes." Whitman dignifies what to Arnold is merely freakish to see it as the precious, compelling imperatives of selfhood; and what to Arnold makes for an anarchic lack of concern for the public good become one half of the rich democratic paradox that centers Whitman's faith, the paradox that a realization of the individual's deepest self leads not to eccentricity and social dissolution but to a discovery of qualities at once unique and universal, individuating and binding, "a typical personality of character, eligible to the uses of the high average of men"—in short, Personalism (396). Arnold's anxiety is admitted exactly when Whitman confesses that "the fear of conflicting and irreconcilable interiors, and the lack of a common skeleton, knitting all close, continually haunts me" (368). But the anxiety is adopted only to be overcome by Personalism, that celebration of difference which yet, as a shared celebration, is "the fervid and tremendous IDEA, melting everything else with heat" (368).

3

The argument Whitman creates with Arnold exemplifies a host of Anglo-American differences we have encountered thus far and points to others that I will limn more fully in the second half of this study. Already, we have seen Whitman and Arnold debate the democratic and we have seen Whitman flog a colonial humility that lags behind political independence.

But it is cultural time, our next interest, that most powers his debate with Arnold. While characterizing Arnold as late and latemaking, Whitman employs for his own ideal a lexicon of earliness spectacular for its variety and evocative power. He provides most profoundly a phenomenology of American earliness.

For instance, what might be larger, grander, more naturally based than Arnold's imagery of light and darkness? The weather itself, which Whitman invokes as an analogous explanation of the paradox of Personalism. Two conditions create "a truly grand nationality—1st, a large variety of character—and 2nd, full play for human nature to expand itself in numberless and even conflicting directions—(seems to be for general humanity much like the influences that make up in their limitless field, that perennial health-action of the air we call weather— an infinite number of currents and forces, and contributions, and temperatures, and cross purposes, whose ceaseless play of counterpart upon counterpart brings constant restoration and vitality," 361). For Arnold, "play" is a complex nimbleness; for Whitman, it constitutes space, the freedom of democracy, and the vast and open and thus early continental expanse. Thus too his title, with vistas implying both a breadth of envisioning and a breadth to be envisioned, the friendly wild as opposed to the cultivated and enclosed garden.

But Whitman does not merely take advantage of a present earliness. He formulates an ideal that will guarantee a culture forever young, of "constant restoration and vitality," by dependence upon the earliest, largest values. We see this when, at last, Whitman apologizes to culture and to Arnold: "Pardon us, venerable shade! if we have seem'd to speak lightly of your office. The whole civilization of the earth, we know, is yours, with all the glory and light thereof." But he would remind Arnold and his light "that there is something greater than you, namely, the fresh, eternal qualities of Being" (403). Apology becomes attack as Whitman equates the early with the spaciously permanent and shows the British apostle of wholeness to be enamored of a fraction.

Earliness lives near origin—Personalism is Nature's "younger brother" (393)—and ideally coincides with it: "As the greatest lessons of Nature through the universe are perhaps the lessons of variety and freedom, the same present the greatest lessons in New World politics and progress" (360). These are lessons, Whitman soon grants, that the New World must learn and cannot yet teach. But Whitman's thrust is to identify origin with essence and to claim a new beginning for the world in an America placed at the source of things. The child America, a national version of Wordsworth's best philosopher, is thus older as well than merely aged Europe in its proximity to original, atemporal truths.

Social America is itself conventionally aged in its borrowed European corruptions; but that is not a sign of intrinsic lateness. It is rather a temporary result of immaturity, for democratic America is not yet quite born: "We see the sons and daughters of the New World"—sons and daughters themselves young—"ignorant of its genius, not yet inaugurating the native, the universal, and the near still importing the distant, the partial, and the dead. We see London, Paris, Italy—not original, superb, as where they belong—but second-hand here, where they do not belong" (411). America is an "embryo" still, though "the throes of birth are about us" and the nativity will, like Milton's Christ, scatter false gods: at America's birth, "our speech, though without polish'd coherence, and a failure by the standard called criticism"—Arnold's near-synonym for culture and another word that at this time belongs to him—"comes forth, real at last as the lightnings" (391) if not possessed of sweetness and light. Alternately, Whitman's America is "in a sort of geological formation state" (387). Or it is in a "nebular state and vagueness of the astronomical worlds, compared with the subsequent state, the definitely-formed worlds themselves, duly compacted, hung up there, chandeliers of the universe" (404). Or America is the primitive land, "Rude and coarse nursing beds, these" from which, however, will spring "flowers of genuine American aroma, and fruits truly and fully our own" (413).

Human, meteorological, geological, astronomical, or horticultural, Nature is the reference, a source of authoritative reality carefully undefined or given multiple, elastic definition to suit Whitman's sense of its larger-than-any-lexicon grandeur. The very variety of Nature is Whitman's rhetorical counterpart to the variety of personalities envisioned by his Personalism, a constellation of images that binds his apparently scattered and repetitious argument as Personalism will bind the human diversity it encourages.

4

This opposition between cultural times leads to wholly different conceptions of the relation between writer and nation, thus returning us to an issue we have confronted heretofore and will consider again. Arnold's imagery consistently implies the poet's need of a wide, elevated view. As early as 1849, in the poem "Resignation," he proclaims, "Not deep the poet sees, but wide."[18] This valuation of breadth against depth implicitly disowns the tendency in romantic poetry to bury ultimate truths in the underlayer of the soul. Like the directional metaphors of romanticism that transferred the above-and-outside locale of ultimates to the under-and-within, Arnold's wide view codifies a crucial shift of cognition. He expounds its significance in a letter of the same year to Clough: "The trying to go into and to the bottom of an object instead of grouping objects is as fatal to the sensuousness of poetry as the mere painting . . . is to its airy and rapidly-moving life."[19]

Arnold's visual metaphor of the wide view implies an elevated location, for how else is the poet to see widely and group objects? Moral valuations attach to images of height, as in the case of the image of the ideal poet in "Resignation" who "from some high station . . . looks down,/At sunset, on a populous town" (164–5) or with the situating of the monks' cloister, home to a spirituality now dead to the society surrounding it, on a mountaintop high above the steamy, smoky Guier stream. In turn, this elevation implies a stoicism that is self-resigning. The speaker who wishes to imitate the "placid" height of the stars and breadth of the waters is advised in "Self-Dependence" by a voice in the night, "Wouldst thou *be* as these are? Live as they" (16). This inspired calm not only demands a renunciation of personal prejudices but a detachment from the embroiling controversies of the time. In another 1849 poem, "Stanzas in Memory of the Author of 'Obermann'," only

> He who hath watched, not shared, the strife,
> Knows how the day hath gone.
> He only lives with the world's life
> Who hath renounced his own.

(101–4)

The "world's life" is best expressed in "Resignation" as "the murmur of a thousand years" (188). It suggests a sense of ongoing natural and historical process with a hint that, despite the horrid brawls of the present, the whole will persist providentially. The wide view is temporal as well as spatial, demanding historical context.

But in its spatial aspect, the ideal of the wide view creates a difficulty with which Arnold would wrestle over the next fifteen years.[20] To group objects rather than delve them assumes that these objects exist on the social plane of life, not in a metaphysical substratum. Yet the elevation implied by the wide view argues for the poet's removal from the social arena. In Arnold's poems of the fifties, fears of sterile inaction alternate with opposing fears of social engulfment. Arnold's Empedocles gains the wide view of an elevated perspective, yet he climbs to the mountain's precipice only to throw himself into its volcano. Finding himself in an age of irrational turbulence, he alienates himself from it only to suffer the fate of one who has sacrificed fellowship to reason and beauty to logic. Reason has taken him to his lonely height but affords him no route back to humanity. He feels keenly the responsibility to lift his age from its mean and violent quarrels, but he finds no way to do so without himself drowning in the "dizzying eddy." Perhaps only the elevated, self-resigning man "knows how the day has gone"; but if it has gone very, very badly and he yet clings to his high perch, he may doubt that he is fulfilling his ideal of the whole man.

Even in the early "Obermann," the wide view depends on "dreams that but deceive," and the poet opts for the world of action in a state of sad schizophrenia: "I go, fate drives me; but I leave/Half of my life with you" (131–32). This resolves nothing, for action and transcendence remain at odds. The wide view becomes available only to the dead. And in "Dover Beach," the speaker and his bride begin with a literally wide view from an elevated perspective. But the beautiful vision of France and England brings thoughts of a postrevolutionary despair fueled anew by the events of 1848, and history is considered as decline and loss: the tide of faith has receded and societies are become desert wastes. In "Obermann," the ideal is a dream in that dreams are inapplicable to reality. In "Dover Beach," the ideal is a dream in the harsher sense of an active deceit. The world only "seems / To lie before us like a land of dreams" (30–31), and the quiet pun on "lie" explodes as the lovers find themselves dropped to a confused reality's "darkling plain" where "ignorant armies" of public controversy and internally conflicted emotions make them victims of war.

Arnold's recovery from the night of "Dover Beach" to the sweetness and light of *Essays* and *Culture and Anarchy* begins in statements that seem only to deepen his despair. In "Stanzas From the Grand Chartreuse," the speaker again pictures himself lost upon the plain but with a difference: "Wandering between two worlds, one dead / The other powerless to be born" (85–86), he waits "forlorn." Forlorn indeed, but with the beginnings of a cyclical theory of historical faith, even as it is negatively expressed. The very mention of a new world, even if unborn, implies that the present despair may not be permanent; and waiting, however forlorn, implies hope. Earliness may follow upon lateness as dawn upon the dark. Likewise, in "The Scholar-Gypsy," we moderns "wait like thee" for "the spark from heaven to fall" but "not, like thee, in hope" (130,120); yet while the new faith is a "long unhappy dream," "The Scholar-Gypsy" is the first of Arnold's major poems in some years to dramatize a speaker actively endeavoring, albeit sceptically, toward a positive goal.

Finally that new world is born. Arnold revisits the grave of Senancoeur, author of "Obermann," hoping for a respite of forgetfulness. Instead, the dreamy Senancoeur becomes a man of action to enforce a scolding:

> Thou fledst me when the ungenial earth,
> Man's work-place, lay in gloom.
> Return'st thou in her hour of birth,
> Of hopes and hearts in bloom?
>
> (77–80)

These lines make historical contextualism a matter for the present: the poetic Arnold has been doing the wrong things at the wrong times, and in his view that is not merely an error but a moral fault. In any case, "the sun is risen," and now elevation need not mean alienation: "One common wave of thought and joy / Lifting mankind again" (324–25). The poem works as well to make Arnold's reentry into the public world one which will not demand the sacrifice of the wide view; no longer must he sink in the "dizzying eddy" for now the world is ready to be drawn up to his high perspective.

But historical change only appears to solve Arnold's dilemma. More truly, Arnold has come to see thought as a form of action rather than an alternative to it. What the literal minded Englishman sees as action is hopelessly local, bulky, and redundant. Instead, Arnold proposes one rich dialectic between a stoical elevation and a participatory involvement and another between imposed circumstance and creative will, "the power of the man and the power of the moment" (*FC*, 261).

Thus in Arnold's historical contextualism of the present, as evidenced in the very title of the essay "The Function of Criticism at the Present Time," the poet must look to his social world's "atmosphere" for his function; and yet that atmosphere is one which he, in his other role as a "critic of life," helps to establish. And finally self-renunciation and self-realization, transcendence and involvement, are solved by his distinction between "the ordinary self" and "the best self" that eschews attitudes based on his social position and looks only to the general good. The wide view comes less to imply a separation from the public world than from one's selfish and limited role in it. As we open upon an era of fresh thought, the philosopher is king.

In "The Function of Criticism" and *Culture and Anarchy*, the imagery of the wide view is triumphantly reasserted. Verbs of rising and nouns of elevation abound; disinterestedness and detachment are calmly asserted as right alternatives to a so-called practical life that is artificial and impractical in comparison to the admittedly slow work of creating a "natural and thence irresistible" atmosphere (*FC*, 275); and culture is exemplified by a free play of thought upon immediate political issues. Detachment becomes socially enabling.

We see evidence of this engaged detachment everywhere. For instance, when Arnold classifies orders of English society as philistines or barbarians or the populace and life-attitudes as Hellenic or Hebraic, the very ability to classify freshly implies a classifier elevated above social space and historical time. And yet what he treats is as pressingly real and concrete as can be. Likewise, Arnold's jibes and sarcasms imply engagement while they are enabled by a freedom, a detachment easily greater than that of his opponents. Finally then, Arnold's voice is his best argument. His style portrays him as an urbane, informal conversationalist who demystifies abstract concepts into commonsense propositions. As John Holloway concludes, Arnold "*is* what he advocates," the flower of cultural maturity.[21] And what he advocates, criticism and culture, have an especially supple dynamism—they are not programs or stolid ideas but methods, atmospheres in themselves—constituting a merger of pure thought and practical action.

5

The refusal of influence is not kind. Read as the culmination of the long, painfully honest struggle invented by the poems, Arnold's essays in their contentious force take on the delicate, personal beauty of a lyric sequence, for we see his primary quarrel to have been with himself. That is exactly the way in which Whitman will not read Arnold, though he seems cannily aware of Arnold's struggle, as when he sneers at culture's defensive reply that it "only seeks to help, systematize, and put in attitude, the elements of fertility and power, . . ." (396). Whitman robs Arnold of his inner struggle, perversely but necessarily, for he must refuse Arnold's terminological basis. What Arnold sees as a perfectly merged detachment and engagement Whitman will see as all detachment, for Arnold (to Whitman) is willing to be participatory only in a salon of rarified debate. Arnold might, by his lights, agree with Whitman's self-ideal in "Song of Myself" as "in the game and out of it," but, for Whitman, being "in the game" means being on the street, means not simply an interest in contemporary life but a ribald living of it.

Whitman's first person shape-changing, often involving his inclusion in a working class which Arnold considers either as an "embryo" too unformed for consideration or as a violent mob, is too familiar to rehearse here. Predictably, as I have emphasized, "the thought of identity" is the "Miracle of miracles" and chief idea of *Democratic Vistas;* and the thought includes an acceptance of all identities, social as well as "the Me in the center," "yours for you, whoever you are, as mine for me" (394). Whitman directly insults Arnold's wide-view-from-a-height as ultimately common: "The common ambition strains for elevations, to become some privileged exclusive. The master sees greatness and health in being part of the mass; nothing will do as well as common ground" (381). Arnold conventionally images by the stars a perspectival, general truth and, in the phrase earlier cited from "Resignation," advises an imitation of their aloofness: "Wouldst thou *be* as these are? Live as they." Whitman replies in parallel rhetoric: "Would you have in yourself the divine, general laws? Then merge yourself in it," in this "common ground." Arnoldian self-resignation aspires to the firmament while Whitmanian personalism means to pull the heavens into the self. Thus Whitman views participation in the present not as a suicidal drop into Arnold's "dizzying eddy" but as "the joy of being tossed in the brave turmoil"; and he minimizes the opposing terms of Arnold's entire struggle by the simple assurance that in this "tossing," a term which transforms Arnold's "clash of ignorant armies" into play, "we have never deserted, never despair'd, never abandon'd the faith" (391). The new prophet, then, does not climb Arnold's mountain; his thoughts are the result "of the ordinary sense, observing, wandering among men" (363). Varied participation replaces Arnold's contemplative breadth as Whitman makes horizontal and democratic all thought.

"Always and more and more": the inclusive assurance of *Demo-*

cratic Vistas goes to charge Arnold's wide view with blind spots and to attack his "whole man" as partial, insufficiently a body, inadequately available to all. Whitman's new poet must be not an alien but both "a kosmos" and "one of the roughs." Arnold's new man of culture is given the task "to draw ever nearer to a sense of what is indeed beautiful, graceful, and becoming, and to get the raw person to live that" as a missionary of cultural maturity; Whitman's earliness urges the man of culture himself to return to the raw.

Both Arnold's self-resignation and Whitman's personalism expand into analogous national ideals, and these ideals abide by another general Anglo-American difference we noted earlier. Arnold urges his countrymen, all too enamored of their freedoms, to conceive of the state as "the nation in its collective and corporate character controlling, as government, the free swing of this or that one of its members in the name of the higher reason of all of them" (122). The state is the national expansion of a best self who refuses bias and idiosyncrasy. But while he wishes England to coalesce he also wishes it to pass beyond its national traits, for these too are provincial, culturally immature, in contrast to the pan-nationalism he espouses. Arnold sarcastically paraphrases liberal jingoism—"Don't let us trouble ourselves about foreign thought; we shall invent the whole thing as we go along" (*FC*, 276)—and calls for "a criticism which regards Europe as being, for intellectual and spiritual purposes, one great federation . . . ; and whose members have, for their proper outfit, a knowledge of Greek, Roman, and Eastern antiquity, and of one another" (*FC*, 284). Arnold's broadening is temporal as well, we see here, but it is not international: he has no use for America or other bastions of chaotic earliness but looks to cultures more sophisticated than England's—to France and Germany in particular.

Whitman of course worries not at all about provincialism but about foreign domination and the inappropriate acceptance of past customs. And while he, like Arnold, does worry about national coalescence—in a footnote he wonders if individualism might too much negate patriotism (373n)—he names a cure not in terms of a controlling state but by the rhetoric of divine national election. As the writer embodies the nation, so the nation embodies God's plan: a "new Metaphysics" (416), enunciated by "races of orbic bards" (407) who hold up "the divine banner of the pride of man in himself (the radical foundation of the new religion)" (412) to be lived out in "the most positive of lands" (410), "inaugurating largeness, culminating time" (423). Only by literary nationalism will America achieve ripe maturity: "I, now, for one, promulge, announcing a native expression-spirit, getting into form, adult, and through mentality, for these states, self-contain'd, different from others, more expansive, more rich and free" (410). American can afford a cultural adulthood on its own terms rather than a British-derived maturity that would constitute a choice for crepitude. Whitman's very cadences, where often each sentence seems the beginning of a new sermon, tinges the national idea with religious principle.

This self-containment makes the past a potentially dangerous intrusion. Thus Whitman exemplifies the struggle against history as authority, which we will consider more generally in a subsequent chapter. Both Arnold and Whitman distrust any narrowly political history, and Arnold would agree with, even might inspire, Whitman's claim that "a single new thought, imagination, abstract principle, even literary style, fit for the time . . . may duly cause changes, growths, removals, greater than the longest and bloodiest war, or the most stupendous merely political, dynastic, or commercial overturn" (366). But Arnold's alternative is to expand the political into a cultural, intellectual history, and then to expand that in turn by making prior ages into permanently, presently applicable modes of being (Hellenic, Hebraic). Whitman essentially shucks history. For an unconvincing moment, he boasts of Columbus and the miracle of an already-present rich American past. But the past to him means Europe and England in particular, the feudalism democracy will supplant. Whitman's anxiety of earliness is such that the past is to be known only so that it can be avoided: "We see that the real interest of this people of ours in the theology, history, poetry, politics, and personal models of the past (the British islands, for instance, and indeed all the past) is not necessarily to mold ourselves and our literature upon them, but to attain fuller, more definite comparisons, warnings, and the insight to ourselves, our own present, and our own far grander, different, future history, religion, social customs, etc." (425). "Like America," an American literature "must extricate itself from even the greatest models of the past" (412). Thus Whitman follows Emerson in praising such grand figures as "Shakspere . . . artist and singer of feudalism in its sunset" (407) but refuses them as models ("ye were, in your atmosphere, grown not for America, but for her foes, the feudal and the old") except in their spirit of audacity. But Whitman goes Emerson one better by suggesting that we learn history to destroy it and to turn tables on British domination: "Yet could ye, indeed, but breathe your breath of life into our New World's nostrils—not to enslave us, as now, but, for our needs, to breed a spirit like your own—perhaps (dare we say it?) to dominate, even destroy what you yourselves have left" (407). It is in this voracious spirit that Whitman sees America "cheerfully accepting the past, including feudalism" (361)—with the cheer of a cannibal.

Still, Whitman is painfully aware of the absence of native models, and his real alternative for history is the authority of the future. If origin is essence, essence also may be identified with purpose or aim, "For our New World I consider far less important for what it has done, or what it is, than for results to come" (361). Whitman's America is both origin and end, surrounding and conquering Arnold's history, "making a new history, a history of democracy, making old history a dwarf" (423).

There is yet an absolute difference between looking to the past and to the future. The past, granting that history is widely conceptual and speculative, has been; Arnold's employment of history is a speculation upon a concrete something. Whitman's prophecies are of what has never been. At most they are speculations upon democratic principles themselves incorporeal, speculations upon speculations. We see in this an American priority of consciousness that we later, more fully, will treat as engendering two central phenomena: actualism, or the American desire to make palpable the poet's vision and live it out on the literal plane of everyday existence; and, opposing such confidence, a sense of having been deprived of the objective world, an ontological insecurity, which yet may be transformed into epistemological freedom.

Arnold's wide view is an attempt, in his repeating phrase, "to see things as they really are"; and while some realities are invisible, a certain mimeticism grounds his ideas. And we have noted the power Arnold grants to particular ages: propitious or unpropitious, to inspire or deaden. People, of course, create eras; but at most the agent is equal in power to his scene with both in a causal whirlygig, and more often the scene or "atmosphere" is made to appear prior. Whitman, in the boundless confidence—or is it infantile egoism?—of earliness can imagine "a new-founded literature, not merely to copy and reflect existing surfaces, . . . but a literature underlying life" (372). Whitman does not say a literature that delves underlying life; "underlying" here is a verb, meaning to *form* life's essence. Literature is to be formative, not reactive, and everything depends on this: "Arrived now, definitely, at an apex for these vistas, I confess that the promulgation and belief in . . . a new and greater literatus order . . . underlies these entire speculations—and that the rest, the other parts, are all founded upon it" (423–24). Carried away by the formative, prior nature of thought to realize a world, Whitman momentarily forgoes his participatory, level, open road to adopt an Arnoldian elevation at "the apex of these vistas."

Nonetheless, it is this very actualism that demands the participatory ethic in terms of the poet's own living-out of his vision. Thus, however much Whitman castigates American politics and generally views the political as shallow, he counsels "I advise you to enter more strongly yet into politics" while he also advises maintaining an Arnoldian godlike distance from parties, "watching aloof, inclining victory this side or that side" (399). Contrarily, Arnold would see Whitman's actualism as akin to the dreamy naïvete of British romanticism, a solipcism that refuses to live in the real world and take its cue from "the circumstances and needs of that particular time." In short, Whitman's actualism would qualify as another example of "the bathos." Yet just as Whitman's priority of thought leads to action, so Arnold's sometimes-priority of things leads to a retirement into thinking. The times dictate, but what they dictate now is a retirement into thought: "Now, and for us, it is time to Hellenise, and to praise knowing: for we have Hebraised too much, and have over-valued doing." At times, Arnold appears to want to make fact into metaphor and render the world into mind, a contention of ideas. Whitman oppositely wishes to make metaphor fact. This is how he can dramatize himself as at once more idealistically speculative and more practical-minded than Arnold. Arnold, of course, in hypothetical reply to Whitman could do likewise.

But there is finally that chief division, chief to the point that I place it at the center of my book as the prime Atlantic contrast. It is simple, even a commonplace, but one that now may be granted its full force. The world really, securely, imposingly exists for the Englishman. It is chiefly mysterious, portable, wispy, and insecure for the American. America elides with Whitman's general reality when he cries, "what prospect have we? We sail a dangerous sea of seething currents, cross and undercurrents, vortices—all so dark, untried—and whither shall we turn?" (422). Whitman's only answer is "the Soul," and this of course returns us to the question. Yet this extreme ontological insecurity, this apparent validation of the West as chaos, is cause for glory too, for only earliness can ask the largest questions, free in its emptiness of ameliorations that blind. In the final pages of *Democratic Vistas*, Whitman more and more emphasizes metaphysics and speaks of "great poems of death" (421) as, paradoxically, the ultimate fruit of earliness, the chief test of its power to subsume. "The poems of life are great, but there must be the poems of the purports of life, not only in itself, but beyond itself" (420). America thereby goes out upon eternity, and Matthew Arnold, himself so little involved in metaphysics, is made to seem left behind, a thin-voiced bard of the dead who cannot contemplate death. Yet Arnold might envision himself most happily left behind, at "the present moment," a wise father chiding the American child, saying, "We are here and it is now. Our prospect is indeed discoverable. Given it, how shall we decide to live?"

Three

AGES OF NATIONAL LIFE

5

CULTURAL TIME IN ENGLAND AND AMERICA

I

The Anglo-American contest is a struggle between two distinct senses of cultural time, British lateness and American earliness. By cultural time, I mean the collective metaphor that expresses an age's view of itself in relation to all of history. But it is not only a reflection of an historical attitude; once established, it directs and helps to determine perceptions beyond a strictly historical field. As John Lynen writes, "The kind of time one assumes determines the kind of experience one will have, because it establishes the horizon of consciousness and therefore locates the positions from which the mind perceives."[1] Lynen's emphases are more immediately metaphysical and less historically minded than my own; but my point is that cultural time has just such ontological and epistemological consequences as Lynen claims.

There are any number of other ways by which a culture may evaluate itself, but cultural time predominates in the nineteenth century. In the first of a series of essays on *The Spirit of the Age*, published in 1831, John Stuart Mill reflects on his title:

> The "spirit of the age" is in some measure a novel expression. I do not believe that it is to be met with in any work exceeding fifty years in antiquity. The idea of comparing one's own age with former ages, or with our notion of those which are yet to come, had occurred to philosophers; but it never before was itself the dominant idea of any age.[2]

In his monumental work *History, Man, and Reason*, Maurice Mandelbaum follows Mill in nominating historicism, "the belief that an adequate assessment of its [any historical phenomenon's] value is to be gained through considering it in terms of the place which it occupied and the role which it played within a process of development," as a prime feature of the nineteenth century. Both the doctrine of Progress, with its sense of culture as advancing toward something new, and the doctrine of Organicism, with its sense of culture as unfolding whatever is implicit within it on the model of the growth of living things, nudged this historical sensibility toward a visionary theory. They also enlarged the meaning of history. "What came to be viewed as the true subject of history was the total way of life and of feeling of a people."[3]

Despite the optimizing tendencies of Progress in particular (for Organicism may imply decay and death), cultural time in England after the Renaissance is predominantly and anxiously late. Walter Jackson Bate quotes Addison in the *Spectator* as Addison himself paraphrases Boileau: "It is impossible for us, who live in the latter ages of the world, to make observations . . . which have not been touched on by others." He quotes Steele in the *Guardian*: "Nature being still the same, it is impossible for any modern writer to paint her otherwise than the ancients have done." He discusses the distress caused by the failure of the "greater genres," tragic drama and epic; and he documents the saddened acceptance of "refinement" and "propriety" as substitutes for "nature" and "genius." Bate's theme is the eighteenth-century origins of the problem that haunts the writer still: "his naked embarrassment (with the inevitable temptations to paralysis or routine imitation, to retrenchment or mere fitful rebellion) before the amplitude of what two thousand years or more of an art had already been able to achieve." Many writers, and Johnson most vigorously, condemned an assumption of decline, but such opposition acknowledged the assumption's prevalence. Solace was available only through the odd idea which developed through the century and was most succinctly stated in the next by Macauley: "As civilization advances, poetry almost necessarily declines."[4]

Such solace, never fully efficacious in the eighteenth century, is less so in the nineteenth, as civilization is increasingly distrusted and the sacrifices demanded by its advance are increasingly resented. Equations between culture and literature become figured differently: the writer's anxiety of influence is not the necessary result of processes by which culture perfects itself; it is part and parcel of the culture's decrepitude.

Bate and Harold Bloom ignore the writer's less solipsistic anxiety for his culture. Bate sees the problem as the accumulation of cultural achievement epitomized by the Renaissance; Bloom wavers between this view and a startling reduction of the problem to the single figure of Milton. Bate sees the problem eased, though not at all eliminated, by the inventions of new forms in the romantic period; Bloom sees the problem as gaining full force only with the advent of romanticism. Neither, in their travels between specific periods and general human responses, stops long enough at the middle place of culture. But British poets and novelists did so and the evidence is everywhere.

Cultural lateness is evidenced in the centrality of a Fall mythology to each of the British romantics' visions—a shared notion that human being, originally unified and harmonious, has become discordant with itself. Each of the major romantics begins his mythic narrative in very late medias res, with Albion sundered, Harold exiled, or Prometheus bound; with a poet-persona bewailing the deprivation of the joys of his youth (Wordsworth) or the joys that belonged to youth and were never his (Coleridge, with his gloomy emphasis on childhood cancelled by enclosure in a city—but then we think of Blake's "Songs of Experience" as well) or a poet-persona blocked from becoming a poet by the cultural loss of mythic consciousness itself (Keats in his "Ode to Psyche" most plainly, but in *The Fall of Hyperion* and *Lamia* as well). Hope consists either in a return, a personal and cultural undoing often dramatized in pastoral landscapes; or, if return is impossible, in a transformation of the lost original perfection into a new, often internalized value. These are major alternatives, for in the second, the conditions of the present may be accepted as a necessary stage for their own subversion. But in all cases the present is weary, and revitalization depends on the regaining of original values—transformed or not—which have been lost or displaced in the aging of self and culture. (Even when the poet, like Wordsworth in the Immortality Ode, accepts as final the loss of certain capacities, he recalls that in his youth each loss provided a first sense of what had been lost and thus constituted a gain; and he demands of himself a return of the power of transformation.) In all cases, the *re*-words of the lateness lexicon predominate.

The prevalence of the Fall myth in romantic literature has been explained variously: as a consequence of the French Revolution and its failure; as the inevitable effect of a Christian heritage; as part of a process whereby the poet at once accepts, rejects, and rewrites Christianity in navigating it into his terms of understanding; as concomitant with a Rousseauian primitive ideal; as a function of the romantic emphasis on myth, since all cosmogonic myths are readings-back from history that devalue historical time in relation to the timelessness that gave birth to history; and even as a near accident, for it is Milton in his supreme poetic power with whom the romantics must negotiate, and his theme happened to be the Fall. None of these explanations is devoid of plausibility. Cultural lateness may seem merely another explanation worth factoring in. But lateness is rather their essence, for each of these explanations implies a conviction that the world is aged.

Cultural lateness figures in many aspects of British romantic poetry. Wordsworthian personal nostalgia (which most plainly in *The Prelude* serves at times as an emblem of a cultural nostalgia for rural dignity and a morality as natural as the landscape); the loss of an imaginative power never fully realized, which Coleridge everywhere dramatizes; the worldweariness of Byron's Harold; Shelleyan forgiveness, which implies a prior history of revenge; more generally, the revolt against the city, the elegiac mode, and the medieval revival—these among many other values, interests, and themes bespeak lateness worries.

They continue into Victorian poetry where, as David Daiches has argued, twilight moods prevail. Tennyson's grief is frequently mused into a fatigued sadness, what Whitman complained of as "languishing melancholy" and "solitary lassitude." Arnold's world is "So various, so beautiful, so new" only in seeming; its reality is as a "darkling plain," which "Hath really neither joy, nor love, nor light," but only "ignorant armies," which "clash by night."⁵

Even Browning, with his drive toward optimism, makes his Roland the last of an apparently failed band of knights. When Roland moves into the "ominous tract," his only gladness is "that some end should be."⁶ His remaining hope has dwindled "into a ghost not fit to cope" with success (IV). His "whole-world wandering" is summarized in the foregoing "day" which "had been a dreary one at best" (VIII). Worse, the fate of this figure of ultimate lateness is to recapitulate all time. Roland passes through a first plain of barren nature that prevents nurture, with its process personified as a demonic god:

> If there pushed any ragged thistle-stalk
>   Above its mates, the head was chopped—the bents
> Were jealous else. . . .
>
> (XII)

And for the jealous "bents" themselves, " 'tis a brute must walk / Pashing their life out, with a brute's intents" (XII).

From this prehistoric Darwinian darkness, Roland passes to a plain of civilization, of history. But in crossing a transitional river of time, Roland stabs a submerged creature that "may have been a water rat" but "sounded like a baby's shriek" (XXI). In rejecting nature for civilization, Roland may, in his progenitor's words from Lear, "prevent the fiend, and kill vermin"; but he also may be guilty of murdering the vital in himself, an act which Browning images as infanticide.

The latter seems likely, as human war on this second plain merely substitutes for Nature's pashing brute: ". . . what war did they wage/ Whose savage trample thus could pad the dank/Soil to a plash? . . ."

(XXII). And industrialism is imaged as "that harrow fit to reel/Men's bodies out like silk. . . ." (XXIV).

Finally, in a "dying suneet," this cultural lateness narrows into the anxiety of artistic influence proper. All of the major arts coalesce as, in the midst of a piece of sculpture (or perhaps anti-sculpture, for the "dark tower" is a "blind squat turret"), Roland becomes a portrait by an act of song that is the title of this piece of literature. The lost adventurers who had preceded him there are

> ranged along the hill-sides—met
> To view the last of me, a living frame
> For one more picture; in a sheet of flame
> I saw them and I knew them all. And yet
> Dauntless the slug-horn to my lips I set
> And blew. *"Childe Roland to the Dark Tower Came."*
>
> (XXXIV)

The vengeful predecessors, "met / to view the last of me," take us back to the jealous "bents" of raw nature. Cultural lateness culminates in a return that is disastrous, to savage aggression.

But that in fact does not happen in Browning's poem, and I have focused on "Roland" not only because it exemplifies lateness but because it also exemplifies the romantic and Victorian attempts to conquer it. Roland does not die so much as he achieves apotheosis. He both reverses and denies linear time. He makes himself a legend upon which the equally bereft Edgar could draw in *Lear:* Browning sources his source. The "sheet of flame" is apocalyptic. The ruined tower *is* the final end of meaning, and Roland conquers it by transforming his quest and himself into the meaning the tower had been expected to provide. The tower is "blind as the fool's heart" (XXXI), a sure allusion to Psalms 14:1 and 53:1, "the fool hath said in his heart, There is no God." But there is a God, which Roland finally discovers shadowed in his human striving. That discovery alters decisively the meaning of Roland's complaint upon his arrival at the tower: ". . . The tempest's mocking elf / Points to the shipman thus the unseen shelf / He strikes on, only when the timbers start" (XXXI). Too late, Roland implies. But the tempest is Shakespeare's *Tempest*, the elf is Ariel, the shipwreck is ultimately educative, and there is a Prospero guiding all. It is never too late and there is no final end to meaning: thus Roland affirms himself and his experience in his last words, which return us to or, more accurately, provide the poem's beginning, its title. In Roland's last moment, linear time is converted to an everlasting presence that defeats cultural lateness.

The British desire to defeat lateness is evidenced in its fullest intensity in Shelley's *Prometheus Unbound,* where the decisive action, Prometheus's forgiving of Zeus, is rushed to an early moment in the verse-drama so that the bulk of the poem can chronicle recovery. Or again, as we saw in the previous chapter, the narrative that Arnold forges from his individual poems does not leave us in mourning upon "Dover Beach" but returns to an earlier poem ("Obermann") for a crucial rewriting that leads the poet from frustration to the efficacious freeing of thought and action. And, as early as in Wordsworth's great "Ode," the desire of a return to an earlier stage of the personal self is viewed as a powerful temptation. Such regression must be eschewed for the forward looking faith of seeing through death to a beyond. That "beyond" is the sphere out of which we are born into the world; and a faith in this larger return is enabled by the poet's looking back on his earlier misgivings and triumphant transitions from stage to stage. Better returns combine to replace a merely nostalgic one.

Wordsworth's fears in the "Ode" are not merely personal. While the narrative of Fall and Return is a permanence in human imagining, it appeals with special power to the English romantics and Victorians because the sole next stage imaginable after cultural lateness is a cultural death without resurrection. And that imagining is the dissolution of meaning.

2

In the fiction as in the poetry of the British nineteenth century, the struggle with an acknowledged cultural lateness figures mightily. We cannot linger to discuss every occurence of this anxiety, but if we take the three British novels of the mid-century that arguably matter most—Bronte's *Wuthering Heights,* Dickens' *Bleak House,* and Eliot's *Middlemarch*—their concerns with cultural lateness may stand for the rest.

The struggle is most plain in that tome on civilization and its discontents, *Wuthering Heights.* The obvious contrast created by the descriptions of the two abodes, Wuthering Heights and Thrushcross Grange, is frequently and correctly interpreted as a contrast between unprotected, emotional tumult and valley mildness, outdoors-nature and indoors-civilization, id and superego. The physical features of the Heights—its rough beams, primitive furnishings, and stone defenses—also signify cultural earliness; and its "deeply set" windows are mirrored by Heathcliff's "deep-set" eyes. In this unity with natural forces and his amoral libidinal energy, Heathcliff is Emily Bronte's hero of extreme cultural earliness. His defeat and subsequent perversion by the forces of advanced, fatigued Christian civilization and Victorian gentility are dramatized in terms of his soulmate's choice for Edgar Linton and the indoor, mild, protected life of Thrushcross Grange. But that soulmate, Catherine Earnshaw, whose choices represent the choices that have been made by civilization, sickens and dies—partly because she cannot resolve the conflict in her character between the early and the late, the unreined vital and the sublimating human, and partly because cultural lateness, when it tyrannizes over and seeks to eliminate the earliness of nature, brings death.

The second half of the romance tends to valorize civilization, not by reversing the values of the first half but by stressing the natural human aspirations expressed in civilized values once civilization is distinguished from the lateness of over-civilization. For example, books are a function of over-civilization in the first half of the novel: Catherine, once she is attracted to the life of Thrushcross Grange, is repelled by Heathcliff's illiteracy, only to find herself placed with the Edgar who remains steadfastly ensconced in his library while she sickens with libidinal hunger. But Catherine's daughter, after ridiculing Hareton for his inability to read, finds her way out of a tragic repetition pattern by repenting and instructing him in the energy of written language. Books, as imaginative and passionate and yet rational artifacts, books like *Wuthering Heights,* harmonize the values that had seemed implacably in conflict; and as nature-terms and civilization-terms merge in the figures of Hareton and the second Catherine, a new garden is (literally) planted, and cultural lateness is defeated.

Cultural lateness may result in part from the passage of time, but its effect is the clogging of time. In *Wuthering Heights,* the tale is told by the work's most repressed, over-civilized, culturally late and attenuated character, Lockwood. He recounts the recountings of Nelly Dean, who is much like him in these respects, and the very enwrapping of the fallible narration serves as another indicator of lateness. The narrative travels backwards from its present-tense beginning (in 1801, significantly—the work lays the basis of the nineteenth century and dramatizes its alternative possibilities), but, upon Catherine's death, any sense of moving forward to the present is made merely statistical. As many critics have noted, Heathcliff comes to imitate his victimizers; his son by Isabella Linton is a living caricature of every Thrushcross-civilized attenuation of energy, the relationship between the offspring, Catherine and Linton, parodies by an exaggerated repetition of events the conflicts of the original Catherine and Edgar; and their dual scorn of Hareton recalls the original rejection of Heathcliff. The tale catches up to the time of the narrative's beginning and frees itself into the literal future only when the younger Catherine and Hareton begin to conspire the purified combination of Heights and Grange values. The couple will marry on New Year's Day. That is, time can go forward once the cultural clock has been turned back to beginnings for a new attempt at historical living.

Dickens plays more openly upon the clogging effects of lateness. The London of *Bleak House* is a senseless garbage heap of cultural accumulation. As J. Hillis Miller observes of the novel's opening, "Things are visible, outlined in the fog, but nothing is related to anything else. Each new object is simply added to others in a succession which makes more and more obvious their disconnection." Miller argues persuasively that the opening description of fogbound London suggests a city backsliding into a prehistoric slime, the disunity of Chaos, and thus mocks the conventionally optimistic view of the city as a sign of human progress. Mistaken progress has resulted in "a continuous nonprogressive present time," and this, in turn, has taken the culture back, not to the vigor of earliness, but to the terror of unmeaning.[7]

Similarly, the clogging of time is expressed—indeed, the reason for this view of the physical scene is provided—by Chancery, with its interminable, heartless legalities. For Dickens, cultural lateness is imaged in systems gone wild, institutions made mechanical and almost all-powerful in their dismissal of human need. Lateness is abstraction. And, as we noted in chapter two, its threatened punishment is imaged in terms not of a return to Chaos—that already has occurred—but of the destructive purification of Apocalypse. The "little Lord Chancellor," Krook, owner of a rag-and-bottle shop whose accumulation of things without relation serves as an emblem not only of Chancery but of the culture at large, dies by that process of spontaneous combustion that we earlier traced to Melville. And, while Miller rightly considers this death as a "notorious example of this return to homogeneity" (he is literally "transformed into the basic elements of the novel, fog and mud"),[8] spontaneous combustion is simultaneously a fire-idea, an apocalypse whimper.

Revolution is the political type of Apocalypse, and Dickens distinctly threatens revolution. The pauper Jo's descendants, treated worse than stray dogs, "will lose even their bark—but not their bite"; the "stillest and politest circles" of self-insulated aristocracy and pastness in which such people as the Dedlocks live (note the similarity of their last name to Bronte's Lockwood, but here more fully a name for the result of giving the present over to the past, a major aspect of lateness) may be broken into violently by the "very strange appearances" of angered sufferers "in active motion outside"; and the French nationality of Mademoiselle Hortense, the murderess of the Chancery lawyer Tulkinghorn, implies the possibility of an English reign of terror.

Apocalypse, as the destructive purification of time gone to its utmost corrupted extent, is the appropriate scourge for cultural lateness just as Chaos is the appropriate critique; but Dickens, having dramatized with some courage the pitfalls to which a Victorian liberal humanism like his own is liable, reformulates the credo to allow for a peaceful return to cultural earliness. It is personified in Esther Summerson. As we noted in our earlier discussion of Melville and Dickens, Esther eventually earns marital bliss in a new Eden, living with a Christlike husband in a pastoral cottage. Dickens's novel states the grounds for possible redemption. Esther's cottage is called the second Bleak House, still "bleak" because social history has been equated heretofore with that adjective, "second" because her marriage, like the marriage of Catherine and Hareton in *Wuthering Heights,* constitutes a return to the good-reasoned beginnings of social living with the hope that history will develop differently, away from bleakness, this time.

Predictably, George Eliot eschews scriptural allusions even as a helpful context for understanding, which is the limited way in which Dickens employs them. Nonetheless, she does begin *Middlemarch* by invoking a religious figure, St. Theresa, to dramatize by contrast the cultural lateness that would-be Theresas of nineteenth-century England must confront. In the sixteenth-century Spain of her childhood, Theresa's heart was "already beating to a *national idea.*" In Theresa's maturity, "She found her epos in the reform of a *religious order.*" In contrast, "later-born Theresas were helped by no *coherent social faith and order.*" My italics highlight the deficiencies of the Middlemarch world, which lacks a social or spiritual ideal to which the self could rise. This compound lack, the narrator reasons, leads modern Theresas like Dorothea and Lydgate to "dim lights," "tangled circumstances," and an inability to join thought and deed in "noble agreement"; that is, failings we otherwise might impute to the individual character are seen, at least in part, as socially caused by a historical decline eventuating in a "brown pond" society that would sully Theresa herself.[9]

Eliot will go on to dramatize the irrelevance of national movements to the Middlemarch community by reducing political action to gossip, scandal, and buffoonery. The debate over the Reform Bill, which serves as the novel's historical center, matters only as an outlet for petty nastiness. Indeed, there is nothing worth reforming given the absence of a really inclusive social faith. As for the official aspects of the life of the spirit, the God of the zealot Bulstrode reassures him of the ultimate justification for his every deceit; clergyman Tyke writes narrow, fiery, dissenting pamphlets and neglects his parishioners: his competitor Farebrother is full of virtues, but the one true Christian spends his free time collecting insect specimens and his Shandyan drawers of insects are not the stuff of which heroic action is composed. Any possibility for a "coherent social faith" is betrayed by the Middlemarch disease, collective schizophrenia. The theoretical reformer Brooke is, in daily life, a usurious landlord. Casaubon's endeavor to find a "key to all Mythologies" is belied by the innumerable pigeonholes which store his notes and represent a hopelessly nitpicking, fragmented intellect. Lydgate is after the more plausible "primary tissue," but his inquisitive spirit is limited to research—"that distinction of mind which belonged to his intellectual ardor did not penetrate his feeling and judgement about furniture and women" (111–12).

Eliot's extended exemplifications of the failings mentioned in her "Prologue" argue against viewing the historical decline she chronicles as a mere metaphor of the crux of tragedy—that we cannot be what we would. Surely the mind is drawn to the nostalgic formula by which the past becomes the time of the ideal and the present its negation. But in the *Prologue* Eliot is careful to treat Theresa with realistic humor; and, as she "found her epos in reform," the claim is not that Theresa's world was ideal but only open. Every sentence in the "Prelude" implies facticity. Indeed, Eliot inaugurates her work by addressing those who wish "to know the history of Man, and how the mysterious mixture behaves under the varying experiments of time." The world *has* aged, and badly.

For Eliot, cultural lateness results in a narrowing by which the possibility of heroism is sacrificed. And Eliot offers no hope for a return to a new initiation of history. In her essay on "The Natural History of German Life," she approves the German historian Riehl in that "He is as far as possible from the folly of supposing that the sun will go backward on the dial, because we put the hands of our clock backward; . . ." And in that same essay, she agrees with Riehl's belief in "the decomposition which is commencing in the organic constitution of society."[10] In her "Finale" to *Middlemarch*, the narrator remarks of heroes and heroines like Theresa, "the medium in which their ardent deeds took shape is for ever gone" (612). Eliot qualifies her pessimism only by stressing that some aspects of life are ahistorical and that an organic society may grow in part out of private actions: because of the unknown Dorotheas and their unknown good acts, "things are not so ill with you and me as they might have been" (612). Domestic virtue provides for the second term, as cultural lateness does for the first, in the title of the final section of *Middlemarch*, "Sunset and Sunrise." Indeed, throughout the novel, the wonderfully versatile narrative attitude organizes itself by two alternating views: a high view that, without compromise, espouses the epic-heroic life and condemns a social situation that frustrates its enactment; and a lower view that seeks out a reduced, domestic equivalent to the heroism now unavailable and examples an intelligent compassion to suit a world of relative failure. Thus, Dorothea's vacant sister is, as Henry James said, "as pretty a fool as any of Miss Austen's"[11] and she is not—not in her flighty egotism, which is an inert hindrance to all who would attempt anything significant. Celia's husband is a "blooming Englishman" and a conforming bigot; Mr. Brooke is yet another Austenian fool, good-hearted withal, and a man whose broken phrases and invariably random thoughts epitomize the bubbleheaded society that believes in nothing.

Each character is treated to his low-high ambivalence. The heroic aspirants like Dorothea only cause a reversal of terms, not of procedure. With her, the high view is sympathetic while the low view ridicules her pretensions and her ignorance. Once she is victimized, however, the compassion of the low view is called upon as well, and by this unity of views we are made to feel for her as for no other character.

By this ambivalence, however, the union of Will and Dorothea is not, as Gordon Haight would have it, the mating of Beauty and Truth.[12] By the time they wed, Will has given up all notions of genius to become a very ordinary legislator, and Dorothea, in the midst of an embrace, is worrying about reduced finances. Even when we are told that, because of Dorothea's small everyday virtues, "things are not so ill with you and me as they might have been" (613), we are in the presence of a negative statement; and we cannot help but recall a comment on Dorothea from an earlier chapter, that "With some endowment of stupidity and conceit, she might have thought that a Christian young lady of fortune should find her ideal of life in village charities" (21). Her good acts, as we may surmise from her actions on Lydgate's behalf, are something more than village charities, yet there is a terrible sense in Eliot's "Finale" of nonfulfillment, of something irrevocably lost. True, "the growing good of the world is partly dependent on unhistoric acts; and that things are not so ill with you and me as they might have been, is half owing to the number who lived faithfully a hidden life, and rest in unvisited tombs." But what of the other half?

The something irrevocably lost in that missing half is historical possibility.

Despite its balances, then, *Middlemarch* marks a moment in the British nineteenth century when cultural lateness is acknowledged, not to be defeated but only somewhat deflected. But I am concerned here less with the development of despair connected to cultural lateness than with its simple existence at, roughly, mid-century. Its existence is publicized further in these three novels by the prevalence of a particular character-type. I will call him the Bachelor for, though he may be married, he is essentially solitary. He is a grotesque with an oversized intellect, a shrunken body, and a shrivelled heart. He refuses the human community; he will not risk relatedness, preferring to experiment upon others or to observe them from a voyeuristic distance. Crippled by self-consciousness, if he loves he often runs away to maintain an equilibrium that is passion's defeat. Impotent and vengeful, highly intellectual yet unwise, he sells his soul for a sullen invulnerability that is itself fraudulent, for his great need is to impress others. He is Bronte's Lockwood (and, to a degree, her Linton and her Nelly Dean, for "he" may be a she), Dickens's Chancery Lawyers (Tulkinghorn, Vholes) and their supposed nemesis Skimpole, Eliot's Casaubon. The Bachelor personifies cultural lateness, the anxiety of overcivilization in which form replaces feeling, hesitation refuses spontaneity, custom murders vitality, nature sickens, and love dies.

I would make two final points concerning this anxiety and then a crucial qualification. First, cultural lateness as we have seen it shows the folly of studying literary influence in a social vacuum. The characteristic forms taken by influence in any age depend on that age's cultural clock. Within *Middlemarch*, for instance, Eliot's narrator says this of Fielding:

> A great historian, as he insisted on calling himself, who had the happiness to be dead a hundred and twenty years ago, and so to take his place among the colossi whose huge legs our living pettiness is observed to walk under, glories in his copious remarks and digressions as the least imitable part of his work . . . We belated historians must not linger after his example; and if we did so, it is probable that our chat would be thin and eager, as if delivered from a campstool in a parrot-house. (104–5)

Eliot substitutes analogous action in her weblike sense of human connections for a generalizing assurance or a large, digressive action because she sees these latter techniques as unavailable or untrue in her (real, not only novelistic) world. Her relation to Fielding is determined by her sense that cultural lateness has reduced history and that the novelist-historian must at once obey that reduction (the novelist no longer can digress because there no longer exists a center—an assumed, collective credo—to digress from) and find within it subversive techniques for the imagination's enlargement.

In short, literary influence is a subcategory of cultural time; to speak only in universal terms of its forms and motives is to court folly. Specifically, influence in a culture with a sense of itself as early not only will be dealing primarily with foreign influences, but individual authors also will tend to see influence as an issue between cultures and not merely individuals or ages—another reason for the American writer's extreme identification with America.

But second, while I am implicitly scolding a colossus "whose huge legs our living pettiness is observed to walk under," I would agree with Professor Bloom that writers can afford kinds of deliberate ignorance that critics cannot. American writers could see the British anxiety of cultural lateness easily enough—how could they miss it? And, by ignoring the earned victories over that anxiety within the English writer's full vision, they could utilize it doubly: by making decrepitude and its signs *the* characterization of Britain and its writers, as we have seen Emerson do, and by viewing this British-acknowledged anxiety as the promise of a free American future.

But it is in speaking of self-conscious Anglo-American comparisons that a qualification becomes necessary. In cultural time, ripeness is all; and if nineteenth-century England often appeared to its literary inhabitants as in the extreme decline of old age, it could as often appear wonderfully mature with its stable identity guaranteed in an assured adulthood. "My native country was full of youthful promise," Washington Irving writes. "Europe was rich in the accumulated treasures of the age."[13] The Progressive doctrine—stated simply, the idea that society is gradually, non-apocalyptically perfecting itself—had real currency in nineteenth-century England: it informs the victories over lateness in the works we have considered. This faith depends on a culture's knowledge that it has faced and capitalized on crises so many times during a long history that this improving perseverance is nationally characteristic. It depends on a culture's sense that each crisis has deepened—not broken—the national character and assured both its continuity and its freshness. Such a knowledge and such a sense depend not only upon long time and its accretions but also upon an appreciation of time, an ability, itself a cultural inheritance, to see the past as a gift, a grace, a support and a stay, not simply as an intimidating crush.

Of all these strengths the nineteenth-century American writer was absolutely deprived.

3

"The youth of America is their oldest tradition," Oscar Wilde has a character say in *A Woman of No Importance*. "It has been going on now for three hundred years."[14] That isn't quite fair. The settlement of the continent was continuing during Wilde's lifetime, the United States was still a relatively new configuration, and, as we have shown to the point of redundancy, American culture awaited definition. But yes, cultural earliness became the tradition to substitute for the lack of more tangible traditions; and this in part because the Americans, glancing at the omnipresent comparative model of Britain, could have no hope of competing for the rewards of cultural maturity. Bryant in 1843 foresees an Anglo-American struggle for "which power holds and governs the world" wherein "the mind of England, old and knit by years and wisdom into strength" is ably combatted by an America "roused to new duties in its youth, and in the van with opinions born of the hour."[15] And Emerson more aggressively tells Carlyle that "England, an old and exhausted island, must one day be contented, like other parents, to be strong only in her children" (*W*, V, 275–76).

Cultural earliness became synonymous with the national faith to the extent that when Melville became an apostate his first move was to deny the benefits of earliness. In *Benito Cereno*, the Spanish and American sea captains are characterized, seated across from each other over a long dinner table, as "a childless couple": the future is made sterile for the American too, as his overripe innocence, his willed naïveté, serves to further the slave trade and, by implication, all of the ills of European history. And we have seen that the New York of "Bartleby the Scrivener: A Tale of Wall Street" is as walled-in, as lifeless and heartless, as devoid of the personal and the possible as the London of *Bleak House*. Alternately, in such paired tales as "The Paradise of Bachelors" and "The Tartarus of Maids," the sterility of British lateness and the savagery of American earliness result in like dehumanizations.

In dissent from the national faith, then, American writers might see the nation not as a new start but as the final, fatal outpost of a decrepit Euro-American civilization. (One could cite here as well the wide variety of Bachelor figures in Hawthorne—Chillingworth, Judge

Pynchon, Coverdale, all of the over-rational scientists of inhuman perfection—as representative of a disastrous lateness.) Or they might render both earliness and lateness irrelevant in comparison to a human
propensity for evil that infiltrates either. But again, such dissents prove
the centrality of the claims for earliness, as when Thoreau, in defense
of "this vast, savage, howling mother of ours, Nature," warns in
"Walking" against a socially centered culture "which produces at most
a merely English nobility, a civilization destined to have a speedy
limit."[16]

Cultural earliness is an organic metaphor and its joys are the joys
of youth. R. W. B. Lewis in *The American Adam* describes these joys
most generally as "a sense of promise and possibility." Specifically,
cultural earliness promises "a life determined by nature and enriched
by a total awareness."[17] Most simply, as Thomas Paine writes, "We
have it in our power to begin the world again." And momentarily in
that spirit, Melville, in his encomium on Hawthorne, defends America
against the assumption he later would apply with a vengeance, "that
the world is getting grey and grizzled now. Not so. The world is as
young today as when it was created; and this Vermont morning dew is
as wet to my feet, as Eden's dew to Adam's."[18]

The Adamic quill would provide specifically literary joys. British
writers who believed that literature in England had declined since the
Renaissance advanced the idea, best put by the artist Constable, that
"In the early ages of the fine arts, the productions were most affecting
and sublime" because "the artists, being without human exemplars,
were forced to have recourse to nature." The Scottish critic Hugh Blair
popularized this idea for Americans, convincing them (and they were
not averse to being so convinced) that, in Benjamin Spencer's words,
"for the highest species of poetry and the grandest reaches of the imagination the vigorous temper of a youthful people was a more likely soil
than that of a polished nation."[19] Thus Emerson in "The Poet"
awaited a "genius in America with tyrannous eye, which knew the
value of our incomparable materials, and saw, in the barbarism and
materialism of the times, another carnival of the gods whose picture he
so much admires in Homer; . . ." (*CW*, III, 21). In Whitman, just such
a genius arrived.

Emerson's hope for a classical revival utterly different from the
British Augustan one, returning barbarism rather than polished wit to
literature, should remind us that cultural earliness is an imaginative
fact, not a historical one. Only by relation to England was there any
historical basis for it. "We are good," writes the senior Henry James at
mid-century, "by comparison, not by position. When compared with

the politics of the Old World, we present the auroral beauty of the morning emerging from the thick night; . . ."[20] Even so, it would have been difficult to have found a true barbarian in Emerson's Boston, or indeed in puritan Boston two centuries earlier.

This helps to answer Wilde's incredulity concerning the three-hundred-year-old youth of America: myth need not age. Leo Marx cites "all the later fictional narrators who begin in the same way, impulsively dissociating themselves from the world of sophistication, Europe, ideas, learning, in a word, *the world,* and speaking in accents of rural ignorance." As myth, then, cultural earliness could claim not only to precede decadent lateness and thus be closer to life's priorities; it could claim to succeed it, as a curative undoing, and thus could defend against the clear absence of those achievements available to cultural maturity. "In its simplest, archetypal form," Marx writes, "the myth affirms that Europeans experience a regeneration in the New World. They become new, better, happier men—they are reborn."[21]

But perhaps one could be reborn with memory intact. If they were sufficiently ingenious, Americans could take Horatio Greenough's dour remark, "the country was young, yet the people were old,"[22] and make it seem cause for utmost celebration. Within its own new history, America could seem final without appearing withered and elderly. It could be seen as the repudiation, the erasure, of all the evils of European history, or as the ultimate achievement of Christian, European culture. David Humphreys, one of the Connecticut Wits, exemplifies the heady rhetoric that could result from this doctrine of first-and-last: "We began our political career, in a great measure, free from the prejudice, and favored with the knowledge of former ages and other nations."[23] Looking before and after at the unprecedented expanse of time granted America by this valuable ambiguity, Americans would be able, sometimes, to ignore the thinness of the cultural present.

Thus the American Puritan myth by which America was the land of apocalypse. In scripture, the apocalypse occurs only at the moment of utmost corruption, when history has degenerated to a waste. But Puritans could load that corruption onto Old World history and see their own historical time as the beginning of the apocalyptic promise, "requiring," in Sacvan Bercovitch's characterization, "one last great act, one more climactic pouring out of the spirit, in order to realize itself." European Christians would look for an end to history, Bercovitch continues, while the Americans could valorize their history as "a preparation, the planting that anticipates a harvest." Theirs is "an errand to the end of time."[24]

Bercovitch errs, however, when he sees this future orientation as invalidating the nostalgic myth of Lewis's American Adam.[25] It is log-ically inconsistent to envision a return and an unprecedented arrival simultaneously, but cultural earliness, an opportunistic myth, is not strictly logical; and, for nineteenth-century writers suffering the recog-nition of emptiness, there would be no fussy discriminations between Old Eden and the New Jerusalem as long as each offered a rebuttal to British jibes. Thus Bercovitch is right to emphasize that, in America, the meaning of the term frontier is sometimes transformed from a sec-ular barrier separating nations to "a mythical threshold," "a *figural* outpost, the outskirts of the advancing Kingdom of God." But to that we must add Edwin Fussell's recognition of the significant synonymity of the terms "frontiersman" and "backwoodsman" as the spatial idea of the frontier takes on a temporal dimension. To Fussell, "back" sug-gests an American fear of cultural regression, "front" a progressive national optimism. But regression, as we saw in considering the myth of the West, may mean a return not to chaos but to paradise, and thus the paradox engendered by these synonyms might be figured all-optimistically. As Eric J. Sundquist writes, "going *back* and going *forth* are the same: the primitive is Past, but it is also West, and West is Future."[26]

At best the paradox triumphs over British cultural lateness and over the American anxiety of mere immaturity as well. The triumph occurs by a surround-and-conquer strategy in each case. This myth of a new beginning that promised as well, by a quickening of time, a millennial ending made English writers, who dealt with society as is and with history as merely secular time, appear narrow and unadven-turesome. The Americans could turn back on the British the charge of provincialism.

The very places of primary perfection to which the British writer hopes to return would seem too socially informed, too temporally provincial. For British Edenic pastorals, Thoreau substitutes the Wild, which is not simply the wilderness but the truly, radically ungoverned, unconditioned spirit raw. Poe and Dickinson emphatically end their return-narratives before any wished-for All is attained because that All by definition cancels the grounds of consciousness and language as we know them. For instance, Poe's "Ms. Found in a Bottle" forwards its narrator back in time, through all temporality, to the edge of atem-poral origin, where the narrator must sign off in language, for over that edge resides not merely silence but the is-not of all being. In *Arthur Gordon Pym,* the white-shrouded figure signals the end of commu-nication; and the editor's postscript only can circle back to earlier mys-teries in the tale without solving them, to emphasize the frustration of language in characterizing a state prior to the self-consciousness that enables words.[27] Similarly, Dickinson's chronicles of dying—"Our journey had advanced," "I felt a Funeral in my Brain," and many others—end with a dash different from other dashes, for these signify a to-be-continued that cannot be continued in the lexicon of ordinary consciousness. The American return is a return at all only most ambivalently, as the Poe narrator or the Dickinson persona emphasizes the exploratory courage, even the radical ignorance, of the adventurer into a realm that may be prior to our life—a realm others may have reached but that the dissolving self reaches for a first time and alone.

The most radical of American returns (or advances) do not attempt an Eden-like harmony of nature and culture; and they are not a metaphor, as the British return often clearly is. They dramatize a shockingly literal-seeming journey to before (or after, or in any case elsewhere than the place of) language, ordinary consciousness, history, all chronology. This is not Esther Summerson's new garden estate, which, in the American metaphysical sweep, appears as part of the cultural habitude that Dickens means to oppose by it.

4

Clearly, cultural earliness allowed Americans to capitalize upon the barrenness of their present scene by considering this barrenness a clearing of the ground for an unprecedented development. Nonetheless, cultural earliness just as easily might mean cultural emptiness. Youth, cultural as well as personal, can be callow. We earlier reviewed the varieties of despair Americans themselves experienced in viewing the present and immediate past of their literary attempts; and while I would not make of the myth of American time (which we have just considered) a merely defensive rationalization—that may have become one of its uses, but it would be entirely too cynical to reduce a cultural faith to an excuse—it demanded a leap of faith that the most springy of the literary nationalists could not make at every moment.

Like the joys, the sorrows of cultural earliness as emptiness and cultural youthfulness as immaturity or a negative savagery are seen most clearly in attempts to refute them. All that we have said of the proposed joys of earliness constitutes, in one sense, the largest refutation of sorrows. But there occurred as well an attempt to disown earliness, either by considering Euro-Americans as the inheritors of a storied Indian past or by foisting earliness upon the Indian and separating oneself from him and it. In its more benevolent form, as an adoption of the Indian as the ancestor of the white American, an instant history might be appropriated. The language of William Tudor, the founder of the *North American Review*, typifies many proposals on behalf of this adoption. He begins by demanding that we not confuse the "degenerate, miserable remains of the Indian nations" with their original state and continues, "They possessed so many traits in common with some of the nations of antiquity that they perhaps exhibit the counterpart of what the Greeks were in the heroic ages, and particularly the Spartans during the vigour of their institutions." They might become, then, heroes for an epic, and an epic would usefully imply that there had been much American time. The more romantic-oriented John Knapp, like Charles Brockden Brown, proposes the Indians as replacements for European gothic mysteries, but he also cites them as providers of a mysterious *genius loci*. "Let us not only revisit the dwellings of the European settler exposed to savage incursions," Knapp writes, "but let us hasten to acquaint ourselves with the earlier native. Let us hasten—for already has the cultivator levelled many a monumental mound, that spoke of more than writings might preserve."[28]

Knapp's statement in particular might seem a proposal for earliness rather than a proposal to escape from it. But in his "let us hasten to acquaint ourselves," a distance is asserted; and Knapp's proposal is preceded by an anxious review of the prevailing opinion that Americans lacked a history.

Irving, Longfellow, and, most ambitiously, Cooper attempted this friendly adoption of native Americans with some real success. But the adoption failed as a means to provide a sense of cultural history. (This is not to gainsay the contentions of Slotkin and others that American writers from Filson and Cooper through Thoreau and Whitman incorporated Indian myths and thus overthrew the assumptions of European myths—for example, the European assumption that the hunter was purely active and never contemplative. But that has to do with a proud cultural earliness, not with the shame we are now considering.) White Americans could not see themselves convincingly as offspring of the natives, especially as their actual ancestors had dispossessed the Indian. Instead, the Indian was employed in a meaner spirit, as we already have noted in discussing the colonists' anxiety occasioned by separation from their felt English ancestry. They became, even in the praisings of such as Tudor and Knapp, "savages" against whom European Americans might advertise their cultural sophistication. This is one of the themes of Roy Harvey Pearce's *Savagism and Civilization*, which begins by asserting that, for the settler, "in the savage and his destiny there was manifest all that they had long grown away from and yet still had to overcome." Richard Slotkin is specific: the complex culture of the Indian is negated, and the Indian comes to represent "the forces of the unconscious, the suppressed drives and desires that undergulf the intellect."[29]

I am interested in the imaging of Indians here only as a sign for the anxieties of earliness. In his negative stereotype, the Indian perfectly projects the essential anxiety, dissolution of the ego. At its most negative, as Marx and Fussell as well as Slotkin have noted, cultural earliness threatened cultural destruction, a horrible regression to a screaming chaos—not a return to Spirit but to an unformed, unformable nightmare place in whose negative timelessness no beginning could be initiated.

By the more settled nineteenth century this was not the leading fear of earliness, though it might remain the underlying one. The fear now, on the surface, concerned a willed banality; and while the century's extraordinary development of cities and machines might further calm the fear of a horrible dissolution of civilized order, this same development would ferment the fear of another kind of unbeing. Perhaps there would be only streets, factories, and masses of people with nothing joining and informing them. All of the brutalities of British lateness might be adapted without any of Britain's cultural richness to soften or control the brutalities. The absence of cultural achievements in a pastoral landscape could be rationalized as the promise of a new kind of achievement that would give significant birth to a new kind of nation. But this same absence of literary achievement within an advanced, urbanized economy could promise nothing but nothingness. If American cultural time might merge the best of earliness and lateness, it might merge the worst of both.

We watch the development of this fear in a transformation we noted earlier. In it, the excuse that Americans had produced no great literature because they were too busy civilizing a continent becomes, as the century continues, a worry that, in the process of civilizing a continent at breakneck speed, Americans had broken their imaginations as well, to become a furiously materialistic people. When Emerson speaks of American materialism as a "carnival of the Gods" fit for poetic celebration, he is reacting against this fear, attempting to incorporate it in the optimistic scheme of earliness. Whitman makes a like assertion when he writes, "It is acknowledged that we of the States are the most materialistic and money-making people ever known. My own theory, while fully accepting this, is that we are the most emotional, spiritualistic, and poetry-loving people also."[30] Whitman's poems, with their absolute acceptance of city life and their notion of commerce as a happy objectification of soulsharing, exemplify this rebuttal. It has old sanction, of course, in the Puritan linking of spiritual and worldly prosperity.

But this fear, which these rebuttals serve to advertise, would not be scattered easily. It is the fear of being at once undeveloped and yet not early enough; and an American fear of lateness might originate not only in the rapidity of material advances or in the uncritical adoption of European manners but in the simple, insistent fact that the generation of the age of Emerson would know itself as not the first generation of Americans. That is, the nineteenth-century Americans may be too late twice: too late as Americans to cure a decadent Western civilization and too late in America to experience the founders' sense of rebirth. George Forgie bases his fine psychohistorical study on this: "The fact of being born too late to experience the Revolution, but in time to be raised by the generation that had fought it, informed the way that many members of this later generation identified and thought about themselves." Again, "The sons had not themselves created or established this fortune of liberty, but were born rich."[31] The members of this "post-heroic" generation, ostensibly deferential to the founding fathers but sometimes subtly angry to the point of patricide, would begin the begun world with a sense of inadequacy that only a continuing, renewed, or altogether new mission might assuage. Mere prosperity would not satisfy this demand for a purpose equal to the founders' own and might seem even a repudiation of that American promise. Emerson's contemporaries thus experienced themselves sometimes as earliness-louts and nonentities and other times as damnable bringers of lateness. By stressing their earliness comparative to England and by redefining the War of Independence as a still-continuing cultural struggle, these sons of the heroes might slip the noose of filial inadequacy to see themselves as a second generation of founders.

Nonetheless, a giddy world in which, because there was no yesterday, everyone lived for today and took no heed of tomorrow; a world which, stripped of the associations granted by cultural maturity, leaves not nature and its invisible spirit but money and its abstract calculations as the sole object of consideration; a world in which class and heritage are removed and the removal results not in brotherhood but the mob, not in social dynamism but social disorder, not in an expansion of familial love but the encouragement of selfish guile—these might seem the results of a cultural earliness tied incongruously to a precocious economic maturity, an idiot's brain in a monstrous athlete's body. These dark imaginings link such disparate writers as Cooper, most particularly in *Home as Found,* and Melville, in *Moby-Dick,* "Bartleby" and many of *The Piazza Tales, Pierre,* and *The Confidence*

Man, and both with James, in *The American Scene*. They constitute the life rejected when Thoreau decides for Walden, and they contribute to the Boston of Hawthorne's *Blithedale Romance* even as that work simultaneously refuses the pastoral alternative. For the English visitor anxious to be disabused of the glories of American earliness, like Dickens in *American Notes* and *Martin Chuzzlewit*, these fears constitute a gold mine of cultural poverty. And in that most American book, *The Adventures of Huckleberry Finn*, Americans ridiculously ape the worst features of British and European lateness to become hicks in tuxedos, and they combine this aping with the worst aspects of a savage earliness to produce a dystopia against which the valued earliness of Huck and Jim barely can contend and never will prevail.

When we wish, more collectedly, to specify the sorrows of cultural earliness, we are drawn back to the quotation from James's book on Hawthorne that opened this study; and, with it, we are drawn back to a central issue, the imagined lack of an American history, with "history" granted its most inclusive meaning. James's rhetorical technique in that passage—a series of parallel phrases each initiated by the negative—is not his own invention but his version of an entrenched convention. The convention is primarily a British one. Americans possess "neither history, nor romance, nor poetry, nor legends, on which to exercise their genius, and kindle their imagination," wrote a journalist who signed no name in an 1818 number of *The British Critic*. We find the same sentiment voiced with a thin sympathy seven years later in *The Literary Gazette*: "America has hitherto had little or no originality in her literature; . . . Unlike other nations, she had no religion, no manners, and, above all, no language, essentially her own. Peopled chiefly by the fanatic, the adventurer, and the criminal. . . ." The Americans "had *no natural imagination*," Hazlitt told Northcote around the same time, but "This was likely to be the case in a new country like America, where there were no dim traces of the past—no venerable monuments—no romantic associations. . . ." Decades passed and the condescension only increased. In 1848, an Englishman wrote in *The Christian Remembrancer*, "since America enjoys no language, church, history, or heroes, it needs no poets." As if to prove the point that Americans lacked native materials and could write only by imitation of the British, Cooper would argue after a return from Europe, "There is scarcely an ore which contributes to the wealth of the author, that is found, here, in veins rich as in Europe. There are no annals for the historian; no follies (beyond the most vulgar and commonplace) for the satirist; no manners for the dramatist; no obscure fictions for the writer of romance; no gross and hardy offences against decorum for the moralist; nor any of the rich artificial auxiliaries of poetry."[32]

Cooper's no-series contains a twist, in that it concludes with a claim for American moral fineness; and other American critics, like W. H. Gardiner and Edward Everett, would concoct a parody of the no-series in ridicule of the British and then go on to suggest rich native possibilities. But the attack of this particular sentence construction struck home. It was especially effective because the absences listed, as in James's version, inevitably were wide-ranging. They jumped from buildings to social institutions and classes to literature and back again to vague experiential terms like "associations" and "manners." By their disarray, they did seem to cover all areas of life and all genres of literature, and all of both under the implied headings of cultural earliness (America "had not worked up her way gradually from barbarism to civilization") and an attendant absence of the historical sense.

We could attempt to categorize the lacks at length; it is more to the point to note that wherever we cut into the whole of literary possibilities, there seems an American Nothing there. If, for instance, we divide literary possibilities into realism and romance, neither seems likely as an American mode. Without the inheritances of classes and manners, and, as De Tocqueville noted, with a commitment to the "principle of equality" that "diminishes the number of objects to be described," realism seems without basis. As we saw in a preceding chapter, Cooper, while claiming that the American Average was a lofty one, nonetheless found that Average so applicable as to negate any potential for the discriminations necessary to realistic portraiture. As for romance, De Tocqueville found the principle of equality likewise nugatory, as it "diverts men from the description of ideal beauty—. . ." Hawthorne himself, in his preface to *The Blithedale Romance,* bewails the lack of an American "Faery Land, so like the real world, that, in a suitable remoteness, one cannot tell the difference, but with an atmosphere of strange enchantment, beheld through which the inhabitants have a propriety of their own" (*CE,* III, 3). Even Brownson, the fiercest of the intellectual literary nationalists, seconds Hawthorne on this: "We have a glorious nature, no doubt, but it is barren of legends, traditions, and human associations, unpeopled with fairies, even with dwarfs. . . . . . Nature, without man, or human association, as Byron well maintained, is not poetical, and cannot sustain a literature that does not soon become fatiguing and repulsive."[33]

The outcome of these dreary recognitions was not despair. Hawthorne did write his romances, in the process enlarging the definition of romance. Or rather, he was enabled to write romances by redefining

CHAPTER FIVE

the genre. Americans would have to redefine all of the genres and literature in general if they were to write at all. And those redefinitions
would depend on a redefinition of history that either would dispel cultural earliness or take greatest advantage of its strengths.

I have been suggesting through these pages that Americans were
capable of this achievement of redefinition, not because of a mysterious
capacity but for a solid reason. As late Westerners and early Americans, they were privy to a rich ambiguity of plural cultural times. It has
become a commonplace to say that all history is an imagined history;
but this conviction that history depends upon imagination possessed a
special, often unwelcome, certainly inescapable certainty for Americans in a period whose only other certainty was that no history had
been provided a priori for them. Within the plural possibilities of
American time, any one element, if fixed upon, might lead to despair;
the plurality itself might cause a confusion, and the confusion might
produce silence. But if the plurality could be seized with a creative
passion, literature not only might be possible; the imagination might
gain unprecedented freedoms from a past and a present that had not
been handed down presupposed.

6

THOREAU'S DAWN AND THE
LAKE SCHOOL'S NIGHT

I

A perfect earliness would be free of influence, and its literary statement would eschew allusion and all debate with other texts. The earliest author would be in immediate relation to Nature, in which, as Bergson tells us, no negatives exist. One foot planted on the first grounds, the other on that ephemeral Ground of Spirit from which Nature spontaneously arises, the colossus of dawn would acknowledge nothing alien with which to bicker.

Such an uninfluenced earliness is Thoreau's goal, and he begins *Walden* by a bombardment of earliness images. He will write in the first person for "it is, after all, always the first person that is speaking."[1] That is, he will speak truly, not just *in* but *as* the first person. He will hear no other voices, least those of elders, for age "has not profited so much as it has lost" (9). He will write for "poor students" (4) who must rely on their own experience for "If I have any experience which I think valuable, I am sure to reflect that this my Mentors said nothing about" (9). Not to "*play* life, or *study* it merely," youth must "earnestly *live* it from beginning to end" (51), where study would afford no authentic beginning from which to set out. The first person's only mentor, the one respected elder, is that "elderly dame," Nature, who "can tell me the original of every fable, and on what fact every one is founded, for the incidents occurred when she was young" (137–38).

To be at the source of myth, "at the fountain head of day" (138) with the "old settler and original proprietor" of Walden, "who tells me stories of old time and of new eternity" (137): this is the only influence Thoreau will accept. Thoreau locates a Walden spun out of the self's morning, "when I am awake and there is dawn in me" (90), a place "to front only the essential facts of life" (90). And like the actual frontiersman/backwoodsman, he moves forward to move backward, though in his act of cultural undoing he moves not at all. With no great interest in in the actual west or the factual frontier, Thoreau temporizes the spatial promise. For him, as Edwin Fussell writes, "it was far more agreeable to step backward in time, while remaining in the same place, . . ."² He wishes to be prelapsarian at a Walden "already in existence" perhaps "on that spring morning when Adam and Eve were driven out of Eden" (179). It is time before time and scope beyond all space.

It is an impossibility. "I am not aware that any man has ever built on the spot which I occupy," Thoreau boasts. "Deliver me from a city built on the site of a more ancient city, whose materials are ruins, whose gardens cemeteries" (264). Yet earlier he had confessed that his hoeing "disturbed the ashes of unchronicled nations" (158). This is an act of recovery, but it shows that the New World is old even if the nation is young; and America in any case is busy refusing what youth it truly possesses. Nature's scope is ignored in favor of a going-indoors. "The nation itself, with all its so-called internal improvements, which, by the way, are all external and superficial" is "an unwieldy and overgrown establishment, cluttered with furniture" (92). Even those unencumbered by an admiration for false improvements must front history and their postheroic moment. Elsewhere, travelling to Concord, N.H., Thoreau confesses, "we found that the frontiers were not this way any longer. This generation has come into the world fatally late for some enterprises."³

The very vocation of writer prevents primacy. Thoreau's first and final dawn is by definition pre- and post-linguistic as it is before and beyond usual consciousness. As Eric Sundquist argues, its only expression would be an *ur* language from "an Eden at the outset of the history of rhetoric, . . . like the speech of a lost God."⁴ And in *The Maine Woods*, Thoreau admits sadly, "The poet's, commonly, is not a logger's path, but a woodman's. The logger and the pioneer have preceded him like John the Baptist: eaten the wild honey, it may be, but the locusts also; . . ."⁵ For his ease, the poet sacrifices priority and the wild.

Thoreau may wish "not to live in this restless, nervous, bustling, trivial Nineteenth Century, but stand or sit thoughtfully while it goes by" (329–30); he cannot. Bedeviled by an enforced lateness, Thoreau's rage at any chosen lateness invades his dawn wonder. "This hostility affects him," Charles Feidelson, Jr. writes. "His writing, explicitly or by implication, is always polemic and never, as he doubtless would wish, blandly indifferent to the assumptions of the enemy."⁶ Thoreau knows that earliness can become American blather, knows, as Stanley Cavell puts it, "that we are not free, not whole, and not new, and we know this, and are on a downward path because of it." But that means only "that the present is a task and a discovery, not a period of America's privileged history; . . ."⁷

Earliness will be an act of will enabled by an acknowledgment of age, one's personal lateness and not alone the nation's or the nineteenth century's: "I long ago lost a hound, a bay horse, and a turtledove, and am still on their trail" (17). But Thoreau's hoeing can renew the lost earliness. If writing is itself notice of a separation from the booming Eternal Now (and it is: "The volatile truth of our words should continually betray the inadequacy of the residual statement," 325), Thoreau will take measures against a too careful appearance of order to stress extra-vagance rather than unity. Finally, as a self-reward, he will melt his structure of words into the seasonal cycle, and then he will surpass nature to create eternal spring. If his very words come out of a language with a history, he will shed their habitual meanings and drive them etymologically back to their origins, not *OED* origins but "a larger sense than common use permits out of what wisdom and valor and generosity we have" (100).[8] If Thoreau is drawn to acknowledge the century's issues and disciplines, these too will be treated to his extra-vagant etymology, as when economy becomes "the cost of a thing" and cost "the amount of what I will call life which is required to be exchanged for it, immediately or in the long run" (31). If he is not as poor a student as he would wish, then he will quote approvingly only from the earliest books from classical and oriental places, eastward, where the sun rises; and his quotings will be signs of confluence, not influence, for "I gaze upon as fresh a glory" as the Egyptian or Hindoo philosopher, "since it was I in him that was then so bold" as to raise "a corner of the veil from the statue of the divinity" just as "it is he in me that now reviews the vision" (99). And if Thoreau must debate and if argument confesses intrusion, if the voice of wonder, epic celebration, and biblical prophecy must sometimes give way to the satirist's thrust, then that voice will be toned as the rustic churl's. Northrop Frye tells us that such a character, whose name connotes the agriculturally early, refuses "the mood of festivity" in comic narratives. Usually we do not like him. But, Frye notes, "The more ironic the comedy, the more absurd the society, and an absurd society may be condemned by, or at least contrasted with, a character that we may call the plain dealer, an outspoken advocate of a kind of moral norm who has the sympathy of the audience."[9] Just so, Thoreau cries, "Simplicity, simplicity, simplicity!" (91) at his "restless, nervous, bustling, trivial Nineteenth Century." In all, if he cannot be prelinguistic and totemic really, he can be so figuratively and drive back time a little bit at least by calling his writing notchings on a stick. Having accepted the latecoming status of woodman in that passage in *The Maine Woods,* Thoreau suddenly makes a choice of what had seemed an inevitability:

"not only for strength, but for beauty, the poet must, from time to time," (and there is a pun here on the imaginative capacity for travel in time) "travel the logger's path and the Indian's trail, to drink at some new and more bracing fountain of the Muses, far in the recesses of the wilderness."

Most largely, as many commentators have noticed, Thoreau secedes from an America that, in its lateness, has lost itself. But he secedes by reenacting the American separation from England. He takes up his "abode in the woods," he reports, "by accident, . . . on Independence Day, or the Fourth of July 1845" (84), a by-accident suggesting not meaninglessness but unplanned and thereby significant coincidence, as the double naming of the day implies. That is, Thoreau refuses the official nation for the American *patria*. Speaking of tea, coffee, and milk, the availability of which his visitor John Field considered a chief American advantage, Thoreau replies, "But the only true America is that country where you are at liberty to pursue such a mode of life as may enable you to do without these" (205). The accusations he must rebut— that he is neglecting his social responsibilities, that he will become a heathen, that his venture is wildly impractical—recall the seventeenth-century British animadversions against the colonists; and his planting activities recapitulate the Puritan settlement.

I would add to this commonplace a simple emphasis on what Thoreau is seceding from it: it is England, or an America gone specifically English. England as a term in *Walden* stands simply and consistently for that which is too premeditated and overcultivated (like English hay) and for that which is too circumscribed (like the hunting grounds of English noblemen or the official English holidays implying the scheduled limiting of joys that should be daily). England stands for that which is decadent ("The government of the world I live in was not framed, like that of Britain, in after-dinner conversations over the wine," 332) or exploitative ("England, which is the great workhouse of the world," 35). England has nothing to tell us: "as for England, almost the last significant scrap of news from that quarter" (notice the employment of Sydney Smith's word from the phrase "In the four quarters of the globe, who reads an American book?") "was the revolution of 1649; . . ." (95). But America's own revolution has done nothing to halt the infiltration of British lateness. Our workers live in conditions "every day more like that of the English" (26), and Irish John Field stands for an America still deeply colonial in "thinking to live by some derivative old country mode in this primitive new country" (208).

Thoreau makes portable the idea of America to take it away from

that Englamerica, the existent America that is a traitor to its own earliness. Part of that removal is explicitly literary, Thoreau's attempt to
separate from English romanticism. And in that rebellion, the idea of
the Wild, which elsewhere Thoreau figures with the fruitful nervousness of a civilized thinker, becomes an unambiguous value.

2

On the title page of the first edition appears, in bold capitals, this
sentence. I DO NOT PROPOSE TO WRITE AN ODE TO DEJEC-
TION, BUT TO BRAG AS LUSTILY AS CHANTICLEER IN THE
MORNING, STANDING ON HIS ROOST, IF ONLY TO WAKE MY
NEIGHBORS UP. Coleridge is Thoreau's chosen opposite, specifically
the night-waking poet of "Dejection: An Ode." He is the insomniac in
rooms who looks out on an ill-omened moon through too literary eyes
that have lost the creative power to unite nature and mind in an act of
Godly joy. And he is everyway rejected as a model by an American who
situates himself outdoors not only at dawn but at the dawn of his
opponent's home literature. Chanticleer is a type-name for a rooster,
but it is Chaucer who is implied by the name in this literary sentence;
and, like Thoreau, Chaucer was another poet of national earliness who
had to battle foreign influence. Coleridge's fatigued self-pity marks a
long English decline from Chaucer's morning cheer. It is Thoreau's
New England neighbors who are to be awakened, but clearly neighbor
England, in its originary spirit, is to be saved from its own lateness as
well.

   Why Coleridge as the negative English representative? I have implied one reason. The most self-disappointed of romantic personae,
one who, even when he proclaims an imaginative faith at ode's end,
sees himself barred from active participation in that faith, would be a
large and likely target. Who better than the author of "Dejection"
could be accused of exporting to America an attitude that would cause
"lives of quiet desperation" (8)? The man who complains that the
"dull sobbing draft" of melancholic weather upon his Aeolian lute
makes him wish that romantic emblem of sounding spirit "mute" announces a death-wish.[10] Thoreau wishes to be awake and all-natural
while Coleridge accuses himself of choosing "by abstruse research to
steal/From my own nature all the natural man" (89–90). Coleridge
chronicles a lateness-decline within the course of his own life, aside
from English literary history. He is set off against a man who self-
approvingly chooses to imitate both an unthinking natural animal and
a god in order to initiate a world.

But of course there is more to Thoreau's choice of Coleridge for a specific rejection. This is not so plainly a case of kicking a good man when he is down. Indeed Thoreau does trivialize the ode. The night of self-pity is spectacularly transformed, first when Coleridge refuses his own melodramatic comparison to Lear to see himself as merely "a little child/Upon a lonesome wild,/Not far from home, but she hath lost her way" (121–24); and then in an act of outgoing generosity as he wishes for the "Dear Lady" (139) that inner joy of which he has become incapable. Hard honesty and a love for the other which survives despair may mark more of a recovery than the poet knows or owns. Indeed, Coleridge's speaker finally enacts Thoreau's own dictum, "We may waive just so much care of ourselves as we honestly bestow elsewhere" (11), another of the poem's implications that Thoreau's allusion discounts.

Thoreau strikes at Coleridge not because Coleridge is a good man down but because Coleridge is a giant keeping him under, an influential poet and thinker whom Thoreau so resembles in many points that differences need to be dramatized for Thoreau to make his own home in an American woods.

Most largely, as Lawrence Buell notes, Coleridge is credited with the importation to America of European pantheisms that emphasize "a metaphysical correspondence between nature and spirit,"[11] and it is precisely this sense that Emerson named Thoreau's best gift, the drawing of "universal law from the single fact" (W,X,474). Further, Coleridge everywhere stresses that "priority of relation over substance," which Charles Feidelson Jr. sees as vital to Thoreau's art of perception.[12] Neither Coleridge nor Thoreau consistently believes in a plain projectivism whereby the self utterly produces the out-there, but both can be drawn to such a view. The Coleridge who writes in "Dejection"

> O Lady! we receive but what we give,
> And in our life alone does Nature live:
> Ours is her wedding garment, ours her shroud!
> . . . .
>
> Ah! from the soul itself must issue forth
> A light, a glory, a fair luminous cloud
> Enveloping the earth—
>
> (47–49, 53–55)

is perfectly met by the Thoreau who argues that architectural beauty "has gradually grown from within outward, out of the necessities and character of the indweller, who is the only builder—out of some unconscious truthfulness, and nobleness, without ever a thought for the appearance" (47). And Thoreau again, perhaps via Emerson, sounds the Coleridgean idea when he devalues the making of beautiful objects by calling it "far more glorious to carve and paint the very atmosphere through which we look, which morally we can do" (90).

Finally, Coleridge and Thoreau share, in James McIntosh's words, a "sense of nature as one, as alive, and as the aggregate of things,"[13] a sense generally romantic. But it is named most succinctly by Coleridge in "The Eolian Harp," where he glorifies "the one Life within us and abroad,/Which meets all motion and becomes its soul" (26–27), and Thoreau takes up Coleridge's image when he writes of distant sound as creating "a vibration of the universal lyre" (123).

Yet McIntosh goes on to insist that "Thoreau and his European counterparts are romantics, not Orphists or Parsees or Buddhists, partly because they share a more or less open awareness of their separation from nature, however much they may desire to be at home in it."[14] Here the two writers begin to differ. McIntosh's generalization is importantly valid, but consider that no other romantic poet stresses depressive isolation so consistently as Coleridge and that Thoreau's isolation issues in self-sufficient joy. "Alone, alone, all, all alone,/Alone on a wide, wide sea" seems Coleridge's motto everywhere. The mariner, Christabel, and the personae of such lyrics as "Dejection," "Frost at Midnight," and "This Lime-tree Bower My Prison" are victimized by a self-absorption pictured as literal seclusion. Granted, this is only a nadir from which many of Coleridge's speakers rise in such acts of outgoing love as we mentioned in "Dejection." In solitude, that is, they may connect to the "one Life" that affords more of a communal sense than any crowd might. But it is only this affirming paradox that Thoreau adapts in his chapter "Solitude": "I have a great deal of company in my house; especially in the morning, when nobody calls. . . . God is alone,—but the devil, he is far from being alone; he sees a great deal of company; he is legion" (137). In "The Eolian Harp" Coleridge finally denigrates and refuses as unholy his pantheistic vision of the "one Life," that sense of an expanded society among nature, man, and God that Thoreau adopts to people his seclusion. And given Thoreau's version of a Coleridge reduced to mere dejection by the lyre of another occasion, Thoreau's affirmation of his own company again accuses Coleridge of an unnecessary despair.

Coleridge as the English writer is not only night-sad but over-civilized and every way barred from the spontaneity that is the only good. Thoreau takes the extraordinary measure of repeating his motto in "Where I Lived, and What I Lived For" as if to guarantee our awareness of these implications. He prefaces it by the sentence, "The present was my next experiment of this kind, which I purpose to describe more at length, for convenience, putting the experience of two years into one" (84). "The present" may mean only the present experiment but it also may mean that the experiment of Walden was an attempt to live utterly in the present: as he writes earlier, "to stand on the meeting of two eternities, the past and future, which is precisely the present moment; to toe that line" (17). Given that Coleridge's "Dejection" is named once more in the next sentence, Thoreau's "present" and the packing of two years into one are in vivid distinction to the lassitude of loose moments with which the Ode opens and to the general sense of an irrevocable Fall throughout.

Immediate participation is the claim of the motto itself. "I do not propose to write . . . but to brag as lustily as Chanticleer in the morning, . . ." Of course, Thoreau *is* writing, but, as we have noted, *Walden* is arranged so as to avoid anything like the tight structure of an ode, with a simulated and-that-brings-to-mind spontaneity rather than the scene, meditation, initial-scene-transformed movement of Coleridge's poem, much less the rigorous ordering of Coleridge's philosophical writings. Bragging is vocal, part of an earlier, oral mode of transmission, and it is early too in refusing the sublimating restraints upon the ego of a Christian-civilized humility. By such means is Coleridge made all too much a poet. (Thoreau mentions "Ode to Dejection" on one other occasion. In his journal, he describes how a tree may be made more beautiful by a diseased swelling of its tissue. "Beautiful scarlet sins they may be. . . . This gall is the tree's 'Ode to Dejection'" [*J*, XI, 210]. This is to give compliment to Coleridge's poem as creating beauty out of personal malaise, but the trope implicitly defines Coleridge's mood as an abnormal, insect-infested disease. He elsewhere calls "Art itself a gall" [*J*, XIII, 10]. More generally, then, Coleridge's Ode simply signifies high art, an injury to inexpressive nature but an injury that is also a benefit. In the context of *Walden*, however, where sublimated acts, including high art, are called into most skeptical question, the paradox of beauty through disruption is removed, and the Ode as the incursion of a diseased art into nature is a gall pure and simple. This is so especially in regard to the motto.) And in his motto Thoreau is libidinally potent, as he brags "lustily," a word that might mean simply "with exuberance" were it not connected to Chaucer's rooster. In "Dejection," contrarily, Coleridge accuses himself of general impotence and is apparently barred (as we know he was factually) from the "Dear Lady" he blesses at ode's end just as he is barred from the source of inner joy he celebrates in absentia. This, Thoreau implies, is where the sublimations of civilized life get you, as he leagues in preference with a barnyard animal.

This is the ultimate difference to which Thoreau's allusion points. The poet of lateness recalls a vision that he no longer can experience internally, much less enact to transform the world. Thoreau, as the bard of the early hour when all is possible, wishes to literalize vision as it has never been made literal before. "When one man has reduced a fact of the imagination to be a fact to his understanding, I foresee that all men will at length establish their lives on that basis" (11). From beans will derive a global village of vision, as Thoreau accepts Coleridge's differentiated terms (the imagination is allied to Reason as a self-referential totality transcending the secondary imagination's Understanding in *Aids to Reflection,* a book Thoreau owned) but demands an actualization of the divine I AM on the most common and available grounds imaginable, democratic American earth. The poet of lateness can barely imagine his imagination; he can recall it only. The bard of dawn lives out his now-forming imagination from July 4, 1845 forward, "about a mile and a half south of the village of Concord" (86) by Walden Pond.

And yet Thoreau does not dismiss Coleridge; he includes the English poet as an item within his emotional range. Coleridge is the poet of night-waking owls. "Tu-whit! Tu-whoo!" they cry at the beginning of "Christabel" (3) and ". . . The owlet's cry/Came loud—and hark, again! loud as before" at the beginning of "Frost at Midnight" (2–3). Thoreau hears in the owls' cries at Walden the words "*Oh-o-o-o-o that I had never been bor-r-r-r-n!*" (124–25). Thoreau grudgingly acknowledges that they speak to one of nature's many truths, "the stark twilight and unsatisfied thoughts which all have" (125); and thus they have their place at a Walden that can afford even despair by placing it within an encyclopedia of other sounds. As McIntosh notes, Thoreau "generally prefers not to exhibit his acquaintance with Wordsworth and Coleridge, Carlyle and Goethe"[15] and so he attributes literary owls to Ben Jonson, while reproducing nearly Coleridge's (admittedly Shakespeare's as well, in the song from *Love's Labour's Lost*)[16] "Tu-whit Tu-whoo" in his next sentence (124). But when he speaks of the owls' meaning, it is the poet of lateness he attacks. They are "expressive of a mind which has reached the gelatinous mildewy stage of all healthy and courageous thought. It reminded me of ghouls and idiots and insane howlings" (125). Yet the owl has its place at Walden and Thoreau can employ Coleridge for incentive. In "Christabel," recall, "the owls have awakened the crowing cock," though Coleridge's rooster crows "drowsily" (2,6), acknowledging English night, while Thoreau's owl makes Coleridge's night of despair itself "a more dismal and fitting day" (125).

3

And now another dawn springs of midnoon, as I wish to unsay, or at least complicate my claim. Coleridge is not the leading figure for England in *Walden*, but only the most overt. Coleridge stands in for the more powerful influence of Wordsworth, as Thoreau makes Wordsworth's claim for the "abundant recompense" of mature age tantamount to Coleridge's dejection.

Thoreau clearly pairs the two, and both together represent what he sees as the going idea of literature itself. "This is my lake country," he says of the ponds surrounding Walden (197). And later, in an 1859 journal entry, "There are poets of all kinds and degrees, little known to each other. The Lake School is not the only or the principal one."[17] Granted, Coleridge is nominating a sleazy muskrat-hunter as yet another poet of sorts, but the entry assumes an agreement that the Lake School is generally thought to define poetry, or at least poetry of natural enthusiasm.

But Wordsworth is not merely an afterthought to be included with Coleridge; it is Wordsworth more. McIntosh quotes an early poem by Thoreau to "surmise that Thoreau professed so vocally his intention not to write an Ode to Dejection in *Walden* because he was personally familiar with the feelings evoked and the questions raised in Coleridge's poem."[18]

> THE POET'S DELAY
> In vain I see the morning rise,
> In vain observe the western blaze,
> Who idly look to other skies,
> Expecting life by other ways.
>
> Amidst such boundless wealth without,
> I only still am poor within,
> The birds have sung their summer out,
> But still my spring does not begin.
>
> (W, I, 366)

But the poem bears a much closer resemblance to the second stanza of a different ode, Wordsworth's "Intimations of Immortality."

> The Rainbow comes and goes,
> And lovely is the Rose,
> The moon doth with delight
> Look round her when the heavens are bare;
> Waters on a starry night
> Are beautiful and fair;
> The sunshine is a glorious birth.
> But yet I know, where'er I go,
> That there hath past away a glory from the earth.[19]

The spiritless praising of an animated nature and a guilty sense that the self's preoccupations, in Wordsworth's phrase, "the season wrong" (26) is imitated closely in Thoreau's poem; and McIntosh himself affirms that "For nineteenth-century New Englanders, Wordsworth was *the* poet of nature" and that Wordsworth's Ode was the single poem "that seems to have affected Thoreau most strongly."[20] It is the figure of Wordsworth, I believe, beyond any single poem, that engages Thoreau, for Americans tend to think in terms of human representatives rather than texts, in confronting what is English.

Wordsworth appears throughout *Walden,* though always incognito. Like Wordsworth, Thoreau worries that the world is too much with us, and he too recommends not augmentations but a purificatory shedding as the means of hope. Like Wordsworth, who saves his awe for the simple individual who is part of a landscape and who hates the crowdings of cities, Thoreau writes, "we live thick and are in each other's way, and stumble over one another, and I think that we thus lose some respect for one another" (136). Like Wordsworth with his leech-gatherer, Thoreau personifies the grandeur of simplicity in a deliberately unheroic-seeming man, the Canadian woodchopper. Thoreau affords his ideal man a more detailed and convincing facticity and allows himself to wonder whether "to suspect him of a fine poetic consciousness or of stupidity" (148). But the woodchopper, like Wordsworth's old man and his other vagabonds, exemplifies that absence of self-consciousness and the concomitant providential assurance that Thoreau directly advises when he writes, "I think that we may safely trust a good deal more than we do. We may waive just so much care of ourselves as we honestly bestow elsewhere" (11). Like Wordsworth too, Thoreau locates a more supernaturally tinged kind of simplicity in the child. Of such as Wordsworth's "best Philosopher," "Filling from time to time his 'humorous stage' " (111,104), Thoreau writes, "Children, who play life, discern its true laws and relations more clearly than men, . . ." (96).

These are not piecemeal similarities. For both writers, they contribute to a program for earliness. More significantly, both writers
travel through a spectrum of descriptions of earliness. This spectrum
ranges in each between a love of earliness-as-nature so intense that the
self is always seen as too late in relation to it and a love of earliness-as-
preexistential vision in which earliest nature itself is too late to fulfill
the demands of the imagination. There is a Wordsworth who frolics in
a simple natural ecstacy and a more mystic Wordsworth who wishes to
look upon natural objects with an eye so intense that object and eye
surpass their material condition and we "become a living soul" that
can "see into the life of things" ("Tintern Abbey," 46, 49) and that
reads in a landscape "Characters of the great Apocalypse" (*The Prelude,* VI, 638).[21] Just so, in Fussell's felicitous phrase, "To the end,
Thoreau seems undetermined whether he means to be on the frontier
or beyond,"[22] with his final goal simple, essential living or the employment of that kind of living to achieve an inexplicable bliss of unity
with the spirit-source.

As much as Wordsworth, Thoreau praises childhood from a position of privation, the vantage-point of adult loss. "I have always been
regretting that I was not as wise as the day I was born" (98), Thoreau
writes in *Walden.* And his later journal entries that mourn a loss of
power could as well quote directly from Wordsworth's crisis poems, as
when he writes "Once I was part and parcel of Nature; now I am
observant of her" (*W,* IX, 378). The famous sentence from *Walden,* "I
long ago lost a hound, a bay horse, and a turtle-dove, and am still on
their trail," employs images that tease us to identify them while they
clearly serve as emblems of a general loss. Just so, Wordsworth in the
Intimations Ode confesses to "a Tree, of many, one,/A single field
which I have looked upon," both of which speak "of something that is
gone" (52–54), the glory and the dream. And in these instances, natural images are employed to dramatize a loss of something not only
natural but preternatural. There is a Thoreau who wishes "to walk
even with the Builder of the universe" (330), who "sometimes expected
the Visitor who never comes" (270), who speaks Plato-like of "the
dark unfathomed mammoth cave of this world" (93–94), who proclaims that "we are not wholly involved in Nature" (135), and for
whom "Time is but the stream I go a-fishing in" (98). Such statements
lead to that anti-natural extreme epitomized in a journal entry from
the period when *Walden* is being written.

We soon get through with Nature. She excites an expectation which she
cannot satisfy. The merest child which has rambled into a copsewood

dreams of a wilderness so wild and strange and inexhaustible as Nature can never show him. (*J*, VI, 293)

That same Thoreau directly quotes Wordsworth in an earlier journal: "Methinks my present experience is nothing; my past experience is all in all. . . . As far back as I can remember I have unconsciously referred to the experiences of a previous state of being. 'For life is a forgetting'; etc." (*J*, II, 306–7). He corresponds to the Wordsworth who finally finds not even the Alps sufficient to the human imagination, which is "A thousand times more beautiful than the earth/On which he dwells, . . ." (XIV, 451–2).

Like Wordsworth, Thoreau represents himself as a walker. His "favorite form," Buell argues, "is the romantic excursion."[23] This natural dynamism is accompanied in both writers by a constant mental travelling between the poles of natural earliness and an earliness that is the ground of nature but is itself incorporeal, as any thing must be defined by what it is not. The characteristic tension in both writers is between idealist and naturalist urgings.

We could enlarge our list of similarities that, in part, bespeak Thoreau's acceptance of Wordsworth's teaching. We could discuss in each the mocking translation of economic terms into considerations of spiritual cash. We could emphasize in each the dramatizations of a childhood wildness which violates nature for a purpose. Or we could cite the recommendation of relaxed reception, Wordsworth's "wise passivity," throughout *Walden*. But it is more to our purpose, as it was to Thoreau's, to discover crucial differences.

First and simply, Thoreau most echoes Wordsworth or Coleridge when he speaks of his own insufficiencies and of Nature's,[24] and *Walden* is predominantly an account of success, the self's ability to find significant life in the earliness of a capacious Nature. "Both place and time were changed, and I dwelt nearer to those parts of the universe and to those eras in history which had most attracted me" (87). Second, although *Walden* is written in the past tense and McIntosh is technically right to attribute to it "a sense of remembered place,"[25] that is not the book's dominant effect. In such of Wordsworth's lyrics as "I Wandered Lonely as a Cloud," the imaginative memory does not merely recollect earlier experience but augments, completes, perfects it. That is not true of *Walden*, which carries us quasi-chronologically through a series of percepts that immediately become concepts. That Walden to which Thoreau attributes a prelapsarian existence is the Walden that he "in the first person" directly experiences.

The verb "experiences" leads to a third and underlying difference that Thoreau marks between himself and Wordsworth. In the Tintern Abbey lyric, Wordsworth is surprised to see "pastoral farms,/Green to the very door; and wreaths of smoke/Sent up, in silence, from among the trees!" He imaginatively infers "vagrant dwellers in the houseless woods" (16–18,20) whom he implicitly praises for a harmony achieved with nature. But Wordsworth himself is not one of them, just as, seated reflectively beneath a "dark sycamore," he is not immediately part of ever dynamic nature, "of sportive wood run wild" (10,16): against that contrast, the rest of the poem must struggle toward an affirmation of age. Thoreau is himself one of those "vagrant dwellers." Just as Wordsworth's pastoral farms are "Green to the very door," Thoreau proclaims of his house, "No Yard! but unfenced Nature reaching up to your very sills" (128). Whereas a civilized Wordsworth looks into nature and a remembered natural self, Thoreau locates himself there: "no gate—no front-yard,—and no path to the civilized world" (128).

Thoreau enacts what Wordsworth contemplates. Again: both Thoreau and Wordsworth horizontalize the universe, find high meaning in low objects; but Wordsworth only in contemplation finds at the conclusion of the Intimations Ode that "the meanest flower that blows can give/Thoughts that do often lie too deep for tears" (203–4) while Thoreau, wishing to know beans, actively cultivates them. Thoreau may allow for characters more primitive than himself, closer to "life near the bone where it is sweetest" (329), such as the woodchopper, but primarily he is himself that Solitary Reaper whose song can inspirit a Wordsworth who is himself too late in time to sing it.

It is not simply that Thoreau describes nature far more particularly than Wordsworth. The claim is that he can be intimately, body-and-soul, amidst nature as the mature Wordsworth spiritually cannot be. When Wordsworth wishes in the Intimations Ode for a simple regression, when he attempts to return to the shores of the ocean of life and leap with the children in festival, the thought of that "Tree" intervenes and reveals the falseness of an adult Wordsworth galumphing about. Yet for the loss of that connection to nature occurs "abundant recompense." Even as a natural child, Wordsworth had felt the loss of an earlier All, and that sense of loss which led to spiritual realization educates him to the good of the present one. Distance from nature affords imaginative space for Faith, for the "philosophic mind" which best appreciates both nature and specifically human courage. Dawn is done but sunset promises a greater return to the state before and beyond time early or late.

For Thoreau, any loss of connection to nature is absolute loss. Men think they are wiser than children, "wiser by experience, that is, failure" (96) and "with years I have grown more coarse and indifferent" (217). Earliness is all, and the return which Wordsworth finally counts folly is exactly what Thoreau desires. "That man who does not believe that each day contains an earlier, more sacred, and auroral hour than he has yet profaned, has despaired of life, and is pursuing a descending and darkening way" (89). As Charles Anderson succinctly puts it, "Thoreau's search to discover his ideal self becomes a quest to recover his lost youth in a second spring."[26] But at his most optimistic, Thoreau contemplates no loss. It is getting earlier all the time.

From this perspective, Wordsworth's "abundant recompense" is hollow rationalization, and he, as much as Benjamin Franklin, is the target of ridicule when Thoreau continues his rhetoric of dawn by asking, "Who would not be early to rise, and rise earlier and earlier each successive day of his life, till he became unspeakably healthy, wealthy, and wise?" (127). In all, Thoreau accounts himself the worshipper of Hebe, "who had the power of restoring gods and men to the vigor of youth" (139).

Of Hebe, Thoreau continues, "wherever she came it was spring" (139). His confessions of decay are confined to a thoroughly personal voice much subordinate in *Walden* to a self who microcosmically speaks for American possibility. Earliness is made all-portable, all-persistent. "Morning brings back the heroic ages" (88). "Morning is when I am awake and there is dawn in me" (90). The "Bhagvat Geeta" expresses a wisdom that should "be referred to a previous state of existence" and "The pure Walden water is mingled with the sacred water of the Ganges" (298). A return to the early is no more difficult than the return of spring. If dawn is not immediately present, that is not because it is irrecoverably lost in an English past—Wordsworth's cultural implication, if we read his personal mythology as partly a social and historical one as well—but because it is yet to come in an American future. "I have never yet met a man who was quite awake" (90). "We loiter in winter while it is already spring" (314). "Only that day dawns to which we are awake. There is more day to dawn. The sun is but a morning star" (333).

Thoreau vacillates cannily between envisioning Walden as the ultimate earliness, the final good in itself, and envisioning Walden as one of any number of paths to an atemporal good. The latter is his escape clause from too literal and didactic a claim. But he need not decide between the alternatives, for earliness is scope and scope makes everything possible. Walden may or may not be it, but Thoreau is after an attainable ultimacy available to the time of our earth. Such a belief makes of Wordsworth's beyond-sunset faith nothing more than fancy work upon Coleridge's plain dejection. Wordsworth tends to assign his natural intensity to childhood, his mysticism to mature thought (though, we need to add, that mature thought is informed by the earlier love of plain nature). Thoreau's paradox of the frontier, whereby he moves forward not to sunset but to sunrise and makes West East, refuses all ordinary temporality, including historical and personal aging. His prize term, "The Wild," brilliantly contains his nature-loving and his spirit-longing aspects, for it means not only "savage, primitive" but also "unconditioned."

Thus, in *Walden*, as Thoreau "rambles into higher and higher grass" (319), the book's seasonal cycle becomes an increasing parabola spinning forward by running backward into the untamed.[27] Thoreau's earliness is not in a place or at a time. "Any prospect of awakening or coming to life to a dead man makes indifferent all times and places" (134). Material fact and spiritual law get transformed instantly, as by instinct, into each other so that earliness becomes less a condition or state than an activity. By its reverse dynamism, we spin ever more rapidly backward until we pass through a vortex of the beginning and through an earlier vortex before that and then an earlier. We must "rise earlier and earlier each successive day" (127) for "each day contains an earlier, more sacred, and auroral hour" (89); and Thoreau's last sentence anticipates yet earlier beginnings as "The sun is but a morning star" (333).

From Beaumont's picture of Peele Castle in a storm, Wordsworth learns that his early view of the castle as exampling "lasting ease,/Elysian quiet, without toil or strife" and, most, "silent Nature's breathing life" was pathetically blind. "But welcome fortitude, and patient cheer,/And frequent sights of what is to be borne!" (25–26,28,57–58). Thoreau eschews Wordsworth's "humanised Soul," sees it as the spirit of defeat, and in his actualist American faith teaches of castles a different lesson: "If you have built castles in the air, your work need not be lost; that is where they should be. Now put the foundations under them" (324).[28] And that is why, for Thoreau, "Wordsworth is too tame for the Chippeway" (*J*, I, 273).

4

In Chapter three, I summarized Sacvan Bercovitch's persuasive theory of a major difference between Protestant theologies in Old and New England. Calvinism in Britain, however radical, always maintains a distinction between the City of God and the cities of man, a gap that New England was founded expressly to close. New England expects an attainable earthly paradise, an ending transformation of historical time into a life of spirit. Especially upon the failure of Cromwell's Commonwealth, Britain would treat with scepticism any such literalisms.

Once we add to this the far more recent and significant failure of human hope in the French revolution, we are a ways to explaining the differences between the Lake poets and Thoreau. The French disaster would teach a stern lesson on the consequences of confusing internal and individual redemption with political rebellion. For Coleridge and Wordsworth, the lesson only would reinforce a privatism, a scepticism toward the utopian, inherited from their culture. Contrarily, the success of the American revolution, though it might seem all too exclusively political to a mind like Thoreau's, could not but rekindle hope for an absolute merge of personal and national salvation. Wordsworth replaces his political dogmatism with personal recovery. Thoreau secedes from the America of fact to found no private domain, whatever Walden at first may seem, but to revive and live out what he calls "the only true America."

By that, we can account too for a final difference. It concerns the structuring of an audience. Coleridge and Wordsworth typically address a like-minded friend, often each other. The intimate tone creates a society of two in quiet defiance of the loveless crowd, which is the world at large. Thoreau takes a far more public stance, that of a Jeremiah haranguing his neighbors, all of them, the nation. It is conversation on one side of the Atlantic, conversion sermons on the other.

You don't live by what you say and what you say does not say far enough: what I described as the typical American critique of English romanticism suits this case. So too does that habit whereby the American, speaking as a national representative, makes the British writer whom he confronts representative as well. To Thoreau, Wordsworth and Coleridge are England, however much these writers themselves insisted on their separate, private country.

It is not surprising, then, that Thoreau's explicit commentaries on England chime with his implicit criticisms of Coleridge and Wordsworth. "The crop of *English* hay" (Thoreau's italic) "is carefully weighed, the moisture calculated" while the wilds produce "a rich and various crop unreaped by man." When he calls his field, and so *Walden,* "the connecting link between wild and cultivated fields" and "half-cultivated," he seems to compromise. But then "They were beans cheerfully returning to their wild and primitive state that I cultivated" (158), and so earliness is retained, even furthered, and cultivation receives a backward definition.

Linear and historical time, English property, are undone in *Walden*. Thoreau's emphasis on dawn and earliness give special meaning to a jibe like "The government of the world I live in was not framed, like that of Britain, in after-dinner conversations over the wine" (333). And in his role as the Salem merchant, peddling a "Celestial Empire" that refuses history's claims and reverses time's decay, Thoreau sells "purely native products . . . always in native bottoms" (20).

Given that England is consistently equated with a public world decaying in its accumulations, with a materialism devoid of spirit and, even in its most visionary aspect, with the open despair of Coleridge and the desperate rationalizings of Wordsworth, and given that Walden is an explicitly American experiment, we are at first surprised to hear Thoreau halloo " 'Welcome, Englishmen! welcome, Englishmen!' for I had had communication with that race" (154). And we are as surprised when he links the two nations in despite in his final pages—"It is said that the British Empire is very large and respectable, and that the United States are a first-rate power" (332)—and lectures John and Jonathan alike, But again we are in the midst of a deceptive compromise. We noted that Thoreau sees the public America as having gone English. Indeed, when he welcomes Englishmen, Thoreau may as well mean village visitors, for he has relived the emigration from England in leaving citied New England for the wild. Despite independence, official America has been annexed to the British again.

But the English visit him, not he them. And as Salem merchant, Thoreau does not merely sell his goods, he "will export such goods as the country affords" (20). If John and Jonathan are to save themselves, they will have to awake to a dawn, a sun, a morning that belongs to the wild, the west, American earliness. *Walden* is a counterannexation.

Four

SUBSTITUTING THE PAST

7

HISTORY IN THE BRAIN, THOUGHT IN THE LAND

I

A contemporary Canadian critic, in the act of surveying the scant literary tradition of his nation and the historical material yet available for literary treatment, exclaims in exasperation, "It's only by our lack of ghosts we're haunted."[1] American writers of the nineteenth century, haunted by the same lack—not only of the classes, manners, institutions, but even of the literary strategies that such a sense of history provides—and by mocking British voices besides, had only one recourse. That recourse was the imagination, since actual ages and events could not be wished into prior existence.

What surprises, as we look back upon the American attempt to find a way to look back, is the number of options these writers developed to supply a historical sensibility. What had appeared a lack became a plethora; and as the desert of history was planted, an American literature flowered.

This is not to assume that literary inspiration requires a historical sensibility to the extent that the nineteenth century imagined: it helps, certainly, but the conviction of its absolute necessity was exaggerated, on both sides of the Atlantic, by an unprecedented excitement with history, legend, and national identity. Rather, American minds discovered their elasticity through working on this centered problem, just as they might have done via any other threatening issue that the British chose to feature and the Americans themselves experienced as hurtful and debilitating. We are not advertising an immutable law of creation here but recounting what occurred. And that was this: as American writers developed various ideas of history or substitutes for history, they came to shape their literature in ways that might afford an American difference even as the question of history lost its potency.

We can discern two basic responses to the British taunt of no history. One was to argue that America indeed did possess a rich past. The other was to argue that a sense of history could be replaced, and decisively improved upon, by considering the entire issue of man-in-time in ways that avoided the linear, secular trail of the past.

These two basic responses can be divided further into four alternatives. In accepting the British challenge to provide a history, one might accept too the usual idea of the secular past and search America's two hundred years for the sense of a culture. One could exploit the materials to their fullest and stretch time to make that past seem more long-distant than the actual number of years in themselves would suggest. Alternately, one might capitalize upon the Myth of the West in such a way as to suggest that America, simultaneously primitive and civilized, recapitulates in its brief span the entire history of man. Or one might refuse the British challenge and substitute a different time sense for the historical, by considering the present not as the result of a long past but as prologue to a glorious future. That is, one could argue that destiny may be as richly definitive as origin. Or, most radically, one might replace horizontal with vertical time and cogitate the present moment with a furious intensity to make the unalterably permanent and ultimate issue from an immediate perception.

As before, but even more strongly, I would qualify my categorizing by a recognition that these four strategies—for shorthand, I will dub them stretched history, archetypal history, futurism, and vertical time—could combine in any number of ways. Most of the American romantics employed all of them, sometimes simultaneously. There is worth in abstracting them for individual examination primarily because the examinations lead to the same result: in employing each of the strategies, American writers would become intently aware of how malleable their American scene was, of how little had been provided and how great the freedoms of individual consciousness thus could become. As each American became aware of his America—became aware, that is, of what he in large measure was creating—he became aware of his own methods for creating meaning and could make that method part of his material. The real American history finally might be the history of dialectics that went into imagining that other, more public history.

2

Stretched time is the least audacious of the four strategies in that it accepts the commonplace definitions of what is meant by history. Yet it is for that reason also the most audacious in its claim that the miniscule American past could fulfill the requisites of conventional historic importance. Henry James's book on Hawthorne is shot through with wonder at this audacity. "History, as yet, has left in the United States but so thin and impalpable a deposit that we very soon touch the hard substratum of nature," James writes; "and nature herself, in the western world, has the peculiarity of seeming rather crude and immature."[2] Yet Hawthorne was, by the most limiting and conventional definition, a historical writer. Even his nature is haunted by ghosts, not by their absence. Hawthorne exemplifies with greatest sophistication what Henry Steele Commager calls the most remarkable fact of early American nationalism, "the speed and the lavishness with which Americans provided themselves with a useable past; . . ."[3]

Stretched history was made available to Hawthorne and others in part by the sense Americans possessed that time itself had speeded up in the New World. This well might be, given the conjunction of an unsettled continent with colonists who carried with them the civilizing techniques developed through the European centuries. Add to that various doctrines that encouraged energetic behavior and the course of each of those European centuries of settlement could be recapitulated in instants. Lowell, writing of the rapidity of change in America, puts the common argument: "Here, as in a theater, the great problems of anthropology—which in the Old World were ages in solving but which are solved, leaving only a dry net result—are compressed, as it were, into the entertainment of a few hours."[4] This compression of historical time, which had a real basis, goes far to justify what might seem hyperbole in the nationalists' claims upon a past, for instance Channing's: "Sometimes," he observes in speaking of Brown's fictions, "the events are placed so far back, that they belong to a somewhat different race from ourselves, . . . ; the wild, adventurous character of the recent settler has become softened by regular and secure industry, and we feel as if we are reading of our antiquities."[5]

Further, epochs are declared not by the passage of a certain number of years but by great events, and the rapidity of settlement with its attendant battles and fierce political crises provided more epochal divisions than two centuries usually might own, especially as viewed retrospectively with the pride of nationhood. William Tudor writes in 1815: "by the great revolutions which have since happened, the connexion between those days" (the colonial period) "and our own is interrupted, and they are so disconnected with the present era that no passionate feeling is blended with their consideration; they are now exclusively the domain of history and poetry."[6] This is hyperbole, as Tudor even pluralizes "revolution." But nationhood in particular might go to make all that went before it seem like a long ago.

More truly, if you want history you can have it, in America or Afghanistan. James argued that "it takes a great deal of history to produce a little literature; . . ."[7] But that is disputable. Not only are we arguing here that it takes only a little history to produce a great deal of literature, but that it takes only a little time to produce a great deal of history. Mircea Eliade argues that "popular memory finds difficulty in retaining individual events and real figures." The person becomes a mythical model, the event is placed within an archetypal category. And Eliade goes on to record the findings of a Romanian folklorist, Constantin Brailou, who became sufficiently interested in a ballad of tragic love, concerning the murder of a young man about to be married by the jealous spirit who adored him, to investigate the historical occurrence of which the ballad told. He found that the actual events, as told to him by the still living fiancee, had been transformed to recurrent mythical patterns. And while all of the villagers believed that this was "a very old story, which had happened long ago," in truth "the event had taken place not quite forty years earlier," that is, at a time when most of these villagers were alive.[8] In this light, the two American centuries appear luxuriously long for the kind of history, allied to myth, that literature most cares about. Indeed, a major industry of instant mythologizing centered on the first national president began even before George Washington's death.

But we must remember that the practitioner of stretched history had to battle not only facts but what was fact raised to myth, cultural earliness. Thus Washington Irving would satirize the old world anachronisms of an Ichabod Crane or a Rip Van Winkle, yet their very presence in Irving's America, as Benjamin Lease remarks, "reaches out to them into an American past as evocative as England's."[9] But no American so marshalled his forces to disarm the debilitating aspects of earliness as Hawthorne, a fact which James alone has appreciated fully. In the history of his family and region, Hawthorne claimed to find the very plenitude of legends, manners, and institutions the English thought disastrously missing in the New World. His claim is persuasive in part because he portrays himself as finding, rather than inventing, far more than was the case; and in part because he dramatizes this discovered past not as the boon it was to him as a freed creative writer but as a something that imposed itself, not always or usually welcome, like a distended superego upon his trapped living self.

The occasional rage and continuing analytical intensity of Hawthorne's narratives toward this cultural heritage deflects our attention from the claim being forwarded silently, that this Puritan past *is* the American cultural heritage. James is getting at this sleight of hand when he comments upon "the spell" that the Hawthorne-character in "The Custom-House" blames for drawing him ever back to Salem: "it is only in a country where newness and change and brevity of tenure are the common substance of life that the fact of one's ancestors having lived for a hundred and seventy years in a single spot would become an element of one's morality. It is only an imaginative American that would feel urged to keep reverting to this circumstance, to keep analyzing and cunningly considering it."[10] The Hawthorne-character *is* a character, a presented persona; his sense of burden cunningly forwards the actual Hawthorne's claim. We are made too busy wondering how anyone can escape the Puritan past to doubt whether that past really is so deep and inclusive. The Hawthorne-character suffers Puritanism; for Hawthorne as subject-searching author, Puritanism is pure joy.

Hawthorne works hard to move the past backward. For example, in the first chapter of *The House of the Seven Gables*, the narrator describes the mansion as "rusty" and "venerable," an "antiquity" (*CE*, II, 5). It is "a specimen of the best and stateliest architecture of a long-past epoch" and "the scene of events more full of human interest, perhaps, than those of a gray, feudal castle—. . ." (10). The description of the house's gothic architecture further serves to obscure the fact that it is not, in reality, a medieval dwelling with all the medieval associational richness. But Hawthorne is travelling backward further still: American time is so lengthy that another structure once stood where this "massive, stable, and almost irresistibly imposing" (25) mansion now stands, the home of Matthew Maule, "hewn out of the primeval forest" (7). That is, the house appears so venerable as to be old as civilized time, and this strengthens in the people's eyes the dubious claim on it of the contemporary Pynchon; but the reason for disputing the claim at all takes us back before civilization itself, to the making of civilization out of "the primeval forest." This seemingly timeless mansion may have been founded in an act of usurpation! Maule's sentencing by the first Judge Pynchon for the crime of witchcraft is itself a claim on the long-ago for the witch trials seem less an event of the late seventeenth century than of a fabled medievalism; Maule's curse on the Judge provides a legendary element that implies long time; and the narrator's report of the speculations concerning Judge Pynchon's mysterious death and its possible ties to Maule's curse further pushes back time, for we associate legend with a distant past.

The house of the seven gables becomes exactly that house of associations that the British had assumed America could not create. Hawthorne even emphasizes the class-conflict aspect of the Maule-Pynchon controversy, thereby providing America with the aristocracy the British claimed America lacked and claimed was necessary to literature. The huge Pynchon Elm, once a strippling of the primeval forest, provides a deep historical shade for all of America.

Hawthorne is so good at this that he can dare to state plainly that the mansion is only 160 years old—he simply lengthens our sense of what a century and a half mean. All through the chapter, his explicit burden concerns the subtle connections between the long-ago and to-day; but to make those connections significant is really the job of his insinuating technique by which the past is cajoled backward, made to look more distant, so that the connections between past and present may have an impressive route of travel.

Another technique for stretching the past is to move the present forward, into cultural lateness. Thus, in the sketch prefatory to *The Scarlet Letter,* Hawthorne's Custom House is seen as dusty and aged, while its inhabitants are made crumbling old men. The banality of the present then is made to contrast with the earliness of *The Scarlet Letter* proper, its city rising out of a wilderness, the passions and restraints of its characters vivid and bare.

Hawthorne goes on in "The Custom-House" to contrast the dead past represented by the "wearisome old souls" (*CE*, I, 16) who are his colleagues with the living past that presents itself to him in his discovery of the burning "A." But by imaging the present in this and other ways as banal if liberalized, he begins a process of pushing that living past backward in time; for again in *The Scarlet Letter,* the past must seem a long-ago to make its presence in the present remarkable. By making the present desultory, easy-going, and (in the personality of the Hawthorne-character) uncertain, the purposive, restrictive, and dogmatic Puritans will seem to characterize the earliest of all civilized pasts.

In this sense, Hawthorne's Puritans have travelled back in time from the Elizabethan England they departed. Richard Brodhead, in his brilliant commentary on the romance's symbols, notes the significance of the details we are given of Governor Bellingham's mansion: "The glass of ale on the table, the comfortable furnishings, and the evidence of a failed attempt to create an English garden show a kind of counterimpulse, a more pleasurable way of life out of which these men of iron try to recreate what they can of the more commodious civilization they have left behind."[11] Indeed, whenever sanctioned pleasure—and with it the compassionate judgment that arises out of a broader and more flexible interpretation of experience than Puritanism affords—is mentioned, so too is the Puritan elders' English heritage. In the scene at Bellingham's mansion, we are reminded that the sweet tempered Reverend Wilson was "nurtured at the rich bosom of the English Church" (109); and later, in describing the measured pomp of the Election Day celebration, the narrator notes that these Bostonians "had not been born to an inheritance of Puritanic gloom. They were native Englishmen, whose fathers had lived in the sunny richness of the Elizabethan epoch; a time when the life of England, viewed as one great mass, would appear to have been as stately, magnificent, and joyous, as the world ever witnessed" (230). This paeon to English cultural maturity is countered by the cultural lateness involved in the unnatural English marriage of a young woman, Hester Prynne, from a decaying aristocratic family, to "a man well stricken in years" (58) and deformed as well, apparently for pecuniary considerations. But my point is that Puritan America is made to seem not only (as it was) contemporaneous with renaissance England but significantly prior to it in the stages of civilization.

Thus too, British nature is characterized as agricultural—"pears and peaches might yet be naturalized in the New England climate" (108), the narrator avers in looking upon Reverend Wilson, that English-nurtured divine—while American nature is the forest wilderness surrounding the city where Hester can propose to Dimmesdale that they throw off civilization utterly. England is the world of middle time, of the ego, while in America a savage id and an equally savage superego (the city is not at all modern, but described by the negative social basics of a prison and graveyard) do battle near the very beginning of civilization.

To Brodhead's succinct statement that *The Scarlet Letter* "illustrates a newer way of imaginatively conceiving of human existence emerging from an older way,"[12] I would add that this newer way is associated with England. And thus by Hester's new epistemology, Pearl is released into the new, to live in Europe. Hawthorne's Americans have travelled back to an originary moment; renaissance England is far closer to the American reader in cultural time than the colony of his forebears. And thereby American history is stretched.

This stretching, to mix metaphors, demands some sidestepping. Hawthorne removes his history a ways from the great publicly acknowledged event. He treats Hester Prynne rather than Anne Hutchinson, though he alludes to a link between the two; the revolution is foreseen but not treated directly in "My Kinsman, Major Molinieux"; the witch trials provide only a backdrop for *The House of the Seven Gables,* just as the French-Indian Wars serve for "Roger Malvin's Burial." By avoiding a central focus on these greater events, Hawthorne avoids a comparison to the crises of British and European history that would make the public American history seem puny and an interest in it provincial and frantic. Hawthorne was perfectly aware of this. In the opening of *The House of the Seven Gables,* his narrator says that he will skip over the stories of the many generations that inhabited the mansion for such a group of lives "would fill a bigger folio volume, or a longer series of duodecimos, than could prudently be appropriated to the annals of all New England, during a similar period" (*CE*, II, 5–6). This is boast and confession at once. America offers so much to tell, yet admittedly, in terms of public importance its story must remain proportionally small in relation to the history of the world.

Hawthorne isn't prudent or proportional. He focuses on a miniature and enlarges it. James understood this: "Hawthorne had, as regards the two earlier centuries of New England life, that faculty which is called nowadays the historic consciousness. He never sought to exhibit it on a large scale; he exhibited it indeed on a scale so minute that we must not linger too much upon it."[13] In going on to note the extreme definiteness of Hawthorne's historical images, James helps us to see what it is that makes for viable history in America: not the event but the method, a symbolic consciousness that the reader is asked not only to imbibe but to exercise. Imagination fills out a spare history; it throws history itself from an objective base into a realm of speculative reconstructions; it may, as its own subject, tend in other writers to replace history utterly as a means for knowing the world.

3

Hawthorne had no need to refuse history as he found rich uses for it; but it would be folly to imagine that he merely stretched history or stopped at it. Symbolism provides for—it cannot avoid—the timeless or universal. And however indirectly symbolism in its speculative freedom heads toward truth, it goes at the beyond-historical truth in a manner shockingly direct relative to any narrative that does not feature symbol-making as an acknowledged activity. The line between stretched (elongated linear) history and archetypal history, which tells in small the history of man and thus asserts a permanent model of the human, becomes so wavy in Hawthorne as to disappear. *The Scarlet Letter* is Hawthorne's *Civilization and its Discontents;* likewise all his other works. At many moments, his characters and their actions represent basic and conflicting forces, and opposed terms like "in the psyche" or "in the historical world of events" blend to lose all autonomy.

Of course we find archetypal histories in all cultures; indeed we briefly treated *Wuthering Heights* in this manner (though its direct approach to the archetypal is mentioned by Leavis and other commentators as making Bronte's work strangely American). What is remarkable is that, in America, stretched history appears to lead inevitably to archetypal history, even when a particular writer is not as determined a symbol perceiver as Hawthorne.

Cooper examples this. He stretched history in an alternate manner—through space rather than time, however illogical this may seem at first. "If American history had been brief," Daniel Boorstin writes, "American geography somehow made up the difference." If Americans "could not be separated from their national popular heroes by hundreds of years, they were in any case separated by hundreds of miles."[14]

This is an alternative kind of instant history, and it goes far to explain how the terms "frontier" and "tall tale" became conjoined. Cooper, following upon Filson (the creator of the "Daniel Boone" legends) and other frontier writers, capitalized brilliantly upon the expanse of territory. That is not to say that he neglected other methods for stretching history. The melancholy of Leatherstocking, by which, from the very first, we see this hero of earliness being pushed westward by an aggressive civilizing force, makes the American present seem advanced, its earliness a long-ago. And, as in Hawthorne, this claim for length is nicely obscured by the authorial attitude—here a balanced resignation tipping toward nostalgia rather than Hawthorne's anger—which draws our attention to itself rather than to the quickened pace of history it is assuming and then attitudinalizing upon.

In American geography, however, Cooper found a means not merely to stretch the past but to juxtapose two cultures that could seem to span all of civilized time. Consider the forces between which Natty Bumppo stands, or rather, wanders. The Euro-Americans are represented most prominently by the Effingham and Temple families. Their dispute, which arises out of opposing loyalties in the revolution, in itself calls into play two times. The white American is culturally early as an American, beginning a new and separate destiny; as an Englishman who has moved, importing European sophistication to a western outpost, he is culturally ripe or late. The Indian natives also exhibit a split. They are placed as extremely early, pre-Christian, and even precivilized in largely negative ways, by the calendar of the Euro-Americans. By their own calendars, Cooper's Indians place themselves as disastrously late and look back upon a time when they were not conquered and degenerate.

But this is only the first step in Cooper's prodigious complication of time. The second concerns the conflict between the two groups. Whatever their differences, the Effinghams and the Temples share the desire to order nature into what they recognize as civilization and thus to create authority in a new land. The Indian's law, in Richard Slotkin's summary, "ordains, not the conversion of the land, but the adjustment of man to the land; not the breaking of the forest to man's will, but the submission of the human will to the laws ingenerent in nature."[15] This is an accurate though loaded description of the conflict in Cooper. But such neat oppositions obscure the divergence of the two groups in cultural time, for they are not even at different places on a shared grid. One represents the pre-Columbian in proud decline, the other the postlapsarian in hopeful recovery. Yet these two utterly distinct senses of a cultural and mythic past are made to interact furiously, to encroach upon each other, in a huge American present that justifies Cooper's panoramas of land.

Time in the Leatherstocking novels is not so much stretched as it is stacked, time upon time. When he chooses, Cooper can draw a nature-against-civilization debate out of the Indian-white conflict; at other times, from a more Indian point of view, a debate between civilizations. His American past, made up of so many senses of the past, thus seems to constitute a compression of all time, even of competing universals. Still beyond this, there is Cooper's insistence upon a moral distinction, applicable to each race, which makes for virtuous and degenerate Indians and Whites, as judged by the conformity of the individual to the generous aspects of whichever moral law his culture espouses. Despite the absolute gaps between the two groups, a universal of honor resists all cultural-temporal difference.

Leatherstocking is a large hero because he, like the land he traverses, contains in himself all of Cooper's American times. But Leatherstocking's own time creates further complications. His relation to the land is mostly Indian, and he shares in what Slotkin calls the Indian's "deeds of violence contained by a moral spirit that transforms them into acts of devotion";[16] his relation to human beings, his social ethics, restraints, and even vanities, as Bumppo never tires of informing everyone, are determined by "white laws." In one sense, he is inclusive; in another, he occupies a lonely middle ground; in still another, in the portrayal of his often uneasy attempt to develop a code for himself, he is earlier than either the Euro-American or the Indian, whose codes are preordained. And finally, he is also later than either of them, even than the Indian, for he is excluded. Leatherstocking is fully at home nowhere and, though he leads (or he is pushed) west, his kind of being dies with him and leads nowhere in historical time. He may merge the nobility of each race and, at his best, purify each code by the other. But (or because of this) he is childless, even celibate.

The only place Cooper can grant him is a mythic one, and this emphasis is most marked in *The Pathfinder* and *The Deerslayer*, the last two novels of the series. They arose out of the cultural despair Cooper suffered in the thirties, after he had killed off Natty Bumppo in the third Leatherstocking novel, *The Prairie*. Even in that work, Cooper's nightmare begins to be asserted in the figures of Ishmael Bush and his family, who have degenerated to a status neither Indian or White but lawless, devoid of values. Eric Sundquist finds within Cooper's social novels of the same period, and in particular *Home as Found*, an America without authority, "a society split between an idle aping of European manners on the one hand and a wholesale repudiation of the past on the other." The Effinghams cannot replace Natty Bumppo effectively, even as heroic losers: "The wall of manners and breeding thrown up by the Effinghams barely keeps out the surrounding chaos, and it does so only by cutting them off into the restricted world where purity comes to equal artificiality in the most disturbing fashion."[17] Cultural maturity looks fatigued when it is invoked in response to paranoia.

In the social novels, American time became a noose that Cooper could slip by closing his eyes once more, by refusing a more immediate historicity for a mysterious one that yet could make claims on the facts of an American past. Leatherstocking is reborn as a mature adult in *The Pathfinder* and grows younger in *The Deerslayer*. By this disordering of chronology, Cooper asserts the permanence of his hero, a spanning permanence, as Natty Bumppo's actions in these works alternate between or merge European and Indian myths.

D. H. Lawrence describes the progression of the Leatherstocking novels as "a *decrescendo* of reality and a crescendo of beauty,"[18] and that progression has to do with something more than a writer's improving craft. In the multitude of pasts joined together in Leatherstocking America, Cooper expanded what history means to escape what history usually means; for, to Cooper, the usual, limited notion of history made for a prophecy of America too terrible to bear.

4

The expansion of history was only one answer to the British taunts. The elimination of history was the more radical other. "No way of thinking or doing, however ancient, can be trusted without proof," writes Thoreau in *Walden*. Then, taking the argument further by personifying the past as age and the present as youth, he continues, "I have yet to hear the first syllable of valuable or even earnest advice from my seniors" (9). As I implied in the previous chapter, Thoreau is talking about influence and about history together. His thrust—that narrow men have set up the part for the whole because their view of life is blinkered—is a familiar one to the student of Anglo-American literary relations. And his personification of the authority of the past as a pompous, tired elder plays on the weaknesses of cultural lateness.

Perhaps, then, it is not to the point to stretch or even to stack history; perhaps that is only to supply a need better left wanting. Not only might history inspire a sick and crippling awe, as Emerson frequently worried; it was a clutter that obscured the archetypes, bollixing the relations of Man to God and Nature available in an open field. David Humphreys in 1790 had called history and its associations "piles of rubbish."[19] Thoreau, in *Walden,* reimages the metaphor and applies it explicitly to England: "I look on England today as an old gentleman who is travelling with a great deal of baggage, trumpery which has accumulated from long housekeeping, which he has not the courage to burn."[20] And Emerson spoke of history as "a vanishing allegory" which "repeats itself to tediousness, a thousand and a million times" (*JMN,* II, 83).

To the fervent literary nationalist, history, England, and cultural dotage were synonyms, and all were reducible to blinding custom. The British had succeeded in playing an impressive trick on the insecure Americans: they had made them forget, in the words of a modern Marxist, that "no mode of production and therefore no dominant social order and therefore no dominant culture ever in reality includes or exhausts all human practice, human energy, and human intention."[21] Raymond Williams's statement puts in surprisingly apt terms Thoreau's discovery in the first chapter of *Walden,* which is, after all, entitled "Economy." Even to answer the British taunts with an American history was to play the British game, and ultimately, in that game limiting tomorrow to the lessons of yesterday, everyone, even and especially the Englishman, was a loser.

More to the point of life than the invention of an American history would be the refusal to take up the challenge. If, as the British claimed, the lack of a history resulted in the absence of social classes, then fine; for that would be a democratic good. And the next link in this British chain of logic, the assertion that the absence of social classes would result in a lack of literary materials, was patently false. "But the truth is," Bryant writes in 1818, "that the distinctions of rank, and the amusements of elegant idleness, are but the surface of society, and only so many splendid disguises put on the reality of things. They are trappings which the writer of real genius, the anatomist of the human heart, strips away when he would exhibit his characters as they are, and engage our interest for them as beings of our own species." When

James asked what, without history and its associations, remains, and answered that the American's "secret, his joke" was "that a good deal remains," he probably was recalling a passage in De Tocqueville: "Man remains, and the poet needs no more. The destinies of mankind, man himself taken aloof from his country and his age and standing in the presence of Nature and of God, with his passions, his doubts, his rare prosperities and inconceivable wretchedness, will become the chief, if not the sole, theme of poetry among these nations." This became a chief tenet of the nationalists, for whom the bombastic Cornelius Mathews spoke in echoing Tocqueville: "the very nakedness of our new condition . . . might be reasonably expected to drive us upon a profounder delineation of the inner life."[22]

In fact, Tocqueville did not get the whole of the American's "secret, his joke." In one sense, the American hero *was* "taken aloof from his country and his age" as from all countries and ages. R. W. B. Lewis defines the American Adam as "an individual emancipated from history, happily bereft of ancestry, untouched and undefiled by the usual inheritances of family and race; . . ." And Richard Poirier finds in American fiction "an ideal of heroic character asserting its independence of oppressive environments and of prefabricated literary styles."[23]

True enough, but if the American's secret was to remove his hero from all history and culture, even his own, his joke was to redefine America in such a way that it could be brought along. Without stretched, stacked, or any history at all, America might be transported into what Poirier calls an ahistorical "World Elsewhere," for America could be imaged as a state of mind rather than as a state, as a flying goal rather than a landed fact, as the harbinger of a never-before future rather than as the bare result of a thin past.

There was still the crisis of authority, but authority itself might be founded anew, away from the past. Cooper and Hawthorne were, in their ways, historians, but they brought forth senses of the past so flexible that history might be thought a product of the mind, cultural time a matter of choice. Thoreau tells us that he lived at Walden Pond for two years and two months; he then relates, with wonderful nonchalance, "At present I am a sojourner in civilized life" (*W*, 3), as if a brief walk may bring him out to extreme earliness whenever he wishes.

As the idea of history was expanded to make for an American history, it was loosened until one might step right out of it toward the West and the future. As I noted in an earlier chapter, we desire a history so that we can trace ourselves to our origins, for one of the ways by which we define ourselves or anything is by discovering its source, its origin. This is what Kenneth Burke calls familial or ancestral definition, by which "the logically prior can be expressed in terms of the temporally prior."[24] But there is an equal possibility of the mind for directional definition, which posits the substance of a thing in its goal or purpose, its destination. Thus Cooper's John Cadwallader, in *Notions of the Americans*, replies to the complaints of an Englishman who longs for historical associations: "The moral feeling with which a man of sentiment and knowledge looks upon the plains of your hemisphere is connected with his recollections; here it should be mingled with his hopes. The same effort of the mind is as equal to the one as to the other."[25] Burke separates directional from ancestral definition by its different question, not "Where are you from?" but "Where are you going?" He conjectures that the ultimate sources of this form of definitional habit (here he himself is practicing familial or ancestral definition) are first, in the human experience of free motion, literal locomotion, and, second, in those experiences that allow more metaphorically for motion, that is, free choices and social mobility[26]—all of which (travel, choice, mobility) were specifically advertised as constituents of a nineteenth-century American experience. Hence arises futurism.

Futurism, which Benjamin Spencer well defines as a "new strategy of association from prospect rather than retrospect,"[27] calls forth a world of earliness and an individual of idealized youth to live in it. World and self become indistinguishable:

> All the past we leave behind,
> We debouch upon a newer, mightier world, varied world
> Fresh and strong the world we seize, world of labor
>   and the march,
> Pioneers! O pioneers![28]

But Whitman received this spirit of futurism from predecessors. "Here," writes Crevecoeur, "everything would inspire the reflecting traveler with the most philanthropic ideas: his imagination, instead of submitting to the painful and useless retrospect of revolutions, desolations, and plagues, could, on the contrary, wisely spring forward to the anticipated fields of future cultivation and improvement, to the future extent of these generations which are to replenish and embellish this boundless continent."[29]

American nature impels such optimism and confidence that Whitman, as heir to the sentiments of Crevecoeur, Cooper, Tocqueville ("Democratic nations care yet little for what has been, but they are haunted by visions of what will be: in this direction their unbounded imagination grows and dictates beyond all measure"[30]), and Emerson ("All has an outward and prospective look"), claimed literally to view the present as if it already had realized the future. "As for native American individuality," he writes in *A Backward Glance*, "though certain to come, and on a large scale, the distinctive and ideal type of Western character . . . has not yet appear'd." Yet the entire persona of Whitman's Walt is the not-yet future American in the here and now. The poet, Whitman writes, "places himself where the future becomes present."[31]

Futurism thus replaces history with American democratic principles, or rather with the hoped for reality that would result from the total and inspired application of those principles. And Melville's demand "to carry republican progressiveness into literature as into life" met with responses so fervent that the imperfect present often dissolved to reveal the perfect future potential in it.

Futurism could be put to naive or hateful uses. Compare Whitman's statement above with this sceptical comment from an English traveller, Morris Birkbeck, in 1817, when he found Pittsburgh, "the Birmingham of America," to be a town with barely any industry at all: "There is a figure of rhetoric adopted by the Americans, and much used in description; it simply consists of the use of the present indicative, instead of the future subjunctive; it is called anticipation. By its aid, what *may be* is contemplated as though it were in actual existence."[32] But what Birkbeck mocks is more than mere rhetoric. Huge hotels were built in the wilderness, ridiculously disproportionate to their present surroundings but so confident that travelers would arrive soon, it was as if they were inhabiting the rooms to capacity already—Trollope notes this as late as 1860. More consequently, Sacvan Bercovitch has traced the means by which the Puritan notion of an American Jerusalem, a special providence, "was shaken loose from its religious framework to become part of the belief in human progress"—which in turn translated too often into rationalizations for industrial growth and the bellicose politics of manifest destiny.[33]

Just as futurism might blind its acolyte to the harsh facts of the cultural present, so it might blind him to his personal reality. Hawthorne's *Blithedale Romance* in part concerns exactly such an illusion. Blithedale's futurist-minded inhabitants wish away their pasts as if rebirth is but a hike from Boston, only to find their pasts, in the persons of Moody and Westervelt, hiking out to haunt them; and the utopian projections of the Blithedalers turn out to be informed by that sin as old as the self, egotism.

Yet in that work, Hawthorne is skeptical of his skepticism, personifying it in the narration of the frosty bachelor Miles Coverdale; and in 1860, Hawthorne told Howells of his interest in the West, which is to say, futurism. He "said he would like to see some part of the country on which the shadow (or, if I must be precise, the damned shadow) of Europe had not fallen."[34] Hawthorne understands that the pull of futurism is strong, that futurism itself has a past. That is why he compares his Blithedalers to the first puritan settlers. And though futurism was dangerously prone to nineteenth-century boosterism, its roots were in the typological thinking of the Puritans, which equally combined a sublime and authentic faith with egotism and excuse-making.

Typology looks back to Christ's earthly experiences as the anti-type, the thing itself, of which our acts are merely shadows; but Christ's incarnation is itself the shadow of the Apocalypse, and thus typology ultimately looks forward. This was the deep source for the nineteenth-century futurism that eschewed all sources; and it was sufficiently potent to engage Emily Dickinson, the writer least involved in literary nationalism, so greatly that her every poem asserts a form of futurism. Dickinson grabs hold of the future-oriented typology of the Puritans to personalize it. She replaces the anti-type, the penultimate fulfillment of Christ's life and the ultimate fulfillment of the Apocalypse, with personal death. Thus Dickinson does not value the crucifixion because Christ suffered it; rather Christ is valued because he suffered crucifixion. His "Compound witness" on the cross is unique only in that it made historically public the internal crosses we all bear: "There's newer—nearer Crucifixion/Than that—" (553). Personal death replaces Crucifixion and Apocalypse as the prime anti-type; and personal states of consciousness, ecstatic or painful, replace historical events as the foreshadowing types. Thus, in one poem, "Looking at Death, is Dying—" (281), for bereavement anticipates the pain of death while the bereaved's questioning of postmortem possibilities anticipates the expansion of consciousness eternity might provide. We are "dying in Drama" all our lives (531); and thus even the poems of mourning, which would seem to be looking back, are looking forward to the postmortem experience the speaker will undergo.

"Adjourns—are all—" (L, 229), Dickinson wrote aphoristically, and she constantly values endings over beginnings, the future over the past tense. One function of her dashes is to announce the "to be continued" of futurism, even when they occur at a poem's end. For instance, in the concluding stanza of "I felt a Funeral, in my Brain" (280), we reach for an ending and find only an unnamed future:

> And then a Plank in Reason, broke.
> And I dropped down, and down—
> And hit a World, at every plunge,
> And Finished knowing—then—

The coffin is lowered into a grave with no bottom; the mind falls through ontological realms until mentality itself is left behind. The journey becomes inexpressible because it goes beyond conceptualization. The poem ends in a dash because any statement of what comes after "knowing" is finished would be a falsification. Whether consciousness is being expanded or violated, whether its final destiny is a heaven or a hell or whether any final ground is to be fallen upon at all, Dickinson moves downward and forward to a personal future beyond all historical projections.

Granting that Dickinson's futurism is more eschatological than social, it is yet thoroughly American. Her aphorisms, "Adjourns—are all—" and "Immortality contented / Were Anomaly" (1036), constitute futurism at its boldest and barest, for there are only endings and, beyond them, endlessness:

> As if the Sea should part
> And show a further Sea—
> And that—a further—and the Three
> But a presumption be—
> Of Periods of Seas—
> Unvisited of Shores—
> Themselves the Verge of Seas to be—
> Eternity—is Those—

> (695)

Futurism is a less organized strategy than either stretched or archetypal history, but we find Dickinson's forward looking in the more socially oriented gazes of other Americans. One thinks of the dashlike endings of many American works of fiction—Twain's *Huckleberry Finn*, Dos Passos's *Manhattan Transfer*, Fitzgerald's *Gatsby*, Faulkner's *Light in August*, Mailer's *American Dream*—in which the hero lights out from the known, historical, and corrupt, the America that has fallen under the European shadow, to a new and unknown locale, delusive perhaps in its promise, but compelling as the only allure.

Or one thinks, not so much of Whitman's programmatic statements of futurism where he speaks, for instance, of "the vast revolutionary arch thrown by the United States over the centuries, fixed in the present, launched to the endless future,"[35] but of the actual techniques of his poetry; in particular his shockingly direct addresses to a future reader so actual to the poet that the Walt persona speaks to him in a present intimacy, as a "You up there" in the phrase from "As I Ebb'd."

Futurism at its boldest, as in *Walden,* imagines that cultural earliness is not a problem but a grace, that it already has been obscured by the British-European shadow cast upon the New World, and that we must strive for a future earlier than the present. Thus, in hoping for a future American poet, Emerson defines him as "the sayer, the namer" (*CW,* III, 5), that is, as originary. In her definition poems, Dickinson takes on this Adamic function of naming: "Hope is a subtle Glutton," "Distance is not the realm of Fox," "Heaven—is what I cannot reach!," "What is—'Paradise'—," and, to end where we began, "'Hope' is the thing with feathers," among many other examples. These first lines acknowledge history, here the history of language meanings, to undo it by revitalizing them. Emerson called language "the archives of history" and Dickinson's refusal of deadened, commonplace usage drives language back to the vitality of poetic origin and thus rejects history.

But in such bold earliness, futurism need not always say, with Whitman's "Pioneers," "All the past we leave behind." Bercovitch notes that the Puritan myth, as expressed by Mather, "reshapes the past into a foreshadowing of the greater things to come, a developing drama whose meaning is accessible only through anticipation."[36] By this formula, Whitman himself can say that American literature is to "complete the inaugurations of the oldest civilizations, and change their small scale to the largest, broadest scale."[37] More importantly, in a poem like "Prayer of Columbus," Whitman can retreat forward: the poem is, in Sharon Cameron's words, "whitman's attempt to intuit the present as if it were future, from the imagined perspective of a figure in the past." In futurism, too, the present can replace the past as history: as Cameron goes on to note, in "Crossing Brooklyn Ferry," Whitman projects himself into time future and "in the imagined retrospect of a future time . . . the present could be recollected as a true past."[38] Futurism finally, like stretched and stacked history, instructs its practitioner in the flexibility of time and thought.

5

The most extreme replacement for history, what I earlier termed vertical time, offers a different means for at once refusing and absorbing history. It is expressed most simply in Emerson's commanding adage that every man "can live all history in his own person" (CW, II, 6). Upon this, Emerson's entire thought rests. That is why the essay on history is placed first in *Essays: First Series,* and that is why this essay is most an essay against history as history is commonly understood. In it, Emerson proclaims, "all the facts of history preexist in the mind as laws" (CW, II, 3). "We are always coming up with the emphatic facts of history in our private experience and verifying them here. All history becomes subjective; in other words there is properly no history, only biography" (CW, II, 6). Just so, Thoreau, in *A Week,* considers whole past cultures recapitulated in our momentary moods: "the history which we read is only a fainter memory of events which have happened in our own experience. Tradition is a more interrupted and feebler memory."[39] "In Chants Democratic," Whitman puts forth the same claim in characteristically more numerous words:

> I was looking a long while for the history of the
>   past for myself, and for these Chants—and now
>   I have found it,
> It is not in those paged fables in the library, (them
>   I neither accept nor reject,)
> It is no more in the legends than in all else,
> It is in the present—it is this earth to-
>   day, . . .[40]

Linear time collapses into an expanded present inhabited by an expansive self. What history can provide, this moment provides as well, to the seer of large vision and perfect empathy. Indeed, it is better to let the present provide an encyclopedic view of life than history, better to look about and within than back, for written history contains inaccuracies as no true knowing of the present will; and the past includes irrelevancies, dross, while the past that matters to the present self is that which is in the self now.

At worst, the study of history may deaden what is of import in it, may lead not to but away from the self and the present, which alone matter. At best, history unfolds the mind and, at worst, obscures it. Thus American vertical time absorbs, subordinates, and distrusts history. "I am ashamed," Emerson writes, "to see what a shallow village tale our so-called History is" (CW, II, 22).

Stephen Spender best describes the Anglo-American split that arises from this: "The American Nowness exploits the truism that the past can only attain consciousness in the minds of the living; the European exploits the opposite truism that the immensely greater part of human consciousness is crystallized in the world of the dead and that to be alive is to be an outpost of that consciousness."[41] Spender too much considers his Nowness the only American idea of historical time; and we should recall once more that it, like the other American times we have considered and even more than them, has a defensive tinge. In Whitman especially, this Nowness is characterized as an extreme democracy of time, since all moments are made equal, each absolutely full. This is democracy made metaphysical with a vengeance, and the revenge is aimed at those who possess the riches of linear time, chiefly the British.

Vertical time, then, like futurism, may show the blushing aspect of an excuse. And, like futurism, its dangers are legion. In its most vulgar form, when a love of the immediate is cut off from the immortal truths to which immediate sensations are thought to lead, it produces the giddy sensationalism, the reckless living and shallow impermanence that Cooper attacks in *Home As Found*. In Cooper's New York, "a town that, in a moral sense, resembles an encampment, quite as much as it resembles a permanent and long-existing capital," an English gentleman's eloquent speech on behalf of permanence—"We love the tree that our forefathers planted, the roof that they built, the fireside by which they sat, and the sods that cover their remains"—is answered by the American Aristabulus Bragg, who says that such a love "must be a great check to business operations."[42] American business itself, and perhaps a good deal more, is characterized by the Exchange, at which wild, speculative trading of foundationless stock occurs; it, with a third of New York, burns to destruction in an apocalyptic fire that emphasizes the frailty of the immediate as much as it does its corruption.

In its dignified literary forms, vertical time may be more dangerous. It assumes a totality of truth and an utmost of consciousness as the twin goals of existence and argues that history and the present moment are alternate routes to it, with the latter the better route as it eliminates the detours of secondhand knowledge. This tends to reduce history from what Spender (showing himself, after all his fairness, delightfully English) calls "a whole experience of living in the world"[43] to mere information. The American critique of history also tends to refuse any final value to the particular and unique, all the interest of individuated character and circumstance, and this in spite of all cries for democratic individualism. Far worse, taken not only as an epistemological strategy but as a guide for living in the world—and we shall see that it insists upon being taken so—vertical time loads such a burden of responsibility on the moment, and thus on the inevitably subjective self whose moment it is, that the self may collapse under its weight.

But precisely because vertical time is the most extreme American replacement for history, it is of special import. And, like futurism, if its doctrine is ahistorical, it is sufficiently rooted in the American past to deserve understanding rather than pejoration. Fred Somkin describes the Puritan founding as "a providential conspiracy against time" and as "an appeal, finally, from time to eternity"; and John Lynen characterizes Puritan epistemology as "the individual in his isolated present moment trying to interpret the immediate by a direct reference to the eternal."[44] The Puritan's notions of the eternal were scriptural, of course; and though scriptural interpretation allows some flexibility in imaging the ultimate, the American romantics gave themselves a great deal more. Christian scripture is only one of their mappings of the ultimate along with the maps of Eastern holy books, various philosophical idealisms, and versions of literary romanticism—these and anything else appealing to the freed individual speculation.

As Melville wrote to his publisher upon completing *Mardi,* "instincts are prophetic, and better than acquired wisdom."[45] Thus for an American romantic as not for an American Puritan consciousness, the flow from the present to the eternal for its interpretation is coupled with a reverse flow by which the eternal is hypothesized out of the present. Nonetheless, Lynen is right to emphasize the Puritan derivation of this epistemological set, the two polarities of the present and eternity with nothing in between. In the nineteenth as in the seventeenth century, "The essential literary program of revealing universals through particulars takes a special form in American writing, because there the contrast between them seems simpler, harsher, more nearly absolute." And Roy Harvey Pearce is equally right to emphasize the degree to which American romanticism rebels against the didactics of the Puritans in its Antinomian trust in spontaneity, intuition, and the divinity within the self.[46]

Lynen may err by claiming too much for vertical time, as there are other times in American romanticism. The supposedly excluded "middle ground" is, of course, history, cultural and personal—yet even Thoreau will cite historical sources, usually classical, for support of his conduct, and both the personal and cultural past figure large in everything Hawthorne wrote.

But within vertical time, Lynen's description is just. If history appears, it is only as a repository of disconnected exemplary actions that may serve to make the self courageous. Whitman's sudden forays into history in the "jet black sunrise" and John Paul Jones episodes of "Song of Myself" have no before or after: they are isolated exempla of a past-present informed by the ultimates of strength and beauty in suffering, Whitman's demonstration of Thoreau's famous adage, "Time is but the stream I go a-fishing in." Similarly, Dickinson will cite Montcalm and Wolfe in one poem as linked heroes loyal beyond death to opposing causes. They characterize the magnificence of obsessive loyalty, they do not provide the history of a particular war. Historical figures—including, as we have seen, Jesus—parade through Dickinson's poetry but only as personifications of internal attitudes. In this pick-and-choose view of history, vertical time is as far as possible from the historical sense that Spender sees the English as possessing, "of moving along a continuous line" with an awareness of "the presence of the past in daily life as a palpable and working influence. . . ."[47]

Still, vertical time is often allied with the other times we have considered, which all include a linear component. In Dickinson's typology, spiritual and secular history is collapsed into the present emotional life of the individual ("There's newer—nearer Crucifixion / Than that—," "Heaven—is what I cannot reach," "Soto! Explore thyself!"); but that personal present is characterized by its mortal or postmortal destination. Thus, vertical time combines with futurism, as we see in her hypothesis, "Each Second is the last / Perhaps" (879). In that phrase, Dickinson utilizes her personalized version of futurism to admonish us to look for ultimate meanings in our every moment as we most likely might in our last.

At times Dickinson appears a pure adept of vertical time. She seems so when she says "Paradise is of the option" (L, 319) or "Forever—is composed of Nows—" (624) or "The Only News I know / Is Bulletins all Day / From Immortality" (827), sentiments whereby history is banished and any present moment becomes the infinite if experienced rightly, fully. And most largely, Dickinson practices vertical time in her basic poetic strategy, which is antimimetic in the extreme. Because "Subjects hinder talk," her poems' concerns are unbounded by place and time, and Dickinson insures their freedom by dramatizing those concerns in locales that are patently illustrative. The typical Dickinson poem provides us a pattern running through a number of carpets and then makes the carpets vanish. This vanishing is achieved by Dickinson's constant analogizing, which mentalizes all images.

But Dickinson needs to acknowledge the distance between the present and the eternal to make the connecting a discovery, and thus a linear future is emphasized even as it is brought into the thinking present. And as thinking has limits (recall the final stanza of "I felt a Funeral, in my Brain,"), sometimes a furthest future cannot be thought in the present and ultimates escape the now. Thus she also can say, in contradiction to some of her other aphorisms, "The power and the glory are the post-mortuary gifts" (*L, 920*).

We discover in all of the American romantics a flexibility of time that allows for surprising combinations within an American earliness. Far from breaking under the weightless burden of historical absence, this earliness can play with a plethora of substitutes.

Perhaps the most surprising occurrence of this flexibility involves the coupling of vertical time with what would seem its negation, stretched history, in American fiction. Fiction-writing in itself would seem a decisive commitment to a historical way of knowing via linear, successive time. But if we look back to the very work I employed to illustrate stretched history, we find that while Hawthorne is emphasizing the factual reality of the Pynchon mansion in terms of its impressive lineage, he is alternately making an eternal emblem of it. He compares the exterior of the "ancestral home" to a "human countenance" whereon an "outward storm and sunshine" (5) betray the vicissitudes of all human living; and as for the interior, "So much of mankind's varied experience had passed there . . . that the very timbers were oozy, as with the moisture of a heart" (27). Hawthorne here stretches time to its breaking point. So much has happened in the house that the domicile represents everything of human import (archetypal time) and represents it instantly to an empathic present perception (vertical time). The mansion is a real domicile proving an American history but it is also a face and a heart, and as such it dissolves temporal difference. This is the American symbol, which pushes mere representation to archetype.

Likewise, Richard Brodhead notes that "at critical moments in *The Scarlet Letter* the story stands still and we are left staring at the scarlet letter itself, at a mute symbol that seems to reabsorb into itself and communicate instantly the 'tale of human frailty and sorrow.' "[48] Melville's *Moby-Dick* provides a variety of such emblems to the extent that it seems often less a narrative interrupted by meditations than a series of meditations on the whale and associated symbols in which narrative is merely one of many methods of getting at those symbols.

Certainly Hawthorne and Melville invoke material facts, terrific social forces, the limits of intellect and the imperatives of the individual psyche as an argument against Transcendentalist high-flying. But Hawthorne and Melville, and especially Poe, make mockery of a log-

ical-positivist reality too, and of any historicism that tends toward naïveté, showing every seemingly hardest fact to be a product of consciousness.

History in the brain: American writers learned to measure kinds of
time against each other or to merge all of them. And among that variety, the American, as we have seen, manages to include the English
time sense of historical fact and rich development that he is also replacing. This surround-and-conquer technique allows the American to
dramatize a scope of speculation by which he can make his British
competitor seem dishearteningly narrow. It is the American's world
that now seems full in comparison. But that world is a world of
thought, and there is a price to pay for this escape from unequal pasts.
Vertical time only makes explicit what is true of all of the Americans'
handlings of history and its substitutes: history is ultimately supple-
mented or replaced by individual consciousness. Not only history but
a historical sense had been passed from generation to generation in
England; in America, some deal deprived of this inheritance, the perceiving self took on the task of the ages, and the self became history's
substitute. Each reader's judgment of this huge substitution largely determines personal bias in the Anglo-American contest.

8

HISTORY, TIME, AND SPIRIT: WHITMAN AGAINST WORDSWORTH, CARLYLE AND EMERSON AGAINST THEMSELVES

I

A gap in British thinking provides the American an opening for a reply to the British historical sense. It is a space between two views of history, as renovative and as ominous decline. The nineteenth-century English writer typically hopes to retrieve a more naturally spontaneous and charged way of living by achieving a return to an earlier, heartier, purer moment in the life of the culture. This is what I have described as the British cure for a sense of lateness, of national fatigue. But the grounds for this hope are self-contradictory. What in an earlier present time then appeared loss, defeat, or decline turned out to be a difficult transition, a vale of soulmaking, which led to a major human advance; so too might the current present time, which appears dark and late, signify yet another furthering. But then how did this present debasement come about if not by a succession of historical ills without redemption? If those previous falls were redemptive, why do we find ourselves here, down in the mire of an ill century?

It is within this gap in attitude that the great British romantics and Victorians work a tense and moving dialectic of secularized faith and doubt. But nostalgia, even a nostalgia nervously faced and defeated, could be made to look pathetically febrile. That is how the American writer typically refused this entire British issue, leaping from its historical worries to proclaim a freedom over time and to celebrate a forward looking continental prospect. History could be kidded in America into undermining itself, leaving the individual enlarged in an unbounded present. From that perspective, British despair would prove the global need for an American fresh start; and, more trickily, British hope would seem unadventuresome—more a part of the problem than a solution, as we saw in Whitman's critique of Arnold—to an America confident that it could realize far more literally and less privately an earlier, wilder beginning.

In the discussion of vertical time, I linked Emerson and Whitman as practitioners of this general strategy. But the two cases I am about to consider to specify kinds of replies to a British historicism—Whitman's "Song of Myself" as a response to Wordsworth's 1850 *Prelude* and

Emerson's *Representative Men* as a response to Carlyle's *On Heroes, Hero-Worship, and the Heroic in History*—are chosen as much for their differences as for their more general likeness. Most obviously, Whitman and Wordsworth redact their views of history into poems more obviously about the individual in time, while Emerson and Carlyle confront public history directly. More crucially, Whitman's return upon Wordsworth is implicit but exuberantly competitive, a brash show of the American advantage in freeing time and self from linear history; Emerson's return upon Carlyle is relatively explicit but ultimately tentative and self-divided, as if in attempting to help Carlyle out of his contradictions Emerson finally gives away to Carlyle much of his own vigor. These two lesser texts make for a more complex relation, though the proof that a relation between them exists is far more obvious.

In linking Whitman and Wordsworth, I must confess speculation, though the connection seems to me a near certainty. "Now the performer launches his nerve," Whitman announces late in "Song of Myself," "he has passed his prelude on the reeds within."[1] Is Whitman punningly meaning to pass Wordsworth's *Prelude* as well as what had gone before in his own poem? Does he mean to imply that Wordsworth's inner pastoral, built in spite of the external world of city squalor and cruel revolution, is not enough? Is "Song of Myself" in more substantial aspects Whitman's deliberate redaction of Wordsworth? I do not know. There is no extra-textual evidence whatsoever to support a claim of direct influence nor are there any obviously telling allusions in "Song of Myself" to *The Prelude* or any other of Wordsworth's poems. Yet I am instructed by Claudio Guillen's insistence, mentioned in my preface, that specific allusion may indicate a far less profound case of influence than an encompassing inspiration, a whole way of thinking or writing that may not display overt allusions at all.

While I cannot know, then, that Whitman is deliberating Wordsworth and *The Prelude* in "Song of Myself," I think it highly likely. *The Prelude* and "Song of Myself" are the two and only examples in English-language poetry in the nineteenth century of a particular genre: the epic-like poem merged with spiritual autobiography, an epic in which the poetic self is hero.[2] *The Prelude* was published finally in 1850 (that is the version of the poem I will employ here), "Song of Myself" five years later. Wordsworth's American fame, late in developing, had not faded; most of the major American romantics, all of them less fearful than Whitman of the consequences of positing one's specific origins, mention Wordsworth prominently. As much as Dickens represents the English mind in prose fiction, Wordsworth means English poetry to the American writer. If direct influence is only probable—

persuasively probable as I believe, for these poems, made to speak to one another, create a dialogue in a manner that two randomly chosen romanticist works would not—indirect influence is definite. For Wordsworth, as Shelley, Keats, and, grumblingly, Byron would attest, defines a British romanticism more fully than any other single poet. And modern critics of American literature, from Matthiessen to Lynen, have been drawn to Wordsworth alone of the English romantics as Whitman's part-compeer, on such grounds as their shared respect for common language and common objects as potentially poetic, their notion of poetry as the underpinning of science, and their deep sense of the interpenetration of human thoughts and apparently inanimate objects.[3] This sure, indirect influence matters most, for in considering Wordsworth and Whitman we can hope to develop a description of American romanticism that sunders the national adjective from the wider territory of the noun.

The proof for Emerson's *Representative Men* as a reply upon Carlyle's *On Heroes and Hero-Worship* is refreshingly more plain, for Carlyle goaded Emerson to this attempt. In response to reading the "Divinity School Address," Carlyle challenged Emerson, "You tell us with piercing emphasis that man's soul is great; *shew* us a great soul of a man, in some work symbolic of such: . . . I long to see some concrete thing, . . . which this Emerson loves and wonders at, well Emersonized: depictured by Emerson, filled with the life of Emerson, and cast forth from him then to live by itself. If these Orations baulk me of this, how profitable soever they be for others, I will not love them."[4] Emerson already had demurred, mentioning some American events and manners worthy of treatment but not for him, "No, not in the near and practical way which they seem to invite. I incline to write philosophy, poetry, possibility,—anything but history" (L,277). In the forties, however, Emerson was testing his distinctive thought to see what it could include—descriptions of bewilderment and doubt, for instance, in such essays as "Experience" and "Fate"—and history would come to seem an attractive challenge in its very lack of attraction. His earlier essay "History" had not been history writing; like *Nature,* a book whose title was playfully misleading in that it belied the content of an argument against the facticity of the world of appearances, "History" was a general debunking of the conventional study and practice of history. Now, beginning in 1846 with a series of lectures that would culminate in the 1850 publication (in Britain and America simultaneously), Emerson would write history according to his own recipe, as biography. Yet to "Emersonize" history is still to debunk it, to dissolve concrete people and events into invisible and unchanging qualities. That is why *Representative Men* is a strange, someways failed book: always in Emerson the study of history leads to the refusal of history in the name of what we have been calling vertical time, and here Emerson wishes at once to make the grubby particulars of history suggestive and to shoo them away altogether.

The book to which he is replying, *On Heroes, Hero-Worship, and The Heroic in History*, contains its own contradictions. Both works (knowingly, I would guess) betray an authorial self-division concerning historical time, and the shape of each conflict is nationally representative. In our second case, we will have a conflict of conflicts to consider.

Together, the Wordsworth-Whitman and Carlyle-Emerson textual debates suggest a range of consequences to the American challenging of history's wisdom. But in this, I do not mean to imply that English writers mindlessly adhere to a simple, linear notion of history. Everyone in the nineteenth century is redefining what history means, and I will treat Wordsworth and Whitman first, against the chronology of the American texts in each pair, because it is Wordsworth who initiates the nineteenth century into a new kind of history linking event and era to metaphysics. It is within that understanding that all four of these works play.

2

History, what we usually mean by that word, matters importantly to Wordsworth; and it matters equally to Whitman to prove that history in its usual sense does not matter at all to a democratically present poet. But we will not comprehend this importance simply by examining each poet's renderings of historical events. What history really means for each is revealed far more tellingly when we take a wider view of each poet's larger idea of time, especially as it is implied by the literary shape of each poet's personal epic. And while epic as a genre usually implies history, commemorating a culture's central public event, *The Prelude* and "Song of Myself" are most surely related as epics that challenge the usual understanding of in what a great event consists, taking it away from the usual notion of history or taking history to mean newly.

We can get at this issue of temporal form by questioning first the two poems' replacements of an epic muse. Wordsworth begins *The Prelude* by scouting a subject for "Aeolian visitations," with "a gentle breeze" importantly substituting for the muse of traditional epic (1:96,1). This substitution inaugurates the poem's creation of a supernatural naturalism whereby, in M. H. Abrams' formulation, God is removed from the triad of God, nature, and mind.[5] But it also implies the poem's epic intent by transforming one of its initiatory conventions. Ordinary if blessed weather replaces all deities of inspiration. So too, as Wordsworth takes us backstage to describe his floundering search for a subject, we may see nothing of the confident authority of the epic bard; but as all of the themes the poet considers only to discard—"some British theme, some old / Romantic tale by Milton left unsung" (168–9), or a Spenserian tale "Of dire enchantments faced and overcome / By the strong mind, and tales of warlike facts" (175–6), in particular the origin of the British nation, or best, "some philosophic song / Of truth that cherishes our daily life" (229–30)—survey epic possibilities, this very confession of poetic trouble characterizes itself as a daring move of the epic address toward inner personality. And this move is borne out in the self-referential subject of "The Growth of a Poet's Mind." It comes unsought, indeed in the midst of a self-complaint that one so favored by early life along the Derwent River should prove incapable. And, presto! arrives the doubly natural subject, of the self's continuity of growth that persists like a river (sometimes running underground) against all apparent strifes, including the present poetic difficulty. The spatial metaphor implies that time is a flow in which the self delightedly discovers personal continuity. This is time's good, available only when the will does not attempt to force the moment.

The Walt persona likewise finds his good in an active passivity, as "I loafe and invite my soul, / I lean and loaf at my ease. . . . observing a spear of summer grass" (1:4–5). His opening phrase, "I celebrate myself," is a far more bold and direct assertion both of epic intent and of a self-reflexive turn upon epic; and while Whitman's muse is part natural, the chiefer source of inspiration is the self in its elemental, physical being, "My respiration and inspiration" (2:15), horrible but engaging pun that it is. Time for Whitman, then, is less a continual flow than it is an alternating momentary exchange, the rhythm of human breathing.

The consequences of such differences to each poet's idea of the self in history will concern us soon. For now, in linking the poems generically, I would stress the like internalization of epic and, as a more specific similarity than genre can account, the identical notion in each that poetic achievement is not a striving but a relaxation, not a task of peak culture but of removing cultural restraints and the self-consciousness that accompanies them. The Prelude is occasioned by Wordsworth finding himself "escaped / From the vast city" (1:6–7) just as the less literal occasion of "Song of Myself" consists in Whitman's refusal of "Houses and rooms . . . full of perfumes" to "go to the bank by the wood and become undisguised and naked" (2:11). Wordsworth turns the punishment of Adam and Eve into an immediate grace by echoing Milton in the phrase "The earth is all before me" (1:14). Whitman avers, "The atmosphere is not a perfume . . . it has no taste of the distillation" (2:9) and prefers it as an unadulterated given. In both cases, the overcivilized world and the god of punishing limits it has fashioned are rejected in favor of trusting the givens of life and the self's free wandering to realize them.

This free wandering is extended from the self to the poem which represents the self in each case, and it is here that Wordsworth and Whitman strain the definition of epic with its assumption of a narrative succession. *The Prelude,* Abrams argues, is "radically achronological." Abrams is typical of recent Wordsworth readers in emphasizing the poem's subjectivizing of time. He notes throughout the poem "a multiple awareness that Wordsworth calls 'two consciousnesses'" and stresses the gaps and interminglings "between the I now and the I then." He quotes a fragment in which Wordsworth writes "I look into past time as prophets look / Into futurity. . . ." and insists upon the primacy of memory as Wordsworth's subject, a power manifesting "the enduring and the eternal within the realm of time and change. Only intermittently does the narrative order coincide with the order of actual occurrence. Instead Wordsworth proceeds by sometimes bewildering ellipses, fusions, and as he says 'motions retrograde' in time."[6]

But Abrams is refusing too much the importance of a continuous narrative time in *The Prelude.* Almost immediately he acknowledges a three-stage plot to the poem: "a process of mental development" essentially unaffected by social circumstances, "violently broken by a crisis of apathy and despair" (the French Revolution as it corrupts Wordsworth's vision), and a recovery "which, despite admitted losses, is represented as a level higher than the initial unity" by the discoveries of suffering. Granting Abrams' point that *The Prelude* is "an involuted poem which is about its own genesis,"[7] granting too that the world's time is constantly rebutted—to the extent that the poet's clock moves by public events he has lost his permanently real being—Wordsworth's notion of a personal *felix culpa* nonetheless depends on linear time. The "growth" of the subtitle emphasizes becoming-in-time. The poem's large units, its books, are arranged chronologically despite "motions retrograde" within them. And meaning depends, at times, upon that chronology. For instance, Wordsworth stresses the invulnerability of his inner state despite the superficial dissipations first of Cambridge and then of London. The narrative shock of the Revolution, its ruinous if temporary triumph over what had been invulnerable hitherto, depends upon our knowledge of these hithertos for its full effect. Further, while Wordsworth daringly makes internal the meanings of history in his treatment of the revolution—it is condemned more, finally, for tempting the poet to a syllogistic, imagination-killing rationalism than for its public cruelties—Wordsworth delays his self-condemnation to book twelve, so that he can dramatize his sad change in the prior few books with only occasional self-knowledge. That is, he imitates the temporal process of error followed by recognition in his retelling. In *The Prelude* then, history comes indoors. And yet, so long as the self considers itself as a history, the historical imagination persists, revised.

"Song of Myself" presents no chronology whatsoever, or so little that any hint of sequence is immediately absorbed into vertical time. It is useless to speak of disruptions to chronos, for no steadily linear time is posited. Whitman's best commentator, John Lynen, notes the futility of dividing the poem into stages to argue instead, "the whole of 'Song of Myself' is a picture of Whitman's state of mind as he loafs on a bank contemplating a spear of grass."[8] And indeed Whitman attempts to go back further in time than Wordsworth, not to childhood intimations of the immortal but directly to a no-time that produces time's events: "you shall possess," he promises, "the origin of all poems" (2:25).

Lynen may be too conservative in insisting upon a scope-defining occasion at all. While "I lean and loafe at my ease . . . observing a spear of summer grass" has the authority of appearing as the close of the brief opening section, it is almost immediately challenged by another potential occasion, "I will go to the bank by the wood and become undisguised and naked" (2:11). Yet another initiating occasion occurs sixty lines later, when "I mind how we lay in June, such a transparent summer morning" (5:78). Whitman goes on to describe body and soul making love, a union upon the hitherto blamed body's terms that refuses the traditional duality, until "Swiftly arose and spread around me the peace and joy and knowledge that pass all the art and argument of the earth" (5:82). This "spread around" suggests a pictorial timelessness that might seem our central moment, but then it is immediately followed by yet another candidate: "A child said, What is grass? fetching it to me with full hands" (6:90). Perhaps the entire poem that follows constitutes Walt's reply.

My point is simple. There are so many competing occasions, each importantly echoing and reinforcing the others, that there is no occasion at all, much less a continuing action. Whitman takes his anti-historical assertion of vertical time seriously enough to structure his poem by it.

There was never any more inception than there is
　now,
Nor any more youth or age than there is now;
And will never be any more perfection than there
　is now,
Nor any more heaven or hell than there is now; . . .

(3:32–5)

Each proposed occasion is equivalent to any moment. There is no specially incarnated moment rising out of the plain of time; any moment
is best and any moment is now. Whitman silently refuses a basic scene
to enfranchise all moments and circumstances as democratically ripe
for inspiration. That is why the poet does not "remember" but
"minds" the June mating of body and soul. Wordsworthian memory
can reinterpret the past to the point of replacing it; but memory depends on temporal difference. Whitman's free roaming through time is
not quite a form of memory, for all moments are identical and the "two
consciousnesses" are one.

For all his acute appreciation of "Song of Myself," Lynen nonetheless agrees with Charles Feidelson Jr.'s conservative complaint: "Whatever the nominal subject, it is soon lost in sheer 'process'; all roads lead
into 'Song of Myself,' in which the bare ego interacts with a miscellaneous world. The result is Whitman's characteristic disorder and
turgidity. When the subject is endless, any form becomes arbitrary."
But "Subjects hinder talk" (L,397), we recall Emily Dickinson proclaiming; and if, as Lynen himself insists, Whitman's only subject is
the inner experiencing, the how-it-feels of a comprehensive perception,
then a canny encyclopaedic randomness creates that reversal of realism
we spoke of earlier, in which the only imitated object is consciousness.
Because "no single object can suffice to represent the moment," Lynen
claims, Whitman does not reiterate the observing of the grass frequently enough to allow it to fulfill its controlling function. "Song of
Myself" is "rather too like a glass of water without the glass." Later
lyrics succeed more fully because they spring from a more continually
evident occasion, "a determinate present."[9]

My view is just the opposite. "Song of Myself" is Whitman's best
work because it most fully enacts vertical time; subsequent poems,
successful as many of them are, allow for a Wordsworthian remembering and a developmental notion of the self that mutes Whitman's individuality. At his most radical, Whitman joins Dickinson in refusing
any referential situation at all. In Dickinson's poetry, I have argued

elsewhere, "apparently mimetic scenes are themselves chance choices from an infinity of possible exemplifications of the poem's unifying proposition. The scenes are not mimetic but illustratory, chosen, temporary, analogous. The poem is finally sceneless." Once more, "Her poems do not dramatize the projection of mind onto matter but the organization of a mind-world continuum in a pattern of chosen language."[10]

Whitman differs from Dickinson in two ways. First, he states blatantly any number of unifying propositions as well as making us derive from analogous events the law that unites them. But this is only a superficial difference: Whitman's laws are so numerously stated that we still must look to define the law of laws. The second difference is real: whereas Dickinson's illustratory scenes are immediately characterized as thought-up, a certain raw reality sticks to the items in a Whitman tally, as if a Warhol frame surrounds each, emphasizing its interest. Whitman's every image attests to a process of "respiration and inspiration," just as successive blocks of the poem stress a creative taking-in and sending-out. It is as if Walt inhales the historical world and then exhales it again, with a loving sheen from this process lighting the most vicious item to beauty. For inside the breathing poet lurks the central self ("Real Me," Whitman would name it in the 1860 lyric, "As I Ebb'd") with its assurance of an ultimate good, now breathed out, made to bear immediately upon particulars. We do not have here an epic hero of action or even Wordsworth's epic hero of developing mind. We have the static essence of a hero, free of time's development, upon multifaceted display.

Objections are obvious. The simplest to disarm would concern those passages that call up past objective history: both official national events like the "jetblack sunrise / . . . the murder in cold blood of four hundred and twelve young men" (34:866–7) or the less official events of Walt witnessing a trapper's marriage to an Indian woman or of Walt harboring a runaway slave. But this is simply to say that the respiratory poet can roam time as freely as God so that history fits within the self's moment. "The student is to read history actively, not passively," Emerson writes in his essay, "to esteem his own life the text, and books the commentary" (CW,II,5). Whitman enacts Emerson's proposition in "Song." Every apparent event is a description of Walt.

More challenging to my view that the poem eschews developmental time is its cyclicity. When Whitman promises the origin of all poems, which I have taken as a proof of a supratemporal intent, he does so in a way which would seem to refute my claim: "Stop this day and night with me and you shall possess the origin of all poems." The early sections of the poem seem dawnlike and, at its close, "The last scud of day holds back for me" (52:1324). This day cycle is also a year cycle (the fifty two sections) and both open out on a still larger cycle of birth, life, death, and rebirth. The mating of body and soul suggests birth; and at poem's end a kind of death occurs—"I bequeath myself to the dirt to grow from the grass I love / If you want me again look for me under your bootsoles" (52:1329–30). Of course, "bequeath" suggests that death is a matter of the will's choice; and its provisional character is guaranteed by the nitrogen-cycle immortality that Whitman employs as evidentiary scientific proof of a spiritual truth. (The grass is also "the hair of graves.") But this is not the point. Cyclicity may round, but a circle is drawn in time. This is where Lynen and I differ. He sees vertical time subsuming all. I see mind subsuming even vertical time in the poem, as one of the many kinds of time the mind enjoys. Here it combines with what we earlier called futurism so that death is made a future state that is not so much anticipated but experienced like the past in the present. And simultaneously, the transmogrified Walt by this ending hurries ahead to be in advance even of his future reader, as the valued dirt, a principle of earthy authenticity, which the reader must seek. A number of time senses uncannily combine to create this amazing result. Vertical time is not all for Whitman, then, though it is indeed chief. Other kinds of time do appear for moments to supplant the *now*, but: in what section is it half past three? where exactly is Walt in late middle age? The cyclical notions are not followed through in continuous fashion. They arise as one of any number of temporal understandings available to a mind above time.

Still, there are sections in which a clear progression occurs. When the sense of touch with its power frightens Walt to cry out against his libido *and then* that fright is accepted (in sections 28–30), even if it is accepted in terms of "perpetual payment of the perpetual loan," the event itself is dramatized as successive. A more obvious succession occurs when empathy leads Walt into despairing with the sufferers—"O Christ! My fit is mastering me!" (37:933). He tricks his way out of that despair by a too hasty, manufactured epiphany—"I rise extatic through all and sweep with the true gravitation" (37:953)—and then he disowns that upward gravitation as false: "I discover myself on a verge of the usual mistake. / That I could forget the mockers and insults" (38:957–8). He decides to "resume the overstaid fraction" (38:961), knowing sorrow is here being inflated beyond its proper scope but knowing too that he must combat its terror by further confrontation. Intermittently, through the next several hundred lines, Walt works himself toward a more enabling empathy—"O despairer, here is my neck, / By God! you shall not go down! Hang your whole weight upon me" (40:1007–8). Walt revises his attitude, changes his mind; and change implies linear time.

Yet, in the second example, this linear progression, after an initial concentration, is dispersed and interwoven with the usual assertions of a perpetual now. And Walt's next statement at the conclusion of this crisis—"I am an acme of things accomplished, and I an encloser of things to be" (44:1148)—reasserts an expansive present that can contain all times. Range and plenitude, not an unchanging perfection, characterize Whitman's poetic godhead. Christ suffered doubt and temptation and remained a god. Here in "Song," movement has been made coexistent with a huge fixity. This Walt is "large" and "contains multitudes" not only in terms of kinds of selves or crowds of images but also in terms of terms, of structural time-principles themselves. We are given an encyclopedia of kinds of time—vertical time, cycles of varied circumference, pasts made present, direct or indirect successions—because the self *in any one moment* experiences time in a rich multitude of ways. This is vertical time squared, containing even its initial self.

It is not a matter of alternatives but inclusions. Thus Whitman's tallyings—say, in small, the lines "The pure contralto sings in the organloft / The carpenter dresses his plank. . . . the tongue of his foreplane whistles its wild ascending lisp" (15:257–8)—depend for their effect on a multitude of time senses. There is simultaneity—one assumes a frozen present in which both of these activities are occurring. There is the claim of vertical time—such activities are occurring at this moment as at all moments; these are acts of a constant creative drive. There is implied causal succession—such objects as an organloft are built by the carpenter's activity. Yet we hear of the resultant object first, and the continuing metaphor of "tongue," "whistles," and "lisp" announces the presence of a mind comparing musics and refusing to give any greater credit to the high culture activity. This mind itself merges kinds of times. The one imaged thought leads to the next; the two are joined by an abstract, fixed logic.

Whitman's carnival of time senses makes Wordsworth's past-present-permanent interlinkings by memory appear impoverished in terms of comprehensiveness. And while each poem concerns the grounds of its own utterance, in "Song of Myself" there is only utterance, which in comparison renders *The Prelude* a report. There is only one scene to Whitman's "Song," the human imagination, all other scenes arising only as experienced by imagination. Wordsworth's imagination "grows" in encounter with reported upon realities and memories of those encounters. Those realities come to be seen as ever imbued with a perceiving sensibility but they are there, the French Revolution is there, there is a *there,* as there is not in "Song."

This point needs exemplification. Both *The Prelude* and "Song of Myself" mean to fulfill in radical manner the epic dictate of making history present by dramatizing the poem as present utterance. But Wordsworth's presence is re-novative. It posits a something to be transformed. In the London book, for instance, the introductory phrase to the city's description,

> Rise up thou monstrous ant-hill on the plain
> Of a too-busy world! Before me flow,
> Thou endless stream of men and moving things!
>
> (7:149–51),

allows a double meaning for its initial verb, the physical erection of this town of pathetically sky-challenging buildings (pathetic because the tallest building possesses an anthill's height when viewed from the proper, heavenly perspective) and the poet's command to his imagination to recreate the scene. It is the second meaning that holds sway, particularly by the time we reach the second command, "Before me flow." It is the imagination primarily, not the Thames or the land-bound city, which is flowing, though there remains sufficient physical shading in these words to sustain a mind-matter continuum. Still, Wordsworth introduces the scene as primarily a mentalized image; and the ultimate criticism of London concerns its effect upon the imagination. That is why it comes as something of a surprise for us to find ourselves taken on a guided tour: "we turn / Abruptly into some sequestered nook" (7:169–70), "We take our way" (174), "Thence back into the throng" (189), "As on the broadening causeway we advance, / Behold. . . ." (199–200). Satirizing the prose of adulatory travel literature, Wordsworth nonetheless represents the real, untransformed London.

We might expect this admission of an exterior reality in a context where that exterior is seen as alien to the self and deadening to the imagination. Yet when Wordsworth wishes to make his furthest claim for the priority of the imagination, "A thousand times more beautiful than the earth" and "In beauty exalted, as it is itself / Of quality and fabric more divine" (14:449,453–4), he does so by remembering raw, even dire experience—for example, the stormy day on which the child, passing a horrific landscape, returns home to see his father die (12:286–335). Wordsworth's idea, illustrated without editorializing, concerns the imagination's power. The scene is "Tempestuous, dark, and wild" because it is remembered in conjunction with sorrow, but this sorrow itself is imaginatively transformed into a solemn joy because the memory is intense and sympathetic. Sublimation derives from its root word here. The terror of death, accepted and appreciated for its power, gives way to mystery, faith, comfort: ". . . So feeling comes in aid /Of feeling, . . ." (12:269–70).

But my point is that something happened. We never view mere occurrence when Wordsworth's imagination is functioning, for it is ever contributory, but it is only by the indication of a raw material that the imagination may display its force. This is appropriate to a poet who defines imagination, in the famous passage on "spots of time," as "A *renovating* virtue" (12:210, italics mine). Imagination grows out of an experience that it imbues all along.

No such paradox exists in "Song of Myself." There is no plain externality, no prior and after divorced from the present, no raw data despite the poem's apparent claim, for data and poem are one. Whitman's claim against Wordsworth is, "I encompass more, I am more bardic in my bolder transcendence of the limits of sense." This in no way implies Whitman's objective superiority to Wordsworth. Much of value is sacrificed to scope. Wordsworth works more intricately with the linkings and disjunctures of past and present; and he can dramatize the rising of the permanent out of the mind's combinings of past and present with a cognitive realism of which "Song" is incapable. Who would deny that "Song" sacrifices dramatic suspense and a warmth of recognizable personality to inclusive exuberance? Yet Whitman's multifaceted immediacy sometimes make us feel that Wordsworth *did write* poems while Whitman is *now acting* to exhale a world. And this is testimony to the potential of the American challenge to history, given that, in plain terms of talent, Wordsworth is the greater poet.

But Whitman's antihistorical resources are still greater than we have accounted, and we need some terms from an earlier discussion to complete this consideration of time and history in these competing poems. To put it most simply, Whitman relies upon American early time to belittle, almost literally belittle, Wordsworth.

Wordsworth is a poet of cultural lateness, and this sense of lateness is multiform. The poet's complete preference for a country life is only its most obvious manifestation. Himself "ill-tutored to captivity" (3:359), Wordsworth finds a modern Cambridge education pompous: knowledge must be

> fit to endure.
> The passing day should learn to put aside
> Her trappings here, should strip them off abashed
> Before antiquity and stedfast truth
> And strong book-mindedness; and over all
> A healthy sound simplicity should reign,
> A seemly plainness, . . .
>
> (3:394–400)

Less is more in Wordsworth's purificatory ethic: this overdressed culture must be stripped, and antiquity must be attended to not for obscure allusions but as a standard of natural simplicity. There is the "passing day"—a scurrilous cultural present—and the past, which is permanent in its unpretension.

This longing for "The unfenced regions of society" (7:57) is personal as well as political, and finally internal. The Golden Age is not so long ago, given "the paradise / Where I was reared; in Nature's primitive gifts / Favoured no less. . ." (8:98–100). But the primitive is not so portable in Wordsworth as we found it in Thoreau. It is available to childhood, but ominously difficult to find in maturity:

> The days gone by
> Return upon me almost from the dawn
> Of life: the hiding-places of man's power
> Open; I would approach them, but they close.
> I see by glimpses now; when age comes on,
> May scarcely see at all; . . .
>
> (12:277–82)

I have described the magnificent tension in Wordsworth's poetry between the loss of childhood ecstasy and the "abundant recompense" of a maturity that alone can comprehend that ecstasy's holiness by a creative memory. It is chicken-and-egg to say whether this tension causes Wordsworth's gloomy view of the culturally-late present or is caused by it. Indeed, Wordsworth hopes for no simple return to a personal or cultural childhood. Instead, as Wordsworth continues the just cited passage,

> I would give
> While yet we may, as far as words can give,
> Substance and life to what I feel, enshrining,
> Such is my hope, the spirit of the Past
> For future restoration. . . .
>
> (12:282–6)

In such a passage, the ideal is more personal than cultural, but it is cultural too. The ideal is a second Bleak House, a going-back that acknowledges a difference, some loss of prelapsarian energy compensated by the humanizing wisdom, the respect for endurance, that a right maturity can provide. Further, Wordsworth's "trust / in what we *may* become" (8:649–50) anticipates the hope of the Victorians, that the domestic hearth will constitute an enclave invulnerable to the corruption that surrounds it, which then will gradually, quietly spread outward to cleanse that corruption: those who are receptive to spirit "from their native selves can send abroad / Kindred mutations" (14:93–4).

Not feudal castles or druidic temples constitute earliness to Wordsworth, as we view them mouldering in *The Prelude*'s scenes of permanent nature. Nature is the earliness and a standard against which all is judged. As a chief example, the French Revolution is finally condemned because, while it promises the earliness of nature "in a people from the depth / Of shameful imbecility uprisen, / Fresh as the morning star" (9:383–5), its leaders "Had plucked up mercy by the roots" (10:332). The revolution was like "the sun / That rose in splendor" but which, "turned into a gewgaw, a machine / Sets like an Opera phantom" (11:364–5,369–70), another victim to lateness and its artificialities.[11]

Yet even nature is finally supplanted, in what is the implicit, then explicit crisis of *The Prelude*, by the imagination: that "awful Power" rising "from the mind's abyss / Like an unfathered vapour. . . ." (6:594–5). It is "unfathered" because beyond or prior to time, even the earliest time of nature; it is linked to an "infinitude," "our being's heart and home," origin and destiny, "whether we be young or old" (6:609–11). This and the apocalyptic reinterpretation of nature following from it would seem a vertical time as audacious as any, and its realization gives force to Wordsworth's restorative hopes, personal and cultural. But it is a hope, *that* is its dwelling, "With hope it is, hope that can never die" (606). But this is also a hope that never will be fully realized, a "something *evermore* about to be" (608). This famous phrase means cheerfully to transform Wordsworth's disappointment by suggesting the imagination's power always to desire a greater. But, as we saw in contrasting Thoreau to Wordsworth, Wordsworth's lateness would seem not only an apolitical retreat from the world but a retreat to a private hope that to an American would be a national despair.

To Wordsworth's "something evermore about to be," Whitman, in the full glory of earliness, would reply "It is":

> It is not far. . . . it is within reach,
> Perhaps you have been on it since you were born and
>   did not know,
> Perhaps it is every where on water and on land.
>
> (46:1209–11)

Like Wordsworth, Whitman desires the early, but he does not ask for a return where none is necessary; and the absence of a developmental biography for Walt is concommitant with this. While Wordsworth longs for a return with a difference to a past Eden, for Whitman the past matters at all only for its contribution to a present from which no escape is desired.

The geographical expanse of the nation, in which different regions display widely varied stages of civilization, takes care of any anxiety caused by a lack of national history; but it is all essentially young, and "Song of Myself" is a hymn to earliness, as the resistless verbs of activity imply the most robust, youthful exuberance. The simultaneity of vertical time accords with this earliness, though a pristine logic would argue that it could not: how can the universal-immediate accord with temporal terms like early and late? The easy answer, for Whitman as for Thoreau, is that only earliness allows for the pure sighting of universals. Whitman refuses Wordsworth's hope, for hope is a historical emotion based on a present lack and a future good. And while that may describe acutely the American cultural situation in Whitman's time, it is the poem's achievement to see that nervous hope as utterly unnecessary to an American present filled to joyful bursting. In other words, it is the poem's achievement to need nothing more and to assign over the anxious, rationalizing aspects of futurism to England and to a poem called, after all, *The Prelude*.

3

The sustained but increasingly difficult friendship between Emerson and Carlyle, begun on Emerson's first visit to England and deepened by his subsequent championing of the American publication of *Sartor Resartus* at a time when Carlyle could find no British publisher, is the best-known fact in Anglo-American literary relations of this period. Yet the friendship issues in one only literary event, Emerson's reply to Carlyle's *On Heroes* in *Representative Men*.

When we turn from the epics of self, those epics-as-lyrics of Wordsworth and Whitman, to this pairing, we are refreshed by the bolder simplicity. History for Carlyle and Emerson, here though not at all everywhere, will mean in a more usual way, as publically authorized social event. Differences will be stark, too, and will issue from a blatant central agreement. Both Carlyle and Emerson wish to defeat various determinisms and mechanical forms of rationalism by insisting, with slight qualifications, upon the priority of unique human personalities in the shaping of the world.

For Carlyle, this implies an anything-is-possible-anytime view of history, and René Wellek is right to assign Carlyle to the general German tradition of Fichte, Schelling, and Hegel, "variously labeled as 'historicism' or 'organology' in which the concept of development is, as it is not in Hegel, unpredictable . . . with no definite goal in history." The historian's method is "not causal, scientific, aiming at generalizations and even laws, but interpretative, intuitive, and even divinatory."[12] The historian of heroes, like the hero himself, enacts God's will but not, to human recognition at least, any progressive plan of God. An informed organicism — "Society has its periods of sickness and vigour, of youth, manhood, decrepitude, dissolution, and new birth," Carlyle writes[13] — and, within that, a casual idea of periodical alternation is as far as Carlyle usually will go toward defining patterns.

But we must hurry to add that Carlyle's universe is not uncontrolled, nor is human personality. Though the divine historical plan is unknowable, it exists; and flux nonetheless tends progressively. Cycles form a spiral, as in Herder's theory; and Charles Frederick Harrold insists rightly that Carlyle combined Calvinism and German Idealism to arrive at a doctrine of "Eternal Growth." Harrold concludes, "behind all transiency he saw the unchanging Ideal, the God behind the Garment. . . . In *Sartor*, time is the world's vast 'seedfield'; and change and death are but evidences of the undying, indwelling force which works out an infinite and eternal design."[14] There, in *Sartor*, Carlyle's Teufelsdröckh finally quiets his rage at the mechanical, God- and life-denying present age by meditating the figure of the Phoenix, from whose ashes of the old way "a new heavenborn young one will arise. . ." Or again, " 'Society,' says he, is not dead: that Carcass, which you call dead Society, is but her mortal coil which she has shuffled-off, to assume a nobler; she herself, through perpetual meta-morphoses, in fairer and fairer development, has to live till Time also merges in Eternity."[15]

Thus is the anxiety of lateness, Teufelsdröckh's "Everlasting No," vanquished in *Sartor,* though even there the Professor represents not all of Carlyle but his youthful and not disowned idealism. In *On Heroes,* Carlyle refuses to proclaim a like victory. He will not allow his faith any longer to underlie his fear. Each will get its voice, rage will rail and hope will promise, deliberately to no resolution.

At times in *On Heroes* a divine progress in human history is implied: in the image of the "Tree Igdrasil," in a fleeting typological trope whereby, for instance, Luther is made a type of Jesus, in occasional comments that call history a revelation. But the very number of these not-coordinated images dilutes their power; and Carlyle's greater stress on the image of fire, here less Phoenixlike than as either the immediate excitement of the cultural spirit's blaze into life, as the Heraclitean symbol of change, or as a moral-prophetic warning against corruption, argue against a seriously held conviction of a scheme operating through time. When Carlyle asserts one or another scheme, it is for the purpose of furthering some other, more central assertion.

Yet the structure of *Heroes* is openly informed by just such a scheme. It is neither apocalyptic or entropic, as some critics have claimed. It is a simple mourning of historical decline in the key of cultural lateness to which we are used—a key that does not sound inevitable dissolution but a call to reform. Carlyle evidences everywhere a worry, much like George Eliot's one-quarter-century later *Middlemarch,* that heroism has been reduced progressively to the point where its very possibility is doubtful. This worry mingles with a more blatant confidence that heroism is potential anywhere, anytime, and has remained a differently clothed constant. What seems a total contradiction results in a Jeremiad, for to the extent that a lateness culture renders heroism impossible, it commits a crime against the very essence of life.

Carlyle's opening chapter poses as a timorous apology for crediting certain pagan ideas. But this is Carlyle having immense rhetorical fun, as he is really putting forth a very aggressive argument for the supremecy of the (not-primitive but) first cultures. He begins "The Hero as Divinity" by posing as a veddy civilized Christian English gentleman looking with proper shock upon the "hideous inextricable jungle of misworships," the "distracted chaos of hallucinations" by which Odin's culture "worshipped their fellow-man as a God, and not him only, but stocks and stones, . . ."[16] Carlyle evinces "sorrow and silence over the depths of darkness" displayed herein, along with a deliberately clichéd, liberal-humanist joy in "the purer vision" to which man "has attained" in present Christian orthodoxy. The study of animism, then, appears worthy only to discover what crudeness has been, and still must be, refined out of our belief.

But with the assertion "Such things were and are in man; in all men; in us too" (4), Carlyle begins to undercut his progressive tenet and moves to an odd second stage in his argument, odd because he seeks at once to establish some validity in pagan animism and to mock the modern world for retaining elements of it. This paganism is not mere quackery, for "isms" that gain currency "have all had a truth in them, or men would not have taken them up." The Tibetans "have their belief . . . that Providence sends down always an Incarnation of Himself into every generation: At bottom some belief in a kind of Pope!" Their "only error" was the belief that this man is discoverable, but if their methods of discovery were rude, what are we to say of "our methods,—of understanding him to be always the eldest born of a certain genealogy?" (5). At once, Carlyle is crediting paganism with a wisdom equal to our own and calling this shared wisdom into question by attaching it to the debased modern facts of papacy and inheritance laws. By now, progressive history has been modulated into a notion of continuity and permanence, a level landscape of then and now always mixing truth and falsehood.

In refusing the other prevalent view of paganism as mere poetic allegory on the grounds that any allegory rests upon a belief, Carlyle at first continues to ply his faint praise: "There was a kind of fact at the heart" of the Pagan ages, "in their own poor way true and sane." But this last condescension leads to Carlyle's third, final, more real view: the pagan is decisively superior to the modern. "This Universe, ah me—what could the wild man know of it; what can we yet know? (8). The mysteries that the Pagan honestly confronts still confront us. Yet we employ our false learnings, our sciences, to circumvent this confrontation: "It is not by our superior insight that we escape the difficulty; it is by our superior levity, our inattention, our *want* of insight." Pagan animism explains the world in ways that retain the world's mystery and encourage awe; in sad contrast, "Hardened round us, encasing wholly every notion we form, is a wrappage of traditions, hearsays, mere *words*" (8). Again, "What in such a time as ours it requires a Prophet or Poet to teach us, namely, the stripping-off of those poor undevout wrappages, nomenclatures, and scientific hearsays—this, the ancient, earnest soul, as yet unencumbered with these things, did for itself" (9). This is, of course, the lexicon of cultural lateness once more, with its declamation against obfuscating clutter and its call for us to return to an originary state, though in Carlyle that return is not to the Christian garden but to the attitude that precedes it and all myths: wonder. From this point of *Heroes* forward, paeons to "the young generations of the world" abound, and always in nostalgic contrast to present thought: the world as Tree compared with "The 'Machine of the Universe,'—alas, do but think of that in contrast" (21). The very worst paganism is better: "Witchcraft worshipped at least a living Devil; but this worships a dead iron Devil; no God, not even a Devil!" (173).

Carlyle thus participates in the nostalgia Walter Houghton sees as a major component of the Victorian heroic ideal. It is to Houghton not just an attempt to embolden the contemporary spirit but equally an escape from it, "a flight *from* thwarted impulses *to* an ideal fulfillment," a compensation for "the ennui and frustration which accompanied the collapse of traditional belief . . . the mood of weakness."[17] All of Carlyle's cries against skepticism; his insistences upon first definitions; and, most, his espousal of hero worship, that "tap-root" of all pagan roots, than which "No nobler feeling. . . than this of admiration for one higher than himself dwells in the breast of man" (11)—in short, his entire project is grounded in the conviction of cultural lateness with its attendant hope for an eternal return.

That hope is real. It depends upon permanent human capacities and responses unaffected by even the steepest historical decline. Yet Carlyle's very announcements of this permanence are infiltrated by the conviction of decline in a rhetoric strained to the breaking point: "Yes, from Norse Odin to English Samuel Johnson, from the divine Founder of Christianity to the withered Pontiff of Encyclopedism, in all times and places, the Hero has been worshipped. It will ever be so" (15). The withered second terms of each pairing call the assertion into some question, qualify it without making it plainly ironic. And the sequence of chapters in *Heroes* which this passage points to—The Hero as Divinity, Prophet, Poet, Priest, Man of Letters, King—makes the same double-statement. The sequence implies both persistence and diminution, and Carlyle plays on the paradox. Of the hero as a man of letters, "with his copy-rights and copy-wrongs," he remarks, "Few shapes of Heroism can be more unexpected," then continues, "Alas, the Hero from of old has had to cramp himself into strange shapes: the world knows not well at any time what to do with him, so foreign is his aspect in the world!" (154,155). Yet this "cramping" has not been mentioned heretofore and seems more significantly peculiar than constant. Indeed, the man of letters serves a purpose "ever the highest; and was once well known to be highest" (155). That it no longer is so well known matters, and there is the implication of a growing skeptical pride that hinders generous worship and diminishes the hero's field of action. But even this diminishment may not be negative. The hero-as-poet is "less ambitious, but also less questionable" (78) than his earlier manifestations. And perhaps there is no diminishment, perhaps "our notions of God are ever rising *higher;* not altogether that our reverence for these qualities . . . is getting lower." But then Carlyle immediately rails against skeptical dilettantism, "the curse of these ages," which makes reverence "all crippled, blinded, paralytic" (84).

The figure of the final lecture, "The Hero as King," Carlyle asserts, "may be reckoned the most important of Great Men. He is practically the summary for us of *all* the various figures of Heroism" (196). We seem to be concluding in affirmation. We are not. The sequence here crucially complicates its hitherto chronological progress. The nineteenth century is not a good one for kings, and we rarely in any time choose the kingly man as our king. The summarizing king is made more an ideal than a living possibility, and this caps the growing split between the ideal and its historical realization. Further, Carlyle's first example, Cromwell, is as much a revolutionary beheader of kings as he is a king himself; and his second and final figure, Napoleon, a disastrous pseudoking who also follows upon revolution, is characterized as "a great implement wasted, till it was useless: our last Great Man" (243). "*Our* last, in a double sense," Carlyle concludes, saying merely that the series of lectures is ending. But the real play is not on "our" but "last," which can mean most recent or final. And by this pun Carlyle carries to the last his ambivalence. "That man, in some sense or other, worships Heroes" is "to me, the living rock amid all rushings-down whatsoever;—the one fixed point in modern history, otherwise as if bottomless and shoreless" (15). But Napoleon, if he is a hero at all, makes hero worship itself "bottomless and shoreless." The "Sceptical World," the "Unbelieving Century" is to blame. "Till this alter, nothing can beneficially alter." Carlyle's "one hope" and "inexpungable consolation in looking at the miseries of the world, is that this is altering" (175). "Here and there" a man is grasping "that this world is a Truth," but we have no hero to dramatize the fact, which seems hope indeed and only.

The hope may consist finally not in a providential history, not positively in the human desire for heroes, which begins to look less and less everlasting: "The Eighteenth was a sceptical century" and its muttering proclamation, that "Heroism was gone forever; Triviality, Formulism, and Commonplace were come forever" (170–71), is yet to be refuted. Still, elsewhere, "Hero-worship never dies, nor can die" (126). Hope consists in the inspirited study of history. For Carlyle's history is the opposite of Thoreau's "accumulated baggage" and "trumpery." By personalizing the mundane shell, he means to strip "the wrappages of tradition"; if the dead word of rationalist science robs mystery, "Do not Books still accomplish *miracles*, as *Runes* were fabled to do? They persuade men" (160). Paganism will never repeat itself but its best attribute, "that, once discovered, we ought to treat him [the hero] with an obedience which knows no bounds" (5), *that* might still be.

"Till this alter, nothing can beneficially alter"—how far is this desperate faith from the tone of Kenneth Marc Harris's otherwise good account of the Carlyle-Emerson relation. For Carlyle, he says, "The purpose of historiography is to clarify the lessons of the past for those engaged in creating the present and future."[18] More truly, for Carlyle, historiography is no schoolboy's tome but the only salvation. "Great men are the inspired (speaking and acting) Texts of that divine BOOK OF REVELATION, whereof a chapter is completed from epoch to epoch, and by some named HISTORY," Carlyle writes in *Sartor*.[19] This is the official Carlyle, who sees secular and spiritual history radically intertwined, and his metaphor of nature as a writing implies his own responsibility as historian and visionary to be heroic. It is to this Carlyle that Emerson's radical Protestant soul is led: to the Carlyle who writes, "The Hero taken as Divinity; the Hero taken as Prophet; then next the Hero taken only as Poet: does it not look as if our estimate of the Great Man, epoch after epoch, were continually diminishing?" and yet can reply to himself, "It looks so; but I persuade myself that intrinsically it is not so" (84). Yet the epochs did not fashion the sequence of the book; Carlyle did. And a part (only a part) of Carlyle is less "persuaded" by immutability or even by an apocalyptic fire than by the slow autumnal drizzle of lateness. This is another Carlyle whom Emerson acknowledged—"a very unhappy man;—profoundly solitary, displeased and hindered by all men and things about him" (W,VI,242). But with this Carlyle, a monument of lateness that "avenged itself by celebrating the majestic beauty of decay," Emerson could have nothing to do.

That makes one reason why the relation of *Representative Men* to *Heroes* is not particularly competitive, certainly less so than the American replies we have considered: Emerson will not engage his worthy friend on the low ground of simple optimism. Nor should we be so purely literary as to discount the friendship as a brake to competition. But more importantly, Emerson's model of heroism refuses the meanness of personal debate. The great man is too involved with expressing his unique selfhood to come out fighting: that would be a self-accusation of reactive, secondary status. "He is great who is what he is from nature, and who never reminds us of others" (W,IV,6). Still, Emerson's lectures, following closely upon the publication of *Heroes* and encouraged by Carlyle's urgings, must constitute a reply. And however self-confident and goodnatured the motive, accentuated difference will be the result.

Scope is the expected strength that Emerson deploys: he will make everything that Carlyle means by "history" a small and dissolving portion of what he means by the world's reality, and in this Emerson takes the usual profit of American earliness. Indeed, magnitude is one implication of Emerson's title. "Representative men" is a phrase first employed by Carlyle himself. Vacillating between an idea of the hero as constituting and as constituent, he emphasizes his second position in calling heroes "representative" of their cultures.[20] Emerson's men are representative "first, of things, and secondly, of ideas" (8). That is, Emerson's men begin as outgrowths of the earth and end by dissolving themselves into timeless aspects of permanent human being. Thus, Emerson begins by punning on nature: "It is natural to believe in great men," children believe in the heroic capacities of their playmates, "All mythology opens with demigods," and "In the legends of the Gautama, the first men ate the earth and found it deliciously sweet" (3). First things—the earliest stages of individual, imaginative, and collective life—bring forth heroes who "make the earth wholesome." Emerson's heroes thus are made, by this striking conjunction, earlier, more earthily primitive, than Carlyle's men who are "a flowing light-fountain" provided "by the gift of Heaven" (12). But Emerson's heroes are later as well, for each of Carlyle's men flourishes in and for a particular era while, to Emerson, "The genius of humanity is the real subject whose biography is written in our annals" (32). If history is biography, biography itself is archetype. Thus Emerson names his first chapter "Uses of Great Men," making even the greatest individual an agency only, "an exhibition, in some quarter, of new possibilities" (32–3). Thus, too, the chapter on Plato quickly becomes a treatise on dialectical thought, the chapter on Montaigne an anatomy of doubt. Indeed, Emerson judges each hero by the size of his representation. Plato merges East and West while the ultimately shabby Napoleon represents only the new men while opposing the old, and new and old together constitute a mere fraction of the human self, the selfishly economic aspect. Emerson dramatizes himself as more supple than

Carlyle as well as larger—larger because Carlyle's men of society exist in the middle time of public history while Emerson's men are the dreams of children and the outlines of being.

This, then, is the chief difference between Carlyle and Emerson. Carlyle's self-conflict pits an historical sense of decline against a wavering belief in a permanent value, still historically visible if infinite at its edges. Emerson blatantly employs history unto its dissolution into invisible qualities.

It is a profound disagreement. It has to do with the nature of the world. In practice, the world is magnificently present for Carlyle even if he can speak in fleeting abstraction of the world as a projection of each person's thought. For Emerson, thought is prior, causal, almost all in all. Five of his six representative men are philosophers or poets and his accounts of his subjects' circumstantial lives are comically rushed, because "Great geniuses have the shortest biographies" (43). It is no surprise that "the biography of Plato is interior," but even in the chapter significantly titled "Napoleon, or The Man of the World," Emerson emphasizes that Bonaparte "won his battles in his head before he won them on the field" (232). Events and lands, trade and travel become thoughts: Plato, "finding himself still capable of a larger synthesis . . . travelled into Italy, to gain what Pythagoras had for him; then into Egypt, and perhaps still farther East, to import the other element, which Europe wanted, into the European mind" (42). Or again, after proclaiming that unity and variety are the basics of all things and all thoughts, Emerson converts the world into "The unity of Asia and the detail of Europe; the infinitude of the Asiatic soul and the defining, result-loving, machine-making, surface-seeking, opera-going Europe" (53–54). When his hero is too European, a social planner, that is cause for allegorical reinterpretation—"All his painting in the Republic must be esteemed mythical, with intent to bring out, sometimes in violent colors, his thought. You cannot institute, without peril of charlatanism" (89)—or for fault finding—"I am sorry to see him, after such noble superiorities, permitting the lie to governors" (89).

This refusal of the conventionally historical is not a mere predilection. It is based on an idea. "History," he had written, "is a shallow village tale," true if at all as an account of immorality, the "old chronology of selfishness and pride" (CW,II,22). And in the chapter on Montaigne, Emerson discloses the ontology underlying these dismissals. The social world argues cynicism. It makes of "free agency . . . the emptiest name" (177), turns practice against theory, and tempts the noble young only to frustrate them. No reply to the bafflements of circumstantial life exists within it; but "The final solution in which skepticism is lost, is seen in the moral sentiment, which never forfeits its supremacy" (183). This alone allows us to see that "through evil agents, through toys and atoms, a great and beneficent tendency irresistably streams" (186). This is Emerson's most pointed response to Carlyle. In 1835, he had criticized Carlyle for being "most limited" in regard to that for which he is popularly praised, "in his Religion and immortality from the removal of Time and Space" (*JMN*,V,111–12). And this was written before Carlyle concentrated his writing upon history. Here in *Representative Men*, Emerson is telling Carlyle plainly that he is looking for salvation in the wrong place, "My dear friend, standing on his mountains of fact" (*J*,VII,125, corrected), in the world of history-as-usual.

But here is Emerson writing a history book or a replacement for it, and how is he to do so with a scorn for the world of facticity? A first response is to recall that Emerson does not scorn the real unless it usurps the ideal and thereby becomes unreal. Still, an historical chronology of a man's outer life will not do honor to Emerson's drive toward qualities while an enumeration of those qualities strictly in terms of what we have been calling vertical time precludes all narrative and particularity. Emerson's answer is to practice upon his heroes Plato's discovery, "a science of sciences,—I call it Dialectic" that "rests on the observation of identity and diversity" (62). The entire work is structured by twos, by opposing terms viewed in their capacity for ascension by merger. Carlyle had scolded Emerson after the publication of *Essays: Second Series* (1844) as "You Western Gymnosophist" (*L*,371). Emerson accepts the epithet punningly. For the claustrophobia of chronological history, Emerson substitutes his "new gymnasium" in which occur "the somersaults, spells, and resurrections wrought by the imagination. When this wakes," he continues, "a man seems to multiply ten times or a thousand times his force. It opens the delicious sense of indeterminate size and inspires an audacious mental habit" (17). That is, Emerson's biographies bespeak Emerson more widely than in his "Emersonizing" of his subjects. They become an autobiographical inscription of the most intimate kind, a record of the rhythms of his spacious thought and an assertion of his power over history.

Carlyle recognized autobiography as the inevitable result of his own writing. He evidences this understanding in his urging that Emerson treat "some concrete thing" in a manner "filled with the life of Emerson." This is so clearly an attempt to persuade Emerson to go Carlyle's way that Carlyle speaks of facts in a manner designed to please Emerson, as mere conduits for vision. But he then advises an obscuring of this subjectivity: the "thing" once Emersonized is to be "cast forth from him then to live by itself" (L,215) in a kind of second-stage objectivity. Instead, Emerson moves his dialectics to center stage and makes his "somersaults" his real subject.

Sometimes the bipolarities are set in play by analogical expansions. Plato combines diversity and unity—the West and East, the real and ideal, the pigment and aether, the limit and the illimitable, which is Socrates and himself, "this Aesop of the mob and the robed scholar," which is Socrates in himself, "rare coincidence, in one ugly body, of the droll and the martyr, the keen street and market debater with the sweetest saint," and which is Plato too in himself, for "The strange synthesis in the character of Socrates capped the synthesis in the mind of Plato" (75).

Emerson's final somersault, nonetheless, is to note the lack of passion in Plato and thus to keep the dialectic free of even his encompassment. Elsewhere, the bipolarities merge to the reduction of each and both. Napoleon is already marked as beneath Plato in occupying only one half of the "standing antagonism between the conservative and the democratic classes" (223). Here, though, the enumeration of each side leads to reiteration more than wholeness, for selfishness and economic materialism propel both classes. When Napoleon, through his illiberal amorality, comes finally to encompass both halves, this is no enlargement, for the terms have been made to dwindle into one fatally narrow strait. "The democrat is a young conservative; the conservative is an old democrat," Emerson decides. "The counter-revolution, the counter-party, still waits for its organ and representative, in a lover and a man of truly public and universal aims" (256–57).

That man is revealed typically to be Emerson himself in the essay on Montaigne. Though Emerson warns in that essay that idealism leads men "like dreaming beggars" to "assume to speak and act as if these values were already substantiated" (151), he is indeed true to that habit of American futurism to find the future good in the present and, most audaciously, in the self. The dialectic here concerns action and genius, the men of practical power and the senses and the men who "have the perception of identity" (150): it is West and East once more, with all the associations built up in the essay on Plato. Here, though, each side "drives too fast" (150). Genius gets ridiculously dreamy while Practicality becomes indifferent, cynical. In the spirit of Montaigne's time, Emerson stresses the middle way and places Montaigne triumphantly there. His skepticism is thus distinguished from the cynicism of the practical. But Emerson is not finally of Montaigne's time, and a middle way is not enough for him. It is not the equal of a transcending merger. Plato "said Culture; he said, Nature; and he failed not to add, 'There is also the Divine'" (67). This third term Montaigne lacks, and his rank is thus itself middle, lower than Plato if above Napoleon. Emerson does include the divine third term and thus becomes his own final representative man. But he is not Carlyle's hero as historian; he is the hero as destroyer of history. If Carlyle derides Emerson as "a *Soliloquizer* on the eternal mountain-tops only" (*L*,371), Emerson will accept the criticism—"Well it is even so"—and return the derision by turning Carlyle's phrase to see him "standing on his mountains of facts." He thus makes his friend representative of the nation that best exemplifies the solid, earthbound, and thus disastrously partial side of dialectical reality. Further, Emerson employs futurism to offset Carlyle's call for a return to an earlier worship with a call for a future never before realized in history. "The mass of creatures and of qualities are still hid and expectant" (9). Each hero has been only a point: "Could we one day complete the immense figure which these flagrant points compose" (33). "All that respects the individual is temporary and prospective" (34) and we continue to await that counterparty of love and universal aims to combat the world as it is now and has been in history ever.

To achieve this, Emerson knows as well as Whitman, we need not simply ways of defeating the past and its limited expectations. We need a man or woman who is one with a nation, and both person and nation must be one with those permanent qualities into which, for Emerson, mere individuality must dissolve. This is as nothing to say: it is the shockingly literal quality of the American saying of it which matters. Thought is to produce the land, not in a trope but in the real time that will replace history. This is American actualism and we need to describe it more fully before we can complete our relating of these two pairs of texts.

Five

REDEEMING THE REAL

9

AMERICAN ACTUALISM

I am naming as American actualism the most dramatic difference between the British and American literatures of the nineteenth century. By actualism, I mean the attempt to make literary vision literally available to everyday living. Actualism is mimeticism in reverse, life imitating art, and in a manner having nothing to do with *fin de siècle* aestheticism and everything to do with the sense of the possible in dawn-driven America.

Before filling out this definition to make it meaningful, I must stress the power of the kind of literary realism that American actualism is meant to oppose. In having emphasized American attempts to challenge the authority of history and its junior partner, linear time, I have not intended to imply that the literary representation of linear or successive time is a simple matter, much less a failure of imagination. Many of the American romantics would characterize realistic literature so, but they speak in part defensively. They are confronted not only by the amazing chronicle of British history but more pressingly by the contemporary British achievement in fiction with its magnificent capacity to create the illusion of an everyday world. Texts are not life, and though print moves down a page and language is successive, such succession has little intimately or inherently to do with the chronology we experience outside of texts. Chronos in the novel is no given but an invention and an achievement; the social realism of any literary work is a persuasive imagining; and there is not one kind of linear time or one kind of social realism attached to it but as many varieties and complications of each as there are writers. These are schoolboy lessons but they need to be repeated ritualistically by grownup Americanists like me, who easily err in adopting the dismissive attitudes of American writers. If they ally successive time and literary realism to a low common sense and an unthinking acceptance of the harshly limited life of society, we must not accept these equations as inevitable; we must ask why the American romantics derogate realism in these terms.

Two replies suggest themselves. There is indeed a defensive aspect to the refusal of Victorian literary realism by American romantic writers. The American sense that England has something of a monopoly upon ordinary reality is as much a judgment of English literature as of English society and history. When Emerson praises "the rude warm blood of the living England," (W,IV,193), is he speaking of the life of the streets or of the life of the streets as presented in the works of Dickens? He perhaps does not know nor do we need to. In literature and in life, America cannot compete with what Emerson calls "the best of actual nations" (W,V,299) on grounds of ordinary reality.

But Emerson's sly ambivalence in his compliment to England suggests a different kind of nation-idea where America might prevail. It derives not just from the need to defend against British influence but from the recovery of a native attitude concerning the relation between thought and living. And it naturally would make Americans skeptical of British realism and the mind-set that realism would imply. Thus in a conciliatory moment the mature Emerson can praise "the fine practical understanding of the English, and the American adventure" (CW, IV, 281). My business here is to show what Emerson means by the American adventure, which is equivalent to what James means by "the American's secret." And the American refusal of British realism is a first consideration.

The philosophical belief that the external world is real and that our senses record that world accurately; the impression of fidelity to human social experience; the emphasis on the dignity and importance of individual experience among ordinary people; the detailed presentation of a social environment with an eye to particulars to create a solidity of setting; the development of human character in the course of time, with time and its circumstances the shaping force of individual and collective history; a liberal-humanist faith in the very gradual improvement of the general human condition; a plain idea of language and literature as socially referential—these are some of the rough definitions by which Ian Watt and other historians of realism attempt to characterize the British tradition of prose fiction that begins with Defoe, extends through Scott and Austen to Dickens, Thackeray, and Eliot, and continues in diminished achievements to the present.[1] Such scholars are quick to point out the insufficiency of these descriptions, especially of any extreme positivist doctrine, to account for the English novel.

But the American romantics, I believe, would find such descriptions true enough, particularly because these descriptions might go to suggest American differences and because differences were what the Americans hoped to find. For instance, a New England writer would locate in his intellectual history an idea of the external world as not real in its own right but as a sometimes baffling hieroglyph of universal law and divine intent. Or again, he would discover a native propensity to view time typologically or cyclically or as a cognitive outcome, not as an external, secular, and successive determinant. More interestingly, however, he also would find himself in agreement with some of the tenets of realism, especially those which can be seen as coincident with a democratic ethic. And it is in the divergent consequences that arise from these initial agreements that American actualism most interestingly defines itself away from British realism.

At times, American writers speak as if they wish to become all-absorbent and to outdo British realism on its own terms by merely representing American scenes. The response to British taunts (and to native fears) of the vacancy of an American scene is a more extreme and even primitive mimeticism than we are accustomed to. Mircea Eliade tells us that, for the Australian aborigine, "every rock, spring, and water hole represents a concrete trace of a sacred drama carried out in the mythical times"[2] and the American landscape is something like that for the Puritan typologist. For our later, secular writers too, America is the place where heightened reality really happens, however reality is defined. James McIntosh, differentiating Thoreau from English and European romantics, writes that he "is attracted not only to mists and crags, as part of the romantic heritage, but also to weeds, swarming insects, small ponds, and individual trees."[3] Likewise, in regard to a different kind of reality, Charles Brockden Brown finds gothic effects historically realized in America:

> Puerile superstitions and exploded manners, Gothic castles and chimeras, are the materials usually employed for this end [of calling forth the passions]. The incidents of Indian hostility, and the perils of the Western wilderness are far more suitable; . . .[4]

That is, the American need wring his imagination less than Europeans because the American experience is so much more imaginatively fulfilling in itself. Just so, when Thoreau wishes to praise savagery, he is not speaking of a "literary" or far-off quality as do English and European writers in comparable discussions; his "wild" is synonymous with his term "the west," and that "west," however metaphorical it becomes, really exists on this American continent and really is a wild.

One need not even search out the extreme since America's most common aspects are remarkable. Thoreau describes his immediate locale as "luxuriously crowded without margin" and Theodore Parker argued: "Common things are not . . . unclean. In plain New England life he [the native writer] finds his poetry, as magnets iron in the black-smith's dust. . . . It is not for him to rave of Parnassus, while he know it not, for the soul of song has a seat upon Monadnoc, Wachusett, or Katahdin, quite as high."[5] Nor need the uncommon common in America be restricted to virgin nature. Emerson found "Our log-rolling, our stumps and their politics, our Negroes and Indians, our boats and repudiations" potentially poetic (CW,III,22), for "Thought makes everything fit for use" (11). And Whitman, who realized the potential Emerson claimed, defines the duty of the modern imagination "to give ultimate vivification to facts, to science, and to common lives, endowing them with the glows and glories and final illustriousness which belong to every real thing, and to real things only."[6]

Is the self of actualism then more nationally absorbent than nationally creative? Not so, for this celebration of American givens depends on a trick we begin to see in the language of Emerson and Whitman above. It is a meditated America, an idea of America, that is so rich; if the writers sometimes humbly obscure the meditative element, that is in defensive reply to the British taunts of American barrenness. Elsewhere they are more frank. E. T. Channing will say that Brown's characters live in a richly gothic world because they are forever "associating every thing around them with their own minds."[7] And Emerson in "The Poet" wishes "to see trifles animated by a tendency." Because "The Universe is the externization of the soul" (CW,III,9), the mystical American Land is really the American, that self we spoke of earlier as a replacement for history. "It is nature the symbol, nature certifying the supernatural" (10) that is imbued with consciousness. Thus, "The poorest experience is rich enough for all the purposes of expressing thought" (11) as Emerson goes on to emphasize "the independence of the thought on the symbol, the stability of the thought, the ascendency and fugacity of the symbol" (12); and by "symbol" here, Emerson means what we usually call "thing," for by this moment of his argument, all things "are emblems" (12). As usual when Emerson seems to argue for the sufficient interest of the world, that world is essentially consciousness.

Emerson is not consistently extreme in his essay: he elsewhere speaks of "the divine *aura* which breathes through forms" (15) and asks the poet merely to give himself up to that. But that aura seems most prevalent in the form we call the mind; and even when Emerson says "America is a poem in our eyes" (22), we sense that our eyes are seeing a vision that they themselves have sent out, for Emerson has insisted earlier, "All form is an effect of character" (8). What Tony Tanner says of Emerson is true of this apparent American realism generally: "Although Emerson is sometimes very specific about individual facts and perceptions, the nature he refers to has no autonomy and very little local identity. It is a mental fabrication."[8] Elsewhere, indeed, Emerson is willing to hypothesize that the first reality, world-as-given, is not truly given but "the apocalypse of the mind." All of our everyday environment, oceans and mountains and not just shops and houses, are our imaginings made real. That is, if a poet self-knowingly can replace the usual environment with his vision, then perhaps even the usual environment that we experience as world-as-given is itself an imaginative projection that we have ceased to acknowledge as of our making. Emerson stands Locke upon his head.

We mistake rhetorical strategy for solid fact, then, if we imagine that the American romantics merely recorded a poem written in the land. American realism—and the term realism is becoming increasingly inapt in this context—means to imitate not any quasi-objective social reality but the divine imagination existent in all beings and then to transfer that divinity into a palpable landscape. "Who hath access to this universal mind," Emerson writes in the opening paragraph of "History," "is a party to all that is or can be done, for this is the only and sovereign agent" (CW,II,3).

This is how American writers, beginning with the same excitement over the literary possibilities of common life and low objects as the English realists—"I embrace the common, I explore and sit at the feet of the familiar, the low," Emerson writes in "The American Scholar" (CW,I,67)—end in major opposition to them. The truly objective reality for them is nothing like what we commonly take as a world of facticity. The imagination alone is fact. There is no unimagined world; that world, which Emerson called "the terrible *is*" in a letter to Carlyle, is a simulacrum created by a failure of imagination. Thus Thoreau in *Walden* simplifies appetites to banish the world of circumstances that the Victorian novelist would insist upon. Thus Dickinson, as Sandra Gilbert writes, transformed the minutiae of her life—the narrow, circumstance-hedged round of domestic events and objects available to her as a woman living in a particular place at a specific time— "into the mysteries of her art," capitalizing on her social circumscription to undo it.[9] Thus and more largely, Richard Poirier writes memorably that American texts "resist within their pages the forces of environment that otherwise dominate the world." By an "eccentricity of defiance," they "both resemble and serve their heroes by trying to create an environment of 'freedom' . . . as if history can give no life to 'freedom,' and as if only language can create the liberated place."[10] But then the vision, as Poirier himself notes, is taken as historical real-

ity—potential in Emerson, realized in Thoreau and Whitman, demonized in Poe. It is a reversed realism, then, not simply in regard to the
British notion of the real but in relation to the authentic reality of God.
Lawrence Buell convincingly argues that the dominant impulse of
American catalogue rhetoric—Emerson's strings of aphorisms, Whitman's tallyings, the enumerations of Melville's Ishmael—is "the sense
of all things in the universe as manifestations of the divine plenitude."[11] Actualism battens on particulars to recreate a holy synthesis
(not always with success, as Melville emphasizes), to put God together
again under the huge aegis of an encompassing American self.

2

We are ready to now to define American actualism on its own terms,
with its positing of a world spun out of the self. Permit me a running
start with the summary of some ideas stated earlier.

Particularly within vertical time, or most explicitly therein, the self
is history's replacement. For the American Puritan, "the connective
between the thing and the thing signified is not the sign, but the re-
generate figuralist in whom the concealed full sense is already manifested." Thereby, Sacvan Bercovitch reasons, "the prominence of the
exemplary life in colonial literature. To be an American is to assume a
prophetic identity; to have been an American is to offer a completed
action that makes destiny manifest."[12] It is not a far distance from that
to Emerson's assertion in his essay "History": "We are always coming
up with the emphatic facts of history in our private experience and
verifying them here. All history becomes subjective; in other words
there is properly no history, only biography" (CW,II,6). Nor are we
very far from Whitman's exemplary Walt, for whom, as Stephen
Spender says, "awareness of his individual self at a particular moment
was everything,"[13] or from the character of Thoreau in *Walden*. Even
as the American romantics soured on a landscape cluttered with factories and with transported Old-World conventions, they could represent
an alternative America in themselves. "Like the later-day Puritan Jere-
miahs," Bercovitch writes, "they could offer *themselves* as the symbol
incarnate, and so relocate America—transplant the entire national enterprise, en masse—into the mind and imagination of the exemplary
American."[14]

Literature, the British argument went, depends on history and its
associations, on the historical sense. Americans replied by inventing
histories out of the self or by making the self tantamount to history.
Then in a final step, the American came to see literature not as the

reflection of history but as the source of a future history. The imagination would produce a world. The self would compel everyday reality into the shape of its vision. History had become an issue of thought; future history would issue from thought. Recall again Emerson's urging, "We must realize our rhetoric and our rituals" (W,XI,530). What is *Walden* but the record of such an attempt at realization? What is "Song of Myself" but a claim that the realization has been achieved by a self who is the nation as well?

These works participate in a program which I am calling actualism. By that term I do not mean a mimetic recording of reality but something quite its opposite, a reality created by literary vision to demolish and replace the hard facts of land and industry. The text leaps beyond its bindings to become actual and informing in daily life. The text is a man, a man a world, as Whitman makes plainest in a poem that emblematizes his enterprise:

> A noiseless patient spider,
> I marked where on a little promontory it stood
>   isolated,
> Mark'd how to explore the vacant vast surrounding,
> It launched forth filament, filament, filament, out of
>   itself
> Ever unreeling them, ever tirelessly spending them.
>
> And you O my soul where you stand,
> Surrounded, detached, in measureless oceans of space,
> Ceaselessly musing, venturing, throwing, seeking the
>   spheres to connect them,
> Till the bridge you will need be form'd, till the
>   ductile anchor hold,
> Till the gossamer thread you fling catch somewhere, O
>   my soul.[15]

In his typically provocative and superb essay, "Notes for a Comparison between American and European Romanticism," Tony Tanner comments on this poem, "America is the 'measureless oceans of space'; the web is the private creation of the writer, constructed with a view of attaching himself somehow to reality, a world of his own making in which he can live on his own terms, assimilating and transforming what the outside world brings his way."[16] Tanner errs only in underestimating the audacity of actualism, for there is here no "assimilating and transforming" of a world prior to mind. That world is abolished—

social America, the one in which Whitman and his compeers live, would hardly be characterized as "measureless oceans of space"—and replaced by the fiction of a vacant, absolute expanse then populated by imaginings made actual.

In describing American actualism, I am not so much making a discovery as publicizing an important agreement that has gone unnoticed. Wherever we look in the most diverse studies of American literature and society, we find this actualist hope of American earliness central. Sacvan Bercovitch distinguishes the American Puritans from their English counterparts by their refusal to separate secular and social history: "They had come to America not to break with either the world or the kingdom, but to fulfill both. . . . Having united the visible and the spiritual, they were free to actualize the metaphors of visible sainthood (for the individual) and national election (for the community)." The idea of national election "takes on a literalness undreamed of by Luthor or Foxe" for "the settlers expected *history* to verify their dream." Leo Marx, whose study of the American pastoral idea includes the Puritans but also many other groups of settlers, states the same law in comparable terms: "With an unspoiled hemisphere in view it seemed that mankind actually might realize what had been thought a poetic fantasy." And again, "In the egalitarian social climate of America, the pastoral ideal spills over into thinking about real life" because, as Marx later explains, "The renunciation of worldly striving in favor of a simpler, more contemplative life always had been the core of the pastoral ethos; but here in the New World, the beneficent influence of an unmodified landscape makes the act credible as never before." A. N. Kaul, with an eye more to the social institutions of the nation, sees this same hope: "the importance of the virgin continent lay precisely in the fact that, as far as society and civilization are concerned, it was a *tabula rasa*, an invitation to create and construct, a visible proof that ideals need not always end in starry-eyed idealism."[17]

These scholars find the actualist hope continuing, and even strengthened, in the great texts of the nineteenth century. And other critics who begin not with a theory of literary or social origins but with a formal analysis of those texts add their agreement. Robert Hertz, comparing British and American romanticism, names as most significant a "divergence in emphasis between English obsession with the unavoidable disparity between the Real and the Ideal, and American assurance that such disparity marks only a temporary and bridgeable gap." And Richard Poirier says similarly of American romanticism, "It is as if the conventions of English romantic poetry could in America take on the life of prose, assume a reality that even history might recognize and that novels could report as news." That reality, which begins with a typically romantic internalization of what is considered real, completes itself in a distinctive act that Tanner, borrowing Emerson's phrase, calls a centrifugal tendency, "a dilation of self, which can become an abandoning of self, into the surrounding vastness."[18]

Are we not, though, claiming too much on behalf of actualism? What of Hawthorne and Melville, with their continuing insistences upon the distorting imperatives of individual and collective psyches? What of Dickinson's admissions of ontological ignorance? What of Emerson's own frustrated cry against "the feeble influence of thought on life, a ray as pale and ineffectual as that of the sun in our cold and bleak spring" (J,IV,467)? American actualism is a hope, particularly vulnerable to defeat by the extent of its claim; and indeed it is only half of a national dialectic completed by an equally extreme skepticism that I will describe in chapter eleven. Emily Dickinson defines her poetic power as consisting equally "in Vision—and in Veto" (528).

But actualism is every bit as present in its recorded failures as in its claims of realization, and this point is best made by the unlikeliest pairing in this (or perhaps any) study. In Jane Austen's *Northanger Abbey*, the heroine, appropriately named Catherine Moreland, has read too many gothic novels and attempts too literally to apply gothicism to life. When she views the ordinary social world through these melodramatic lenses, she stumbles blindly into gullibility and even unkindness. Worst, by looking for gothic villainy, she overlooks more subtle forms of real human failings. In *Pierre*, Herman Melville creates a hero who also wishes to live out romantic literature, and for his pains Melville rushes Pierre through a sunny romantic ideal to a dark, socially rebellious, romantic ideal that turns out to be equally naïve and from there to a final bewilderment approaching nihilism.

Both works are in part satires upon kinds of literature that bloat human capacity to a disguised emptiness and upon attempts to transform life into literature. But from that point they diverge to display the actualist difference. By satirizing spectacular action and overstuffed passion, Austen argues for her own way of writing. For her, the novel should find its meanings in the ordinary. It should not create another world that distorts our view of the one in which we really live, must not dismiss the surfaces of social life for abstract idealisms. Literature must help its reader to an uncommonly keen perception of the common life.

Melville's path is nowise so certain in *Pierre*. He may make a reductio ad absurdum of romantic idealism via Pierre's self-simplifying, cloyed, and unconsciously clichéd enthusiasms; but this is accompanied by a high respect for Pierre's "sterling charity." Melville ultimately satirizes his very satire by Pierre's discovery of the pamphlet "Ei" authored by one Plotinus Plinlimmon. Plinlimmon's Carlylean dichotomy between the chronometrical and the horological, between the forces of the world and divine truths, and his injunction against attempting to live in the world by other-worldly laws, might seem just the advice Pierre needs. It is not. In Warwick Wadlington's words, it "fails to carry authorial approval because with its icy temper of 'non-Benevolence,' utterly unaffiliated with the contingent, suffering human action it is distantly conscious of, it can be no more than the 'restatement of a problem' rather than 'the solution of the problem itself.' "[19] The actualist hope is a folly and a vice in a world of ambiguities; but the refusal of it is a cynicism no more responsive to the reality of warm nature and immensely less fine. Melville's satire becomes a tragedy leading not back to realism but forward as an anticipation of the literature of despair. Melville can debunk actualism's veracity but not its desire. That actualist desire, as Hawthorne's famous comment on Melville insists, is precisely what makes Melville's negations so self-terrifying.

3

Even in a chronicle of actualism's defeat—and Hawthorne's *Blithedale* is just another such—the norms of English realism are refused; for, as Ishmael poses the question punningly, "Who the devel ain't a dreamer?" The relation of American actualism to English romantic literature is far more problematic.

Certainly American actualism begins in the generally romantic aesthetic of expression whereby the external world is credited as a source for literature only as it is converted by the writer's projective imagination. But I have noted a basic difference between American and British romanticisms in other contexts at just this point of conversion. The British romantic's conversion of a factual world is private, inner, to an extent uncompetitive but grudgingly coexistent with the world out there. The American romantic wishes not only to convert the world of fact within himself but on its own external, historical ground.

We can explain and extend that difference by asking who it is making the conversion. The American "I" is not the isolated ego but the representative American we spoke of in chapter three, a self who blends his most immediate and personal being, his very seeing, with a national epistemology. Bercovitch argues that while the European-English romantic employs the creative imagination as intermediary between self and God, the American's intermediary is "the text of America."[20] The distinction is not so absolute as claimed, for the text of America is actively, differently rewritten by each writer's imagination. But the sense of the self as participating in or containing a communal destiny creates a self-nation continuum leading to the particularly American symbolism that Charles Feidelson, Jr. describes as an attempt to obliterate the old dualities of external-objective and internal-subjective.[21] Feidelson does not sufficiently credit English romanticism with its own attempt to defeat the self's alienation from otherness, but even so the English attempt is one of interpenetration (by Wordsworth's "half perceive, half create" formula) while the American attempt is one of absolute self-nation-God identity.

I am trying to describe what are finally two different views of the relations between writer and text and writer and world. My clue to this final aspect of actualism comes from poor students, not Thoreau's poor students who refuse influence and make riches of their poverty, but my own usually good students who become shockingly literal minded in reading many American texts. Why do students who fully comprehend the difference between an actual person and his or her literary persona suddenly desire to see Dickinson's lyrics as absolutely real confessions or to confuse Ishmael with Melville, Walt with Whitman, Coverdale with Hawthorne? Perhaps it is because these writers desire such a confusion, though not quite in this literalist form. Perhaps they wish to be present in their works in a way to which we still are not used.

American works assert their ontology with what John Lynen calls "the odd self-consciousness" of their symbol-making. Stephen Spender, in different terms, agrees with Lynen: "More than the European (except for a Shelleyan Romantic) the American writer *exists* in his fiction or poetry . . . One feels, reading Melville, Whitman and Hemingway, that the writer's subjective consciousness permeates the objects created." And Richard Brodhead shows Hawthorne exemplifying this process in his alternative interpretations of the red rose bush whereby "we watch a mind calling . . . multiple life into being by making use of all the resources of its own imagination."[22] It is possible to discuss the world-hypotheses of any work, but all works do not lead their own discussions of their epistemology and its results as American works tend to do. And this is no sterile, intellectualized self-consciousness. It is self-making. In his book on Yeats and American poetry, Terrence Diggory emphasizes the attraction of the Irish poet, himself concerned by British influence in his land, to that Whitman who discovers "the self as an alternative to tradition that was at the same time a new source of tradition." In British romanticism, the self is expressed; in American romanticism it is created, then externalized, and finally granted sway over externality. "To enjoy the sanction of external authority and yet to recognize that authority as the self is the definitive experience of the tradition of the self."[23]

Diggory is wrong to equate so utterly a Walt with Yeats's masks or antiselves, for Whitman's Walt is not presented as a wrought fiction but as Whitman's truest national center of being. But Diggory's claim that, in this tradition, "the self is not merely a seer but a man of action whose deeds are his poems" is persuasively supported by C. Carroll Hollis's discovery that Whitman employs performative or illocutionary utterances (phrases that perform actions, like "I christen thee the Titanic") with a frequency unparalleled in any other writer.[24]

The American text is an action that discovers the self who represents the nation. The writer's life is to be present in the text with an unprecedented immediacy—"It makes a great difference to the force of a sentence if there be a man behind it or no," Emerson writes in *Representative Men* (W,IV,282)—but the writer's essential life and identity are to be discovered in the act of creating the text. This creates a round of art and life placing extraordinary demands on both. For Thoreau, each wise man must answer the eternal questions "according to his ability, by his words and his life" (*Walden*,108) and Thoreau requires of himself this interchange of writing and living when he expresses the desire to "improve the nick of time, and notch it on my stick too" (16).[25] Likewise, Sandra Gilbert wisely remarks that Emily Dickinson consciously constructed the mysteries of her life that baffle biographers still, just as she created her poems: "the 'real' Emily Dickinson was as much a 'supposed person' as the so-called 'Representative of the Verse'."[26]

Mircea Eliade sees the primitive distinguished from modern man by his obligation "not only . . . to remember mythical history but also to re-enact a large part of it periodically,"[27] and in that sense the Puritan, with his typological view, is a culturally early primitive re-enacting a still-earlier myth. But the American romantic is earlier still, in that he is creating a myth while simultaneously attempting to live it out. And because essence can be allied to origin, so that the question of what a thing is gets answered by from what it arose, the actualist often portrays himself as originary in a supersocial guise: as god or prehistorical primitive. (Whitman's Walt is both.)

What he, like a god, apparently sees outside of his all-expansive self is in truth a world that his vision creates: but as his vision is not subjective but essential, the very categories of self and world are abolished. This finally results in the reversal of mimeticism whereby literature claims not to imitate or even to interpret reality but to create it. Actualism is not reducible, then, to the characteristic project of all romance, which is to present essences of social reality as if those essences were apparent and immediately operative on the everyday surface of reality, for it refuses the "as if" to make the surface and the essence, stance and substance, one. Within and beyond literature, the actualist's final task is to live out his vision literally.

He is to make the word flesh. In the text, this making occurs when a speculative idea is portrayed as if it were most literally existent in everyday reality, with the peculiar insistence that this is no mere trick, no yarn, because one way or another the impalpable *is* immediately apparent. Hegel's distinction between the inner and outer eye is refused just as the distinction of essence and appearance is.

But making the word flesh also demands a refusal of any boundary between literature and life. Essence must become appearance, persona must become personality, in the writer's living. However unreasonable the demand that any being literalize on the public surface of his life his private delvings, this is precisely the continuing requirement of American authorship. The writer does not happen to be American; he contains America within himself. Not only his writings but his life must actualize the dream. His daily doings must be informed by the grandeur of his words. Writers may be prone to all sorts of self-disaster, but the American writer, from Thoreau to Hemingway to Mailer, has been particularly vulnerable to one in particular: the impossible, always awkward attempt to find in his literary persona his essential self and live it literally out. Emerson knew the danger as well as the thrill of this attempt. "The world is full of renunciations and apprenticeships," he wrote to his prospective poet, "and this is thine; thou must pass for a fool and a churl for a long season . . . And this is the reward; that the ideal shall be real to thee, and the impressions of the actual world shall fall like summer rain, copious, but not troublesome to thy invulnerable essence" (CW,III,24).

How persistent is this actualist strain? In Saul Bellow's *Henderson the Rain King,* an African King educated in part in New England speaks to Henderson his deepest belief:

> "The career of our specie," he said, "is evidence that one imagination
> after another grows literal. Not dreams. Not mere dreams. I say not
> mere dreams because they have a way of growing actual. . . . All
> human accomplishment has this same origin, identically. Imagination is
> a force of nature. Is this not enough to make a person full of ecstasy?

Imagination, imagination, imagination. It converts to actual. It sustains, it alters, it redeems . . . What Homo sapiens imagines, he may slowly convert himself to."[28]

The king fails ultimately to convert his own life into his imagined good and he turns out to be part confidence man as well; and Henderson, the American protagonist, must learn to modulate his demands upon the world. Yet here is Bellow wrestling with the angel of actualism still, as Emerson and Melville had and as future American writers will.

10

THE ACTUALIST HERO:
WHITMAN AND WORDSWORTH,
EMERSON AND CARLYLE
ONCE MORE

I

Literary actualism is a result summed from many of the strategies of nineteenth-century American writers to differentiate an American sensibility from what they considered the general mind-set of England. Because actualism constitutes part of a sensibility, it is difficult to define abstractly. It is not a literary genre or technique. It is not a particular moral understanding separable from its dramatizations and it is least of all a dogma: the American romantics are each determined to place all convictions within the changeful flow of consciousness so that no belief can ossify or become restrictive. If actualism means to imitate the Universal Mind, it assumes that Mind to be dynamic, even at times contradictory to itself. Actualism is an atmosphere of self, with all the vague diffusion that phrase suggests. Here, more than anywhere else in this study, we must look to cases for any real clarification. And by returning to the two cases I earlier considered in relation to their views of time and history, we can add actualism to our informal lexicon of terms by which American writers refuse the British limits of possibility for self and world. We find most generally that where the British self is placed within a world (though there are choices within that world and though the self can improve upon that world), the world is placed within an expanded American self.

In our first case, for instance, Whitman deems himself larger than his competitor. It is as the poet of the both-and that Whitman most decisively differentiates himself from Wordsworth. Wordsworth's *Prelude* is a drama of subtle choices—the primacy of nature or imagination, social involvement or personal renovation, the fleshy ecstacies of youthful, firsthand experience or the spirit's mature wisdom achieved by the mind working upon that recalled experience—to each of which alternatives Whitman replies, "Why not both?"

For instance, if we recall the traditional description of the epic bard as one who defies sensory limitation, we find that Whitman not only attempts a more complete transcendence but that he also more completely credits and trusts the senses. For Wordsworth, the senses at best make palpable essential truths beyond sense, as when the skating child

> reclining back upon my heels,
> Stopped short; yet still the solitary cliffs
> Wheeled by me—even as if the earth had rolled
> With visible motion her diurnal round!
>
> (1:457–60)

More than the earth's physical turning, the spirit's vital dynamism is revealed by this sensory illusion. Just so, the child who steals a boat and imagines a mountain pursuing him unknowingly credits a truth by this guilty illusion, the vitalism of nature. But note that the senses must be tricked or placed *in extremis,* the self hanging on a "perilous ridge" to perceive a sky that "seemed not a sky / Of earth—and with what motion moved the clouds!" (1:338–39), to reveal the real. At best, sight intensifies until it flashes itself out, giving way to "an eye made quiet by the power / Of harmony"; through that corporeal blindness, in the phrase from "Tintern Abbey," "we see into the life of things." At worst, the bodily eye is "The most despotic of our senses," which, in company with the revolution, overcomes imagination and "held my mind in absolute dominion" (12:128, 131). Body and sense are dangerously neutral for Wordsworth, leading to spirit when controlled by an extrasensory joy, but ever capable of tempting us to that world too much with us when the mind's harmony is unsettled. Wordsworth exemplifies Tony Tanner's general thesis that "for the English Romantics a purely visual relationship to the outside world betokened a state of deprivation, a loss of intimacy, a failure of poetic vision."[1]

The American actualist closes any gap and refuses any opposition between vision and Vision. Surfaces bespeak essences, *are* essences, in this world spun out of a mind. It is a world in which "the unseen is proved by the seen, / Till that becomes unseen and receives proof in its turn" (3:45–46). Whitman acknowledges a bipolarity of soul and body, thought and sense, only to assert the equality of the parts— "Clear and sweet is my soul. . . . and clear and sweet is all that is not my soul / Lack one lacks both. . . ." (3:44–45)—, then to proclaim their interdependence, and finally, as in the shocking sexual mating of soul and flesh, to insist upon their identity. Thus, Whitman assumes his corporeal vision to be so endlessly imbued with the incorporeal visionary that he can trust it utterly, as in his tallyings. The Wordsworthian process of actual vision leading to a blanking out that itself leads to supraphysical seeing into the life of things is all collapsed into Whitman's ordinary eyesight, so that the first and third stages become one.

Kenneth M. Price has documented Whitman's notes upon reading romantic texts in the years before 1855, and we should not be surprised that Whitman enthuses over the meditative ecstacies of Wordsworth and Coleridge but criticizes the cancellation of the senses the English poets require for the experience.[2] And Matthiessen helpfully quotes from one of Whitman's notebooks his version of a Wordsworthian mystic moment—"a trance, yet with all the senses alert"—to contrast it to Wordsworth's "serene and blessed mood" in which "we are laid asleep in body and become a living soul." This insistence on "the *senses* not lost or counteracted"[3] is not merely declamation on Whitman's part. The nudity of the items in his typical catalogue of sights, the absence of commentary, enacts the trust that every physical fact has its spiritual counterpart and that unembellished sight is thus sufficient. By that, while each item seems as potentially representative as Wordsworth's best few—a Mount Snowden in every line—and while we are constantly aware that each item is the product of the mind's eye, yet when we read "The pavingman leans on his twohanded rammer—the reporter's lead flies swiftly over his notebook—the signpainter is lettering with blue and gold" (15:292), we experience a corporeal immediacy because mind's eye has been given an as-if-physical actuality. Thus Whitman can seem at once more transcendent-abstract and more physically accepting and visually precise than Wordsworth. For this, again, he sacrifices Wordsworth's intricacy, and his drama of successive mind-matter borrowings and transformations. Instead, all stages become one simultaneous total vision. And while, for Wordsworth, the mystic moments blessedly interrupt the flow of time, even as they may underlie that flow, for Whitman any chronological crisis merely interrupts a continually sustained mystic moment.

Whitman also complained that "Wordsworth lacked sympathy with men and women."[4] The actualist drive for inclusion and the actualist faith that all fact is immediately redeemable unto spirit differentiates Whitman's social vision from Wordsworth's. The self-referential quality of each poet's ethic implies that poetry is no longer to be considered a subcategory of any doctrine but a way of knowing. So Wordsworth implies when he acknowledges within him "that first great gift, the vital soul," and only secondarily "general Truths," which are defined as merely "subordinate helpers to the living mind" (1:150,153). Everything, however commonplace, must be seen as within the mind's holy ken. But what things are included in this "everything"? Both poets acknowledge a counterreality—for instance, Wordsworth's confused immersion in the immediate history of the French revolution— which opposes a poetic reality allied to the rhythms of the earth and the sonorities of a blooming sacrament. Yet the opposition must be eliminated; else the poetic vision condemns itself as partial. How each poet battles the enemy, a world of overcivilized manners and brutish materialism, has all to do with Wordsworthian choice and Whitmanian inclusion.

Here is Wordsworth describing London in Book Seven of *The Prelude*, in a passage seemingly inspired—the seeming is, of course, impossible—by Whitman.

> The comers and the goers face to face,
> Face after face; the string of dazzling wares,
> Shop after shop, with symbols, blazoned names,
> And all the tradesman's honours overhead:
> Here, fronts of houses, like a title-page,
> With letters huge inscribed from top to toe,
> Stationed above the door, like guardian saints;
> There, allegoric shapes, female or male,
> Or physiognomies of real men,
> Land-warriors, kings, or admirals of the sea,
> Boyle, Shakespeare, Newton, or the attractive head
> Of some quack doctor, famous in his day.

(7:156–58)

Or again:

> A raree-show is here,
> With children gathered round; another street
> Presents a company of dancing dogs,
> Or dromedary, with an antic pair
> Of monkeys on his back; a minstrel band
> Of Savoyards, or, single and alone,
> An English ballad-singer. . . .
> . . . .
> The Nurse is here,
> The Bachelor, that loves to sun himself,
> The military Idler, and the Dame,
> That field-ward takes her walk with decent steps.
> . . . .

THE ACTUALIST HERO

> The begging scavenger, with hat in hand
> The Italian, as he threads his way with care,
> Steadying, far-seen, a frame of images
> Upon his head; with basket at his breast
> The Jew; the stately and slow-moving Turk,
> With freight of slippers piled beneath his arm!
>
> (174–80, 207–10, 213–18)

As Wordsworth says at this junction, "Enough"; for, while this catalogue of viewed images creates a syntax rarely employed by Wordsworth but ever characteristic of Whitman, the quickest second glance reveals an absolute contrast. What for Whitman will constitute a plenitude of human activity attesting to the one spirit is for Wordsworth a noxious bedlam-let-out of misspent energy and ambition. Preceding the first quoted passage occurs the famous condemnation of London and the urban that I quoted earlier:

> Rise up, thou monstrous ant-hill on the plain
> Of a too-busy world! Before me flow,
> Thou endless stream of men and moving things!
>
> (149–51)

London is not only the egotistic heap of a prideful pettiness. As anthill it is the ridiculously failed man-built competition for the sublime mountains of *The Prelude*'s nature. As too busy, endless stream, it is a demonic version of *The Prelude*'s Derwent river, that water by which Wordsworth affirms the deep continuities in the growth of a poet's mind. And the inhabitants of this London in their scurrying, antlike commercial industriousness are played off against the dignified and earth-related toilers of Wordsworth's rural solitudes. These Londoners seem to bear no inner life. They cannot maintain individual status but assume types; or if they strive to be individual they are merely bizarre— "Extravagance in gesture, mien, and dress, / And all the strife of singularity, / Lies to the ear, and lies to every sense—" (578–81). That they are unnatural is clear; whether they are truly alive at all is questionable. The notice taken of Nurse, Bachelor, Idler, and Dame is preceded by a contemplation of signboards; and it is made purposively difficult to discern whether these types are living or painted images. The Dame, "That field-ward takes her walk," apparently away from London, has a good idea.

A cheap thrills spectacle, the city is itself a degraded raree-show. London's Fair, with its

Albinos, painted Indians, Dwarfs
The Horse of knowledge, and the Learned Pig,
The stone-eater, the man that swallows fire,
Giants, Ventriloquists, the Invisible Girl,

(707–10)

is inseparable from the city's squalid reality—"true Epitome / Of what the mighty City is herself" (722–23). In its frantic and false joy in the unnatural, the Fair, "Holden where martyrs suffered in past time / And named of St. Bartholemew" (677–78), images a cultural decline and lateness which Wordsworth's nostalgic phrasing—"Holden" and "named of"—deepens.

Indeed, Wordsworth here anticipates Whitman less than he looks back to Pope. The rhythms and conventions of the rhymed couplet underlie the free verse. Bathos is the prevailing mode, zeugma a frequent technique, satire the result: "foolishness and madness in parade" (594). Wordsworth turns conservative, in literary as well as social terms, when confronted by this urban menagerie. With the inspiring breath of nature so disastrously absent, "For once the Muse's help will we implore" to waft the poet "Above the press and danger of the crowd" (682, 684), as Wordsworth's natural realism must submit to tradition for imaginative survival.

For Whitman, as we have noted, the city is merely one port of call on the route of a continually flying vision: "By the city's quadrangle houses . . . in log-huts, or camping with lumbermen" (33:715). Urban corruption is noted, even emphasized, in Whitman's tallyings, yet more emphasized is the poet's silence in response, his refusal of condemnation in favor of an enjoying wonder founded on the faith that joy and agony resolve in joy:

> The blab of the pave . . . the tires of carts and
>   stuff of bootsoles and talk of the promenaders,
> The heavy omnibus, the driver with his interrogating
>   thumb, the clank of the shod horses on the
>   granite floor,
> The carnival of sleighs, the clinking and shouted
>   jokes and pelts of snowballs;
> The hurrahs for popular favorites . . . the fury of
>   roused mobs,
> . . . .
> The souls moving along . . . are they invisible while
>   the least atom of the stones is visible?

What groans of overfed or half-starved who fail on the
flags sunstruck or in fits,
What exclamations of women taken suddenly, who hurry
home and give birth to babes,
What living and buried speech is always vibrating
here . . . what howls restrained by decorum,
Arrests of criminals, slights, adulterous offers made,
acceptances, rejections with convex lips,
I mind them or the resonance of them . . . . I come
again and again.

(8:146–49, 154–59)

Whitman's silence, his lack of editorializing, his refusal of despair, is
meant to shock. The undifferentiated pleasure of sound, or more accurately of hearing, leads the poet through the city; and every social,
sexual, and biological corruption is surrounded and conquered, in-
fused and resolved, by the faith that neither death nor trivialization,
aggression or torpor, is final. This is Whitman's broil of life. Every
prostitute and criminal is a soul moving along.

In short, Whitman's is an inclusionary vision while Wordsworth's
is exclusionary. Whitman's good accumulates, Wordsworth's good purifies. Wordsworth brings God down into the countryside, to abide
within the natural rhythms of life and in those relatively few men who
will make those rhythms their own. Whitman opens the gates of the
city to God, for He resides everywhere and in everyone.

This actualist rallying in a surface seen as essence makes for a
difference even in the poet's response to his poetry. Whitman's inclusive, accumulative ethic, by which plethora is a good, interprets his
tallyings as a proof and a boast. Wordsworth, when he adopts the
catalogue mode, is fatigued not more by the city than by his own ver-
sification. "Enough," he cries, to stop himself from multiplying upon
the examples of "the same perpetual whirl / Of trivial objects" (219
and 725–26). The city cannot but "weary out the eye, / By nature an
unmanageable sight" (731–32). "I mind them or the resonance of
them," Whitman makes rejoinder, "I come again and again."

The opposition I have stated needs qualification, yet every qualification comes to reinforce the difference. Wordsworth verges momentarily on a Whitman-like affirmation: though the city is "an
unmanageable sight,"

It is not wholly so to him who looks
In steadiness, who hath among least things

> An under-sense of greatest; sees the parts
> As parts, but with a feeling of the whole.
>
> (733–36)

Not only is the city thus redeemed, but it has contributed to the wisdom which is its redemption:

> This, of all acquisitions, first awaits
> On sundry and most widely different modes
> Of education, nor with least delight
> On that through which I passed. . . .
>
> (737–40)

Still, one must respond that this acquisition of an underlying good, to which the city contributes and by which the city is saved, has not been enacted even in Wordsworth's recollection. At most, his underlying faith has served not to transform the city but to shield the poet against its temptations. He puns of the city, "yet the storm / Passed not beyond the suburbs of the mind" (475–76). It is a city of failed empathy and understanding:

> How oft, amid those overflowing streets,
> Have I gone forward with the crowd, and said
> Unto myself, "The face of every one
> That passes by me is a mystery!"
>
> (626–29)

This is not a holy mystery but an ignorance occasioned by an anonymity that empties out any hope of communication with innerness. Against the deprivation of fellow feeling it occasions in Wordsworth, the poet can respond only by focusing hard on an individual and, in a sense, making the city recede "as a solemn background, or relief, / To single forms and objects. . ." (622–23).

To the extent that London represents British culture, Wordsworth is a countercultural poet. He can prosper in London only by seeing it away; he can see into its inhabitants only by locating central human qualities unaffected by a too busy world. London is his "foil," like Cambridge an opponent showing the resistant strength of his "dedicated spirit." But little of the enemy's ground without is conquered and transformed by that strength within. Thus Wordsworth turns in the next book of *The Prelude* to agricultural life as his recommended alternative.

THE ACTUALIST HERO

It is this very issue of including the urban in a vision of the good that occasions Whitman's brag, "Now the performer launches his nerve. . . . he has passed his prelude on the reeds within" (42:1054). *The Prelude* is passed as Whitman affirms "This is the city. . . . and I am one of the citizens" (1070), with the "I" of the poet who is not countercultural but representative American. Yet this affirmation occurs in the midst of another largely negative tallying of the city that seems to draw Whitman closer to Wordsworth: the people walk "with dimes on the eyes" (1065). And we recall as well Whitman's early preference of the bank by the woods to those "Houses and rooms. . . full of perfumes" (2:6). Houses and rooms separate us from each other, civilized luxuries separate us from the lifegiven essentials, and both separate us from our free and real selves. In Wordsworth, the city misdirects and trivializes our energies; in Whitman, the city is not scattering or paradoxically barbarizing but repressive. In both, the intoxication is resisted by attention to what always matters. But Whitman's negatives are themselves negated, as Wordsworth's are not. Whitman can affirm citizenship by affirming "They who piddle and patter here in collars and tailed coats" as "the duplicates of myself under all the scrape-lipped and pipe-legged concealments" (42:1074–5). Central spirit persists under all of the human failures to recognize and enact it. Here the multitudes do multiply the holy mystery, as Whitman typically cures all corrupt repressions not by isolating his gaze but by enlarging it to include more. This is what Wordsworth wishes, "a feeling of the whole"; but it is what Whitman does. Of his thoughts he says, "If they do not enclose everything they are next to nothing" (17:335), and the tallyings are the enactment of an enclosing which never reaches an "enough."

We are not discussing here merely the attitudes of two poets toward urban life. We are contemplating a distinction between an English romantic who locates his paradise securely within—the title of Wordsworth's entire proposed epic was, of course, *The Recluse*—and an American romantic whose paradise is equally within and out there in the "blab" of the actual pavement. We are contemplating as well Whitman's nineteenth-century version of the New England Puritan tenet that the City of Man and the City of God could become one, not figuratively in one man's inner being but in historical reality. For Whitman, the open road includes city streets.

Wordsworth is not left in an ultimately hypocritical or self-contradictory situation. Wordsworth's All, that "empire we inherit / As natural beings in the strength of Nature" (3:195–96), does not include urban reality; and while, to an American actualist, this exclusion argues a failure of vision, faith, and nerve, to Wordsworth it constitutes a re-enforcement of faith. Wordsworth reduces the powerful, historical force of urbanization to a sideshow, a freakish mutation. If his All cannot include modern life, life given over to the merely modern, that does not accuse his vision of circumscription but condemns a cultural choice that undermines life itself.

Whitman cannot think in this manner because he cannot be without being representative. We see in this the actualist reliance upon American early time; and we can return to the issue of time and history in these two poems to deepen it by the concept of actualism into the underlying question of address.

It is most by voice that we know each of these poets. And each speaks in a tone and via a mode of presentation befitting the poet's time. The Wordsworth of *The Prelude* is a man not only living in a late world but affected, however little, by that lateness: "the recreant age *we* live in" (3:404), he writes, humbly italicizing his inclusion. He represents his poem as a best conversation with the Friend, Coleridge, who becomes with Wordsworth a party of two, separate from and opposed to that greater society variously represented by Cambridge, London, and Paris. Conversation is a cultural achievement, and the sincerity of this poem of conversation is a rebuke to a decrepit culture's trashing of human relationships. In the very form of his undertaking, Wordsworth creates an enclave, a micro-society, against the decaying world; he admits his own lateness but purifies it into a rich maturity that restores the early purpose of a convention, here conversation. We discover this same compounding of early and late when Wordsworth seeks a voice that will combine spontaneity and the sophistication of traditional order, the best of youth and age:

> Thus far, O Friend! did I, not used to make
> A present joy the matter of a song,
> Pour forth that day my soul in measured strains
>
> (1:46–48)

Somewhat nonplussed at finding his poetry in a pure present (though even the present-joy song is now being recalled), Wordsworth indicates the song's spontaneity by the verb "pour" and qualifies that spontaneity by "measured strains." Yet this is not qualification, for a ripe maturity can be spontaneous and ordered at once.

This ideal is at a remove from the earliness of Whitman's "barbaric yawp" or "belched words," where poetry is not the spontaneous overflow of emotion recollected in tranquility, but the spontaneous, even incompletely digested overflow of emotion now. If both poems posit poetry as a way of knowing, then poetry not only must embrace all being, but the voice of poetry must make its peace with the language of everyday living. Poetic decorum must be redefined. Wordsworth knew this well, as it becomes a leading subject of his critical thought. His solution is to imitate a conversational tone which, as his friend was the first to point out, is not really ordinary language at all. Wordsworth's metrics, never obtrusive, are intricate; and he will employ a simple vocabulary only to set up such a latinate as "abundant recompense," a phrase like a gorgeous orchestra coming in to supplement an a cappella voice. He blends the plain speech of earliness with the grace and resources of maturity to create a rich, best middle time outside of the world's time.

With Whitman, "an American, one of the roughs, a kosmos/Disorderly, fleshy, and sensual" (24:499–500), worlds of diction do not complement each other but collide:

> I resist anything better than my own diversity
> And breathe the air, and leave plenty after me
> And am not stuck up, and am in my place.
>
> (16:349–49)

Yet the collision is also an encompassing by earliness of sophisticated lateness, bringing the delicate and abstruse to fertile common ground as in the phrases just quoted. And significantly, Whitman does not address a friend in private conversation. He imitates what is simultaneously the pose of a soapbox orator addressing the world, and particularly the nation—"A call in the midst of the crowd, / My own voice, orotund sweeping and final" (42:1050–51)—and the reader's own inner voice—"I teach straying from me, yet who can stray from me?," "It is you talking just as much as myself. . . . I act as the tongue of you / It was tied in your mouth. . . . in mine it begins to be loosened" (47:240,1244–45). The orator's call and the language of the central self, by which Wordsworth's middle ground of private conversation is skipped over, are not two different tones, much as some of Whitman's interpreters wish to section them. They are one, for Whitman wishes to cleanse public rhetoric so that it will speak heart's truth—"To make the people rage, weep, hate, desire, with yourself," in a phrase from "Poem of Joys"[5]—as befits a national poetic in which self and nation are one and any private/public sundering condemns each. Whitman's metaphysical colloquialism is the stylistic enactment of a democratic self-definition.

This actualist self, as we noted earlier, subsumes all experience. Whitman's genius would be projective while Wordsworth's would be renovative. Whitman, dogged by influence, attempts the act of purest creation, a poem that will not interpret life but be alive. We must not overdraw the difference. Tony Tanner generalizes of the English romantics, "With Wordsworth they could consider 'man and nature as essentially adapted to each other.' In discovering nature they were at the same time discovering themselves; in internalizing what was around them they were at the same time externalizing what was within, ..."[6] By the end of *The Prelude*, Wordsworth would have to qualify this view by proclaiming that nature never can fulfill the imagination's further sightings. Yet this is still short of where Whitman begins, with Emerson's belief that "That which once existed in intellect as pure thought has now taken body as Nature" (*CW*, I, 123). The matter of "Song of Myself," which Whitman so insists upon, comes after the dissolution of a socially given matter. But the most audacious claim of "Song of Myself" consists in presenting this mind-spun, second matter as one with given matter.

Which is to say that "Walt" is not a person in the sense that the poet of *The Prelude* is. Whitman is aware of the difference and employs it to pass the interiority and past-ness of *The Prelude*. The entire drama of *The Prelude* is encapsulated within Whitman's single line, "Backward I see in my own days where I sweated through the fog with linguists and contenders" (4:71). The statement seems a minor exception to Whitman's refusal of any linear biographical account. But it is also a subtle boast, for it makes of *The Prelude* a prelude, "Song of Myself" its fulfillment. Or to put it otherwise, *The Prelude* becomes a commentary upon "Song of Myself," a developmental explanation of "my own days" by which Whitman became Walt and all old days were replaced and contained by the present moment. Given the vastness of the achieved moment, all the past, including Wordsworth, dwindles to a phrase.

2

Emerson never attempts to belittle Carlyle so extremely. But we can cite actualism as a prime cause both of Emerson's attraction to Carlyle and of these friends' increasing sense of their crucial differences.

The usual litany of reasons for the initial attraction will not do. In his intelligent book on the friendship of Carlyle and Emerson, Kenneth Harris helpfully recounts his subjects' similarities of attitude. They shared a sense of their age as self-conscious and analytic and desperately in need of a new spiritualism that could brook the assaults of skeptical thought. Both men, in a generally Coleridgean spirit, sought to oppose mechanical forms of rationalism by an idealist trust and a thorough awe toward human and universal mysteries. Both particularly opposed any insistence on social circumstance that would make of man a mere product; and both would insist upon the individual's shaping force, as Carlyle's "strength" and Emerson's "power."[7]

But these agreements are too large to matter much; one can imagine a similar list of correspondences that could be drawn between any two late-romantic writers. And our list of agreements issues in predictable ways into sharper disagreements. Carlyle saw the analytical bent of the age as dangerously disrespectful of greatness and deference and order, and thus on the verge of dissolution. Emerson dramatized contemporary intellection in nearly opposite terms. He begins *Nature* by asserting, "Our age is retrospective. It builds the sepulchres of the fathers. It writes biographies, histories, and criticism. The foregoing generations beheld God and nature face to face; we, through their eyes. Why should not we also enjoy an original relation to the universe?" (*CW*, I, 7). Carlyle warns of a selfish refusal of influence and threatens chaos; Emerson warns of a sycophant attitude and threatens mere repetition and a secondary existence. Both disparage cultural lateness, but for the Englishman, that means a loss of continuity while for the American it means all too much continuity, the importation of stale Europe to these otherwise fresh shores. Again: Carlyle's attitude of awe could match Emerson's "flying perfect" for an appreciation of mystery—"Force, Force, everywhere Force; we ourselves a mysterious Force in the centre of that" (*On Heroes*, p. 8). But to Carlyle, the special man, the hero, is particularly open to existence in an attitude of awe which other men must replicate in response to the mysterious force of the hero himself, while in Emerson all share in the primary awe alike and learn thereby the partial, limited greatness of any single great man. Or again, Carlyle's "strength" means "wager-of-battle in this world" (143), the sway of one's idea upon others, while Emersonian "power" means self-actualization with total disregard of competition.

In spite of these eventual differences, many of which Emerson could sense upon his earliest meeting with Carlyle, the American had cause to see his friend, if a bit wishfully, as a transatlantic brother in actualism. Carlyle became a magnet for Emerson most, I believe, by reason of his vocation. As quasi-novelist, quasi-philosopher, quasi-politician, and quasi-prophet, Carlyle, in his wild rural retreat, seemed to be combining human roles now sadly held separate and to be living them out with an impressively literal tenacity. Emerson praised this living virtue in the writing—"a poetic use of the spoken vocabulary"—and in the living of a man whose immediate conversation is "altogether as extraordinary in that as in his writing; I think even more so" (*W*, VI, 241–42). He exemplified, to a far extent, the self-realization that Emerson desired for himself and for all others.

But not far enough. The second lesson of this famous friendship reinforces our sense of the British-American difference. We recall that, in his journal entry upon his return from England, Emerson included Carlyle in his list of living disappointments. Carlyle's call, in *On Heroes, Hero-Worship, and the Heroic in History*, for men of letters to make practical their imaginations and become religious and political heroes—even if he was living up to this call—was not sufficient for an Emerson who wished not merely to enter into and reform the social sphere but to dissolve it entirely and remake it without compromise to the demands of vision. In their meeting at Stonehenge, challenged by Carlyle to define "an American idea," Emerson reports in *English Traits* his assertion that there was such an idea, "but those who hold it are fanatics of a dream which I should hardly care to relate to your English ears, to which it might be only ridiculous,—and yet it is the only true" (*CW*, V, 287). No wonder that, when each writer creates an avatar, Carlyle qualifies the idealism of his Teufelsdröch while Emerson extends the idealism of his Orphic Poet, who employs the temporal metaphor of a Fall and a recovery where Emerson would argue against even the historical-seeming metaphor of a Fall whatsoever.[8]

The Carlyle who can write "for us in these days *Prophecy* (well understood) not Poetry is the thing wanted: how can we *sing* and *paint* when we do not yet *believe* and *see?*"[9] sounds like an American actualist. And his desire to substitute literature for a dead religion and to become a lay prophet, as it is a desire of many of the English Victorians, explains not only Emerson's attraction to Carlyle but the more general American interest in the British Victorians.

But this commonality is only apparent, for it arises, as we have seen, out of nearly opposing worries, British lateness and American earliness; and thus it lays the grounds for what would seem to the Americans a British betrayal. In our particular case, the titles of the two works by which Emerson means to dun Carlyle's "English ears" with his "American idea" are once more significant. *Representative Men* seems at first only an immediate democratic challenge to the nostalgically medieval sound of *On Heroes, Hero-Worship, and the Heroic in History*, and that is part of its effect. Emerson's men adore what is common and available to all. Plato is "a great average man" (60) whose created hero Socrates "valued the bores and philistines," "Plain old uncle as he was" (71–72); Montaigne, growing sick of the courts, "will indulge himself with a little cursing and swearing; he will talk with sailors and gypsies, use flash and street-ballads" (166); Napoleon is "the incarnate Democrat," perfectly representative of "the young and the poor," "the class of industry and skill" (224).

More profoundly, Emerson's title refuses Carlyle's two classes of heroes and worshippers on the actualist grounds that every man is potentially great. "The imbecility of men is always inviting the impudence of power" (18) for "We are all wise in capacity, though so few in energy" (25). Hero-worship for Carlyle is to deference as chastity is to virginity, its divine essence: "There is no act more moral between men than that of rule and obedience" (199). For Emerson, hero-worship is never without the taint of toadyism. "The aid we have from others is mechanical compared with the discoveries of nature in us" (8); "The soul is impatient of masters and eager for change" (19); the great hero is found "drawing all men by fascination into tributaries and supporters of his power. . . . But I find him greater when he can abolish himself and all heroes, . . . destroying individualism" (23). Momentarily, Carlyle and Emerson will seem alike, as in arguing for a receptivity to influence. Carlyle's statement "that a man be self-subsistent, original, true, or what we call it, is surely the farthest in the world from indisposing him to reverence and believe other men's truths!" (126) finds an echo in Emerson's adjurations, "Serve the great. Stick at no humiliation. Grudge no office thou canst render" (29). "The greatest genius," he says in introducing Shakespeare, "is the most indebted man" (189). But this is deceptive, for Emerson has been arguing that "Nothing is more marked than the power by which individuals are guarded from individuals" (28) in that "We cloy of the honey of each peculiar greatness. Every hero becomes a bore at last" (28). "Rotation," the multiplying succession of heroic influences, indemnifies us from "excess of influence of the great man" whose "attractions warp us from our place" (27). Thus, the very progression of Emerson's book, random as it is, carries meaning as a sequence, always leaving one great figure for another, each chapter ending with a series of disparagements to guarantee a next.

Finally, though Emerson does not announce it, there exists a more positive guard against the soul's coercion. It is transubstantive, the selfhood redefining its borrowed constituents in terms of its distinction. "Plato, too, like every great man, consumed his own times" (41) and even travelled through other nations to absorb still more; but "this grasping inventor puts all nations under contribution" (42) only because his huge, merger making individuality could afford such influence: "his forerunners had mapped out each a farm or a district or an

island, in intellectual geography, but . . . Plato first drew the sphere"
(86).

Emerson himself practices a ventriloquism that answers to this
claim. Each of his heroes for a time becomes Emerson. Plato "represents the privilege of the intellect, the power, namely, of carrying up
every fact to successive platforms and so disclosing in every fact a germ
of expansion" (81), a perfect description of Emersonian symbolism.
And it is this expanding, synthesizing quality that Emerson most remarks in Shakespeare, Swedenborg, and Goethe as well—all but
Napoleon, with whom Emerson wishes no final identification. More
locally Emerson's paraphrasings of both Plato and Montaigne turn out
to be the short, declarative aphorisms of Emerson and no one else.

"All men are of a size" (31)—every man can be a hero. The germ
of greatness exists in the common life of all men and in the central soul
of each man. No hero exhausts nature's possibilities. Even Plato,
"making it impossible to think on certain levels, except through him"
(44), is insufficiently passionate and insufficiently systematic, so that
"unconquered nature lives on and forgets him" (77). Emerson gains
scope over an exclusive-seeming, facticity-bound Carlyle by these
tenets.

The difference here has centrally to do with each writer's relation
to his Calvinist background. Charles Frederick Harrold, after fifty
years still one of Carlyle's great commentators, argues persuasively
that Carlyle's idea of heroism merges Calvin and German idealism.
"Calvin's exaltation of action appeared, in new dress, in Fichte's emphasis on the moral deed, rather than on the pretensions of the Understanding" just as "Predestination became Fichte's doctrine of the
progressive and inevitable realization of the Divine Idea in the world's
history." To these Carlylean combinations, Emerson could himself add
the American promise. But Harrold also notes that, for Carlyle, "The
Calvinist sense of 'election' was satisfied in Fichte's doctrine of the
Gelehrt (scholar, or great man),"[10] and Emerson would rebel violently
against this. Calvinist Election presupposes an elite class, in which a
few men, obedient to the Divine, would rule in a patriarchal, the-
ocratic manner over the multitude, whose responsibility was to be obedient to the Elect. Such unequal access to the Divine, and the super-
state structure of society it implies, must appear wildly evil to a democracy minded actualist. Emerson's attitude to Calvinism is various and
complex; but Calvinism à la Carlyle's heroes is pure anathema. That is
why one of the major meanings of *Representative Men* consists in an
omission. While Emerson takes up some of Carlyle's heroes—Shake-

speare, Napoleon, Goethe—he refuses, in Carlyle's phrase, to "Emersonize" Carlyle's chapter on Calvin and Luther or to mention the Protestant founders at all. It is a silence that speaks protesting volumes.

3

We have yet to say why *Representative Men* ultimately fails as an actualist enactment, and for that I need to return to a text considered earlier, Thoreau's *Walden*. In *Walden*, the chapter "Higher Laws" contradicts many of the claims I made for Thoreau in his debate with Coleridge and Wordsworth. This is the chapter James McIntosh finds "in opposition to the whole drift of argument and feeling in *Walden*" and Frederick Garber terms "markedly schizophrenic" in itself.[11] In it, Thoreau for a time rejects the wild, the West, the early. He substitutes for his dawn-demands a loose, powerless adaptation of the very Wordsworthian myth of abundant recompense in a sublimating Good which he rejects so strenuously elsewhere in *Walden*. In "Higher Laws," Thoreau dislikes himself for his likings, with nervous guilt defending and then condemning hunting and fishing. And as for the Good he espouses, it reduces to not hunting, not fishing, and not eating meat. Throughout *Walden*, Thoreau appeals for purification, but here the purifications lead not to the vital but to what Thoreau calls the chaste and I would call the effete. Elsewhere in *Walden*, Thoreau openly exploits self-contradiction, but here the contradictions are unorganized, and attempts at consistency lead to mumbly qualification. As much in his first two and last two chapters as here, Thoreau scolds our excesses. But only here does he tempt us, in response to his cry against "this slimy beastly life, eating and drinking" (166), to say with Emerson, "I hate goodies. I hate goodness that preaches. . . . Goodies make us very bad. We will almost sin to spite them. Better indulge yourself, feed fat, drink liquors, than go straitlaced for such cattle as these" (*J*, IV, 491–92). Excuse us for living, chaste Henry.

Thoreau begins the chapter wonderfully and typically. He wishes to rip into a woodchuck "and devour him raw; not that I was hungry then, except for that wildness which he represented" (210). This is the wildness of cultural youth that Garber defines accurately as "primordial life not yet made into forms of civilization," a "burgeoning fertility."[12] In translating a material, natural savagery into a spiritual trope, Thoreau manages to retain the material, to merge body and spirit, by making the trope's goal wildness.

But now Thoreau ruins the saving ambiguity by which, throughout *Walden*, nature and earliness mean both the physical marrow of basic living and the immaterial essence of material living at once. He writes,

> I found in myself, and still find, an instinct toward a higher, or, as it is named, spiritual life, as do most men, and another toward a primitive rank and savage one, and I reverence them both. I love the wild not less than the good. (210)

The quasi-iconoclastic claim for an equality between the wild and the good cannot mask the retreat into dualism. Compare the foregoing passage with this from "Where I Lived, and What I Lived For."

> Let us settle ourselves, and work and wedge our feet downward through the mud and slush of opinion and prejudice, and tradition and delusion, and appearance, that alluvion which covers the globe, through Paris and London, through New York and Boston and Concord, through church and state, through poetry, philosophy, and religion, till we come to a hard bottom and rocks in place, which we can call *reality*, and say, This is, and no mistake; . . . . . . Be it life or death, we crave reality. (97–98)

This passage ends by saying that the good is defined by the real. The good—be it life or death, what we conventionally call good or immoral—is determined by the wild. Thoreau at Walden would reply to the moralist as Emerson does in "Self-Reliance": "'if I am the Devil's child, I will live then from the Devil.' No law can be sacred to me but that of my nature" (*CW*, II, 30). But in "Higher Laws," the good is something other than the wild, something even opposed to it, something else, something imposed. *That* good is what the earlier passage calls "the mud and slush."

A comparison of the two passages reveals not simply an ideational reversal but a disastrous change in imaging, which is where literature lives. In "Higher Laws" Thoreau refuses his own directions. Higher Laws? A "higher, or spiritual life"? In the earlier, far more characteristic passage, Thoreau plays on the word "substance" to locate the ideal at the center of the earthly real. We must descend to it, through and fighting against the muck of culture's sublimations that falsify the real.

Back, down, youth, and origin are replaced by a lateness lexicon of forward, up, maturity, and culture in "Higher Laws." The earliness terms, promising the greatest true culture, had combined what in

"Higher Laws" become alternatives. Elsewhere in *Walden,* Thoreau descends to basics and rises to truth at once.

When Thoreau foregoes that, the result is a mess of time-terms. Within two paragraphs, we are told first that "the embryo man passes through the hunter stage of development" (213), as if the early is savage and unfortunate but just a stage. (Later, more true to his overall vision, Thoreau will translate Mencius: by "a return to goodness," we are schooled, "one approaches a little the primitive nature of man" [315]). Then, feelings of guilt for fishing are made "a faint intimation, but so are the first streaks of morning." Thoreau recalls his dawn-demands but empties them of meaning, for what can guilt, which augurs self-division, have to do with the healthy air of morning? Next, "There is unquestionably this instinct in me which belongs to the lower orders" and then, "The repugnance to animal food is not the effect of experience, but is an instinct. It appeared more beautiful to live low and fare hard in many respects; and though I never did so, I went far enough to please my imagination." Well, decide. Which is instinctual? If the instincts are contradictory, are not we, is not morning? But the sun rose clear. This is desperate stuff, reversals less mutually enriching than cancelling and neurotic. And throughout, the self pictures himself a compromised failure—"though I never did so"—until he confesses, "with every year I am less a fisherman, though without more humanity or even wisdom" (214), which makes us wonder what all of this discussion is for.

Aside from its other failings, the chapter is too personal, merely personal, for the Thoreau of *Walden* is the American exemplar. And where in other places Thoreau's dramas of self-conflict are charged and brave, here they seem trivial and tortured. We are in the realm of seatbelt legislation, a good, no doubt, but of no interest to the vision of *Walden.*

It is not even Wordsworth's complex tale of a fortunate Fall that eventuates, but the weakest liberal-humanist gradualism in the West. Let boys hunt; they will become "mighty hunters at last, so that they shall not find game large enough for them in this or any vegetable wilderness—hunters as well as fishers of men" (212). This is not Thoreau's usual punning, it is Christian-derived cliché. And when he speaks of "the destiny of the human race, in its gradual improvement" (216), he seems to forget that everywhere else he sees what is called improvement as taking us farther and farther from the dawn of what we truly are.

What scatters Thoreau? It is not merely a desire to be a good boy.

It is, in one of its far reaches, the Anglo-American struggle. The myth of the West, we recall, had its negative counterpart by which the West was the land of nightmare anarchy, of savagery ugly and unredeemed, of sensuous entrapment and the loss of the human in human being. We recall, too, that the first settlers were at pains to prove themselves still civilized to the England they had abandoned. Badgered by continuing British taunts, Thoreau, in his emigration, is rabid to show what he does not mean by wildness. But his better strategy, employed in every other chapter, is to accept the negatives and translate them into a new tongue. The voice that transforms meanest thing into finest thought is Thoreau's real, his only proof.

"Higher Laws" is created out of a native imperative as well, the American aim to envision heaven on earth and really mean it. Making vision practical works poetically when the practical is lifted to the visionary. When the literalism operates in descent, when the ideal is made to clarify what we might call editorial issues, as when Emerson's self-reliance refuses the beggar's request or as here, when Thoreau adopts the thin voice of vegetarianism, the author misunderstands his own project.

But there is another problem in *Higher Laws*, not a misapplication of actualism but a misbegotten attempt to add to it a vision of how America can develop once a perfect earliness is realized. All of the claims for earliness cannot quiet the imagination's query of where we go from there. In "Higher Laws," Thoreau is attempting to imagine a maturing America, an America which would mature not by a repressive refusal of wildness but by a sublimating translation of it: "mighty hunters at last." The chapter is nothing less than Thoreau's attempt to imagine a linear succession of time that yet could avoid the pitfalls of British historicism and lead to a distinctly American maturity. And it fails because the rest of *Walden* is so stridently antitemporal and because the contradictions are never sufficiently resolved.

Representative Men is yet another actualist tome that far more ambitiously attempts to add a national sophistication and development to the early All of actualism. It too fails, but in a heroic way that refutes the going idea of Emerson's decline. Harold Bloom concurs with Stephen Whicher's perspective on the career when he "dated 1841 as the end of Emerson's 'Period of challenge' and the start of his long 'Period of acquiescence,'" though Bloom must exclude the year 1846 from this "useful enough categorization. . . ."[13] R. A. Yoder concurs in this simple disparaging (though not in Bloom's unexplained exclusion of 1846) when he takes his title for an essay on American romantic retreats, "The Equilibrist Perspective," from Emerson's praise of Montaigne as a figure of equilibrium. He generalizes:

> The Equilibrist is indeed the high Romantic "Central Man" become a centrist, one who seeks a point of balance determined by his own compensatory responses to forces outside him. Essentially passive, . . . he is a diminished thing, no longer a Giant Form but an "Ephemeral" well on his way to post-Romantic "little man" and the modern "anti-hero."[14]

This is decisively wrong, and not only because Yoder enshrines solipsist assurance as an unquestionable good. Yoder ignores the very context of the phrase he borrows. "Every superior mind will pass through this domain of equilibration," Emerson concludes (171), having characterized his own awe of Montaigne as a postcollegiate enthusiasm. The mature Emerson writing now writes himself a spiritualist, one who can employ the skepticism he has passed through to refuse the clichéd "generosities of the day." But Emerson continues, "he denies out of more faith, and not less. He denies out of honesty. He had rather stand charged with the imbecility of skepticism, than with untruth" (182).

Emerson stands so charged today. But in truth he can afford his skeptical–seeming "power of moods, each setting at nought all but its own tissue of facts and beliefs," his "rotation of states of mind" (175–76) precisely and only because "All moods may be safely tried and their weight allowed to all objections" in that "the moral sentiment as easily outweighs them all, as any one" (183). As in "Song of Myself," a permanent vertical time can allow for other kinds of time, say a succession of mere attitudes, within it.

But there is an attempt at developmental national time in Emerson's book, and it is by this that the book more truly disappoints. In *Representative Men* and in his other writings of the forties, Emerson is attempting, as I mentioned earlier, to extend his range, and now we can define more specifically the new territory within his new circle. Call it cultural maturity. True, Emerson continues to deploy the advantages of earliness, as we noted in chapter eight. Nonetheless, *Representative Men* praises maturity: Plato represents, among all else, that "moment in the history of every nation, when, proceeding out of this brute youth, the perceptive powers reach their ripeness and have not yet become microscopic; . . . That is the moment of adult health, the culmination of power" (46–47). Carlyle and his England have "become microscopic" while in *Representative Men* Emerson seems to enact the perfect maturity he finds in Plato. "The philosophy we want," he writes in "Montaigne" (160), "is one of fluxions and mobility" (though as we have seen these fluxions must be underwritten by spiritual conviction) and the dialectical somersaults of *Representative Men* achieve just this. So too Emerson's enlarged range of appreciations and of rhetoric. The hortatory aphorisms of his earlier essays persist but they are blended into a gradated spectrum of tones extending to colloquialisms and jokes. ("It does not appear that he listened at key-holes," Emerson writes of coarse Napoleon, "or at least that he was caught at it," 256.)

Emerson had never been monotone but his voice had not before been so obviously variegated. His range here anticipates James as much as it does Whitman. It is spectacularly cosmopolitan and its flexibility goes to make Carlyle appear unripe even while the prospective dismissals of history make Carlyle appear decayed. In other words, Emerson is attempting here, before Henry James, to represent in himself the maturation he wishes for his culture without giving up a jot of youthful energy, without losing anything at all.

It is an impossible task. Even as we acknowledge that Emerson has become more, not less, audacious than he had been, we must admit a degree of failure both in relation to the earlier essays and to Carlyle. In the thirties, Emerson created an uncompromising, assertive voice, which one would expect never to be supportable by the thought. Yet it was so supported, not just perfectly but with constantly astounding turns of logic. The wonderful dialectics of *Representative Men* nonetheless pale in comparison to the bafflement of dialectics occurring in *Nature* or "Self-Reliance" or "The Divinity School Address." "Life is not Dialectics," he writes even in "Experience" (*CW*, III, 34). The earlier essays eschew conventional dialectics so that where we expect a qualification we are given instead a further extravagance. Time itself is baffled by a sequence of sentences that undermine their own linear movement, for they present an exfoliation of a permanent instant of belief.

The back-and-forths of *Representative Men* do not so. They are not enlarging circles of a thorough thought, at once center and circumference. Though Emerson concludes his essay on Montaigne by quoting Channing, "If my bark sink, 'tis to another sea" (186), this does not describe the method of the book. It is aptly inapt that this chapter ends with the words of another man, and a man without the power to threaten any overwhelming of Emerson. In replacing the history of facts with the dialectics of thought, history has smuggled itself inside, for Emerson's dialectic is often sequential in ordinary ways that disappoint. In "Montaigne," he presents himself as a man of personally historical stages, not as exemplary of qualities. Earliness, dissatisfaction, maturity; innocent confidence, skepticism, faith: in rejecting Carlyle's conviction of decline ("Things seem to tend downward, to justify despondency . . . yet, general ends are somehow answered," 185), Emerson has reverted to the three-stage paradigm of English romanticism and of Carlyle's own Teufelsdröckh. To speak of this drama of stages next as a mere "rotation" is to falsify.

Something is the matter here, but the matter is hidden. In "The Uses of Great Men" Emerson carefully defeats a fear of influence by reasserting from earlier writings the repellent power of that particular individuality created "by transferring my *Me* out of the flimsy and unclean precinct of my body, my fortunes, my individual will . . ." (*JMN*, V, 336–37). That *Me* is insufficiently sustained in *Representative Men*, for while Emerson ultimately refuses ordinary biography for others, his own troubled biography informs too much. When he writes, "Each man woke in the morning with an appetite that could eat the solar system like a cake" (184), Emerson is indeed and archetypically "Each man." But as he goes on to speak of disillusion, the boldly gross appetitive image declines into tired words ("this chasm is found,—between the largest promise of ideal power, and the shabby experience" 185). We experience, as in "Higher Laws," not only the merely personal life but an understanding of it given up to others' understandings. Emerson is so involved in a love-hate relation with his influence upon himself that the struggle with earlier figures, wrapped into the form of a struggle with Carlyle, comes to be an obfuscation that damages itself.

If the somersaults are systematic, then we have only what Emerson himself scorns, "the gymnastics of talent" (174), despite whatever protestations of a deeper devotion. Everything in *Representative Men*, though momently wild and civilized at once in the vigor of expression, seems arranged, unspontaneous, *canned*—in particular the debunkings that end each chapter with relentless regularity. Shakespeare is too little a delver into mysteries and too little a giver of laws, Goethe too much so. Plato is too unsystematic, Swedenborg's "theologic cramp" (137) systematizes all too much and "Nature avenges herself speedily on the hard pedantry that would chain her waves" (121). But these critiques are systematic themselves in the low sense of formulaic repetition. That most and least systematic of writers, Emerson is scattering and disguising a question to himself.

Running from an open self-confrontation, Emerson runs into a competition with Carlyle. The result is an unhappy, unfruitful contradiction to Emerson's own assertion that all competitions are debased: "a man comes to measure his greatness by the regrets, envies and hatreds of his competitors. But in these new fields there is room: here are no self-esteems, no exclusions" (22). Emerson toils competitively in a well-tilled field. Of all our writers, he was the one who meant to employ the very terms of our Anglo-American argument to take himself away from it. In that regard, *Representative Men* is a book that never should have been written.

That is why, with what Kenneth Marc Harris well terms its "cool dialectics,"[15] Emerson's book is without a strongly stated motive for its existence: its motives are too many and too confused. Carlyle in comparison is a man with a mission, like the earlier Emerson. In attempting to go beyond the hortatory prolegomenae of his prospective early essays to an enactment of them in relation to a subject-world, Emerson disowns a trust in prophecy as itself enactment. In becoming cosmopolitan, Emerson inadvertently makes Carlyle appear more energetically youthful. Earliness and old age exchange continents as Emerson pushes himself beyond maturity into what we may cruelly call the effete. Nothing seems really crucial in *Representative Men*.

I am ending this consideration as Emerson ended each of his lectures in *Representative Men*, with a debunking; my point being how difficult it will be for American writers successfully to imagine a national maturity, the challenge I will consider in my final two chapters. But again, if this is defeat, it is because Emerson had become more ambitious than he had been, not less so. He leads us, knowingly I believe, to an inevitable conundrum. Influence dies to be born again in a grim resurrection. This is the other way to look at the sequence of chapters in *Representative Men*. "The Uses of Great Men," with its magnificent title already transforming the hugest agents into mere instruments, brilliantly moves to fearlessness. Yet the very first chapter following, on Plato, not only takes up a figure of apparently universal dominion, but a figure who boa-like swallowed his figure of dominion, Socrates, along with anything and anyone lesser. Emerson frees himself and nature finally from this Plato cum Emerson. Yet there is a next chapter that repeats the tale and a next after that. We are made to ask, Why is this man still writing? The reply bespeaks something less inspiriting than an acknowledgment that there are no once-and-for-alls in the quest against influence, especially as the challenging figures do not, as in romance narratives, grow more challenging. Emerson means to show us how a multitude of heroes proves each one partial and guarantees our freedom from each and all. Rather, he dramatizes repetition, which is to say influence as a series of successive traps, each vulnerable to escape but all together forming an inescapable labyrinth, with the self's own prior being a culminating warden and executioner. This is "Childe Roland" in America, without self-apotheosis. But if Emerson will not tell his tale truly, he is yet one of the few sons of God who will tell it at all.

Six

THE AGING OF AMERICA

II

ONTOLOGICAL INSECURITY

I

From an Actualist position, we can see how the American, without a merely personal and mean rancor, could consider his English contemporary as weary, limited, and ultimately insincere. But he also might have a fugitive wish to be more like him. Aside from the danger, noted so often, that this utopian nationalism might discount too grandly the great good and the combatable evils within truly ordinary society, there was the fragility of vertical time and of the actualist self that envisioned it into being. Richard Poirier remarks upon "a necessary discontinuity between revelatory moments, always sporadic and infrequent, and the 'environment' in which people ordinarily pass time." He concludes, "American writers are at some point always forced to return their characters to prison."[1] Dickinson employs the same metaphor when, claiming for the soul "moments of Escape" during which "she dances like a Bomb, abroad, / And swings upon the Hours," she goes on to acknowledge

> The soul's retaken moments-
> When, Felon led along,
> With shackles on the plumed feet
> And staples, in the Song,
>
> The Horror welcomes her again,
> These are not brayed of Tongue.
>
> (512)

The inspired moment that seems to sum eternity is not itself eternal; and, once revoked, it may serve only to make ordinary reality unbearable. Dickinson again:

> Had I not seen the Sun
> I could have borne the shade
> But Light a newer Wilderness
> My wilderness has made—
>
> (1233)

"In theory," John Lynen writes, "the transcendentalists seek to unite the two selves by asserting that the 'I' and the Oversoul are in fact one, and in portraying their own experience, they are most interested to show it developing toward this self-realization. In practice, however, the union is never achieved, except faintly, as an intuition glimpsed, a momentary insight." Such a small portion of success not paradoxically may intensify the actualist attempt, for Lynen goes on to say that the very transitory nature of the union makes one's existence "a continual repetition of the effort to discover one's transcendent identity."[2] Lynen may not acknowledge sufficiently the considerable success of a Thoreau, a Whitman, an Emerson, or a Dickinson in living publicly their literary selves (or for Dickinson in *not* living publicly at all, as intense privacy or innerness was the character of her poetic persona). But the extraordinarily brief periods of full achievement for the American romantics—a decade each for Emerson, Hawthorne (as novelist), and Melville, half of that for prime Whitman—argues the fragility of the actualist state of mind. Even Emerson acknowledges an "I" that could not be merged permanently with the national utopian self in a famous passage: "The worst feature of this double consciousness is, that the two lives, of the understanding and the soul, really show very little relation to each other; never meet and measure each other; one prevails now, all buzz and din; and the other prevails then, all infinitude and paradise; and with the progress of life, the two discover no greater disposition to reconcile themselves."[3] And Emerson confesses in "Experience" that America is not always a poem: "I know that the world I converse with in the city and the farms is not the world I *think*. One day I shall know the value and law for this discrepancy" (CW, III, 48). Now, however, he merely and movingly mourns it.

But without the doubt of discrepancy, in the full confidence of the actualist American, dissatisfactions yet might arise. This personal-corporate self is, after all, some ways unreal; all psychological occurrence could not be contained by it, nor all forms of worldly pleasure. Unlike Emerson, Dickinson never doubted the immanence of the Oversoul; nonetheless she found occasion to refuse it. Sometimes the refusal is based on her assumption that the actualized self would have to experience all emotions to the utmost ("Peril as a Possession / 'Tis Good to bear," 1678) while a partially blinkered reality offers not only a necessary self-protection but also its own joys and capacities:

> Crisis is sweet and yet the Heart
> Upon the hither side

Has dowers of Prospective
To denizens denied. . . .

(1416)

Conversely, the actualized self is sometimes refused because its advertised confidence is all too safe: in "I should have been too glad, I see"
(313), Dickinson's persona refuses a "new Circumference," presum-
ably the Emersonian-Whitmanian certainty, because "I should have
been too saved—I see—/Too rescued—Fear too dim to me."

The actualized American self, then, demands a suppression of any
number of wayward elements in the renegade personality. "All evidence," Bercovitch writes of Emerson generally, "indicates that an
enormous anxiety underlies the affirmation of national identity,"[4] and
this has become a commonplace of Whitman criticism. What is most
suppressed by the invocation of vertical time and the actualized self is
doubt, in particular those doubts concerning self and nation that arise
out of the negative aspects of cultural earliness. We have seen Whitman's "vacant vast," his "measureless oceans of space," as the middle
term in an instantaneous three-part process where hard reality is dissolved and then replaced by an imagined vision made to appear real.
But we could as easily see these "oceans of space" as a terrifying cultural void. There is surely a nervousness in the image of Whitman's soul
"seeking the spheres to connect" these oceans, with actualism a promise not realized—"Till the gossamer thread you fling catch somewhere,
O my soul."

Alongside the assertions of actualism, then, an ontological uncertainty exists; alongside the American self as history's ultimate substitute exists the American self as not quite or at all formed, just as
American history does not quite or at all make a history. With all of the
cultural lacks in Henry James's list, an ego may not collect itself. "*Who
are we? Where are we?*," Thoreau cries as he climbs Katahdin. "*Contact! contact!*" Without a sufficient sense of the "where"—and one
way we must locate any given spot is historically—, the "who" may
dissolve, even the boldest actualized self like Thoreau's. "A mere collection of atoms," he calls himself in a letter to Harrison Blake, "a spiritual foot-ball." Just so, Emerson writes to Samuel Gray Ward, "Can
you not save me, dip me into ice water, find me some girding belt, that
I glide not away into a stream or a gas, and decrease in infinite diffusion?"[5] Emerson recoils less boastfully from the exhortatory confidence of his actualized persona in the crisis essay "Experience."
"Where do we find ourselves?," he begins by asking. "In a series of

which we do not know the extremes, and believe that it has none" (*CW,* III, 27). We are on an intermediate step of a staircase, ignorant of its first and final steps, of origin and goal alike: And in this, Emerson's adaptation of Shelley's dismal "Triumph of Life,"[6] the vacancy of middle time is experience not as a moment from which we will climb to an end glory but as the constant, immobile human condition itself: "Sleep lingers all our lifetime about our eyes, as night hovers all day in the fir-tree." Not only do "we lack the affirmative principle," but the essay refuses to afford one. "Up again, old heart!", Emerson cries in a conclusion which rings with actualist hope, ". . . the true romance which the world exists to realize will be the transformation of genius into practical power" (49). But this familiar aim seems now a far-off and desperate solace, for Emerson just has told us, "I have not found that much was gained by manipular attempts to realize the world of thought. Many eager persons successively make an experiment in this way, and make themselves ridiculous" (48).[7]

Whitman will accuse himself of just such eagerness in his lyric of actualist recoil, "As I Ebb'd." Only five years after the writing of "Song of Myself," the standard-bearer of actualism will attack and refuse its claims:

> Aware now, that amid all the blab whose echoes
>   recoil upon me, I have not once had the least
>   idea who or what I am,
> But that before all my insolent poems the real ME
>   still stands untouched, untold, altogether un-
>   reached,
> Withdrawn far, mocking me with mock-congratulatory
>   signs and bows,
> With peals of distant ironical laughter at every word
>   I have written or shall write,
> Striking me with insults till I fall helpless
>   upon the sand.
>
> O I perceive I have not understood anything—not a
>   single object—and that no man ever can.[8]

Whitman also recovers partially: the poem ends with a futurist vision of Walt and his poems as a debris which may be gathered into a wholeness by a "You, up there," who is simultaneously God and the future reader. But again, the literal realization of vision is made not an immediate possibility but a dream to console present ill; and when actualism partakes of a vague hope, it draws closer to Old World romanticism and ceases to be itself anymore. Neither Emerson or Whitman, in their subsequent works, recover fully the actualist grace.

The actualist begins to quiet his claims, then, when he doubts that his diffusion, his spinning out of his authentic self, may not constitute a truth but a horribly bloated false pose. And this doubt is easily come by, for actualism heads toward kernel tenets while each of the American romantics is persistently aware of fluidity. "There are no fixtures to men, if we appeal to consciousness," writes Emerson in "Circles." "People wish to be settled; only as far as they are unsettled is there any hope for them" (CW, II, 182). The actualist self can accommodate this dynamism of thought—Whitman's self-contradictions, indirections, and "whirlings" and Emerson's "flying perfect" attempt such accommodation—but only briefly, for, flying from dogmatism, the actualist may find himself not spinning out a world but hopelessly scattered within himself. And then, after all the strenuous world-makings, he is left back where the British consigned him, in a vacancy all-negative.

One can argue forever whether the silencing of that actualist shout constitutes a failure (as Harold Bloom implies when he frequently characterizes the career of the American romantic as one of a sudden, triumphant flood followed by an equally startling, painfully slow ebb) or a laudable maturing of visionary honesty. Surely the recantation and the subsequently chastened claims of realizing one's world themselves imitate the dramatized career patterns of the English romantics and make the American romantics less distinctly American: but that too need not be judged an ultimate value.

My point here simply concerns the ambivalence of earliness. The incapacity of the world to fulfill imaginative hope is a theme constant to the literatures of all cultures. But the literalizing insistence of an American actualism can go to crate an especially dire skepticism, and this extremity of opposition is *the* American dialectic. Gather the strengths of earliness, place greatest stress on them in actualism, and they will break into an acknowledgment of the disasters of earliness. These, taken together, constitute ontological insecurity. It is, though refashioned, the same ambivalence that allowed the seventeenth century its alternative visions of the New World, as Jerusalem West or Chaos. Typically, it is Brownson who faces that chaos most squarely. "As parvenus," he writes, "we seek rather to forget than to recall our own past. We are in a position which we were not born to, which we were not brought up to, and which we feel that we may at any moment lose. We do not feel ourselves at home, or settled for life; we are ill at ease; care sits on our brow, anxiety contracts and sharpens our features."[9] This is the anxiety of being early all too late.

2

As the failure of the ego to collect and know itself, ontological insecurity implies death or a failure to be born at all. But cherished, this insecurity may afford widest life. Whitman's persona regains a chastened hopefulness in "As I Ebb'd" as he trades the terrible dualism of a moral body and an untouchable "Real ME" for the fluid identity of water whereby life issues from death: "see, from my dead lips the ooze exuding at last" (XVI). And, not accidentally, the two greatest prose fictions of American romanticism dramatize the progress of ontological insecurity from disaster to triumph.

In the "Custom-House" preface to *The Scarlet Letter,* Hawthorne's persona claims that he is terribly burdened by the heavy history of Salem; yet while overtly he is stretching history to advertise a cultural maturity, he cannily displays the chief symptoms of earliness: he does not know who he is. He begins by praising "the few who will understand him"; a moment later, this poor, misunderstood author who wishes so badly to be seen aright will claim for himself the privilege to "still keep the inmost ME behind its veil" (*CE,* I, 3,4). Later, he generalizes of himself, "Unless people are more than commonly disagreeable, it is my foolish habit to contract a kindness for them" and remarks of his subordinate officers in the Custom House that he "soon grew to like them all" (15); yet in his very next paragraph, the Rotarian becomes misanthrope in describing these same officers "generally as a set of wearisome old fools" (16) and proceeds to pages of caustic merriment at their expense ("Looking at him merely as an animal,—and there was very little else to look at. . . ." [17]).

The real Hawthorne indeed keeps "the inmost ME behind its veil" by concocting for himself a character wildly self-divided, whose comic contradictions prepare us for the warring impulses of Hester and Dimmesdale. This "Hawthorne," taken out of his self-confusions by the burning letter, goes on to create a fiction dependent on the narrator's speculative freedom, his will to put forth a multitude of sometimes contradictory significances and to forgo the valorization of any one. Hester and Dimmesdale, too, dramatize the challenge of transforming ontological insecurity into epistemological breadth. Both rebel against a tyrannical actualist society and become chaotic; Hester allows her thought its full, distraught expanse and finally achieves a coherence that is large; Dimmesdale refuses, even punishes, this free-dom, to the point where his greatest moment—his public confession of sin—is sullied by a despair which is pride. When Dimmesdale cries that he is "the one sinner of the world!" (254), we might reply, "No you're not; but you are the most extreme Puritan." For he, more than his society, has become Stevens's man of one idea in a world of ideas. The Puritan community is able to differentiate between Hester's "A" of adultery and the "A" that may appear in the sky on the night of Gover-nor Winthrop's death, which is interpreted to signify "angel"; to Dimmesdale, every A is adultery. What Hester and "Hawthorne" can do in embroidering that A is to create a vast possibility, which is the strength of American earliness.

Their progress is the progress of Melville's Ishmael as well. He begins his book-life so stuffed with self-contradictions as to appear ultimately bogus. The early Ishmael counterfeits iconoclasm while courting convention. He mocks the safety of land life while quaking at the merest physical discomfort. He advertises easy empathies while his actions are prone to violence and his attitudes to condescension. Most largely, his off-hand, witty, casual tone consorts not at all with a cynical death wish which has him following funerals, eying windowed gravestones, and boarding at the Coffin Inn.[10] But Ishmael learns to be, as he says, "friendly with horrors." His progress is measured by the extent to which he can relax in contradiction, can be grasped by phan-toms without returning upon mystery the grasp that a strangulating single-mindedness could afford. As this progress is equated with Ish-mael's relation first to Queequeg and then to mankind in general, it is equated with the transformation of aggression and death into love and buoyed life.

Accepted, ontological insecurity becomes epistemological play; and the cultural earliness which threatens dissolution comes to afford that clean, unfinished universe promised by the disparagers of history. "I unsettle all things" (CW, II, 188), Emerson can boast in "Circles," and Dickinson's apparent plaint "I'm Nobody!" (288) likewise be-comes a boast of the protean ego, free to identify with the dynamism of thought: "How dreary—to be—Somebody," for to be "Somebody" is to stop. Thus "The Soul should always stand ajar" (1055), open to the trauma of unexpected attitudes. Whitman's pride of inconsistency is of the same nature.

James McIntosh tellingly describes the American romantics as "acutely aware that the mind lacks fixtures, and they look for ways to express belief or disbelif that will be true to the unfixed temporal flow of consciousness." McIntosh quotes a letter from Melville to Hawthorne in which Melville mocks Goethe's emphasis on "the 'all' feeling," then admits a personal recognition of that feeling, and concludes, "But what plays the mischief with the truth is that men will insist upon the universal application of a temporary feeling or opinion."[11] Just so, Emerson will, with some sympathy, criticize Swedenborg in *Representative Men* because he "fastens each natural object to a theologic notion" while "Nature avenges herself speedily on the hard pedantry that would chain her waves" (*W*, IV, 121). This is a perfect description of Melville's Ahab and his fate. There is a demonic form of actualism in which the self mistakes the mere ego's subjectivity for the universal mind, and Emerson as much as Melville or Dickinson employs his ontological insecurity as a veto power, though often in the form of counterassertions that keep doubt subtle.

But the case may be put more positively. Ontological insecurity need not be dramatized always as a recoil from actualism or as a function of American barrenness but as an attempt to validate immediate spiritual emotions, in McIntosh's words, "so as to allow for one's own intruding skepticism."[12] And if ultimate spirit is unattainable or given for a moment only to be revoked, that is no woe if epistemological vitality itself is seen as the greatest good. "The moment that a Plot is plumbed," Dickinson writes, "Prospective is extinct—" (1257); and conversely, "How destitute is he / Whose Gold is firm" (1477). Just as, for Dickinson, "'Heaven'—is what I cannot reach!" (239), so Thoreau can write in an early journal entry, "Let me forever go in search of myself; never for a moment think that I have found myself: be as a stranger to myself, never a familiar, seeking acquaintance still" (*J*, II, 314–15).

However much it may oppose actualism, then, this ontological insecurity never does so finally on the basis of nihilism. Melville certainly entertains nihilism regularly and increasingly. And in *The Confidence Man*, he not only parodies "the radical transfiguration and rebirth of the world by the apocalyptic power of faith," as Warwick Wadlington argues;[13] he attacks his own raw material, language, and its and his own claim for communication. In the first chapter, crazed circumlocutions like "not wholly unobnoxious," "as if not wholly unaffected," "accidentally or otherwise," and (my personal favorite) "Illy pleased" describe and obscure a crowd's brutal reaction to the man of charity who is given added reason by Melville's language to appear as a deaf-mute. Yet Melville is never nihilistic because nihilism is a position, and Melville is far more concerned with unmooring all beliefs than with despairing in public. *The Confidence Man*, as Wadlington insists, sponsors this same rebirth of the world that it hazes; and while the human self is given increasingly fuzzy boundaries in Melville's fiction of the 1850s, so that identity seems sometimes a leaky boat, that is as often a source of empathic delight as of bewildering terror.

Once again here, American writers acknowledge an anxiety and make it a resource. It is a resource more powerful than I have yet suggested, for the epistemological thrust that develops out of insecurity itself develops into an unprecedented freeing of literary form. In fiction alone, from Blithedale to Bly, from Yoknapatawpha to Yoyodyne, American writers have unsettled every novelistic given they could recognize—all, one presumes, on the assumption that cultural and literary inheritances bind as much as they enable. Against them, a floating uncertainty is a first move to a larger truth.

Nervous, edgy, actively heuristic: American texts place their own epistemological coming-into-being at center stage. One can write about the metaphysics of Dickens—J. Hillis Miller has done so with superb insight—but one could choose not to and still write well of Dickens; one could not with that same impunity ignore the jostling of attitudes in Hawthorne, Melville, Dickinson. Emerson describes the proper role of the American Scholar as "Man Thinking," and works of American romanticism bear an intense present as the persona tries on one attitude after another. At extreme times, as when Dickinson writes, "It was not death, for I stood up" (510), we go beyond "Man Thinking" to what we can term thought manning, as the self thinks itself into an ego, one ego after another. "Every thought is also a prison," Emerson declares in *The Poet*. "But the quality of the imagination is to flow, and not to freeze" (W, III, 19,20). To place Emerson's image against De Tocqueville's muse of ontological insecurity—"In democratic ages it sometimes happens . . . that men are as much afloat in matters of belief as they are in laws"[14]—is to view an anxiety transformed.

3

If the American can so transform his anxiety, then the English Victorian, the Victorian Sage as John Holloway characterizes him, is liable to discrediting. The Victorian novelist or essayist has it figured; now he is instructing us. He is past tense, man having thought, late even in his moment of writing. Again, from this American stance, English works could be devalued in relation to American works in terms of a dichotomy stated by Roland Barthes:

> Text of pleasure; the text that contents, fills, grants euphoria; the text that comes from culture and does not break with it, is linked to a

comfortable practice of reading. Text of bliss: the text that imposes a state of loss, the text that discomforts (perhaps to the point of a certain boredom), unsettles the reader's historical, cultural, psychological assumptions, the consistency of his tastes, values, memories, brings to a crisis his relation with language.[15]

Barthes goes on to qualify his opposition by noting the anarchic coexistence of pleasure and bliss in all examples of literature; and to characterize English and American works by this extreme dichotomy is simplistic and unjust. But all's fair in the overthrow of influence, and this dichotomy is, as we have seen in specific cases, the root attitude by which the American writer could render impotent his British counterpart. Cheerfully transformed, ontological insecurity would team with its apparent opposite, that confident literalizing of vision that we have termed actualism, to make the English writer appear safe, narrow, superficial, tired, past, imprisoned, dead. If actualism tells the Englishman, "You have not meant what you said," ontological insecurity taunts, "You have not searched deeply enough; what you imagine as answers are merely beginning questions." The case of Melville and Dickens, considered in chapter two, we now can see as exampling this aggressive employment of the American epistemological demand.

But just as often, perhaps more often, ontological insecurity promotes a peace between American and English writers. This is so because its free-moving skepticism is bound to call all attitudes and projects into question, especially those most dearly held. Fighting the British would start to look silly or boring. More positively, in calling a writer's actualist hopes into question, ontological insecurity would create within the self an opposition of encompassing interest; the British enemy would be less and less necessary as the anxiety of demand (in Geoffrey Hartman's phrase), a writer's worry about what he should do next *vis-à-vis* his own prior works, replaces the anxiety of influence. I want to look briefly at three examples wherein American writers employ the British romantics in a spirit we have not yet seen—a friendly one—to consider the quality of this peace.

If we return momentarily to Wordsworth and Whitman, this peace looks like a rationalization of defeat. In Whitman's case, the route of actualist retreat leads to British romanticism. The only crises of "Song of Myself" had been crises of the too-much kind: aesthetic receptivity is so acute and full that "the trained soprano . . . she convulses me like the climax of my love-grip"; or that climax itself, in terms of "touch . . . quivering me to a new identity," is "too much for me"; or a too-complete empathizing leads to an oath that is an identification,

"O Christ! My fit is mastering me!" (26:602; 27:618; 37:933). But these crises are equally boasts of vitality, and Walt as suffering Christ has only to accept and increase the full force of his experience to become Walt as triumphant Christ. There is a momentarily sarcastic inner voice externalized in "Song of Myself" to tease, "Walt, you understand enough . . . why don't you let it out then?" but it is easily met by the reply "My final merit I refuse you . . . I refuse putting from me the best I am" (25:570, 578); and as this temporary reticence is progressively conquered throughout the rest of the poem, no more self-directed sarcasm occurs. This confidence is diametrically opposed by the sarcastic, externalized voice of the Real Me in "As I Ebb'd" who, "with peals of distant ironical laughter at every word I have written or shall write," makes a "baffled, bent" Walt admit "I have not understood anything"; and the phrase "or shall write" precludes even hope for the future on the actualist grounds of realizing one's rhetoric. Indeed, the shift to a present tense following upon the poem's confident opening (from "As I wended the shores I know" to "As I wend the shores I know not") announces a perpetual incapacity, a terrible cancelling of the actualist *now*.

The grounds shift to the Lake district. Whitman's "As I Ebb'd," with its ocean of eternal life spitting temporal beings onto the shore as debris, owes its chief drama to Wordsworth's Immortality Ode, though the symbols are demonized to the extent that debris can hardly "sport along the shore." More essentially, the poem is enacted in the Wordsworthian stages of primary confidence, wreck and deprivation, and humbled regathering. In the other great lyric of the 1860 *Leaves*, "A Word Out of the Sea" (later "Out of the Cradle Endlessly Rocking"), the retreat to Wordsworth is more fully marked. This is distinctly a poem of the Wordsworthian two consciousnesses sung by "A man—yet by these tears a little boy again" with its main body entitled "REMINIS-CENCE." The poem's major form is a doubled elegy, an elegy upon the deserted he-bird's elegy for his lost mate, just as "As I Ebb'd" had been Whitman's elegy for a deserted confidence in himself, just as all of Wordsworth's great lyrics are transformed elegies mourning and then justifying the loss not of a youthful friend but of a youthful heart within the self. Here, too, employing Wordsworthian developmental time, Whitman traces his origin as poet to this specific occasion, the child's hearing of the he-bird's mournful, wildly desirous chant:

> Bird! (then said the boy's Soul,)
> Is it indeed toward your mate you sing? or is it mostly
>   to me?

For I that was a child, my tongue's use sleeping,
Now that I have heard you,
Now in a moment I know what I am for—I awake,
And already a thousand singers—a thousand songs,
    clearer, louder, more sorrowful than yours,
A thousand warbling echoes have started to life within
    me,
Never to die.

(XXIX)

The bird's sorrow is terrible. But it occasions an intensity of song that leaves the boy more in awe than in despair. It awakes the child to significant life and to a song "Never to die." Even before the sea "Lisped to me constantly the low and delicious word DEATH," death's finality has been translated into life.

"A Word Out of the Sea" enacts the very process Wordsworth dramatizes in such memories as the Christmas of his father's death in book twelve of *The Prelude*. Whitman's imagination has become, like Wordsworth's, renovative upon a harsh reality existing external to the imagination but available to the mind's transvaluation.

Wordsworth confesses of his youthful self elsewhere in *The Prelude*, "when spring had warmed the cultured Vale, / moved we as plunderers where the mother-bird / Had in high places built her lodge; . . ." (1:326–8). Whitman twits his predecessor by a greater delicacy: "When the snows had melted, and the Fifth month grass was growing," he too seeks "every day the she-bird, crouched on her nest"; but though "a curious boy, never too close, never disturbing them, / Cautiously peering, absorbing, translating" (I). This would be a febrile jibe were we not to see it as significant of actualist traces in Whitman's lyric. His *then* and *now* are not so clearly separable as Wordsworth's. His child is more meditative than Wordsworth's, more empathically capable. He is given "the key" all at once; at that moment, in that moment, he becomes much of what he now is, the poet. Further, the mature Whitman becomes by his reminiscence "a little boy again," collapsing time as Wordsworth never fully does nor wishes to. Nonetheless, for the little boy the sea's lisping of death replaces the bird's distraught complaint while the mature self can pledge, "I do not forget, / But fuse the song of two together" (XXXIV). "Two together" had been the repeated phrase of the he-bird celebrating his companionship with his mate. "Two together" now means severally that lost union, the he-bird song of terrible loss and the sea's answering lisp, and the little boy and the mature poet. But for two to be together, there must be differentiation, and the mature poet, more fully than the little boy, can fuse the song of mourning and the mystery that gives it ecstatic answer. Like Wordsworth, if for once more hesitantly and hintingly, Whitman admits and celebrates a difference brought by time: a deep distress hath further humanized a soul earlier humanized in the moment of awaking.

It is a strange business. The poet who had fought Wordsworthian influence to inaugurate his career is, within five years, adapting Wordsworth's vision, sometimes to rebuke his earlier self. This action is fascinating, the result powerful in these superb lyrics, but that may be because the 1855 Walt of actualism remains nearby. From 1860 forward, as C. Carroll Hollis strikingly proves by a consideration of style elements, Whitman "tries to invade the high formality of English traditional poetry"[16] to the clear detriment of his art.

But that is Whitman only. The unfraught acceptance of a British model, I said earlier, is sometimes part of an American writer's attempt to reach a visionary maturity on behalf of his culture via ontological insecurity. (It is paradoxical that this insecurity results from cultural earliness and then becomes a means of aging; but then the extreme cognitive sophistication of our major nineteenth-century writers— mingled with whatsoever barbarisms—is likewise a surprise.) But I do not mean that this is a decisive change in mid-career for the other writers of Whitman's period. And I do not find in that process an inevitable harm. One of Hawthorne's finest short stories, "Rappaccini's Daughter," is primarily based on Keats's "Lamia," though it includes allusions to Dante, Spenser, Milton, and other figures of a large Western tradition; and rather than marking a new direction for Hawthorne, the tale is an extension of Hawthorne's most characteristic techniques into new Old World territory.

Two scholars, Julian Smith and Norman A. Anderson, independently made this discovery.[17] Each finds in "Rappaccini's Daughter" numerous verbal echoes of "Lamia" and I will quote Anderson's summary at length to suggest the density of Keats's influence on the story.

> The resemblances of "Rappaccini's Daughter" to "Lamia" are of two
> kinds, the narrative and the conceptual (allegorical). Of the first kind are
> these details: (1) a young student living apart from his family meets and
> falls in love with a ravishingly beautiful girl who is possessed of super-
> natural powers; (2) the student idealizes the girl but is persuaded by her
> to realize her essential womanliness; (3) the pairs of lovers dwell in a
> bower of extravagant (but unnatural) splendor; (4) the young student
> secludes himself from the world, avoiding his tutor in the street; (5) the

tutor intrudes upon the bower and upon the lives of the lovers; (6) the tutor opposes the beautiful enchantress and destroys her, killing or ruining his student-friend at the same time. Of the second kind are: (1) the characters themselves—the deluded, imperceptive dreamer-lover, the innocent but corrupt serpent-woman, and the coldly rational scientist; (2) the depiction of "sweet sin"; (3) the impact of the busy world of reality upon the beautiful, enchanted world of illusion; and (4) the author's ambivalence toward his subject, manifested in an ambiguity in the meaning of the story.[18]

Given this particularity of borrowings, what astonishes is how little we can make of it. Smith concludes lamely that both writers are depicting the intermixture of good and evil and the woes of selfishness. Anderson, promising grand results, decides that Hawthorne stresses moral issues more openly than Keats. And I cannot do any better. Keats is more concerned with the loss of a mythological imagination, Hawthorne with ill ideas of feminine sexuality, but so? Both ladies are traditionally or officially deluding and evil but in these renderings they are dominantly sympathetic. But so? Keats and Hawthorne are both criticizing and overturning literary traditions that appear frightened of imaginative passion as embodied in women, but Hawthorne is nowhere criticizing and overturning Keats.

He is instead testing his own usual vision on new materials. Perhaps to alert us that his tale is full of sources, the narrator claims to be retelling a story written by a certain "M. de l'Aubépine" ("Hawthorne" in French), author of a series of volumes titled "Contes deus fois racontées." This is a delightful joke—poor Aubépine is "unknown to many of his own countrymen" because "he seems to occupy an unfortunate position between the Transcendentalists" and popular "pen and ink men"; viewed properly, his tales "may amuse a leisure hour as well as those of a brighter man; if otherwise, they can hardly fail to look excessively like nonsense" (CE, X, 91–92). But this is more than a self-deflating joke, too. Hawthorne is naming himself as his own chief source; and he is giving himself a European name because he is transferring his usual New England material to a European locale. More importantly, he is mating his sense of things to a British and Western literary tradition. The Italian Giovanni Guasconti displays the usual problems of Hawthornian young men with women and with their own sexuality. Beatrice is for him either poisonous-passionate or angelic-sisterly. In Giovanni, as in Goodman Brown or even Arthur Dimmesdale, lust and fearful repression feed each other. And Giovanni is another Aylmer as an empiricist who attempts an inhuman purification of a woman that results in her death. "Seemed" is the verb whenever Giovanni, king of the voyeurs and prince of the narcissists, takes his eyes from his mirror long enough to spy Beatrice withering insects with her breath. For Hawthorne, she is poisonous by perspective—not so in relation to Giovanni, whose hybrid emotions, as the girl tells him, make for "more poison in thy nature than in mine"; poisonous indeed in relation to the protective and possessive father Rappaccini, a demented actualist whose creation of hybrid plants do not reveal God but compete with Him.

Hawthorne's own experiment with his hybrid story is far more successful. He is able to extend his materials, let them be infiltrated by Dante (who, as I said in chapter one, views *his* Beatrice initially with lust but who then sublimates his desire, as Giovanni never can, to experience his beloved as an example of divine bounty), Milton, and, especially, Keats, without at all sacrificing his distinctive identity. The characters belong to Hawthorne's usual gallery as much as to the cast of "Lamia"; the narrative indirection and even misdirection, whereby the narrator will show momentary sympathy with any number of views, is a constant in all of Hawthorne's more ambitious writings from "The Maypole of Merry Mount" forward; the hideous final paragraph, in which Baglioni enjoys his triumph while ignoring his responsibility for Beatrice's death, is a match for the ironic close of "Roger Malvin's Burial" in which a protagonist imagines himself saved by the killing of his son. Hawthorne can borrow from Keats as we earlier saw Dickens borrowing from Hawthorne: without repayment, borrowing as pure theft. It is an incorporative act, but it is more friendly than competitive, for Hawthorne in no way dramatizes a going-beyond in relation to Keats.

Whitman retreats to Wordsworth; Hawthorne extends to Keats, finding an epistemological playmate. A final example of peacemaking is more complex. When Poe employs the major motifs of Coleridge's "Kubla Khan" and Shelley's "Alastor" in "The Domain of Arnheim," he appears to debunk these poems of visionary frustration by picturing a paradise that can be realized successfully upon literal, common land. But this infinite oneupmanship turns out to be less aggressive and significant than it promises, for Poe's major rebellion in this remarkable, insufficiently acknowledged story-essay is against his own other works. He works here so furiously against his usual American tension that it is his British predecessors who appear contrastingly fraught, self-divided, epistemologically nervous, American. Poe achieves less a peace than a role reversal. But again, his main opposition is to himself.

Poe's typical self combines an actualist thrust—his protagonists voyage back in time to the edge of the All in circumstances that, though increasingly strange, are described realistically—with an equally insistent ontological insecurity, for as the self approaches the All his identity begins to dissolve. For Poe, as not for Emerson, you cannot become a transparent eyeball on the Boston Commons, for as you possess the "Heart Divine" you will cease to be you. In his insistence that temporal experience can be manipulated to lead back to its own grounds of nonbeing, or preexistence, Poe is something of an actualist. But in that temporal experience is thereby cancelled, in that, as Lynen writes, "Poe considers the now and eternity as exact opposites,"[19] Poe opposes an Emersonian actualizing of vision within our common lives. But thus too, Poe does not sponsor Wordsworth's flashing out of the senses in a bodiless ecstacy. Instead he claims to have experienced "psychal impressions" in which "it is as if the five senses were supplanted by five others alien to mortality."[20]

Thus too, in many of Poe's tales, a tension develops within the hero between his immortal longings and his fear of personal extinction. A barely recognized drive for unification rages against an earthly existence that is a tortured and bewildering block to the All; and an equally tenacious will struggles to stay alive. The tension is dramatized in shockingly physical terms, so that the reluctant flesh speaks its terror to us. But Poe manipulates the voice of the flesh so that it must confess or unwittingly disclose self-defeating impulses, the impulses of the desiring spirit. Because the metaphysical and psychological parties of critical discourse on Poe each tend to feature one pole of this tension and discount the other, what to one critic is a quest for unity is to another a sinking into primitive anarchy.[21]

This argument can be resolved. While an individual story may emphasize the protagonist's psychological disintegration or his spiritual completion, in Poe's full vision these are not alternative poles but the same process as seen from incongruent perspectives. As Ellison, the artist-hero of "Arnheim," speculates, "There *may* be a class of beings, human once, but now invisible to humanity, to whom, from afar, our disorder may seem order—our unpicturesqueness picturesque."[22] With Poe, it is always a question of stance. Where the *Eureka*-minded reader finds in a Poe hero excitation unto a final ecstasy, a psychologically minded reader finds intolerable self-conflict amounting to a dissolution of the personality. In Poe's most complex stories like "Ligeia" or "Usher," neither perspective is sacrificed to the other: the protagonist himself experiences a cognizance of both views and the result is a self-fright that is equally a cherished terror.

But not quite always. In his earlier story-essay "The Landscape

Garden," a rewritten version of which constitutes the first two-thirds of "Arnheim," Poe had introduced Ellison as a mortal who achieved the same shadowing forth of heaven's beauty for earthly eyes. With the addition of the narrator's voyage into Ellison's creation, "Arnheim" became Poe's most ambitious effort to dramatize the fulfillment of his hope for timeless experience within the temporal and to specify through imagery the nature of this experience.

In "The Landscape Garden," Ellison refuses neoclassical rules for his creation, praising instead the free beauty of a "Nightingale," such as that of Keats, or the "Sensitive Plant" of Shelley.[23] But Poe is rarely frank in his acknowledgments, and "Kubla Khan" is surely his most general model. In Coleridge's greatest lyric, Kubla Khan is envisioned as creating a compendious landscape which combines all oppositions—life and death, love and aggression, intellect and passion, male and female, transient intensity and permanent order—so as to include and thereby defeat all negations. But while the eternal may be captured in real time, past, present, and future are made to confess the hatefulness rendering temporary that achievement: "ancestral voices prophesying war." And the poet's alternative, to rebuild that dome "in mid-air," is hedged, as everyone says, by "coulds" and "woulds" even as the poem's description of Xanadu may seem the very achievement hoped for.

In "Arnheim," Ellison does achieve his vision, and on land rather than in language only. His, too, is a *discordia concours*. There is solitude without isolation, nature and mystery coexisting, foreboding answered by security. The narrator travels through the domain in a vessel buoyed by a phantom bark like the boat of Wordsworth's Peter Bell or Shelley's Witch of Atlas, a conveyer of swift spirit. Unlike the usual vessel of a Poe protagonist, however, this "phantom bark" is not destructive but sustaining, affording the physical boat "a substantial floor." Nature is modified by a "wizard propriety" and yet "the clear water still tranquilly flowed" (191). Spirit and matter cooperate. Hills come into view which Poe describes by piling noun upon contrasting noun—"richness, warmth, color, quietude, uniformity, softness, delicacy, daintiness, voluptuousness"—in holistic resolution, and finally, after changing to a canoe that directs itself and whisks the narrator beyond any fearful self-control, the narrator is able to view at once a savage range of hills and a cultivated bank, the wild and civilization, at once. The wild is purified ("There is not one token of the usual river *debris*," 194); primitivity is cured of violence as if, where id was, there shall sane spirit be. But the boat does veer toward the cultivated bank, in the direction of Poe's belief that man's "savage condition—his condition of action *without* reason—is his unnatural state" and that "not until he has stepped upon the highest pinnacle of civilization will his *natural* state be ultimately reached, or thoroughly determined."[24] Ellison adapts the English writer's claim for cultural maturity thereby. Finally, a wall covered with the mourning weed of clematis and a forbidding gate come into view. But the gate, that final barrier, musically separates its wings as the last beams of the setting sun take on a flamelike effulgence. Death becomes a passageway into the "Paradise of Arnheim" for a visitor still ruddily alive.

Death is defeated as well by Ellison's postmortem transformation into his domain. Every quality of his landscape is related to the personal harmony of its maker. In other words, Ellison and Poe have achieved what Kubla Khan and Coleridge could not. Or have they? Ellison's attempt is finally more modest. It is to provide "this sense of the Almighty design to be *one* step depressed—to be brought into something like harmony or consistency with the sense of human art" (187). This may be a redacted statement of Coleridge's imagination, that "repetition of the eternal I AM," but the "*one* step depressed" sounds more humble, and Ellison's character displays far more a natural moderation than it does the dangerous delight of the poet-speaker of "Kubla Khan." The architecture of his ultimate place is described as midair too, but midair means differently here. It is the handiwork of sylphs, fairies, genii and gnomes—that is, the "Almighty design . . . *one* step depressed." It is Poe—Poe of all people—who appears sensibly earthbound in relation to his British source.

So too in relation to Shelley's two voyage-poems, "Alastor" and "The Witch of Atlas." The latter had been written to oppose explicitly the overly naturalized moralizings of Wordsworth's "Peter Bell," which in turn had been written to show Coleridge that one did not need the supernatural machinery of "The Ancient Mariner" for moral purposes. "Arnheim" is thus the final term in this natural-supernatural to and fro, merging its predecessors.

But "Arnheim" is more interestingly related to "Alastor."[25] In Shelley's poem, a visionary voyager is unsatisfied by nature, even as he visits the places of civilization's origins. He spurns human love only to be visited in a dream by a veiled maid who treats him to the "All feeling" and then disappears when he wakes. The maid personifies in her sexual-spiritual being something of the same life totality as Xanadu and Arnheim and also represents the visionary's own ideal self. But her departure leaves Alastor spiritually bereft. His previously unanswered longings become intolerable as he wakes to "The cold white light of morning, . . . / . . . the clear and garish hills, / The distinct

267

ONTOLOGICAL INSECURITY

valley and the vacant woods,"[26] a nature impoverished by the mating that could not be sustained. He wanders through gloom-increasing landscapes, a "blind earth, and heaven / That echoes not my thoughts" (289–90). He enters a boat, a self-directing "little shallop," which leads him finally to a whirlpool, "Reflecting yet distorting every cloud" (385). The whirlpool threatens death in a grim, root-twisting landscape, but it leads to a beautiful and calm vista hitherto un-discovered. Alastor nonetheless refuses nature's virgin paradise for the solitude of his vision, which even nature's best cannot return to him. He wills his death in the doubt-invaded hope that death will lead to a pre-natural origin, to the maid.

Poe's Ellison accepts the natural best vista that Shelley's visionary hero refuses. He collapses the schism that rends Alastor into the happy natural supernaturalism of Arnheim. The contrast is further particu-larized. Alastor had spurned human love—there is even a suggestion that nature may revenge itself upon Alastor for his refusals by the vi-sion of the veiled maid. For Poe's hero, "above all, it was in the sympa-thy of a woman, not unwomanly, whose loveliness and love enveloped his existence in the purple atmosphere of Paradise, that Ellison thought to find, *and found,* exemption from the ordinary cases of human-ity . . ." (188, Poe's italics). The landscape of Arnheim is suffused by relational love, just what Alastor's gloomy projections lack.

There is a whirlpool in the Arnheim voyage as well, at least a cir-cular basin. It too seems threatening but leads to that wider vista of the hills. That vista is then itself gone beyond until we reach a realized vista of vistas as the gate swings open into the natural/beyond-natural paradise that is deemed sufficient.

Poe everywhere combines what Shelley had sundered. Shelley had rent even himself in "Alastor," into the nature-spurning visionary and the nature-worshipping narrator who tells the tale as an admonition. But this Wordsworthian narrator is himself divided, for his disapproval of Alastor is equalled by an unscheduled strong awe of him. At places, Shelley even manages his tone to make some cruel fun of the narrator's relatively low satisfactions. The two Shelleys are combined in Poe's story. While there are two characters in "Arnheim" as well, this nar-rator actively voyages through Ellison's legacy—Shelley's visionary had bequeathed only "pale despair and cold tranquility" to his narrator (718)—and consistently praises his subject rather than veering in self-contradiction like the narrator of "Alastor." Again, it is the American who appears more ontologically settled and mature than Shelley, while Shelley is conducting a twisty debate with Wordsworth (and with Col-eridge, for the poem's opening alludes to "The Eolian Harp" and

"Frost at Midnight" as well as to Tintern Abbey and The Intimations Ode) inside himself.

But Poe is debating himself as well, and the imagery of his tale bears greatest relation to his usual images, in contrast. For instance, crucial to Ellison's achievement is the deceptively simple "chief principle" of "free exercise in the open air" (176). This principle protects Ellison from the dangers of those forms of isolation, those self-obsessed "indoors" of consciousness that preclude the natural world and surround a Roderick Usher or a Prospero in "Masque of the Red Death." Poe's typical hero places himself in a tightly enclosed space that is both a magic circle and a trap—again our dual perspective—in which, as Richard Wilbur says, "he is in the process of dreaming his way out of the world."[27] The locale in these narratives is invariably isolated, the atmosphere overripe, stifling, and rich, and finally as inescapable as Poe's paradox of existence and fulfillment. Though "thrown back on self" by his creative idea, Ellison does not lose hold on a natural life for the sake of his vision. Rather, he discovers in landscape gardening a form of art that includes the physical and immediate and affords the dream within this world. Too, the principle of "free exercise in the open air" warns Ellison against the absolute seclusion of Poe's typical protagonist and against that protagonist's usual scorn of others as well. The meaningfully sociable Ellison declares, "as yet I am not Timon. I wish the composure but not the depression of solitude." Roderick Usher take note, as Ellison builds his domain near a city, not only to gain "control over the extent and duration of my repose," but also to enjoy the benefits of citizenly friendships, "the sympathy of the poetic in what I have done" (189).

Not fame but moderation is Ellison's principle. His reaction against solitude is, almost literally, measured. It is certainly mirrored in the landscape he creates. Robert L. Carringer notes that, on the few occasions when Poe allows his protagonists an infinite expanse, such as in the sea voyage of Arthur Gordon Pym, he manages somehow to place the protagonist in a succession of narrow enclosures. Carringer argues that Poe is driven to employ these claustrophobic locales by his theme of inescapable self-confrontation.[28] But Poe may see, rather, that an endless vista will create its own reaction, that giddy exposure will lead back to solitude. For this reason, Ellison also rejects a "panoramic prospect" for his site. Its constant view would overwhelm him and make him feel all too "abroad in the world" (190). Ellison wishes to limit, interestingly, his voyagings.

Ellison's ability to fulfill the intense longings of Poe's typical seekers while he self-consciously excludes their destructive elements also evidences itself in the limited aim of Arnheim. It will express "a nature which is not God, nor an emanation from God, but which still is nature in the sense of the handiwork of the angels that hover between man and God" (188). At the same time that Ellison wishes to assert his humanity fully, he never forgets the limits of his mortal being. His desire to humanize nature, to make it significant and fulfilling, and his desire to protect himself and his fellows from the terror of an encounter with the "Heart Divine" give two meanings to another principle of Arnheim: "Its adaptation to the eyes which were to behold it on earth" (177), an adaptation never achieved or even seen as a possibility by Poe's more frenzied seekers. But then too, Ellison is Poe's only happily married man, and his whirlpools are not destructive-ecstatic but open out to a more complete world.

And yet not only Arnheim the domain but "Arnheim" the tale is prone to the limits of any vision meant to mediate. The story-essay does deserve greater recognition, but one can see why it has not gripped the imagination of readers. Poe's imperfect art depends on those incongruent tensions that "Arnheim" is designed to relax. We prefer Poe's American unease to his more-than-British sanity here.

My effort, though, has been to suggest that epistemological issues may provide a neutral ground where American and British romanticisms can meet. I do not mean to imply that, once that occurs, the American struggle against the British automatically ends. None of the works I have considered here has the power to perform such a wide cultural resolution, and literary history is hardly so ordered in any case as to proceed by the effect of single works. It will take an American-British imagination just a crucial bit more American than British to end our tale; ah, it will take Henry James. But I have meant to propose that epistemological questings provide an Anglo-American basis for James's resolution.

4

Until James, though, any such reconciliation occurs between American writers and the English romantics, not the Victorians. Ontological insecurity in fact tends to differentiate more fully the Americans from a going British realism. If we look back on our last two examples, we note the authors of American works of prose fiction choosing for their influences British poems. That is, at a moment in England when a socially oriented realistic fiction is becoming ascendent to the point that poetry (say, in Browning's monologues) is borrowing from it, American fiction writers head toward the more obviously mythy and wonder-creating realms of verse. But more largely this may suggest a genre-freeing result once ontological insecurity becomes epistemological experiment. I will neglect some other obviously important facets of this insecurity: the American refusal of fictional endings that would imply a stolid settling upon a too packaged moral lesson; and, allied to this, the affective demands upon the reader to discover a work's springs of meaning, which are deliberately left unadvertised to afford the democratic reader his participatory chance. Instead, I will focus on this single, large effect of the epistemological thrust, for it carries us to a final point concerning the American struggle with history. It also bears implication for any mapping of American literary history.

This effect, again, is generic. I wish to claim that the prevalent genre of American romantic texts is the encylopaedic. Northrop Frye defines encyclopaedic form proper as "a scripture or sacred book in the mythical mode" but he then broadens his term to include any work attempting to be the story of all things. Not only the Bible but Dante's *Commedia*, the epics of Homer, Virgil, and Milton, Yeats's *Vision*, and Joyce's *Finnegans Wake* qualify as encyclopaedic. Each appears exhaustive in its treatment of human matters; each treats origins and endings, Genesis to Apocalypse and, apparently, everything in between.[29]

The demand for a national epic, so prevalent in America during the eighteenth and early nineteenth centuries, was really a demand for a central cultural myth. On its own somewhat mistaken and nostalgic terms, the demand went unanswered in any significant way. (Such attempts as Joel Barlow's *The Columbiad* make us wish it had gone unanswered wholly.) The American romantics replaced the ideal of epic by an encyclopaedic form that was less the story of all things than the telling of all tellings of some things. These works are methodologically encyclopaedic.

That is, *Moby-Dick* is not encyclopaedic because we find in it many imitations of epic commonplaces or because every inch of the whale is surveyed or even because every thought anyone ever has had about a whale is presented. It is encyclopaedic because it seems to provide an exhaustive repertoire of all possible methods for thinking about the whale, with whale-thoughts metonymic for all human experiencing of the world. Again, it is not so much that Ishmael examines every aspect of the whale but that he tries out every system of explanation. Simultaneously, the book surveys literary possibilities—epic gives way to prose lyric, which gives way to satire, which gives way to Renaissance tragedy, which gives way to the social novel, and such subliterary genres as the potboiler and the dirty joke get included as well. *Moby-Dick* is Melville's best book but all of his books proceed similarly. Richard Brodhead argues persuasively that "Hawthorne's and Melville's common tendency to tell a story in several ways" affords "what Yeats calls an 'emotion of multitude' less by representing a large variety of occasions or relations or attitudes or feelings, than by *seeing* their subjects in a large variety of ways." And it is epistemological action that finally becomes the real subject, for "Hawthorne and Melville do not try to merge the representational modes they use, nor do they try to efface their differences by moving among them gradually and transitionally. If anything, they enlarge the differences: they allow each mode to write its own chapters, to bring its own kind of world into existence."[30] Or, as David Lodge puts this same distinction, "The English novelists create and sustain their own distinctive authorial voices which give unity of form and feeling to their versions of experience. . . . It may be an anonymous voice, but it is strongly charged with personality: urbane or energetic, jolly or meditative. It is always civilized and reliable. The reader knows where he is." But in an American work like *Moby-Dick,* "The jocular, yarn-spinning style of the early chapters shifts into passages of prophetic declamation, Shakespearean pastiche, poetic lyricism, and discursive prose."[31]

This same process occurs within the single speaker of a poem or essay. "Song of Myself" is not encyclopaedic because it lists everything but because its grand tallymaster is everything. The Walt of the poem is on occasion a mythic hero, an omniscient god; a hero of romance, a mortal with godlike empathic powers; a leader of society, mortal but powerful, the American spirit personified, out of what Frye calls the high mimetic mode; one of us, "one of the roughs," full of colloquialisms out of Frye's low mimetic mode; and even for repudiated moments the hero of bondage in what Frye calls the ironic mode. Within a single phrase of self-description—"Hankering, gross, mystical, nude"—Whitman illustrates Lodge's dictum that "the American writer puts words together which, according to the canons of traditional literary decorum, just don't belong together."[32] Likewise, in a single paragraph of *Nature,* Emerson identifies himself as an ordinary, low-mimetic fellow "Crossing a bare common, in snow puddles, at twilight" and then as a "transparent eyeball" who is "part and parcel of God" (*CW,* I, 10). And this is appropriate to a writer who is also an orator because in oratory, as he says in an 1839 journal entry, "everything is admissible, philosophy, ethics, divinity, criticism, poetry, humor, fun, mimicry, anecdotes, jokes, ventriloquism, all the breadth and versatility of the most liberal conversation: highest, lowest, personal, local topics, all are permitted and all may be combined in one speech;—it is a panharmonicon. . . ."[33]

Lodge finds these juxtaposings evidence of the American writer's uncertainty "about how to address himself to his subject and to his audience." But that is to fail to recognize the happy transformation of ontological insecurity. Whether American encyclopaedic form is given comic treatment (as in the works of Whitman and Emerson where the diversity of the self is celebrated) or tragic implication (where, at times in Hawthorne, Melville, or Faulkner, the distance any mode of perception takes us from a unitary truth is mourned), it implies the freedom and largesse of human possibility. The methodological encyclopedia is the literary equivalent of the New World myth by which America at once would recapitulate rapidly all history and yet end history to usher in a new existence beyond the bounds of the temporal. Granted that genres travel through historical periods without being contained solely inside one or another, we tend to associate genres and periods (poetic drama, say, with the late Renaissance); and by employing conventions of language the tie can be tightened. Thus a work like *Moby-Dick* surveys the past, brings universal history aboard the American whaling vessel. America thus recapitulates all time. But as historical ages, through literary genres, are being presented self-consciously and examined for their possibilities, the work itself exists beyond temporal strictures; and as these genres are equally characterized as permanent methods for seeing rather than as artifacts of this or that past period, history is dissolved into significance. History is exhausted so that the capacious *now* of vertical time may subordinate it. The burden of Britain is escaped simultaneously, as the genres most easily associated with its literature—Shakespearian tragedy, realistic fiction—become a few possibilities among many more.

But in a different sense, no literary text escapes time. Two paragraphs above, in discussing the juxtaposed selves of the Walt persona, I employed Northrop Frye's terms for five stages of literary development: myth, romance, high-mimetic, low-mimetic, and irony. Each stage is defined by the hero's status—a god in myth, a miraculous but still-human being in romance, a leader in high-mimetic, one of us in low-mimetic, a nearly subhuman sufferer in irony—and by the hero's environment—supernatural in myth, mixed in romance, natural in both high- and low-mimetic, hell-on-earth in irony. Frye argues that European fiction over fifteen centuries "has steadily moved its center of gravity down the list"; and, when he claims that the history of classical literature, "in greatly foreshortened form," evidences this same descent, he comes close to claiming a universal literary history.[34] It is easy to question his map: the aspects (hero's power, environment) by which Frye defines the modes seem arbitrary and the trust he places in a permanent norm of everyday experience seems naive. As a helpful formulation, then, rather than as an ultimate truth, we can apply the terms to question the status of American romantic literature.

That body of literature becomes dominant in the second quarter of the nineteenth century, which for European literature marks the heyday of the low-mimetic. And Emerson, right on the temporal spot, would seem to agree with this categorization. In "The American Scholar," he celebrates the recent literary development by which, "instead of the sublime and beautiful, the near, the low, the common was explored and poeticized" (*CW*, I, 67). But for Emerson, who once proclaimed "All meaning in a potato!," the ordinary world of low-mimetic realism is acknowledged only to be freed of the limits of the low-mimetic proper. By an American calendar, Emerson's works, *Moby-Dick*, and "Song of Myself" are first-phase, mythic works: they have had nothing nationally before them to descend from. Later writers have alluded to the works of Emerson, Whitman, Melville, and Hawthorne as proposed central cultural myths. And in more apparent terms of internal form, though there are no American stories of the gods, American romantic literature invariably emphasizes a sense of mysterious spirit largely absent from the surfaces of Victorian fiction.

And yet these works are, in their own way, low-mimetic: they concern "Man Thinking." It is the implied author, not his characters—though author and hero merge in much of Emerson, Thoreau, Whitman, Dickinson, and Melville—who is one of us, in that attention is called to his creating process. Realism goes indoors and verisimilitude becomes a matter of accurately describing important but obscure states of consciousness. Further, this inward move has much to do with European romanticism, with a nineteenth century that exists everywhere.

And yet again: the consciousness prescribed by Emerson, exemplified by Whitman's Walt, gained only to be revoked or disowned by Dickinson's persona, is godly. And myth is redefined as the allegory of ordinarily available human power. We go back and forth, and in so doing the aim should not be to decide on myth or low-mimetic as the correct characterization but to view their interaction. If we admit Frye's stages of development or anyone else's, we must allow a vertical, national axis to be crossed horizontally by a European axis. Any time is many times, and any history of American literature must be generous enough to allow at least for two, national and western.

It is not mapping or categorization that ultimately interests me, but what the problems of such mapping suggest for characterizing the

Chapter Eleven

national qualities of a body of literature. We can say what is distinctly American only by showing how it is not universal, and the sharpest way to show that is by comparison to another body of literature; if that other national literature historically has influenced American writers, the distinctions become more definite still. That should not need saying, but too often claims of American difference and rebuttals to those claims depend on equally naïve subordinations of time to place or of place to time. This study on the American attempt to escape the burden of Britain thus heads to a final chapter with a plea to bring Britain back into the treatment of American literature; and my concern with American attempts to escape from linear history here concludes with a plea for a broadened historicism.

12

HENRY JAMES AND THE TREATY
OF GARDENCOURT

I

Simply to be alive and thinking in the American nineteenth century consigned one to a place in the struggle with British influence; to ignore the struggle was a position too, just as all apolitical omissions constitute the very strongest political support for the status quo. But it is never an entirely happy fate for an American to be bossed by his historical moment, especially if one of his claims against the British is a greater freedom to delve all of life's ahistorical deeps. He must, then, engage in the struggle but not devote his entire being to it. And upon any writer's recognition that he somehow must participate in it, a natural next thought would be of reconciliation or transcendance.

Likewise, upon the writer's recognition of an American cultural earliness relative to Britain, he may interpret and rally its strengths while attempting to cure its ills by creating a distinctly American maturity. This desire to ripen American letters may accompany a desire to get beyond Anglo-American animosities or it may not. We saw earlier how Emerson, in *Representative Men,* attempted to retain the scorn of history-worship endemic to earliness while adding elements of maturity—a skeptical wit, a more fully dramatized dialectical play—to a hortatory, oracular earliness. And in his subsequent work, the canny *English Traits,* Emerson more openly takes the role of American cosmopolitan (and cosmos-politican) to turn tables on American earliness and British cultural maturity. There, Emerson employs a capacious sense of human possibility to characterize himself as something of an enlightened Gulliver amid British Lilliputians.

But we also have considered Poe's attempt to mature his vision by fitting it to an attainable world, and there the tableturning upon the British romantics was only incidental and, I believe, wholly without debunking intent. And we have seen as well Whitman's maturing, where a partial repudiation of his own visionary audacity led him into the arms of his truest combatant Wordsworth.

Peacemaking, then, may coincide with an attempt at American maturity but it need not. Nor can we see such peacemaking as a linear progress, a gradual lessening of hostilities. Years after he makes his accommodation with Wordsworth, Whitman is ripping Arnold in *Democratic Vistas*. By the examples of Poe and Whitman, we might surmise that the American achieves a peace with British romanticism only to enlist the dead British romantics in struggle against a Victorian literature busy in repudiating its English predecessors. There is truth in this but nothing like law. Melville's epic poem of the seventies, *Clarel*, most clearly contradicts the rule.

Melville's questioning of all supposed certainties would lead him to qualify more and more harshly the messianic nationalism he had shared. Pure metaphysical angst finally would not be contained by a place. Yet the specifically Victorian questioning of God's disappearance appeals most to the writer who earlier most aggressively opposed British habits of thought. "Where is the foundling's father?" Ishmael asks in a question which is less personal than culturally collective and universally human. Not in England, Melville decided early, as in *Redburn* the map of Liverpool left to the young hero by his father proves as disconcertingly outdated as his father's love of England. But, astonishingly, Melville's search for origins did lead him, after all the repudiations, back to England in the seventies. In Arnold and Clough, Melville found his spiritual likeness: men hounded by the thought of a disappearing God. *Clarel* is as Victorian-seeming a work as one could wish, or not wish; and its pilgrimage-structure full of monologues relates it to an English tradition extending from Chaucer to Browning. Yet one of the pilgrims is named Derwent, after Wordsworth's nurturing river in *The Prelude;* and Melville characterizes the genial Derwent as an optimism-seeking coward of perception.

Once an American is willing to distinguish among kinds of British literature, accepting some influences and belittling others, we are heading away from the monolithic figure of the Englishman and toward a perspective freed of nationalism. But my point is that peacemaking is a fitful matter for a long time. And it is largely unsuccessful. *Clarel*, Melvillians notwithstanding, is a fascinating failure. *Moby-Dick* may be a series of meditations interrupted by a plot, but Melville required a powerful central action to catalyze and make exigent his ideas; and the central action of *Clarel*, a spiritual quest, is itself too much an idea to perform this good. *Representative Men* and *English Traits,* for all their audacity, sacrifice the drive of Emerson's essays of the 30s, their force of archetypal autobiography, to transform Emerson too much into a mere reporter on the world. Whitman's self-repudiation is an exciting moment that makes for a few great poems, but it eventuates in a loss of original power. And Poe's intelligent and lovely "Arnheim" is too atypical and insufficiently large to provide an American assurance of sustained cultural maturity. Whether it takes a Civil War or whether it takes a certain passage of time for American literary achievement to be credited by Americans (one thinks, for example, of James's youthful refusal of Whitman and his more generous reconsideration of the American bard in his middle years), or whether it takes something else entirely—the accident of one man's capacities—not until Henry James does the Anglo-American struggle get treated with a fullness that allows it to be authentically left behind. Not until James does American ripeness, which *is* concomitant in James with making the peace, get asserted persuasively.

Before James, Hawthorne came closest in attempting a peace with England by way of a calmed certainty of American virtues. By his strategy of stretched history, Hawthorne attempts to validate America according to English standards, while the archetypal history growing out of the quasi-factual record adds an insistent American emphasis. But we need not make the case so abstractly. Very early in his career, Hawthorne achieves a complex and balanced view of winning independence best dramatized in "My Kinsman, Major Molineux." In that tale, by tying a boy's personal initiation to a colonial town's savage overthrow of an Andros-like loyalist governor who is the boy's uncle, Hawthorne justifies revolution (and, by extension, literary independence) as an organic necessity while he fully confesses, as idealizing national historians would not, the hateful violence that necessity itself demands. And in the tale's conclusion, the friendly adult figure, whom the boy has earned by living through his conflicted emotions toward authority, urges him to stay in the city—that is, taking the boy as nation, to grow up culturally rather than to return to a pastoral ideal too past its real time to be anything but puerile.[1] James is nascent in all of this.

Hawthorne avoided literary violence himself in two ways. First, he chose as influences the British romantics' most collected and restrained works. It is not Coleridge as guilt-ridden poet but the confident author of the *Biographia Literaria* who stands behind Hawthorne's formulation of romance, even when the actual romances make guilt their burden. It is not the wildly visionary Shelley of *Prometheus Unbound* who enters into Hawthorne but the socially concerned, ambiguity-minded Shelley of *The Cenci* (in both "Rappaccini's Daughter" and the Hilda of *The Marble Faun*). Keats, given his collected employment of ambiguity, Hawthorne could afford to take whole, as we noted in the case of "Rappaccini's Daughter."

Second, Hawthorne limited his direct confrontations with British writers to his tales that tend toward witty parable: the aforementioned

"P's Correspondence," "A Virtuoso's Collection," and "Earth's Holocaust." That is, Hawthorne kept his opinions in a light, rational realm. Even when he makes Wordsworth into a character, as the model of the poet in "The Great Stone Face," his characterization is generous. At times it seems that Hawthorne gives himself over most to what least touches him. He is the only writer of the era to involve himself with the eighteenth century, in the conventional epithets, the formal parallels and antitheses, and the Johnsonian balanced syntax of his style; yet that Augustan style is employed self-consciously to create an exploitable gap between Hawthorne's manner and his meanings. Only in "Old Feathertop," where Hawthorne plays on Dickens's name to depict the English novelist's art as mechanistic demonry, does Hawthorne evince the competitive scorn typical of American influence-freeing gestures; but this too is qualified by the tale's fabulist humor.

Hawthorne would seem the best prepared of the American writers to take up the entire British-American quarrel. But in this he failed. *Dr. Grimshawe's Secret,* in which an American travels to England as the claimant of an estate and wrestles with questions of national loyalty, is one of Hawthorne's botched and unfinished final attempts. This failure might be predicted by *Our Old Home,* Hawthorne's lesser counterpart to Emerson's *English Traits,* in which the English are obsessively described as obese, lugubrious, and earth-bound. Here too, Hawthorne's depictions of English poverty depend so heavily on Dickens's famous passages that they are less affecting than stale. Hawthorne, even Hawthorne, was not yet ready to sacrifice the emotionalism of the Atlantic quarrel to gain a perspectival freedom.

James, who everywhere wishes to complete Hawthorne, does so most in this. One should not imagine James as automatically above the struggle. Specifically, James's first successful novel, *Roderick Hudson,* criticizes Arnold's ideas on Hellenism and Hebraism throughout; *The Princess Casamassima* begins in as complete and brilliant a parody of Dickens as Melville's "Bartleby" had achieved, and it too works to render Dickens dangerously (though here regretfully) irrelevant; that novel's main character is based in part on Keats, both Keats and Blake are central to *The Golden Bowl,* and in the story "The Velvet Glove" James partly rewrites "Endymion"; and James consistently refashions George Eliot—*Adam Bede* in *The Bostonians, Middlemarch* and *Daniel Deronda* in *Portrait of a Lady, Middlemarch* and *Romola* in *The Golden Bowl.* Yet James's idea of Eliot, both in his explicit critical commentary and in the implications of these texts, displays none of the competitive turmoil marking the American attempt to cut loose from the British. There is a particular tone of rich and richly qualified admiration, the tone which is James's most characteristic, that runs through even the famous sallies. And it is clear that James, in writing international novels, is really writing the Anglo-American novel, with the characters and situations of Eliot and Hawthorne often mingled and mutually transformed.

At times, James can sound the note of defensive nationalism perfectly. At age twenty-one, with an American's pride in epistemological probing, he writes, "Mr. Dickens is a great observer and a great humorist, but nothing of a philosopher."[2] In "A Passionate Pilgrim" (1871), he has his character Searle praise American earliness: "Naked come we into a naked world. There is a certain grandeur in the absence of a *mise en scène,* a certain heroic strain in those young imaginations of the West, which find nothing made to their hands, which have to concoct their own mysteries, and raise high into our morning air, with a ringing hammer and nails, the castles in which they dwell."[3] In the next year, James gives a reason for such characterizations in his own famous sentence, "It's a complex fate, being an American, and one of the responsibilities it entails is fighting against a superstitious valuation of Europe."[4]

But James writes that sentence just after he admits that he is himself guilty of such a valuation of Europe and he tends everywhere to hold the American-British debate within himself. In an 1875 review of Howells, James acknowledges that "civilization with us is monotonous" and then makes that monotony a virtue by considering the apparent blanks of American life an encouragement to devoted vision. He admits the "limited authority" of American writing and yet praises its "great charm," a charm especially evident in contrast to the "ponderous, shapeless, diffuse piece of machinery" that is the English novel.[5] Or again, in "The Future of the Novel," James can praise general literary earliness, when "the novel took the same robust ease as society," and will go on to blast the English novel's lateness, with its "mistrust of any but the most guarded treatment of the great relation between men and women, the constant world-renewal" and its squeamish neglect of "too many sources of interest" out of a misplaced idea of "safety."[6] That extends the usual American criticism of Victorian writers to the questions of love and sexuality. And James sounds the American note too in "The Art of Fiction" where he disdains "the moral timidity of the usual English novelist; with his (or with her) aversion to face the difficulties with which on every side the treatment of reality bristles." This is not only an attack against "delicacy" but against epistemological naïveté as well, and it seems almost Walt-like until James adds, with a delight in surprise, "In the English novel (by which of course I mean the American as well), . . ."⁷ And, as we have seen, James's paeons to American barrenness are at best double-edged.

James evidences a certain self-conflict in forwarding American claims just as Melville had, but James fashions his divided attitude to more of a purpose. We can get at that purpose by quoting at length from the famous 1888 letter James wrote to his brother William:

> For myself, at any rate, I am deadly weary of the whole "international" state of mind—so that I *ache,* at times, with fatique at the way it is constantly forced upon me as a sort of virtue or obligation. I can't look at the English-American world, or feel about them, any more, save as a big Anglo-Saxon total, destined to such an amount of melting together that an insistence on their differences becomes more and more idle and pedantic; and that melting together will come the faster the more one takes it for granted and treats the life of the two countries as continuous or more or less convertible, or at any rate as simply different chapters of the same general subject. Literature, fiction in particular, affords a mag-nificent arm for such taking for granted, and one may so do an excellent work with it. I have not the least hesitation in saying that I aspire to write in such a way that it would be impossible to an outsider to say whether I am at a given moment an American writing about England or an Englishman writing about America (dealing as I do with both coun-tries) and so far from being ashamed of such an ambiguity I should be exceedingly proud of it, for it would be highly civilized.⁸

This appears simple enough: James is tired of the theme that earned him his fame. England and America constitute "a big Anglo-Saxon total" and James will sum himself from that totality. But as soon as James employs the phrase "big Anglo-Saxon total," he begins a pro-gressive undercutting of it. From achieved fact this totality becomes a destiny and then a destiny dependent on imagining that it has oc-curred. (Here is American futurism for the first time employed against the marking of a national difference.) By the phrase "different chap-ters" James nudges the social question into a literary one, but he also retreats further from a no-difference claim. And finally he subtly re-verses his first statement in two ways. He is going to continue to write about America and England, and about them distinctly and not merely as a totality. If James' national identity is to be ambiguous and in-terestingly so, that ambiguity will depend on a sustained and notice-able meshing of sustained differences. A "big Anglo-Saxon total" would make for no ambiguity at all.

James knows exactly what he is about, and the payoff occurs in the

final phrase, where he calls his Anglo-American ambiguity "highly civilized." It is the British, of course, who assume their more advanced
civilization. This is, after all, an American speaking, and he is pressing
an American claim by defining the "highly civilized" as half-American.
It is a wonderful surprise, this sudden, subtly booming nationalism at
the end of a passage that had seemed to be heading to the mid-Atlantic, and the claim can be filled out by a comment James made two
decades earlier.

> I feel that my only chance for success as a critic is to let all the breezes of
> the west blow through me at their will. We are Americans born—*il faut
> en prendre son parti.* I look upon it as a great blessing; and I think that
> to be an America is an excellent preparation for culture. We have ex-
> quisite qualities as a race, and it seems to me that we are ahead of the
> European races in the fact that more than either of them we can deal
> freely with forms of civilization not our own, can pick and choose and
> assimilate and in short (aesthetically etc.) claim our property wherever
> we find it.[9]

Thus and wittily, James employs the French language to insist on his
American identity: "*il faut en prendre son parti.*" American earliness
by a paradox makes for maturity. By the strength of the American *now*
to employ history as a collection of human possibilities from which
one can choose favorites to form a self, James hopes for "a vast intellectual fusion and synthesis of the various National tendencies of the
world."

James really does wish to get the novel free of the old quarrel but
he understands that it has been far more of a struggle for Americans,
that they—and he—have been the underdogs and may still be. The
downtrodden side of the Atlantic quarrel must be a tiny and decisive
bit favored, and so James adopts the tie-in-favor-of-America strategy of
the phrase "highly civilized." It is this strategy that James adopts more
largely in works of fiction distinguished, despite his "fatigue" of English-American differentiations, by an unprecedented thematic display
of what heretofore had been a matter of sly allusion or complex innu-
endo. Like an effective psychologist, James knows that he must bring
to the surface the concealed national animosities and the rationalized
American fears if he is to free the nation and himself of their presence.
For James had decided that the defensive national pride, if it had been
creative in Hawthorne's time, was not so now. He knew too that only
an American could end the quarrel, an American authentically international with a special, felt loyalty to England and yet a self-confirmed

American still. And he could end that quarrel only in an American way, by that actualist figuration of the self as culturally representative. James thematized the Anglo-American struggle and, by that, stole from the struggle its guerilla force. Then, secondarily in his presented social person but most by the qualities of his style, he presented himself as the fine result of a won peace, "a big Anglo-Saxon total" as an individual writer.

2

I mean here to end this book, not to begin a new one, and that would be the minimum requirement for a full consideration of James as the concluding term of our topic. Instead let me take one best-loved book, *The Portrait of a Lady*, and try to be only suggestive about only some of its aspects that might engage our special concern.

"Lady" flatters an achieved maturity and a "Portrait" is an effect of high (or middle-high) culture, and both relate to an American heroine. This is James's "highly civilized" claim once more, although, as a portrait is static and a novel developmental, it is the act of maturing that James holds forth here as a potential, a goal of American culture. This claim blends into the ideal of an Anglo-Saxon total when the novel opens with a still life of Gardencourt at teatime. Two of the figures in this "peculiarly English picture I have attempted to sketch"[10] are nonetheless the American Touchetts, father and son, owners of the estate, who yet retain frankly their native qualities unlike those deracinated, Europe-aping expatriates James always despises. These two permanent visitors to England are themselves being visited by an English lord, the third figure in this opening portrait, and are shown in playfully loving discourse with him. Gardencourt, then, is named as it is to imply not only a best merging of ordered nature and noble civilization but a best merging of America and England, with each retaining its distinctive features.

This kind of rough-hewn inferring does not falsify the novel—James never feels the need to eschew broad strokes, for he is confident of his finer detail work—but neither can it account for very much of the reader's experience. Everything in my last paragraph demands qualification. Isabel Archer, the lady-in-making, is not merely an American type, a Christopher Newman or Daisy Miller. She *is* an Emersonian girl, who reads German idealist philosophy in the locked office at Albany that occludes a view of the street; she *is* an overly theoretic self-realizer, ignorant of circumstantial living. But Henrietta Stackpole, whose characterization is based in part on Margaret Fuller in her role as European correspondent for the New York Herald, exists to draw off the typical American designation from Isabel. And as soon as Mrs. Touchett inquires whether Isabel wishes to be told what actions are conventionally indecent "so as to do them" and Isabel replies "So as to choose" (67), she has shot ahead of James's typical American girl Daisy Miller. As to Gardencourt, while it expresses an English-American ideal, it is in danger of dissolution. The Americans are nearing actual death; and their visitor, that member of an English aristocracy that no longer knows what to do with itself, is later posed in Rome standing on cracked pavement by the portrait of "The Dying Gladiator." After Isabel struggles to an understanding of Gardencourt's high value, she will have to transform the lost place into an aspect of her spirit and have it inform her actions in a world where even civilized Edens are always being lost.

If we stay another moment with the novel's title, we can sample James's finer and further-reaching national implications. In a fine unpublished essay, Barbara J. Walker considers James's allusions to specific works of art. She notes, for example, Ralph Touchett's metaphorical response to Isabel's arrival.

> Suddenly I receive a Titian by post, to hang on my wall, a Greek bas-relief to stick over my chimney piece. The key to a beautiful edifice has been thrust into my hands and I'm told to walk in and admire it. (63)

Keys and the politics of entering in upon another's privacy make for a continuing image-cluster throughout the work, and architecture is a constant source of characterization. But more importantly, in mentioning Titian and a bas-relief, James is gesturing toward a Titian painting of a woman posed by an antique bas-relief. Of this painting, critic David Rosand remarks that Titian not only flatters the woman by associating her with classical antiquity but, by its historical reach into the past, implies the preservative persistence of art. Further, "creating a work of art within a work of art he accepted the challenge of the PARAGONE, the comparison of the arts . . . he turned his painting into a triumphal declaration of the power of painting itself."[11] The title of Titian's painting is "Portrait of a Woman."

James's incorporation of the painting into the novel creates a third perspective, a work of art within a work of art, all within a work of literary art; and, to paraphrase Rosand, this is James's triumphal declaration of the power of fiction, an extension of the prestige of painting to a form of narrative art still shedding its relatively low status in James's era. But it is also, I would argue, a claim for America forwarded through and by a representative man and artist. By this and other allusions, James realizes that American power he had praised years earlier, "to deal freely with civilizations not our own," to "pick and choose and assimilate and in short (aesthetically etc.) claim our property wherever we find it." James is employing his cosmopolitan culture in a distinctly American manner, by taking history less as linear and successive than as an open store of permanently illustrative images. And yet he is adding to the free-dipping into historical moments practiced by Emerson and Whitman a cultivated aestheticism. It is art history, after all, that he is employing, and that employment is accompanied by a respect for tradition not at all Emersonian. Yet James keeps himself and his avatar Ralph clear of an overcivilized aestheticism by Ralph's remark previous to the comparison, that Isabel's "passionate force" is "finer than the finest work of art—than a Greek bas-relief, than a great Titian, than a Gothic cathedral" (63). Art is to serve life, which surpasses it.

James's network of allusions furthers the claim of American high civilization that the author personifies. Titian's is a "Portrait of a Woman," not yet of a lady, as Isabel at this early stage has not earned the epithet. Much later, Gilbert Osmond tells Isabel that one of the chief events of his life had been in "discovering, as I once did, a sketch by Correggio on a panel daubed over by some inspired idiot" (223). James alludes here to a Correggio originally attributed to Lorenzo Lotto and finally identified correctly by one Lorenzo Longhi, whom James alludes to within a few pages. The Correggio Longhi (or Osmond) discovered is "The Portrait of a Lady."

Osmond is the deracinated American culture-vulture that Ralph is not. Like Ralph, Isabel thinks, life to Osmond "was a matter of connoisseurship"; but she makes a distinction in her wrong admiration, for "in Ralph it was an anomaly, a kind of humorous excrescence, whereas in Mr. Osmond it was the keynote, and everything was in harmony with it" (220). Well, not quite everything, Isabel will learn. And the aestheticism of Osmond's life in any case is ugly. His taste is atrocious, as young Ned Rosier asserts, and his motives have more to do with self-advertisement than aesthetic emotion. Beyond that, James clearly means by Osmond to show that art replacing and denying life is exactly what he does not approve.

Some readers plead for Osmond's complexity. This is fine so long as it is recognized that his complexity is a multifaceted compounding of human inhumanity created by James in a simple spirit of unrelieved disgust. There are few creepier beings in the history of literature. Yet, by alluding to Correggio's "Portrait of a Lady" and its discovery by

Osmond, James implies that Osmond's intervention is the negative means to Isabel's achieving of the epithet. He, himself, trying to turn her into a work of art, is the "inspired idiot" who daubs over a brilliant original. Yet unknowingly his attempts at obscuration only develop the portrait's—Isabel's—potential.

James's internal cross-references of allusions to paintings—and there are numerous others—help to create a self-portrait of the American artist as artist indeed. Yet accompanied brilliantly by an admonition against making art rather than life the final goal, the cross-references reconfirm James's American freshness by refusing any going over to an Osmond-like aestheticism. Art is preservative and some ways permanent, but the second portrait, the Correggio "Portrait of a Lady," has undergone obscuration and recovery, the vicissitudes of the world's time in which portraits as well as people exist. In all, James's refusal of a "superstitious valuation of Europe," his refusal of that burgeoning aestheticism expressed by Osmond in his wish "to make one's life a work of art" (256), does not prevent a sensible valuation and use of Europe. This is the all-telling distinction between Osmond and Ralph as it differently is between Henrietta Stackpole (whose jingoist refusals of Europe determines that she will go all the way over to the mediocre Englishman Bantling at last) and Isabel Archer as she finally inherits Ralph's values.

3

It is a carefully hedged but wonderfully detailed pact that James negotiates between England and America, involving author, work, and reader. Not least important in this is James's combining of elements we associate with Victorian realism with elements we associate with American romance. Eliot and Hawthorne appear the prime national representatives of James's merge and, given the existing and detailed treatments of their influences on James, I will say only a little. Isabel is often compared to Gwendolyn Harleth, the heroine of *Daniel Deronda;* but both her essential fineness of character and the novel's comparing of her to subjects of portraiture link her more interestingly to Dorothea Brooke and *Middlemarch*. Of course, as an American Dorothea, Isabel's idealism resides in self-realization more than in performing social good; but she is developed in this American way out of the English tradition, going back to Jane Austen, of the remarkable but self-deluded young woman. (James is making claims not only for fiction in general and for the American artist but for the male writer in adding to the Austen-Eliot tradition here.) But it is Hawthorne who is most profoundly informing. It is not in the centrality of an adulterous affair nor in the Aylmer-like characterization of Osmond nor in his daughter Pansy's link to Hawthorne's Pearl ("pure as a pearl," Pansy's hidden mother calls her, 206) that this profundity resides. Hester Prynne and Zenobia have something to do with Isabel Archer but that too is at once too large and too particular an influence to suggest what Hawthorne means for James. It is the resonance of Hester Prynne's decision to return to Boston in Isabel's final decision to return to Osmond and Italy that provides our clue. James is completing Hawthorne's drama of individual choice and social environment, of how we are to interpret the world's history and our own.

The novel's first words, "Under certain circumstances" (17), acknowledge the reality of a world not created by the self but independent and sometimes governing. They also alert us to the importance of rational discernment and its dependence on a detailed appreciation of context. James is telling us how to read his book; and his narrator's continual demands for the reader's perceptual patience through the early chapters carries forth American emphases on epistemology and reader-participation but in the tone of a Victorian sage and with an insistence on an attainable right judgment all-English.

We are shown Gardencourt before Isabel is allowed to enter the grounds and the book because Gardencourt and England and Europe and the world exist prior to Isabel's entrance into them. In this insistence and in his frequent criticisms of Isabel's over-literary, sometimes unhinged and fantastic imagination—she will guess at Madame Merle's entire character, for instance, before having spoken one word with her, indeed seeing only this complicated creature's back as Merle plays artfully upon the piano—James joins Austen and the Victorians in warning against fantasies spun out of the self and mistaken for the world. He joins them, too, in directing the perceptual drive to what is truly out there, an everyday world, which will appear easily comprehended and insufficiently rich only to the misguided intelligence.

James votes, at least initially, against American actualism. Yet the novel is structured as much by moments of choice as by all emphases on circumstance. It is as a young woman all undetermined and yet capable of choosing a self and a life that Isabel garners the reader's admiring affection beyond all the annoyances she provides. She is not just any American girl; but in her sense of possibility and, for better as well as worse, in her preconceived determination to create a self, Isabel *is* an American and a version of James's America. Further, her refusals of the American businessman and the English lord are refusals of circumstance and circumscription. Each of these men, despite whatever protestations, belong to life-systems she must fit. Isabel sees truly here and James appreciates her determination against a hand-me-down social existence. The irony everyone recognizes, Isabel's choice of Osmond on the basis of the apparent freedom of life that Osmond offers, in no way undercuts the courage of her earlier refusals. Between the warnings and the approvals, James is steering a mid-Atlantic course.

It is emotional circumstance that most engages James, as it had Hawthorne, the self's personally historical determinants more than the world's. True, society is something more solid in James that it is in Hawthorne, where society sometimes seems only a collective and neurotic psyche. But Isabel's two major choices, for marriage to Osmond and then again (only apparently) for the same at story's end, have immediately to do with emotional circumstance, personal context, however much that is ultimately determined by social inheritances. (It is worth remembering that all the major characters in the novel, save Warburton, are American. Their variety urges against any monolithic idea of national determination.) And this is where the reader is afforded a stern lecture on the importance of history. On each of these occasions, Isabel will make a decision that will surprise and disappoint the reader to the point of incredulity. This is James's daring, to have Isabel choose in a way that might appear perfectly at odds with her presiding spirit, but that is completely, even lavishly prepared for by what James has told us of her. In other words, James makes the reader conscious of those failings, those barbarisms of perception, to which that reader as well as Isabel is prone. The epistemological emphasis, again, is roughly American; the solid prospect of an accurate perception is British; and James's demand for British context and American scope is his Anglo-Saxon total. But for the reader to correct his incomplete perception, James makes that reader reread, makes him perform that least American of all tasks, to look back. Or, to avoid the controversies of reader-response criticism, we can say simply that the linear, progressive development of Isabel's character earns its way to this disastrous moment when she chooses Osmond.

This is to argue that James employs linear fictional time more resourcefully and wholeheartedly than any American predecessor had. But it is a particular kind of linear development that retains an American epistemological emphasis. Later, James will skip time. He leaves Isabel unaccounted for several years of her marriage, and in resuming her tale he presents a full disclosure of this terrible period in Isabel's life by horridly delicious, excruciating, gradual and delaying recapitulative hints. We learn that Isabel has, in a sense, lost her consciousness under Osmond's civilized tyranny; and it is only just before Isabel is to rediscover her individuality (when Osmond requires her to become a Merle in manipulating Pansy and inadvertantly causes her to recognize most painfully what has happened to her) that the narrative resumes. The strategy is wonderfully effective in immediately juxtaposing the last moment of Isabel's magnificent freedom with the gored remains of an Isabel enslaved. But it also enforces the sense that James's linear time runs by the mentalized clock of consciousness.

When we do look back from the moment of Isabel's first choosing Osmond, we discover a startling fullness of motivation. James does not display that encyclopaedic variety of forms that go to make form self-evaluating in Hawthorne and Melville, but he substitutes for this a seemingly encyclopaedic range of interlinked motives for a single act. It is as if everything we have been told of Isabel is a gene pool, and her acceptance of Osmond's proposal is the relentlessly logical, worst possible combination of genetic possibilities.

Briefly: "Isabel had in the depths of her nature an even more unquenchable desire to please" than her sister (40); Osmond, with his judgmental reserve, encourages this desire in Isabel as Warburton and Goodwood, falling over themselves, do not. Isabel initially rebels against the desire: "'I'm under no obligation that I know of to charm Mr. Osmond'," she sharply remonstrates to Madame Merle's for once indiscreet coachings (209). Yet soon she is worrying about "her possible grossness of perception" and Osmond's potential disapproval (221). But Osmond also makes himself appear in need and this too plays upon Isabel's "unquenchable desire to think well of herself" (53) and upon that "deepest thing" in her, "a belief that if a certain light should dawn, she could give herself completely" (55). That certain light, Osmond, will become a darkness visible; but Isabel's very fear of this capacity to give plays into Osmond's and Merle's game. Warburton exacts a price in terms of social freedom; Goodwood offers a passional servitude. Osmond appears wonderfully unconditioned—as Merle describes him, "'No career, no name, no position, no fortune, no past, no future, no anything'" (169), above it all in his hilltop home. The hilltop will become Isabel's suffocating dungeon and these negatives certainly could be taken at face value or worse, as a Satanic emptiness. But Merle counts rightly upon not only Isabel's fear of constriction but also upon her "certain nobleness of imagination which rendered her a good many services and played her a great many tricks" (53). Thus, when Osmond counts his discovery of the Correggio as one of the major moments in an uneventful life, "her imagination supplied the human element which she was sure had not been wanting" (223). As in her first journey to Rome, while Isabel puts off a final decision, so here Isabel is "seeing often in the things she looked at a great deal more than was there, and yet not seeing many of the items enumerated in her Murray" (240). But even without her mixture of imaginative generosity and careless perception, Isabel would find Osmond's "studied, my willful renunciation" attractive. It confirms her own decisions against a conformist marriage and against Goodwood and Warburton more immediately. Yet a fear of a too embracing renunciation frightens Isabel of herself, and she dimly perceives the cold, dry results of a refusal of human devotion in Mrs. Touchett. Approving Isabel's European tour, "'I should like to see you when you're tired and satiated,' Osmond added in a moment. 'I shall prefer you in that state'" (256). What a ghoul! But Isabel is already tiring, and Osmond offers her a way to renounce renunciation while embracing it.

Of course, Osmond actually renounces nothing. In the midst of a tale striving for an American cultural maturity, Osmond stands as a deceptive simulacrum of that, a living compendium of what James wishes for not at all. Osmond does not value art but opinion, and he employs art objects as he does other people, to achieve a social recognition that is the only basis of his negative being. He is egotistical, competitive, envious, small, and materialistic, self-proclaimed convention in its emptiest form and dishonest even in that. This man's life is as much a work of art as a stuffed bat. Worse still, Osmond is a near double for the dissolute father Isabel worshipped with a child's loving error. Free choice indeed! Yet Isabel's final decision to return to him is no return at all to the conditions of her first acceptance. It is substantially a reversal—that is why Isabel must return to Gardencourt and re-experience the major persons of her earlier time there. This second decision differs sufficiently in its achieved self-consciousness to make Isabel the lady of the novel's title.

Again here, the reader must rebel against the novel and then must quell his rebellion by acknowledging context, the full fabric of Isabel's development, as the only relevant material for judging her choice. When we consider that choice, we find James not only incorporating Hawthorne but struggling, really struggling for the first American time, with John Milton, and by that struggle exhausting the Anglo-American dispute so that his work can achieve a human truth unfettered by nationalism—on American grounds nonetheless.

4

Let us note what does not determine Isabel's final choice. Most largely it is not a renunciation in any way. "Deep in her soul—deeper than any appetite for renunciation—was the sense that life would be her business for a long time to come" (458). This verbal echo of Isabel's long-ago "deepest thing," to "give herself completely," marks a change. It is in its very formulation an advance, as its terms are no longer self-concerned but acknowledge a world with which the self interacts. And "her business" suggests a new acceptance of the necessity to struggle. The real quest is just beginning at the end of this novel.

Isabel's decision, then, has nothing to do with a Victorian ideal of self-refusing duty. She returns not at all to save Osmond; and we need to acknowledge the vulgar fact that Isabel could ruin Osmond now. Though she never will and he may never know that she can ruin him in the only way possible, by public repute, power in this marriage has shifted absolutely. Isabel is strong as God in her return. Nor does she return simply to fulfill her promise to Pansy. She confesses to Henrietta that she no longer sees with certainty why she made the promise. But when Henrietta says "'If you've forgotten your reason, perhaps you won't return,'" Isabel replies "'Perhaps I shall find another'" (467).

She finds more than one other, and her promise to Pansy, transfigured, counts in them. We can get at a first reason by one sentence, as Mrs. Touchett reacts to her son's death. "'Go and thank God you've no child,' said Mrs. Touchett, disengaging herself'" (472). Mrs. Touchett has been disengaging herself all of her life, and this disengagement has withered her. Madame Merle has denied her tie to her child, and her disengagement has demonized her and made her pitiable at once. It is perhaps James's most daring ploy to place the resultant truth in the lying mouth of Osmond: "'. . . I think we should accept the consequences of our actions, and what I value most in life is the honour of a thing'" (438). Honor is not to the point here: and while *Portrait* fulfills the typical pattern of the Victorian novel by challenging a convention that has been emptied of meaning only to reinvigorate that convention with felt, experiential meaning, Isabel is doing something more. The self is not in James, as it also is not in Hawthorne, an abstraction or an ideal. It is the result of accumulated experience. Isabel must return to Osmond, as Hester must return to Boston, to affirm her identity. Anything else would be a dissolution. That is the kind of necessity James enforces, a duty only to self. And Isabel's return also affirms her freedom, not only her present freedom but the freedom of her history. If she is to see her earlier choice of Osmond as the result of a manipulation, and she has almost every reason to do so, then she defines her self as Osmond's walking-stick indeed. If she instead reasons that there was a someone present who allowed herself to be manipulated, then by the confession of her complicity she retains a view of her earlier choice as free. In returning to Osmond, Isabel thus literally defeats his freedom-killing powers and affirms herself, then and now.

Like Mrs. Touchett, Goodwood tells Isabel that "'The world's all before us'" in part because "'You've no children; that perhaps would be an obstacle'" (481). We think again of Pansy here; but Pansy would be no real obstacle because Goodwood's idea of freedom would obliterate Isabel's past and thus Isabel. The theory that Goodwood's white-lightening kiss frightens Isabel back to Osmond is essentially ridiculous, and not alone because if everything came down to an imagined frigidity ("something cold and dry an unappreciated suitor with a taste for analysis might have called it," 55, surely the very least reliable judge), the reader would have good reason to feel sold. More, freedom exerts itself only against the limits of chosen circumstance, and the world as free vista is a wide vacuity. Much earlier, in London before her marriage, "The world lay before her—she could do whatever she chose." And Isabel "chose simply to walk back from Euston Square to her hotel" (257). She does lose her way "almost on purpose, in order to get more sensations" (another, most tricky reason for her initial choice of Osmond). Now, much later, Isabel discovers "a very straight path" home (482), not to Osmond but to herself. Her response to Goodwood's "act of possession" recalls to Isabel "those wrecked and under water following a train of images before they sink" (482). Earlier, in a state of fatigue unto suicide, Isabel envies Ralph his dying, his perpetual rest: "To cease utterly, to give it all up and not know anything more—this idea was as sweet as the vision of a cool bath in a marble tank, in a darkened chamber, in a hot land" (457)—as dangerously sweet, that is, as death and Goodwood's embrace. For to return with Goodwood to America, the land of the unconditioned, would be Isabel's suicidal regression, her unamerican uncreating of her self. It would make of freedom what the despairing contemporary song says it is, "just another word for nothing left to lose."

Isabel chooses instead to make her world. Her final choice achieves her youthful naïve ideal to realize her spirit in the world, to "move in a realm of light" (53), though that light has been made into a dark night at Gardencourt and her selfhood is affirmed most unexpectedly. James makes his peace with the American actualist ideal finally, on his own terms, terms which include the British appreciation of a reality not all-centered in the self's pleasurable egoism.

Isabel's world-making is the final, fullest reason for her choice, and this intricate self-determination involves James with Milton and his great epic. Any number of American writers had referred to Genesis in depicting or disputing an American Eden. But James, as half-English

American, must take his Genesis via Milton; and particular and general allusions to Milton abound. (Indeed, James' very plethora of allusions, exampled earlier, makes him an American Milton.) Gardencourt is a civilized Eden and Isabel's "nature had, in her conceit, a certain garden-like quality" (53). But Isabel is a prideful Eve, "very liable," the narrator playfully admits, "to the sin of self-esteem" (53); and, like Eve, she bears a "general disposition to elude any obligation to take a restricted view" (99). She wishes to view "the cup of experience" without touching it (132). Mr. Touchett, with his "unlimited means," is something of a god with whom Ralph as a sort of Christ intercedes on behalf of Isabel-as-humanity. In her confusion, Isabel mistakes this god and his free gift of money (which is also free will) for Satan, naming him "the beneficent author of infinite woe" (351). And Ralph, like Christ, heals humanity in the act of his dying.

Osmond, of course, takes that freewill money Mr. Touchett and Ralph had provided Isabel. He is the dissembler, who possesses for Goodwood "a kind of demonic imagination" (415). Like Satan, he corrupts the Church, wishing to be Pope and converting the convent where he places Pansy to a penitentiary to keep his daughter pliable to his wishes. "His egotism lay hidden like a serpent in a bank of flowers" (353) and, like Satan, he is a disappointed, envious revenger. He has, as his faithful assistant Merle says, enacted his revenge on Isabel, who mistook the devil for something of heaven. "Instead of leading to the high places of happiness, from which the world would seem to lie below one, so that one could look down with a sense of exaltation and advantage, and judge and choose and pity, it led rather downward and earthward, into realms of restriction and depression where the sound of other lives, easier and freer, was heard from above, and where it served to deepen the feeling of failure" (349).

This is Isabel's language of "infinite dismay," the counterpart of the pride she confesses to. In its grip, she cannot confess her unhappiness to Ralph, much as "he made her feel the good of the world"; she "had an idea she was doing him a kindness" in hiding from him as Adam and Eve hide from Christ after their fall, but then "women find their religion sometimes in strange exercises" (357). It is in "a tone of far-reaching, infinite sadness" that Isabel finally "must see Ralph" (448). Ralph "spoke at last—on the evening of the third day" (469). And Ralph, who earlier, in recognizing Isabel's hidden misery, "feels as if I had fallen myself," releases Isabel's sorrow in a theologically tinged emotion: "'Oh my brother!' she cried with a movement of still deeper prostration" as Ralph tells her that "'if you've been hated, you've also been loved. Ah but, Isabel—*adored!*'" (471). The next morning, her confession of suffering wins her a witnessing of the ghost of Gardencourt, a holy rather than gothic ghost as Ralph's spirit becomes hers.

Yet in that beautiful final interview, Ralph tells Isabel never to wish for death. "'Dear Isabel, life is better; for in life there's love. Death is good—but there's no love'" (470). This is hardly a Miltonic-Christian sentiment. And in fact, while James has employed the Miltonic echoes as a helpful if rough context for understanding his characters, he finally urges the overthrow of that context as a basis for moral understanding. When Isabel, now informed of Merle's deceit, asks herself "whether to this intimate friend of several years the great historical epithet of *wicked* were to be applied," (424), all of the foregoing allusions and more prepare us for an answer in the affirmative. Merle, who cannot shed tears even when she would, who is beyond redemption, who is in Ralph's description "the great round world itself" and thus, with Osmond, constitutes the world, the flesh, and the devil—God yes, she is wicked. But that is not where Isabel's thought leads her, even as she is for the first time recognizing the full brutality of Merle's sacrifice for her. The long paragraph of thought opening with the question of the epithet—"She knew the idea only by the Bible and other literary works"—ends with Isabel questioning how Osmond must be punishing Merle for procuring him a marriage partner so little to his ultimate liking.

> What must be his feelings to-day in regard to his too-zealous benefactress, and what expression must they have found on the part of such a master of irony? It is a singular, but a characteristic, fact that before Isabel returned from her silent drive she had broken its silence by the soft exclamation: "Poor, poor Madame Merle!" (425)

The Miltonic understanding, in its moral extremes, comes to be too much like that modern "scientific criticism," which James as narrator warns the reader to forgo. It is insufficiently flexible in its allegorical understandings, too impoverishing of a full consciousness, a complete recognition of self and other. Cleansed of this proclivity, Milton and his Christianity can be recalled in their happier, heavenly, suffering-justifying aspect in the interview with Ralph that Isabel earns by her "soft exclamation."

James's heroic American always refuses revenge. Christopher Newman gets the goods on the Bellegarde family that has deprived him of a wife in *The American* but he finds that he cannot return happily to San Francisco with revenge in mind. The American cannot enter into revenge for revenge is the basis for the nightmare of European history that the American Adam seeks to disown. Still, as Newman throws the incriminating note in the fire, word reaches him that the Bellegardes expected him to do just this. He has fulfilled his type so perfectly that James tilts his halo.

Isabel Archer takes a bit of revenge. She exults in saying to Osmond of his desire to procure Warburton for Pansy and the English lord's reflected title and fortune for himself, "How much you must want to make sure of him!" (388). Her "horrible delight" (389) precedes the moment of her pity for Merle, but even after that Isabel does say enough to banish the cosmopolitan Merle back to her hated origins in a Brooklyn of an America. Nonetheless, essentially and internally, she refuses Countess Gemini's encouragement to be a little wicked and take a revenge.

Isabel's reason, however, is far more precise and affecting than Christopher Newman's. Isabel chooses, with eyes painfully open, not to live in a world of moral absolutes, not to be wicked herself or to act upon others as if the historical epithet summed them. It is not so much that she would become like her enemies in taking a revenge as that the revenge would be based on a simplification of experience that again robs the self. She must experience others as James requires the reader to experience her. People are not allegories, and John Milton is not enough. The world is now truly all before Isabel and all before us, we who have been shorn of all the comforting reductionisms, and who now must live in ontological insecurity, by our wits and by our love.

5

And this could seem a deprivation. In *The Portrait of a Lady* James finally plunged beneath England and America to unsettle the Christian foundations of both cultures. He opened life beyond the strictures of nationality in an act which yet would complete the American-universal intention. It is a triumphant peace.

But later in his career James would speak of the imagination of disaster and initiate a century of shocked literature. He would write his *Turn of the Screw,* in which the village church is never reached; in which the god-like master does not care about his charges and enquiries to him are never truly sent, much less answered; in which the authorial God refuses a final frame for his tale to match the opening one because final truth is an illusion, and the individual imagination is set free from any socially binding ethic to become nothing more than a result of the low irrationality of that self-justifying monster, the psyche. Still later, he would write his *Golden Bowl* as yet another farewell to the international theme, in which power and manipulation become so inescapably necessary as to make Isabel's achievement seem sentimental in retrospect.

In retrospect too, the American attempt to throw off British literary influence can appear quaint. This book has been written in part against previous studies that tend to make a John-and-Jonathan joke out of what was a battle for cultural existence. And yet, after all, it is impossible not to feel a certain nostalgia for the struggle, given the diminished England, the gigantically sinning America, and the emptied universals which are our present. James brought to his conclusion—there were others—the Anglo-American battle to get at larger, more terrifying prospects. In the triumph of peace was no long joy. And that is why we look back with desire upon that now-exhausted American hope, to begin after all other endings and to end at a moment of Spirit where beginning is.

Notes

Preface

1. Henry James, Jr., *Hawthorne* (New York: Harper & Brothers, 1880), p. 43.

2. Margaret Fuller, "American Literature. Its Position in the Present, and Prospects for the Future," rpt. in *Margaret Fuller, American Romantic: A Selection from Her Writings and Correspondence,* ed. Perry Miller (1963; rpt. Ithaca, N.Y.: Cornell University Press, 1970), p. 232.

3. John Krapp, "National Poetry," *North American Review* 8 (1818), p. 171.

4. Walt Whitman, "Poetry To-Day in America—Shakspere—The Future" in *Prose Works 1892,* 2 vols., ed. Floyd Stovall (New York: New York University Press, 1964), II, p. 480. Whitman's article first appeared in *The North American Review* 132 (1881), pp. 195–210, with the title "The Poetry of the Future." Whitman revised the essay in small details for *Specimen Days & Collect* in the following year.

5. Edward Everett, "Review of a Tour on the Prairies," *The North American Review* 88 (1835), p. 12; Henry David Thoreau, in a remark to Ellery Channing, quoted without ascription by Benjamin T. Spencer, *The Quest for Nationality: An American Literary Campaign* (Syracuse, N.Y.: Syracuse University Press, 1957), p. 168.

6. Meyer H. Abrams, *The Mirror and the Lamp: Romantic Theory and the Critical Tradition* (New York: W. W. Norton, 1958), p. 22.

7. James, *Hawthorne,* pp. 42–43.

8. Raymond Williams, *Marxism and Literature* (Oxford: Oxford University Press, 1977), p. 189.

9. Lionel Trilling, "Manners, Morals, and the Novel" in *The Liberal Imagination: Essays on Literature and Society,* Anchor Books ed. (1950; rpt. in soft cover, Garden City, N.Y.: Doubleday & Co., 1953), p. 200.

10. My terms "actualism" and "ontological insecurity" correspond in a rough manner to what Tony Tanner views as the twin anxieties of American thought. In his superb book on recent American fiction, *City of Words* (London: Cape, 1971), Tanner argues that the American writer fears that conspiracies are about to rob him of his self-realizing autonomy; but alternately he fears that, in a land of insufficient historical associations, he will be left too much alone, and the ego will fail to collect itself.

11. Edward Tyrell Channing, "On Models in Literature," *The North American Review* 3 (1816), p. 206.

12. I am thinking here of Eliot's famous essay "Tradition and the Individual Talent" (1919), rpt. in *Selected Essays, 1917–1932* (London: Faber and Faber Ltd., 1932), pp. 13–22.

13. Walter Jackson Bate, *The Burden of the Past and the English Poet* (New York: W. W. Norton, 1970); Harold Bloom, *The Anxiety of Influence: A Theory of Poetry* (New York: Oxford University Press, 1973); and see also Bloom's subsequent, more explicit study *A Map of Misreading* (New York: Oxford University Press, 1975).

14. Claudio Guillen helpfully differentiates between allusion and influence in *Literature as System: Essays Toward a Theory of Literary History* (Princeton, N.J.: Princeton University Press, 1971).

I

1. Quoted in this order: "Literary Importation," in *The Poems of Philip Freneau,* ed. Fred Lewis Pattee, 3 vols. (New York: Russell and Russell, 1963), II, pp. 303–304; Charles Brockden Brown, *Clara Howard* in *Complete Works,* 6 vol. (Port Washington, N.Y.: Kennikat Press, 1963), VI, p. 329; William Cullen Bryant, "Early American Verse," originally published in *The North American Review* (July 1818), rpt. from corrected copy as "An Essay on American Poetry" in *Life and Works,* ed. Parke Godwin, 6 vols. (New York: D. Appleton and Co., 1884), V, pp. 54–55; Henry Wadsworth Longfellow, Review of *Defence of Poetry, The North American Review* 34 (January 1832), p. 75; Orestes Brownson, "Specimens of Foreign Literature" (review of Ripley), *Boston Quarterly Review* (October 1838), p. 436; Orestes Brownson, unattributed, 1864, in *The Native Muse: Theories of American Literature,* ed. Richard Ruland (1972; rpt. in soft cover New York: E. P. Dutton, 1976), pp. 399 and 406; Willis and Morris quoted by Spencer, *The Quest for Nationality,* pp. 85–86; Margaret Fuller (Ossili), *Papers on Literature and Art* (New York: Wiley and Putnam, 1946), II, pp. 126–7; Whitman quoted by Perry Miller in *The Raven and the Whale: The War of Words and Wits in the Era of Poe and Melville* (New York: Harcourt, Brace and Co., 1956), p. 187; James Russell Lowell, "On a Certain Condescension in Foreigners," *Prose Works,* III (New York: Riverside, 1870), p. 272.

2. Williams, *Marxism and Literature,* pp. 45–49 passim.

3. Spencer, *The Quest for Nationality,* p. 32.

4. Charles Brockden Brown, "Preface" to *Clara Howard,* quoted in *Literary History of the United States,* ed. Robert Spiller, Willard Thorp, Thomas H. Johnson, and Henry Seidel Canby (New York: Macmillan, 1948), p. 184.

5. Benjamin Lease reviews contemporary British and American responses to Irving fully and well in his intelligent study, *Anglo-American Encounters: England and the Rise of American Literature* (Cambridge, London, and New York: Cambridge University Press, 1981), pp. 13–35.

6. In *The Complete Works of Washington Irving: The Sketch Book of*

Geoffrey Crayon, Gent., ed. Haskell Springer (Boston: Twayne, 1976), pp. 31, 34, 37.

7. Royall Tyler, "Prologue to *The Contrast*," ed. James Benjamin Walker (New York: AMS Press, 1970), pp. 20–21.

8. See Cooper's "Preface" to *The Pilot* for his criticism of Scott. See also Warren S. Walker, "A 'Scottish Cooper' for an 'American Scott'," *American Literature* 40 (1969), pp. 536–37. See also George Dekker's chapter, "An American Scott," pp. 20–32 in *James Fenimore Cooper the Novelist* (London: Routledge & Kegan Paul, 1967).

9. For Cooper's development, see Dekker and Richard Slotkin, *Regeneration Through Violence: The Mythology of the American Frontier, 1600–1860* (Middletown, Ct.: Wesleyan University Press, 1973), pp. 466–516.

10. W. B. Gates, "A Note on Cooper and *Robinson Crusoe*," *Modern Language Notes* 67 (1952), pp. 421–22.

11. I am relying here on Gerald Grubb's impressive, three-part essay, "The Personal and Literary Relations of Poe and Dickens," *Nineteenth Century Fiction* 5 (1950), pp. 1–22, 101–20, and 209–21. As for Poe's relation to British periodical writing, the major source is now Michael Allen's thoughtful study *Poe and the British Magazine Tradition* (New York: Oxford University Press, 1969).

12. Orestes Brownson, "An Oration, delivered before the United Brothers Society of Brown University," *Boston Quarterly Review* 3 (1840), pp. 60–61.

13. Quoted in this order: Charles Brockden Brown, "Why the Arts are Discouraged in American Life," *Literary Magazine* 6 (July, 1806), pp. 76–77; Bryant, "An Essay on American Poetry," rpt. *Life and Works*, V, p. 47; Brownson, "Specimens of Foreign Literature," p. 435; Longfellow, "Graduation Address, Bowdoin College" (1825), rpt. in *The Native Muse*, p. 238; Lowell, Review of Longfellow's *Kavanagh*, *The North American Review* 69 (July 1849), p. 200.

14. Theodore Parker, "Ralph Waldo Emerson," *The Massachusetts Quarterly Review* 10 (1850), p. 203; *The Dial*, I (1840), p. 3.

15. *Myths, Rites, Symbols: A Mircea Eliade Reader*, ed. Wendell C. Beane and William G. Doty (New York: Harper and Row, 1975), pp. 51–52.

16. William Cullen Bryant "The Prairies," *Poetical Works*, ed. Parke Godwin (1883; reissued New York: Russell and Russell, 1967), I, p. 228.

17. Eaglesfield Smith quoted by Spencer, *The Quest for Nationality*, p. 27.

18. Longfellow, *Kavanagh*, ed. Jean Downey (New Haven, Ct.: College and University Press, 1965), p. 87; Brownson, "Specimens," p. 436.

19. Robert E. Spiller, "Critical Standards in the American Romantic Movement," *College English* 8 (1947), pp. 344–52.

20. The cited articles are reprinted in full or in part in Richard Ruland, ed., *The Native Muse*. (See fn. 1.)

21. Grubb mentions several other examples (see fn. 11). For the satire on Dickens in Poe's "Tarr and Fether," see William Whipple, "Poe's Two-edged Satiric Tale," *Nineteenth-Century Fiction* 9 (1954), pp. 121–33.

22. *Great Short Works of Herman Melville,* ed. Warner Berthoff (New York: Harper and Row, 1969), p. 79.

23. Melville, *Works* (New York: Russell and Russell, 1963), XVI, p. 233.

24. Stephen Spender, *Love-Hate Relations: English and American Sensibilities* (New York: Random House, 1974).

25. *Moby-Dick,* ed. Harrison Hayford and Herschel Parker (New York and London: W. W. Norton, 1967), p. 165.

26. Henry F. Pommer's *Milton and Melville* (New York: Cooper Square Publishers, 1970) affords no surprising conclusions but provides a useful survey of allusions.

27. Melville, "Hawthorne and his Mosses" (part 2), *Literary World* 7 (24 August 1850), p. 146; Thoreau, "Walking," *Atlantic Monthly* vol. 9, no. 56 (1862), p. 667; Whitman, "A Backward Glance O'er Travel'd Roads," *Prose Works 1892,* II, pp. 720–21.

28. For Spencer's overview, see *The Quest for Nationality,* pp. 212–13; Cooper, *Notions of the Americans,* excerpted in *The Native Muse,* p. 223; Lowell, "Review of Kavanagh," pp. 199 and 202.

29. The Irving controversy has been treated by Ben Harris McClary, "Mr. Irving of the Shakespeare Committee: A Bit of Anglo American Jealousy," *American Literature* 41 (1969), pp. 92–95, and by Lease in *Anglo-American Encounters,* pp. 19–22. Quoted material from *The Westminster Review* rpt. in *The Native Muse,* p. 394.

30. Spencer, *The Quest for Nationality,* p. 213.

31. Bate, *The Burden of the Past and the English Poet,* pp. 99–100 fn.

32. Evert Duyckinck, from *The Literary World* (1847), rpt. in *The Native Muse,* 332.

33. Freneau quoted in *The Quest for Nationality,* p. 20; Spencer's comment, *ibid.,* p. 82; Webster quoted, *ibid.,* p. 212.

34. Henry David Thoreau, *Early Essays and Miscellanies,* ed. Joseph J. Maldenhauer and Edwin Moser (Princeton, N.J.: Princeton University Press, 1975), pp. 106–108.

35. I am relying here on Sidney E. Lind, "James's 'The Private Life' and Browning," *American Literature* 23 (1951), pp. 315–22.

36. Clarence Gohdes, *American Literature in Nineteenth Century England* (Carbondale, Ill.: Southern Illinois University Press, 1944), pp. 45–46.

37. For Arnold's lecture comment, see *Discourses in America* (London: Macmillan, 1885), p. 196. For the other quotations and for a general commentary, see John Henry Raleigh, *Matthew Arnold and American Culture* (1957; rpt. in softcover, Berkeley and Los Angeles: University of California Press, 1961), pp. 68–72. More generally, see William J. Sowder, "Emerson's Early Impact on England: A Study of the Periodicals," *PMLA* 77 (1962), pp. 561–76.

38. R. H. Super, "Emerson and Arnold's Poetry," *Philological Quarterly* 33 (1954), pp. 396–403. Super quotes Tinker and Lowry on p. 402.

39. See Allan Casson, "*The Scarlet Letter* and *Adam Bede,*" *Victorian Newsletter* 20 (1926), pp. 18–19, and Jonathan R. Quirk, "*Silas Marner* as

Romance: The Example of Hawthorne," *Nineteenth Century Fiction* 29 (1974), 287–98.

40. See, for instance, William H. Hall, "Hawthorne, Shakespeare and Tess: Hardy's Use of Allusion and Reference," *English Studies* 52 (1971), 533–42.

41. John Vincent Fleming, "Browning's Yankee Medium," *American Speech* 29 (1954), pp. 26–32.

42. See William J. Goede, "Swinburne and the Whitmaniacs," *Victorian Newsletter* 33 (1968), pp. 16–21.

43. See James Hazen, "Whitman and Hopkins," *American Transcendental Quarterly* 12 (1980), pp. 41–48.

44. Gohdes, *American Literature in Nineteenth-Century England*, pp. 46, 144.

45. The best treatment of Whitman's British reputation remains Harold Blodgett, *Walt Whitman in England* (Ithaca, N.Y.: Cornell University Press, 1934).

46. Samuel Clemens, *Alta California*, 5 Feb. 1868. Rpt. in *The Twainian* 7 (1948), p. 4.

47. Spencer, *Quest for Nationality*, p. 213.

48. I rely here on Joseph H. Gardner, "Mark Twain and Dickens," *PMLA* 84 (1969), pp. 90–101.

49. Peter Conrad, *Imagining America* (New York: Oxford University Press, 1980).

2

1. Charles Dickens, *Bleak House,* ed. Morton Dauwen Zabel (Boston: Houghton Mifflin Co., 1956), Riverside edition, p. 69. I am employing this popular edition for this and subsequent quotations because of its easy availability. Page numbers in parentheses follow quotations.

2. Hyatt Waggoner, *Hawthorne: A Critical Study* (Cambridge: The Belknap Press of Harvard University Press, 1955), pp. 160–71; Edgar Johnson, "The Anatomy of Society" in *Charles Dickens: His Tragedy and Triumph* (Boston: Little, Brown and Co., 1952), rpt. in *Dickens: Bleak House, A Casebook,* ed. A. E. Dawson (London: Macmillan, 1969; and Nashville: Aurora Publishers, 1970), p. 139.

3. E. Stokes, "'Bleak House' and 'The Scarlet Letter'," *AULMA Journal* 32 (1969), pp. 177–89. See also Ghulam Ali Chaudhry, "Dickens and Hawthorne," *Essex Inst. Historical Collection* 100 (1964), pp. 256–73.

4. Herman Melville, "Hawthorne and his Mosses" (part two), *Literary World* 7 (1850), pp. 145–46.

5. Bloom categorizes such cases as *Apophrades*, or the return of the dead, pp. 15–16 and 139–55 in *The Anxiety of Influence*.

6. For other views of Esther's guilty psyche, see Taylor Stoehr, *"Bleak House:* The Novel as Dream" from *Dickens: The Dreamer's Stance* (Ithaca, N.Y.: Cornell University Press, 1965), rpt. in *Dickens: Bleak House, A Case-

book, pp. 235–43; and A. E. Dyson, "*Bleak House:* Esther Better Not Born?," pp. 247–73 in the same volume.

7. *The Letters of Charles Dickens,* ed. Walter Dexter (London, 1938), II, p. 335.

8. Elizabeth Wiley, "Four Strange Cases," *Dickensian* 58 (1962), pp. 120–25. See also George Perkins, "Death By Spontaneous Combustion in Marryat, Melville, Dickens, Zola, and Others," *Dickensian* 60 (1964), pp. 57–63, for the particular influence of Melville.

9. Herman Melville, "Bartleby," in *Piazza Tales,* ed. Egbert S. Oliver (New York: Hendricks House, 1962), p. 54. All quotations from "Bartleby" are to this edition.

10. Herbert F. Smith, in "Melville's Masters in Chancery and His Re-calcitrant Clerk," *American Quarterly* 17 (1966), pp. 734–41, details the Amer-ican adoption of English Common Law in matters of inheritance. He does not discover Melville's link to *Bleak House,* but he does provide a good discussion of the ways in which Melville sees Chancery as a terrible corruption of the the-ological ideal on which it is based—just as, I would note, Dickens does.

11. Reprinted in *Bartleby the Inscrutable,* ed. M. Thomas Inge (Hamden, Ct.: Archon, 1979), p. 39.

12. Edward Rosenberg, *Melville and the Comic Spirit* (Cambridge: Har-vard University Press, 1955), p. 145. This is the first mention of a Melville-Dickens link, though Rosenberg dismisses its import. It was briefly noted as well by Richard Harter Fogle in *Melville's Shorter Tales* (Norman: University of Oklahoma Press, 1960), pp. 17–18; by William Van O'Connor in *The Gro-tesque: An American Genre and Other Essays* (Carbondale, Ill.: Southern Illi-nois University Press, 1962), p. 97; by Kingsley Widmer in *The Ways of Nihilism: A Study of Melville's Short Novels* (Los Angeles: The California State Colleges, 1970), p. 108; and, with more specificity, by Lauriat Lane, Jr., in "Dickens and Melville: Our Mutual Friends," *Dalhousie Review* 51 (1971), pp. 322–23. More recently, four other critics have noted specific echoes of *Bleak House* in "Bartleby," generally in terms of characterization. They are Charlotte Walker Mendez, "Scriveners Forlorn: Dickens' Nemo and Melville's Bartleby," *Dickens Studies Newsletter* 11 (1980), pp. 33–38; Robert F. Fleissner, "'Ah, humanity!' Dickens and Bartleby Revisited," *Research Studies* 50 (1982), pp. 106–9; David Jaffe in a 15-page pamphlet, "Bartleby the Scrivener and Bleak House: Melville's Debt to Dickens" (Arlington, Va: Mardi Press, 1981); and my former student in the Ph.D. program in English at the University of Michigan, Brian Foley, whose essay, "Dickens Revised: 'Bartleby' and *Bleak House,*" was written at my suggestion and is forthcoming in *Essays in Criticism.* Foley's is the only discussion other than mine which finds Melville's attitude to Dickens hostile. (The other critics either bypass conclu-sions altogether or imagine an agreeing and grateful Melville.) He also very helpfully draws out the implications of Melville's Dickensian characters—Tur-key, Nippers, and Gingernut—in far greater detail than I will here. I am grate-ful to Mr. Foley for extending my ideas and for his very helpful research into secondary sources which he generously shared with me.

Three recent book-length studies pair Melville and Dickens as well, but each eschews questions of direct influence. In *Dickens and Melville in Their Time* (New York and London: Columbia University Press, 1975), Pearl Chesler Solomon places the two writers in partial contrast on the relation of the indi- vidual to the social nexus, an issue so large as to hinder real specificity. More interestingly, in *The Metaphysical Novel in England and America: Dickens, Bulwer, Melville,* and *Hawthorne* (Berkeley, Los Angeles and London: Univer- sity of California Press, 1978), Edwin M. Eigner links the writers as practic- tioners of a fictional genre "in which experience is presented first in purely materialistic or associational or positivistic terms, which are then contradicted from the idealist point of view so that experience is mystically transformed and a new reality is established" (p. 9). Here again, though, I find the brush too broad, for Melville clearly finds Dickens insufficiently metaphysical in just these terms. More general still is the comparison of the two writers in Jonathan Arac's *Commissioned Spirits: The Shaping of Social Motion in Dickens, Car- lyle, Melville,* and *Hawthorne* (New Brunswick, N.J.: Rutgers University Press, 1979). The link here is simply a concern with social organization ex- pressed, in imitation of the centralizing society these writers confronted, by a systematizing, totalizing overview. But Arac delivers more than this vague ar- gument promises in his local observations, for instance when he writes that "Melville typically focuses on one specific setting that is related by narrative metaphor to the larger world outside that sphere of action, while Dickens proliferates instances within a work that he links to each other" (p. 34). This provides a sharp and helpful differentiation which I treat later in this chapter when I discuss Melville's answer to the kind of epic novel which Dickens attempts.

13. Kingsley Widmer, "The Negative Affirmation: Melville's 'Bartleby'," *Modern Fiction Studies* 8 (1962), pp. 276–86.

14. Further, Christopher W. Sten argues to some persuasive effect that Bartleby is modelled upon Emerson's "The Transcendentalist" in "Bartleby the Transcendentalist: Melville's Dead Letters to Emerson," *Modern Language Quarterly* 35 (1974), pp. 30–44. But Sten sees Bartleby as self-dependent and uncharitable and he imagines Melville as disputing Emerson thereby, in- terpretations with which I disagree. Up against Wall Street, Melville could put aside his antagonisms to Emerson.

15. J. Don Vann, "*Pickwick* and 'Bartleby'," *Studies in American Fiction* 6 (1978), pp. 235–37.

16. Charlotte Walker Mendez, "Scriveners Forlorn," p. 36.

17. Herman Melville, *The Confidence-Man: His Masquerade,* ed. H. Bruce Franklin (Indianapolis and New York: Bobbs-Merrill, 1967), p. 96.

18. Here and elsewhere in this study, I am beholden to Sacvan Berkovitch, whose work with colonial and nineteenth-century materials over the last fif- teen years has invigorated the study of American literature and thought. Other scholars will qualify some of Bercovitch's claims, and I do so myself in chapter three. But such partial disagreements honor his work. *The American Jeremiad* (Madison: The University of Wisconsin Press, 1978) informs my argument at

this point and well may shape some ideas elsewhere beyond specific acknowledgment.

19. Quoted by Vann in *"Pickwick* and 'Bartleby'," p. 237.

3

1. Geoffrey Hartman, *Beyond Formalism: Literary Essays 1958–1970*
(New Haven and London: Yale University Press, 1970), p. 375.

2. Thomas Paine, *Common Sense* in *Complete Writings*, 2 vols., ed. Philip S. Foner, (New York: Citadel, 1945), I, 45; Melville, "Hawthorne and his
Mosses" (part two), p. 145.

3. Franklin is quoted by Spencer in *The Quest for Nationality,* p. 20.

4. *The Knickerbocker* and *The North American Review* are quoted in
Miller, *The Raven and the Whale,* p. 99.

5. Lowell, "Review of *Kavanagh,"* p. 199; Longfellow, *Kavanagh,* p. 86.

6. Spencer, *The Quest for Nationality,* p. 37.

7. Kenneth Burke, *A Grammar of Motives,* "California" edition (1945;
rpt. Berkeley: University of California Press, 1969), pp. 21–33.

8. Eliade, *Myths, Rites, Symbols,* p. 99.

9. Brownson, "Specimens," p. 63.

10. Hartman, *Beyond Formalism,* p. 377.

11. Spencer, *The Quest for Nationality,* p. 90.

12. Bryant, "Review of Mrs. Sedgewick's *Redwood,"* *The North American Review* 20 (1825), pp. 249–50; for Channing and Thoreau, see *The Quest
for Nationality,* pp. 190–91.

13. Williams, *Marxism and Literature,* pp. 51–52.

14. William K. Wimsatt Jr. and Cleanth Brooks, *Literary Criticism: A
Short History* (New York: Random House, 1957), p. 290.

15. Quoted in this order: Webster in Spencer, *The Quest for Nationality,*
p. 27; *North American Review* 29 (1829), p. 231; Poe quoted in Spencer, *The
Quest for Nationality,* pp. 78–79; Bryant, "An Essay on American Poetry," p.
48; Cooper and Freneau quoted in Spencer, *The Quest for Nationality,* pp. 72,
195; Southey quoted in Wright, *Life of Landor,* I, p. 361.

16. Brownson, "Specimens," p. 60.

17. Daniel Boorstin, *The Americans: The National Experience* (New
York: Random House, 1965), pp. 393–98 and 414; Henry Steele Commager,
"The Search for a Usable Past," *American Heritage* 16, no. 2 (1965), p. 4;
Robert Spiller, "Critical Standards," p. 346; George B. Forgie, *Fratricide in the
House Divided: A Psychological Interpretation* of *Lincoln and His Age* (New
York: W. W. Norton and Co., 1979), p. 13.

18. Brackenridge quoted in *The Quest for Nationality,* p. 12; John
Lathrop Motley, *Morton's Hope; or, The Memoirs of a Provincial* (New York:
Harper and Brothers, 1839), I, p. 96.

19. Gerald Critolf, "The Evolving Images of the United States," *Mississippi Quarterly* 16 (1962–1963), pp. 4–5; Jay Fliegelman, *Prodigals and Pil-*

grims: *The American Revolution against Patriarchal Authority, 1750–1800* (Cambridge, London, and New York: Cambridge University Press, 1982), pp. 3, 4, 26.

20. Quoted in this order: *Monthly Review or Literary Journal* 78 (1788), p. 377; Arnold, *Letters,* ed. G. W. E. Russell (London and New York: Macmillan, 1902), I, 151; Ruskin, *Fors Clavigera,* Letter of June 1, 1874; Trollope, *North America* (New York: Harpers, 1862), pp. 578–79; W. H. Channing quoted in Sowder, "Emerson's Early Impact on England," p. 572.

21. In *Leaves of Grass, 1891–1892,* ed. Sculley Bradley and Harold W. Blodgett (New York: W. W. Norton and Co., 1973).

22. Slotkin, *Regeneration Through Violence,* pp. 40, 121. For additional commentary on this issue by Slotkin, see pp. 38, 98, 108.

23. Sacvan Berkovitch, *The Puritan Origins of the American Self* (New Haven and London: Yale University Press, 1975), p. 113.

24. Slotkin, *Regeneration Through Violence,* p. 117.

25. *Ibid.,* p. 15.

26. *Dublin Review* 23 (1874), p. 68.

27. Quoted in this order: Melville, "Hawthorne and his Mosses" (part one) *Literary World* 7 (1850), p. 126; Brownson, "Specimens," p. 436; Whitman, "Poetry To-day," *Prose Works 1892,* II, 476–77. Harold Kaplan's *Democratic Humanism and American Literature* (Chicago and London: The University of Chicago Press, 1972) is the most ambitious and helpful consideration of democratic effects upon American literature in the nineteenth century.

28. Quoted in this order: Anon., "America and American Writers," *The Atheneum* (1829), p. 639; Alexis De Tocqueville, *Democracy in America,* The Henry Reeve Text, rev. Francis Bowen, ed. Phillips Bradley, 2 vols. (1840; rpt. New York: Alfred A. Knopf, 1945), pp. 71–72; Cooper, *Notions of the Americans,* quoted in Ruland, ed., *The Native Muse,* p. 225; Whitman, "A Backward Glance O'er Travel'd Roads," *Prose Works,* II, pp. 726–27.

29. Fred Somkin, *Unquiet Eagle: Memory and Desire in the Idea of American Freedom, 1815–1860* (Ithaca, N.Y.: Cornell University Press, 1967), pp. 20–21. See also 11–54 passim.

30. Bryant, "Review of *Redwood,*" *North American Review* 20 (1825), p. 251.

31. Mrs. Catherine Gore, *Peers and Parvenus* (London, 1846), I, p. 252.

32. Gohdes, *American Literature in Nineteenth Century England,* p. 132. See as well D. P. Crook, "The British Whigs on America: 1820–1860," *British Association of American Studies Bulletin* 3 (1961), pp. 4–17.

33. Edwin Fussell, *Frontier: American Literature and the American West* (Princeton, N.J.: Princeton University Press, 1965), p. 5.

34. Columbus' *Book of Prophecies,* quoted in Charles L. Sanford, *The Quest for Paradise* (Urbana, Ill: University of Illinois Press, 1961), p. 10; Stowe quoted in Edmund Wilson, *Patriotic Gore: Studies in the Literature of the American Civil War* (New York: Oxford University Press, 1962), pp. 84–85.

35. Eliade, *Myths, Rites, Symbols,* pp. 75 and 76.

36. Karl Löwith, *Meaning in History* (Chicago: The University of Chicago Press, 1949), p. 208.

37. Jonathan Edwards, *Images or Shadows of Divine Things*, ed. Perry Miller (New Haven: Yale University Press, 1948), p. 70; Adams quoted in Spencer, *The Quest for Nationality*, p. 22.

38. Hartman, *Beyond Formalism*, pp. 317–19.

39. Quoted without ascription in Spencer, *The Quest for Nationality*, p. 22.

40. J. Hector St. John Crèvecoeur, *Letters from an American Farmer* (New York: Fox, Duffield & Co., 1904), pp. 54–55.

41. Thoreau, "Walking," p. 667.

42. John Adams, *Old Family Letters: Copied From the Originals for Alexander Biddle*, Series A (Philadelphia, 1892), pp. 143–44; eighteenth-century poet quoted without ascription in Spencer, *The Quest for Nationality*, p. 23.

43. Thoreau, "Walking," p. 662.

44. Whitman, "A Backward Glance" in *Prose Works* (1892), II, pp. 478–79.

45. Slotkin, *Regeneration Through Violence*, p. 27. See also p. 117.

46. George Herbert, *Works*, ed. F. E. Hutchinson (Oxford: Clarendon Press, 1941), pp. 196–97; John Keats, *Selected Poems and Letters*, ed. Douglas Bush, Riverside ed. (Boston: Houghton Mifflin Co., 1959), p. 249.

47. "Walking," p. 665.

48. Fussell, *Frontier*, p. 6.

49. Bercovitch, "The Image of America: From Hermeneutic to Symbolism," *Bucknell Review* 20 (1972), p. 3. Oakes quoted in Bercovitch, *Puritan Origins*, p. 52.

50. Bercovitch, *Puritan Origins*, pp. 28, 35–36.

51. Bercovitch, "Image of America," p. 8; Eliade, *Myths, Rites, Symbols*, p. 8.

52. Slotkin, *Regeneration Through Violence*, pp. 22, 39, 94.

53. Bercovitch, *Puritan Origins*, pp. 74, 81, 90–91.

54. Ibid., p. 165.

55. Meyer H. Abrams, "English Romanticism: The Spirit of the Age" in *Romanticism Reconsidered*, ed. Northrop Frye (New York and London: Columbia University Press), p. 53. See also pp. 26–72 passim.

56. Bercovitch "Image of America," pp. 4–5.

57. Bercovitch, *Puritan Origins*, p. 166.

58. Williams, *Marxism and Literature*, p. 122. See also pp. 121–37 passim.

59. Leo Marx, *The Machine in the Garden: Technology and the Pastoral Ideal in America* (London, Oxford, New York: Oxford University Press, 1964), p. 27.

60. Spender, *Love-Hate Relations*, p. xxiii.

61. Whitman, "Poetry To-Day," *Prose Works* (1892), II, pp. 486–88.

62. "An American Abroad," *Partisan Review* 33 (1966), p. 78.

63. Whitman, "Starting from Paumanok," stanza 4 in *Complete Writings*, 10 vols. (New York and London: G. P. Putnam's Sons, 1902), p. 18.

NOTES

4

1. Horace Traubel, *With Walt Whitman in Camden,* I (Boston: Small, Maynard, and Co., 1906), p. 45.

2. Whitman, *Democratic Vistas, Prose Works 1892,* II, p. 396. All quotations of *Democratic Vistas* are taken from this edition and are followed by page numbers in parentheses.

3. "The Function of Criticism at the Present Time" in *The Complete Prose Works of Matthew Arnold,* 11 vols., ed. R. H. Super, vol. 3, *Lectures and Essays in Criticism* (Ann Arbor: The University of Michigan Press, 1962), p. 268. All quotations of this essay are taken from this edition and are followed by the symbol *FC* and page numbers in parentheses.

4. Arnold, "Preface" to *Culture and Anarchy: An Essay in Political and Social Criticism* in *The Complete Prose Works,* ed. Super, vol. 5 (Ann Arbor: The University of Michigan Press, 1965), p. 233. Quotations from "Preface" are followed by the symbol *P* and page numbers in parentheses; quotations from the essay proper will be followed by page numbers only in parentheses.

5. Raleigh, *Matthew Arnold and American Culture,* p. 52.

6. Traubel, *With Walt Whitman in Camden,* V (Carbondale, Ill.: Southern Illinois University Press, 1964), p. 481.

7. Thomas Carlyle, *Critical and Miscellaneous Essays,* 5 vols. (New York: Charles Scribner's Sons, 1901), V, pp. 5, 7.

8. For a more extended discussion of Whitman's relation to Carlyle, see Joseph Jones, "Carlyle, Whitman, and the Democratic Dilemma," *English Studies in Africa* 3 (1960), pp. 179–97.

9. I am relying here on Edward F. Grier, "Walt Whitman, the *Galaxy,* and *Democratic Vistas,*" *American Literature* 23 (1951), pp. 332–50, esp. pp. 337 and 345.

10. The phrase occurs at least five times in *Democratic Vistas.*

11. Arnold, "Preface to *Essays in Criticism,*" *The Complete Prose Works,* ed. Super, III, p. 288.

12. Whitman, "Our Eminent Visitors: Past, Present and Future" in *Prose Works 1892,* II, p. 541.

13. Raleigh, *Matthew Arnold and American Culture,* p. 59.

14. Traubel, *With Walt Whitman in Camden* in this order: III (New York: Mitchell Kennerly, 1914), pp. 189, 400; II (New York: Kennerly, 1915), p. 112; I, p. 45. Arnold's returning of the favor, his low view of Whitman's poetry, is discussed well by Lionell Trilling in *Matthew Arnold* (1939; rev. Cleveland and New York: World Publishing, 1955), pp. 360–62. Trilling quotes from a letter in which Arnold sees in Whitman "an eccentric and violent originality": "while you think it his highest merit that he is so unlike anyone else, to me this seems to be his greatest demerit: no one can afford in literature to trade merely on his own bottom and to take no account of what the other ages and nations have acquired: a great original literature America will never get in this way, and her intellect must inevitably consent to come, in a considerable measure, into the European movement." Trilling notes that Arnold refused to support the

protest led by Whitman's friend, W. D. O'Connor, on the occasion of Whitman's dismissal from the Indian Department for the publication of *Leaves of Grass*. Arnold replied that "here, too, or in France, or in Germany, a public functionary would . . . have had to pay for the pleasure of being so outspoken," and Arnold implies the payment is just, merited by a culture's need to require behavior.

15. Traubel, *With Walt Whitman in Camden*, I, p. 232.

16. Arnold, "Preface to *Essays in Criticism*," *Works*, III, p. 288.

17. Traubel, *With Walt Whitman in Camden*, III, p. 400.

18. Line 124. All quotations of Arnold's poems are taken from *Poems*, ed. Kenneth Allott (London: Longmans, Green and Co., 1965). Quotations are followed by line numbers in parentheses.

19. Quoted by Allott in *Poems*, p. 92n.

20. The finest, fullest account of the development of thought in Arnold's poetic career is A. Dwight Culler, *Imaginative Reason: The Poetry of Matthew Arnold* (New Haven: Yale University Press, 1966).

21. John Holloway, *The Victorian Sage: Studies in Argument* (1953; rpt. New York: W. W. Norton, 1965), p. 208.

5

1. John F. Lynen, *The Design of the Present: Essays on Time and Form in American Literature* (New Haven: Yale University Press, 1969), p. 21.

2. John Stuart Mill, *The Spirit of the Age* (rpt. Chicago: The University of Chicago Press, 1942), p. 1.

3. Maurice Mandelbaum, *History, Man, and Reason: A Study in Nineteenth-Century Thought* (Baltimore: The Johns Hopkins Press, 1971), pp. 42, 44–45, 54.

4. Bate, *The Burden of the Past and the English Poet*, pp. 39–40, 42–44, 61–62, 64, 95.

5. David Daiches, "Imagery and Mood in Tennyson and Browning" in *English Studies Today*, second series, ed. G. A. Bonnard (Berne: Francke, Verlag, Bern, 1961), pp. 217–32, esp. pp. 217–18.

6. Stanza III, "'Childe Roland to the Dark Tower Came'" in *Robert Browning's Poems and Plays*, 5 vol., intro. John Bryson (1906; rev. 1919; rpt. London: Dent and New York: Dutton, 1964), II, p. 299. All quotations of the poem are taken from this edition and followed by stanza numbers in parentheses.

7. J. Hillis Miller, *Charles Dickens: The World of His Novels* (Cambridge, Mass: Harvard University Press, 1958), pp. 159–61, 163, 165.

8. *Ibid.*, p. 200.

9. I am quoting from pp. 3–4 of the "Riverside" edition of *Middlemarch*, ed. Gordon S. Haight (Boston: Houghton Mifflin, 1956). I am employing this edition because the novel's text is established and the edition is widely available. Subsequent quotations are followed by page references to this edition in parentheses.

NOTES

10. In the "Rosehill" edition of *George Eliot's Works,* 24 vols. (Boston: Estes and Laurent, 1874), X, pp. 311, 317.

11. Henry James, "George Eliot's Middlemarch" (1873), rpt. in *A Century of George Eliot Criticism,* ed. Gordon S. Haight (Boston: Houghton Mifflin, 1965), p. 85.

12. Gordon S. Haight, "Introduction" to the Riverside *Middlemarch,* p. xiv.

13. Irving, *The Sketch Book* in *The Complete Works,* ed. Springer, p. 3.

14. Oscar Wilde, *Complete Works,* ed. Robert Ross, 10 vols. (Boston: Wyman-Fogg, 1909), VII, p. 20.

15. Bryant quoted in Spencer, *The Quest for Nationality,* p. 86.

16. Thoreau, "Walking," *Atlantic Monthly* 10 (1862), p. 670.

17. R. W. B. Lewis, *The American Adam: Innocence, Tragedy, and Tradition in the Nineteenth Century* (1955; rpt. in softcover Chicago and London: The University of Chicago Press, 1958), pp. 1, 25.

18. Paine, *Common Sense* in *Complete Writings,* I, p. 45; Melville, "Hawthorne and his Mosses" (part two), p. 145.

19. Spencer, *The Quest for Nationality,* p. 10.

20. Henry James Sr., "Democracy and its Issues" in *Lectures and Miscellanies* (New York: Redfield, 1852), pp. 5–6.

21. Marx, *The Machine in the Garden,* pp. 109, 228.

22. Quoted in Spencer, *The Quest for Nationality,* p. 128.

23. David Humphries, "Preface" to "On the Happiness of America" in *Miscellaneous Works,* Facsimile Edition, intro. William K. Bottorff (Gainesville, Fla.: Scholars' Facsimiles and Reprints, 1968), p. 24.

24. Bercovitch, *American Jeremiad,* pp. 71, 94, 96.

25. Bercovitch argues that the Puritan myth of national election attempts "to turn the nostalgia for paradise lost into a movement toward the future." (*American Jeremiad,* p. 169.)

26. Bercovitch, *Ibid.,* pp. 163–64; Fussell, *Frontier,* p. 15; Eric J. Sundquist, *Home as Found: Authority and Genealogy in Nineteenth-Century American Literature* (Baltimore and London: The Johns Hopkins University Press, 1979), p. 45.

27. See Daniel Hoffman's reading of "Ms." in his study *Poe Poe Poe Poe Poe Poe Poe* (Garden City, N.Y.: Doubleday and Co., 1973), pp. 140–46. John Irwin's extraordinary reading of *Pym* as a never-completed return to pre-linguistic origin is the highlight of his book *American Hieroglyphics: The Symbol of the Egyptian Hieroglyphics in the American Renaissance* (New Haven: Yale University Press, 1980).

28. William Tudor, "Address to the Phi Beta Kappa Society," *The North American Review* 2 (1815), p. 19; John Knapp, "American Poetry," *The North American Review* 8 (1818), p. 176.

29. Roy Harvey Pearce, *The Savages of America* (1953); revised and reissued as *Savagism and Civilization* (Baltimore: The Johns Hopkins University Press, 1965), p. v.; Slotkin, *Regeneration Through Violence,* p. 205.

30. Whitman, "Poetry To-day" in *Prose Works 1892,* p. 484.

31. Forgie, *Patricide in the House Divided*, pp. 7–9. See also pp. 3–87 passim.

32. All quoted material in this paragraph is taken from essays reprinted in part or in full in Ruland, ed., *The Native Muse*, pp. 155, 185, 195, 224.

33. De Tocqueville, *Democracy in America*, II, 72; Brownson, in Ruland, ed., *The Native Muse*, p. 403.

6

1. P. 3. All *Walden* quotations are taken from the *Walden* volume, ed. J. Lyndon Shanley, vol. II in *The Writings of Henry D. Thoreau*, ed. Walter Harding (Princeton, N.J.: Princeton University Press, 1971). Page numbers in parentheses follow each quoted passage.

2. Fussell, *Frontier*, p. 200.

3. Thoreau, *A Week on the Corcord and Merrimack Rivers* (Boston: Houghton Mifflin Company, 1961), p. 323.

4. Cooper, *Home as Found*, p. 52.

5. Thoreau, *The Maine Woods, The Writings of Henry David Thoreau*, 20 vols. (Boston: Houghton Mifflin, 1906), III, pp. 211–12.

6. Charles Feidelson, Jr., *Symbolism and American Literature* (Chicago and London: University of Chicago Press, 1953; rpt. in softcover, 1959), p. 137.

7. Stanley Cavell, *The Senses of Walden* (New York: Viking Press, 1974), p. 58.

8. See Cavell *passim.* on the expanding meaning of recurrent words in *Walden*. See also F. O. Matthiessen, *American Renaissance: Art and Expression in the Age of Emerson and Whitman* (London, Oxford, New York: Oxford University Press, 1941; rpt. in softcover, 1968), pp. 95–96, though Matthiessen takes Thoreau's etymological intent too literally.

9. Northrop Frye, *Anatomy of Criticism: Four Essays* (Princeton, N.J.: Princeton University Press, 1957; rpt. New York: Atheneum, 1966), p. 176.

10. Lines 6–8. All quotations from Coleridge's poems are taken from *Selected Poetry and Prose*, ed. Donald A. Stauffer (New York: Random House, 1951) and are followed by line numbers in parentheses.

11. Lawrence Buell, *Literary Transcendentalism: Style and Vision in the American Renaissance* (Ithaca, N.Y. and London: Cornell University Press, 1973), p. 149.

12. Feidelson, *Symbolism and American Literature*, p. 139.

13. James McIntosh, *Thoreau as Romantic Naturalist: His Shifting Stance Toward Nature* (Ithaca, N.Y. and London: Cornell University Press, 1974), p. 50.

14. *Ibid.*

15. *Ibid.*, p. 51.

16. As Walter Harding claims in a note to *The Variorum Walden* (New York: Twayne, 1962), p. 291, note 53.

17. Thoreau quoted in Matthiessen, *American Renaissance*, p. 175.

18. McIntosh, *Thoreau as Romantic Naturalist,* p. 51.

19. Lines 10–18. Quotations from Wordsworth's lyrics are taken from *The Prelude, Selected Poems and Sonnets,* ed. Carlos Baker (New York: Holt, Rinehart, and Winston, 1954), and are followed by line numbers in parentheses.

20. McIntosh, *Thoreau as Romantic Naturalist,* pp. 59, 63. And Charles R. Anderson, in *The Magic Circle of Walden* (New York: Holt, Rinehart, and Winston, 1968), writes (p. 225) that "Thoreau not only knew this famous ode but adopted it as a kind of spiritual autobiography, with recurrent allusions to it in his journal."

21. All quotations from *The Prelude* (1850) are taken from *The Prelude, 1799, 1805, 1850,* ed. Jonathan Wordsworth, M. H. Abrams, and Stephen Gill (New York and London: W. W. Norton, 1979). Quotations are followed by book numbers in roman and line numbers in arabic.

22. Fussell, *Frontier,* p. 231.

23. Buell, *Literary Transcendentalism,* p. 188.

24. Frederick Garber also takes this view, though in a different context and with differing emphases, in *Thoreau's Redemptive Imagination* (New York: New York University Press, 1977), pp. 168–69.

25. McIntosh, *Thoreau as Romantic Naturalist,* p. 59.

26. Anderson, *The Magic Circle of Walden,* p. 223.

27. See *Thoreau's Redemptive Imagination,* p. 215, where Garber persuasively argues for the figure of the parabola as indicating the structure of *Walden.*

28. And so too for "that dome in air" which the Coleridge of "Kubla Khan" "would build" if he could: if, if, if. I am not claiming an actual influence in these "castle" passages, but simply employing their fortuitous differences to dramatize real contrasts.

7

1. Earle Birney, quoted by Adrian H. Jaffe, "Canadian Literature," *Comparative Literature Studies* 5 (1968), p. 145.

2. James, *Hawthorne,* p. 12.

3. Commager, "The Search for a Usable Past," p. 6.

4. Lowell, "Cambridge Thirty Years Ago" in *The Works of James Russell Lowell,* ed. Charles E. Norton, 16 vols. (Boston and New York: Houghton Mifflin, 1904), I, p. 13.

5. E. T. Channing, "Brown's Life and Writing," *North American Review* 9 (1819), p. 69.

6. Tudor, "Address to the Phi Beta Kappa Society," *North American Review* 2 (1815), p. 14.

7. James, *Hawthorne,* p. 3.

8. Mircea Eliade, *The Myth of the Eternal Return: or, Cosmos and History* (Princeton, N.J.: Princeton University Press, 1954), pp. 43–45.

9. Lease, *Anglo-American Encounters,* p. 24.

10. James, *Hawthorne*, p. 14.

11. Richard H. Brodhead, *Hawthorne, Melville, and the Novel* (Chicago: The University of Chicago Press, 1976), p. 47.

12. *Ibid.*, p. 64.

13. James, *Hawthorne*, p. 66.

14. Boorstin, *The Americans*, pp. 401, 333.

15. Slotkin, *Regeneration through Violence*, pp. 488–89.

16. *Ibid.*, pp. 499–500.

17. Sundquist, *Home as Found*, pp. 6, 8–9.

18. D. H. Lawrence, *Studies in Classic American Literature* (1923; reissued New York: The Viking Press, 1961), p. 50.

19. Humphreys, "On the Happiness of America," rpt. in Ruland, ed., *The Native Muse*, p. 55.

20. Thoreau, *Walden*, ed. Shanley, p. 66.

21. Williams, *Marxism and Literature*, p. 125.

22. Quoted in this order: Bryant, Review of *Redwood, North American Review* 20 (1825), p. 252; De Tocqueville, *Democracy in America*, II, p. 76; Mathews, quoted in Spencer, *The Quest for Nationality*, p. 139.

23. Lewis, *The American Adam*, p. 5; Richard Poirier, *A World Elsewhere: The Place of Style in American Literature* (New York: Oxford University Press, 1966), p. 27.

24. Burke, *A Grammar of Motives*, p. 26.

25. Quoted by Commager, "A Usable Past," p. 3.

26. Burke, *A Grammar of Motives*, p. 33.

27. Spencer, *The Quest for Nationality*, p. 16.

28. Whitman, "Pioneers! O Pioneers" in *Leaves of Grass* (1891–92), p. 229, ll. 17–20.

29. Quoted by Commager, "A Usable Past," p. 3.

30. De Tocqueville, *Democracy in America*, II, p. 73.

31. Whitman, "A Backward Glance" in *Prose Works 1892*, II, p. 726; and *Uncollected Poetry and Prose*, 2 vols., ed. Emory Holloway (Garden City, N.Y.: Doubleday, Page, 1923), II, 93.

32. Quoted by Boorstin in *The Americans*, p. 296.

33. Bercovitch, *American Jeremiad*, p. 93.

34. William Dean Howells, *Literary Friends and Acquaintance: A Personal Retrospect of American Authorship*, ed. David F. Hiatt and Edwin H. Cady (Bloomington and London: University of Illinois Press, 1968), p. 49.

35. Whitman, "Poetry To-Day" in *Prose Works 1892*, II, p. 478.

36. Bercovitch, *Puritan Origins*, p. 133.

37. Whitman, "Poetry To-Day" in *Prose Works 1892*, II, p. 479.

38. Sharon Cameron, *Lyric Time: Dickinson and the Limits of Genre* (Baltimore: The Johns Hopkins Press, 1979), pp. 224–25.

39. Thoreau, *A Week on the Concord and Merrimack Rivers*, p. 310.

40. Whitman, "Chants Democratic," no. 19, in *Leaves of Grass, 1860, Facsimile Edition*, intro. Roy Harvey Pearce (1961; rpt. in softcover, Ithaca and London: Cornell University Press, 1969), p. 192, lines 1–4.

41. Spender, *Love-Hate Relations,* p. 45.
42. Cooper, *Home as Found* (New York: Capricorn Books, 1961), p. 23.
43. Spender, *Love-Hate Relations,* p. 47.
44. Somkin, *Unquiet Eagle,* p. 60; and Lynen, *Design of the Present,* p. 47.
45. *The Letters of Herman Melville,* ed. Merrill R. Davis and William H. Gilman (New Haven: Yale University Press, 1966), pp. 70–71.
46. Lynen, *Design of the Present,* pp. 4 and 5; Roy Harvey Pearce, *The Continuity of American Poetry* (Princeton, N.J.: Princeton University Press, 1961), pp. 41–42.
47. Spender, *Love-Hate Relations,* p. 46.
48. Brodhead, *Hawthorne, Melville, and the Novel,* p. 11.

8

1. "Song of Myself" in *Walt Whitman's Leaves of Grass: The First (1855) Edition,* ed. Malcolm Cowley (New York: Viking Press, 1959), section 42, line 1054. I am employing the 1855 version of "Song of Myself," Whitman's un-amended first publication of the poem which I, with most contemporary readers, much prefer to his subsequent, revised versions of it. Quoted passages are followed by section and line numbers in parentheses. For the 1850 *Prelude,* I am relying once more on the Norton edition noted in chapter 6.
2. James E. Miller, Jr. seems to me significantly right in considering the entirety of *Leaves of Grass,* not "Song of Myself" alone, as an epic. See *A Critical Guide to Leaves of Grass* (1957: rpt. in softcover, Chicago and London: The University of Chicago Press, 1966), pp. 256–61. But it is possible to see "Song of Myself" as epic-like and Roy Harvey Pearce does so in a very fine discussion in *The Continuity of American Poetry,* pp. 69–83. I disagree strongly with Pearce's four-part structuring of the poem, however, and I stress widely different aspects of epic intent.
3. See Matthiessen, *American Renaissance,* pp. 540, 613–17; and see Lynen, *Design of the Present,* pp. 304–305, 318–22.
4. *The Correspondence of Emerson and Carlyle,* ed. Joseph Slater (New York and London: Columbia University Press, 1964), p. 215. Subsequent quotations from the letters will be followed by the symbol *L* and the page numbers in parentheses.
5. Meyer H. Abrams, *Natural Supernaturalism: Tradition and Revolution in Romantic Literature* (New York: W. W. Norton, 1971), pp. 88–94.
6. *Ibid.,* pp. 71, 76.
7. *Ibid.,* pp. 77, 79.
8. Lynen, *Design of the Present,* p. 293.
9. Feidelson, *Symbolism,* p. 25; Lynen, *Design of the Present,* pp. 299, 301.
10. Robert Weisbuch, *Emily Dickinson's Poetry* (Chicago and London: The University of Chicago Press, 1975), pp. 16, 19.
11. Geoffrey Hartman considers Wordsworth's standard of nature as a judgment upon the revolution at much greater length and to real effect. See

Wordsworth's Poetry 1787–1814 (New Haven and London: Yale University Press, 1964), pp. 248–51.

12. Rene Wellek, *Confrontations: Studies in the Intellectual and Literary Relations Between Germany, England, and the United States during the Nineteenth Century* (Princeton, N.J.: Princeton University Press, 1965), p. 87.

13. Carlyle, *Miscellanies* in *Works*, Centenary Edition, ed. H.D. Trail, 30 vols. (London: Chapman and Hall; New York: Charles Scribner's Sons, 1896–1901), II, p. 82.

14. Charles Frederick Harrold, "Introduction" to *Sartor Resartus: The Life and Opinions of Herr Teufelsdröckh*, ed. Harrold (New York: Odyssey Press, 1937), p. xxxviii.

15. Carlyle, *Sartor*, pp. 236–37.

16. Carlyle, *On Heroes, Hero-Worship and the Heroic in History* in *The Works*, Centenary Ed., p. 4. All quotations are taken from this edition and are followed by page numbers in parentheses.

17. Walter E. Houghton, *The Victorian Frame of Mind 1830–1870* (New Haven and London: Yale University Press, 1957), pp. 332, 340.

18. Kenneth Marc Harris, *Carlyle and Emerson: Their Long Debate* (Cambridge, Mass. and London: Harvard University Press, 1978), p. 118.

19. Carlyle, *Sartor*, p. 177.

20. Carlyle, *Miscellanies* III, p. 90.

9

1. See in particular Ian Watt, *The Rise of the Novel: Studies in Defoe, Richardson and Fielding* (Chatto and Windus, 1957; rpt. Berkeley and Los Angeles: University of California Press, 1967), pp. 9–34. See also the helpful distinctions between the novel and the romance summarized by Northrop Frye in *Anatomy of Criticism*, pp. 303–14; and Richard Chase must be honored for the first real attempt to distinguish American romance and English novel in *The American Novel and its Tradition* (Garden City, N.Y.: Doubleday & Co., 1957), pp. 1–28. I am not in the present study attempting a history of generic development but I would cite Michael Davitt Bell's historically rigorous *Development of American Romance: The Sacrifice of Relation* (Chicago and London: University of Chicago Press, 1980) as particularly helpful. I disagree with some aspects of Bell's emphasis on an American distrust of fiction-making, but his consideration of the major romancers as outcasts and even outlaws is well-argued and important.

2. Eliade, *Myths, Rites, Symbols*, p. 54.

3. McIntosh, *Thoreau as Romantic Naturalist*, p. 61.

4. Charles Brockden Brown, Preface ("To the Public") to *Edgar Huntley*, ed. David Lee Clark (New York: Macmillan, 1928), p. xxiii.

5. Thoreau and Parker quoted in Spencer, *The Quest for Nationality*, pp. 168–69.

6. Whitman, "A Backwood Glance O'er Travel'd Roads," *Prose Works*, II, p. 716.

7. Channing, "Brown's Life and Writings," *North American Review* 9 (1819), p. 72.

8. Tony Tanner, "Notes for a Comparison between American and European Romanticism," *Journal of American Studies* 2 (1968), p. 90.

9. Sandra Gilbert, "The Wayward Nun Beneath the Hill": Emily Dickinson and the Mysteries of Womanhood" in *Feminist Critics Read Emily Dickinson,* ed. Suzanne Juhasz (Bloomington: Indiana University Press, 1983), p. 37. See also pp. 22–44 passim.

10. Poirier, *A World Elsewhere,* pp. 13, 29.

11. Buell, *Literary Transcendentalism,* p. 169.

12. Bercovitch, *Puritan Origins,* pp. 111, 121.

13. Spender, *Love-Hate Relations,* p. 13.

14. Bercovitch, *American Jeremiad,* p. 181.

15. Whitman, "A Noiseless, Patient Spider," in *Leaves of Grass* (1891–1892), p. 450.

16. Tanner, "Notes for a Comparison," p. 84.

17. Bercovitch, *Puritan Origins,* pp. 90, 108, 124; Marx, *Machine in The Garden,* pp. 3, 130, 239; A. N. Kaul, *The American Vision* (New Haven and London: Yale University Press, 1963), p. 14.

18. Robert N. Hertz, "English and American Romanticisms," *The Personalist* 46 (1965), p. 82; Poirier, *A World Elsewhere,* pp. 3–4; Tanner, "Notes for a Comparison," p. 87.

19. Warwick Wadlington, *The Confidence Game in American Literature* (Princeton, N.J. and London: Princeton University Press, 1975), p. 111.

20. Bercovitch, *Puritan Origins,* p. 165.

21. Feidelson, *Symbolism and American Literature,* p. 56 passim.

22. Quoted in this order: Lynen, *The Design of the Present,* p. 45; Spender, *Love-Hate Relations,* p. 21; Brodhead, *Hawthorne, Melville, and the Novel,* p. 16.

23. Terrence Diggory, *Yeats and American Poetry: The Tradition of the Self* (Princeton, N.J. and London: Princeton University Press, 1983), pp. 5–6.

24. *Ibid.,* p. 7; and C. Carroll Hollis, *Language and Style in Leaves of Grass* (Boston Rouge and London: Louisiana State University Press, 1983), pp. 65–88.

25. Cavell makes this final point in *Senses of Walden,* p. 9.

26. Gilbert, "The Wayward Nun," p. 33.

27. Eliade, *Myths, Rituals, Symbols,* p. 5.

28. Saul Bellow, *Henderson the Rain King* (1959; rpt. New York: Viking Press, 1965), p. 271.

10

1. Tanner, "Notes for a Comparison," p. 88.

2. Kenneth M. Price, "The Margin of Confidence: Young Walt Whitman on English Poets and Poetry," *Texas Studies in Language and Literature* 25 (1983), pp. 541–57.

3. Matthiessen, *American Renaissance,* pp. 539–40.
4. Whitman quoted in Matthiessen, *American Renaissance,* p. 613.
5. Later retitled "A Song of Joys." I quote from section 30 of the first version (1860), as reprinted in *Leaves of Grass, 1860: Facsimile Edition,* ed. Roy Harvey Pearce (Ithaca and London: Cornell University Press, 1961; rpt. in softcover, 1969), p. 268. All quotations of the 1860 poems are from this edition.
6. Tanner, "Notes for a Comparison," pp. 89–90.
7. Harris, *Carlyle and Emerson,* pp. 1–28, 71. Robert N. Hertz contrasts Emerson and Carlyle on the bases of "tone, emphasis, form, and language" in "Victory and the Consciousness of Battle: Emerson and Carlyle," *The Personalist* 45 (1964), pp. 60–71.
8. Barbara Packer shows that only the Orphic Poet of *Nature,* not Emerson himself, creates a mythology of the Fall. Emerson's own "axis of vision formula" repudiates the idea of a past failure for which we are not responsible. "It evades temporality" so that we cannot evade our present failure by employing the Fall as an excuse. See "The Instructed Eye: Emerson's Cosmogony in 'Prospects,' " in *Emerson's Nature: Origin, Growth, Meaning,* 2d ed., enlarged, ed. Merton M. Sealts, Jr. and Alfred R. Ferguson (1969; Carbondale and Edwardsville, Ill.: Southern Illinois University Press; London and Amsterdam: Feffer & Simons, 1979), pp. 209–21.
9. *Letters of Thomas Carlyle: 1826–1836,* ed. Charles Eliot Norton (London: Macmillan, 1889), p. 378.
10. Harrold, "Introduction" to *Sartor Resartus,* p. xxxvi. See also xxxiii–xxxvii *passim.*
11. McIntosh, *Thoreau as Romantic Naturalist,* p. 25; Garber, *Thoreau's Redemptive Imagination,* p. 120.
12. Garber, *Thoreau's Redemptive Imagination,* p. 43.
13. Harold Bloom, "Bacchus and Merlin: The Dialectic of Romantic Poetry in America," *The Southern Review* 7 (1971), p. 142.
14. R. A. Yoder, "The Equilibrist Perspective: Toward a Theory of American Romanticism," *Studies in Romanticism* 12 (1973), p. 712.
15. Harris, *Carlyle and Emerson,* p. 88.

II

1. Poirier, *A World Elsewhere,* pp. 13, 29.
2. Lynen, *The Design of the Present,* p. 3.
3. Emerson quoted in Matthiessen, *American Renaissance,* p. 3.
4. Bercovitch, *Puritan Origins,* p. 178.
5. Thoreau in *The Maine Woods* (Boston: Ticknor and Fields, 1864), p. 71; and *The Correspondence of Henry David Thoreau,* ed. Walter Harding and Carol Bode (New York: New York University Press, 1958), p. 302. Emerson in *Letters from Ralph Waldo Emerson to a Friend, 1838–1853,* ed. Charles Eliot Norton (Boston and New York: Houghton Mifflin, 1899), pp. 35–36.

NOTES

6. Emerson's prefatory poem to "Experience," "The lords of life, the lords of life,— / I saw them pass, / In their own guise, / Portly and grim," makes a self-conscious gesture to Shelley's parade of despair.

7. Joel Porte affords a brilliant and moving interpretation of this essay, and I have adapted here his main view and his tone. See *Representative Man: Ralph Waldo Emerson in His Time* (New York: Oxford University Press, 1979), pp. 179–86. Porte proposes the opening of Keats' "Ode to a Nightingale," with its "confusion and uncertainty," as a possible influence on Emerson's first paragraph. Whichever English romantic Emerson is imitating, he is in a realm of sleep, of cultural lateness.

8. "As I Ebb'd" in *Leaves of Grass 1860, Facsimile edition*, ed. Pearce, sections V and VI. All quotations of Whitman's poetry in this chapter are taken from this edition and followed by section numbers in parentheses.

9. Brownson quoted in Ruland, ed., *The Native Muse*, p. 403.

10. The fullest, best interpretation of the early Ishmael is Robert Zoellner's, in *The Salt Sea Mastedon: A Reading of Moby-Dick* (Berkeley, Los Angeles, and London: The University of California Press, 1973).

11. Melville quoted in McIntosh's unpublished essay, "Nimble Believing: Dickinson to Melville," given as a lecture at the University of Michigan, 15 November 1983. The note on Goethe can be found in a letter to Hawthorne. See *The Letters of Herman Melville*, ed. Merrill R. Davis and William H. Gilman (New Haven: Yale University Press, 1960), pp. 130–31.

12. McIntosh, "Nimble Believing."

13. Wadlington, *The Confidence Game in American Literature*, p. 137.

14. De Tocqueville, *Democracy in America*, II, p. 72.

15. Roland Barthes, *The Pleasure of the Text*, trans. Richard Miller (New York: Hill and Wang, 1975), p. 14.

16. Hollis, *Language and Style in Leaves of Grass*, p. 223.

17. Julian Smith, "Keats and Hawthorne: A Romantic Bloom in Rappaccini's Garden." *Emerson Society Quarterly* 42 (1966), pp. 8–12; Norman A. Anderson, "'Rappaccini's Daughter': A Keatsian Analogue?" *PMLA* 92 (1977), pp. 271–83.

18. Anderson, "'Rappaccini's Daughter': A Keatsian Analogue?," p. 281.

19. Lynen, *The Design of the Present*, p. 213.

20. Poe, "Selections from *Marginalia*" in *Major Writers of America*, 2 vols., ed. Perry Miller et al. (New York: Harcourt, Brace, & Ward, 1962), I, p. 472.

21. See for instance Richard Wilbur's metaphysical view of Poe in his introductory essay to Poe in *Major Writers of America*, I, p. 373 in particular, and in his essay "The House of Poe" in *The Recognition of Edgar Allan Poe: Selected Criticism Since 1829*, ed. Eric W. Carlson (Ann Arbor: University of Michigan Press, 1966), pp. 258–63, and the psychological emphases of Robert L. Carringer, "Circumscription of Space and the Form of Poe's *Arthur Gordon Pym*," PMLA 89 (1974), pp. 508–10 in particular.

22. "The Domain of Arnheim" in *The Complete Works of Edgar Allan Poe*, ed. James A. Harrison (New York: Thomas Y. Crowell, 1902), VI, pp.

184–85. All quotations of the tale are taken from this edition and are followed by page numbers in parentheses.

23. In *The Complete Works,* IV, p. 197.

24. "Selections from *Marginalia,*" p. 473.

25. The relation between Shelley's poem and Wordsworth's is noted by Earl R. Wasserman, but I am indebted more largely to his superb interpretation of "Alastor" in *Shelley: A Critical Reading* (Baltimore and London: The John Hopkins University Press, 1971), pp. 11–41.

26. Lines 194–96. Quotations of "Alastor" are taken from *The Selected Poetry and Prose of Percy Bysshe Shelley,* ed. Carlos Baker (New York: Random House, 1951). Line numbers in parentheses follow subsequent quotations.

27. Wilbur, "The House of Poe," p. 271.

28. Carringer, "Circumscription of Space and the Form of Poe's *Arthur Gordon Pym,*" pp. 508–10.

29. Frye, *Anatomy of Criticism,* pp. 316–28.

30. Brodhead, *Hawthorne, Melville, and the Novel,* pp. 15 and 19.

31. "Anglo-American Attitudes: Decorum in British and American Fiction," *Commonweal* 83 (22 October 1965), p. 85.

32. Ibid., p. 86.

33. Whitman quoted in Hollis, *The Language and Style of Leaves of Grass,* p. 5.

34. Frye, *Anatomy of Criticism,* pp. 34–35.

12

1. For the national allegory in the tale, see Q. D. Leavis' well-known article, "Hawthorne as Poet," Part I, *The Sewanee Review* 59 (1951), pp. 179–205. See as well Benjamin Lease's discussion of the tale in *Anglo-American Encounters,* pp. 102–104.

2. Quoted in Cornelia P. Kelley, *The Early Development of Henry James* (Urbana, Ill: The University of Illinois Press, 1930), p. 53.

3. Henry James, *Complete Tales,* ed. Leon Edel (Philadelphia: The University of Pennsylvania Press, 1960), II, pp. 293–94.

4. *The Letters of Henry James,* ed. Percy Lubbock (London: Macmillan, 1920), I, p. 13.

5. James's review of Howells appears in *Nation* 20 (1875), pp. 12–13.

6. Henry James, *The Future of the Novel: Essays on the Art of Fiction,* ed. Leon Edel (New York: Random House, 1956), pp. 38–39.

7. Henry James, "The Art of Fiction," rpt. in *The Future of the Novel,* p. 25.

8. *The Letters of Henry James,* ed. Lubbock, I, pp. 143–44.

9. *Selected Letters of Henry James,* ed. Leon Edel (New York: Farrar, Straus, and Cudahy, 1961), pp. 20–21.

10. Henry James, *The Portrait of a Lady,* Riverside reprint of the New York edition, ed. Leon Edel (Boston: Houghton Mifflin Co., 1963), p. 17. All

NOTES

quotations are taken from this widely available edition and are followed by page numbers in parentheses.

11. David Rosand, *Titian* (New York: Henry M. Abrams, Inc., 1978), p. 76.

INDEX